CW01186903

Franklin's Fate

an investigation into what happened to the lost 1845 expedition of Sir John Franklin

John Roobol

Franklin's Fate

Published by The Conrad Press in the United Kingdom 2019

Tel: +44(0)1227 472 874
www.theconradpress.com
info@theconradpress.com

ISBN 978-1-911546-49-8

Copyright © John Roobol, 2019

The moral right of John Roobol to be identified as author of this work has been asserted in accordance with the Copyright, Designs and Patents Act 1988.

All rights reserved.

Typesetting and Cover Design by:
Charlotte Mouncey, www.bookstyle.co.uk

The Conrad Press logo was designed by Maria Priestley.

Printed and bound in Great Britain by Clays Ltd, Elcograf S.p.A.

This book is dedicated to the memory of the Inuit, named herein, whose acute observations and oral history made possible this investigation into Franklin's lost expedition.
J.R.

We left King William Island on the 31st May, after having been a month on its most inhospitable coast. In no part of the world have I ever experienced such a continuation of bad weather. From the 8th, the day we left Cape Franklin, to this date I scarcely saw the sun. It snowed almost incessantly. The wind held almost continuously from the NW varying in force from a strong breeze to a hard gale. The force of the wind was generally sufficient to raise snow drift.

Lieutenant Hobson of the McClintock expedition in search of ships, records and relics of the Sir John Franklin expedition, 1859

Please note:

Interpolations in square brackets as [...] are by the author.

All distance measurements are straight-line distances taken from Google Earth. They often differ from historic published measurements.

M'Clintock and M'Clure were the nineteenth-century spellings and have been replaced by the modern spellings - McClintock and McClure.

In 1845 some words were spelled differently to today. A list of these and their modern equivalents follows:

Old Spelling	Modern Spelling
Disco in Greenland	Disko
Behring Strait	Bering Strait
Kamschatka	Kamchatka
Petro Paulowski	Petropavlovsk
Back's Great Fish River	Back's River
Poctes Bay	Poet's Bay
Eskimo/Esquimaux	Inuit
See-pung-er	Su-pung-er
Eskimaux language	Inuktitut

Distances are given in miles as the many inserts into the manuscript use this style. Some reports mention '5 leagues'. 5 leagues is equivalent to 15 nautical miles, 17.26 geographic miles and 27.78 kilometres.

The following distances in geographic miles have their kilometre equivalents in brackets:

10 miles (16 km), 17 miles (28 km), 20 miles (35 km), 80 miles (130 km), 100 miles (160 km), 112 miles (180 km), 150 miles (245 km), 1,700 miles (2,800 km).

Contents

AUTHOR'S NOTE..13

PREFACE..17

1: SEARCHES CARRIED OUT FOR THE LOST
   EXPEDITION..27

2: THE RELIABILITY OF INUIT TESTIMONY...........................37

3: KING WILLIAM ISLAND, ITS SEASONS AND THE ICE
   STREAM..40

4: THE DREAM OF A NORTH-WEST PASSAGE.......................46

5: THE SENIOR OFFICERS...53

6: DESCRIPTIONS OF COLLEAGUES ON THE
   OUTWARD VOYAGE BY COMMANDER FITZJAMES....68

7: SOME FINAL LETTERS SENT BY EXPEDITION
   MEMBERS..75

8: THE LAST SIGHTINGS OF *EREBUS* AND *TERROR*..........81

9: SUMMER 1845 TO SUMMER 1846 – EXPLORATION
   AND WINTER QUARTERS ON BEECHEY ISLAND..........84

10: SUMMER 1846 – EXPLORATION OF POCTES/POET'S BAY AND INTO THE ICE STREAM..................94

11: WINTER 1846 TO SPRING 1847 – MAPPING OF A NORTH-WEST PASSAGE AND THE DEATH OF SIR JOHN FRANKLIN..................105

12: SUMMER 1847 TO SPRING 1848 - NO RELEASE OF THE SHIPS, TERROR THROWN ONTO HER BEAM ENDS & PREPARATIONS FOR ABANDONMENT..................133

13: SUMMER 1847 TO SPRING 1848 – HEALTH PROBLEMS 160

14: THE FAILED RETREAT OF 1848..................178

15: SUMMER 1848 - THE CAPTAINS FACE DEFEAT 199

16: SUMMER 1848 TO SUMMER 1850 – AN OCCUPIED SHIP AND CAMP AT IMNGUYAALUK ISLAND AND THE DEATH OF CAPTAIN CROZIER..................209

17: THE 1850 RETREAT..................220

18: THE BLACK MEN..................244

19: THE UTJULIK SHIP..................250

20: LAST ACTIVITIES ABOARD *EREBUS*..................256

21: THE ARRIVAL OF A DESERTED SHIP WITH BODIES ABOARD, SOUTH OF CAPE CROZIER..................267

22: 1851 TO 1854 - THE LAST SURVIVORS 272

23:	SOME EVENTS AT HOME	285
24:	SOME NARROW MISSES IN LOCATING THE LOST EXPEDITION	311
25:	THE PRESENT LEVEL OF KNOWLEDGE ABOUT THE FATE OF THE LOST FRANKLIN EXPEDITION	316
APPENDIX 1:	CREW LISTS	322
APPENDIX 2:	SOME NUMERICAL ESTIMATES	326
APPENDIX 3:	SOME SUGGESTIONS FOR FUTURE DIRECTIONS OF SEARCH FOR THE LOST FRANKLIN RECORDS AND HISTORY	328
APPENDIX 4:	TWO REJECTED TESTIMONIES	330
ACKNOWLEDGEMENTS		333
NOTES ON SOURCES		335
REFERENCES		347
MAP 1		356
MAP II		358

AUTHOR'S NOTE

The complete disappearance of the 1845 Arctic expedition led by Sir John Franklin remains a mystery even to the present day. Two well-equipped ships of the Royal Navy with 129 men sailed in search of the North-West Passage and never returned. The puzzle has generated a whole library of speculation as to what might have happened. A massive international search for the lost ships produced almost nothing.

It was not until 1854 that Scottish explorer and Hudson's Bay Company explorer Dr John Rae unexpectedly heard of the lost expedition from the Inuit and purchased relics from them. The Royal Navy at the time was heavily engaged in the Crimean War and could not spare any more ships for searching. So Sir John Franklin's widow, Lady Jane, organised another search ship. She purchased the steam yacht *Fox* and obtained the voluntary services of Captain (later Admiral Sir) Leopold McClintock. The latter met with Dr Rae before he sailed to ensure he had all the information available of where the lost expedition had been seen in retreat by the Inuit, and where relics were found.

McClintock's book is a masterpiece of courage and endurance. He faced almost insurmountable difficulties. He failed to reach the search area in the first year. In the second year (1859) he had to leave his ship some 300 miles from the search area. He and Lieutenant Hobson led two sledge parties and crossed the line of retreat but at a time when the ground was still covered with winter snow. He brought back a naval message form with two brief messages, numerous relics and heard from the Inuit of a ship wreck that came ashore and was much salvaged and of another that sank abruptly and was little salvaged. In 1864, American Charles Francis Hall set out in search of survivors and spent five years collecting Inuit testimony. He did not find survivors but brought back many relics and one skeleton. Later, in 1879, American Lieutenant Frederick Schwatka led an overland expedition to the area of the retreat. His was a summer search but failed to find the missing records, but collected many relics, Inuit testimony, buried skeletal remains and brought back one skeleton.

Because Dr John Rae's report included reference to cannibalism by some of the last survivors, there was a great outcry in England and the blame was placed on the Inuit whose testimony was ignored for a long time. There was insufficient information to explain how the expedition came to be entirely lost.

My own interest in the lost expedition began in 1963 when as an undergraduate at London University, I was given a copy of McClintock's book 'Voyage of the *Fox*'. This sowed the seeds of curiosity and as a geologist working around the world on smaller expeditions I often found myself wondering how the 1845 expedition was lost. In the early 1970s, well before desktop computers were around, I tried to make sense of the information available. But it was inadequate and resulted in a lot of pieces of paper. Still the puzzle bothered me in quiet times, usually in some desert camp where there was little distraction. Meanwhile I was gaining lots of experience of expeditions in remote places including two sailing expeditions, one to the Caribbean and another to the Pacific.

Having always been dissatisfied with the problem, when I returned to the UK to retire, I decided that I had waited long enough for somebody to deliver a better understanding for the loss of the expedition. Unless I undertook the project, it seemed likely I would never know what happened. So I made the Franklin expedition my first retirement project. It took seven years to collect all the literature needed, read it and assemble the fragments into a coherent whole. The two books of David Woodman (1991 and 1995) that were based largely on his reading of Hall's notebooks at the Smithsonian Institution were a major step forward as they took the Inuit testimony seriously. But there was still insufficient evidence to fully understand the catastrophe. Then, Dorothy Harley Eber's 2008 book produced previously unrecorded Inuit testimony that added much to the story, in particular a description of one ship that was reoccupied and sailed south. Lastly, the Canadian Government's search for the two lost ships under the direction of Parks Canada succeed in 2014 with the discovery of the wreck of *Erebus* and in 2016 with the discovery of *Terror*.

Finally there were enough pieces to put together a reasonably complete account of the actions of the lost expedition. This was done in the form of a compilation of all the known evidence arranged into chapters that might reveal the history of the expedition. The Inuit testimony was critical but usually lacked dates and often place details, although the time of the year was known from the major seasonal changes. However some publishers said that the manuscript (Franklin's Fate) was too academic. So I sat down and wrote what I thought had happened as a novel (Trapped). The latter was accepted for publication by James Essinger of The Conrad Press in

Canterbury, UK. James became interested and decided to publish both books simultaneously with his editing.

PREFACE

On July 26 1845, Sir John Franklin, accompanied by 129 men (Appendix 1) aboard the two exploration ships H.M.S *Erebus* and H.M.S. *Terror* (referred henceforth as *Erebus* and *Terror*) was last seen by whaling ships. The two ships were moored to an iceberg awaiting passage through pack ice into Lancaster Sound, a body of water in the far north of Canada, between Devon and Baffin Islands (Map 1).

The twenty-three sections of Admiralty orders to Sir John Franklin were to proceed directly to Lancaster Sound and advance along it and Barrow Strait at approximately latitude 74 degrees 15 minutes, until they reached Cape Walker (about 98 degrees west). He was not to examine any channels extending north or south from Barrow Strait. Then he was to steer to the southward or westward towards Bering Strait. If obstructed by ice at Cape Walker, he was to pass between Cornwallis Island and North Devon, if the strait between them (Wellington Channel) was open. The two ships were not to separate and Captain Crozier was to be kept fully informed of his intentions.

The expedition was seeking to complete the North-West Passage – a sea route north of the American continent linking the Atlantic and Pacific Oceans. It was the best equipped Arctic expedition ever, with many new scientific inventions including two railway train engines to drive propellers that could be raised and lowered, and even a central hot water heating system.

The expedition never returned and the mystery created numerous searches and a library of writing.

An examination of the fate of the lost expedition has to be made in three fundamental parts.

The first stage, the preparations and the voyage to Disko Island in Greenland and the final sighting by whalers in July 1845 is well documented. A crowd of 10,000 watched the expedition leave Greenhithe on May 19.

The second part of the expedition, from July 1845 to April 1848 is known from the remains of their 1845/46 winter quarters on Beechey Island located by Captain Erasmus Omanney and others in 1850 – a year when there were thirteen ships in the Arctic looking for the lost expedition. It is also known from two messages recovered by the *Fox* expedition led by Captain Leopold McClintock in 1859. The first message reports the successful exploration of Wellington Channel and a circumnavigation of Cornwallis Island. The second message reports the death of Sir John Franklin on June 11 1847, and that the ships had been abandoned on April 22 1848 and the 105 survivors were marching south. In addition, there is Inuit testimony of ship activity in Poctes/Poet's Bay to the East of King William Island.

For the third part of the expedition after April 1848, there is a considerable amount of Inuit testimony as well the physical remains of the men and the boats which retreated to the south. The 1848 retreat appears to have failed and a remanned ship and her crew is described by the Inuit as spending two years at Imnguyaaluk Island – the smaller of the two Royal Geographical Society islands off the western cape of King William Island.

Present-day Inuit at Gjoa Haven on King William Island have found a 'fireplace trail' including a camp on Imnguyaaluk Island where western men cooked seal meat over blubber fires. This evidence of hunting is not surprising as the two ships carried enough food and fuel for only three years.

Probably in 1850, a senior officer believed to be expedition leader Captain Crozier died and was buried ashore as witnessed by Inuit. A second retreat (dominated by men from *Terror*) took place to the south and was witnessed by the Inuit. One small group of survivors was befriended by the Inuit and wintered with them. They set out for Fort Churchill but did not arrive,

The ship, believe to be *Erebus* with a small crew and one officer shortly afterwards sailed south to the Adelaide Peninsula or Utjulik. The abandoned ship was found in good order by the Inuit and became known as 'The Utjulik ship', and was salvaged over a least eight years. A small group of survivors travelled onto the Melville Peninsula where their trail fades.

In 2014, a Parks Canada led consortium, after years of searching, located the sunken wreck of *Erebus* and in 2016 *Terror*. The former was found in Utjulik as described in Inuit testimony, strengthening the reliability of Inuit testimony, that had been rejected in Victorian times because it contained reports of cannibalism. Modern studies are revealing new information. Autopsies have been carried out on three frozen bodies of crewmen from graves at the expedition's 1845-46 winter quarters on Beechey Island. Modern forensic studies have been made on skeletal remains of the retreat and on a skeleton recovered in 1869 and interred at Greenwich Old Royal Navy College, London. The contents of the two wrecks have yet to be appraised, although *Erebus* is in poor condition after being salvaged for years by the Inuit and *Terror* is in excellent condition and locked up with the crews possessions removed.

This volume is a reappraisal of all the available data. This is dominated by Inuit testimony but includes the correspondence of some of the officers, archaeological remains including relatively recent discoveries, and the results of modern forensic studies. Identification of the missing flagship *Erebus* (described in Inuit testimony as being seen in two places - Imnguyaaluk and Utjulik) and her consort *Terror* (a deserted ship with many bodies aboard), has clarified the picture by eliminating other possible interpretations. A summary of the present reconstructed fate of the expedition is given below.

Until the summer of 1847 the expedition had great initial success, mapping new areas by sailing up Wellington Channel and back via Cornwallis Island to a winter harbour at Beechey Island. Here, a scientific program was carried out until the ships were released the following summer. From there they sailed south but failed to penetrate the reef-filled waters of Poctes/Poet's Bay on the east side of King William Island. *Erebus* had a seventeen foot draft and *Terror* sixteen. One ship went aground and many stores were abandoned to lighten her. This shallow-water passage was used by Amundsen in 1903-06 (in *Gjoa* with a nine foot draft) to make the first sea voyage through the North-West Passage.

Franklin then made a fatal decision to force a passage to the west of the King William Island. Both ships became trapped in a branch of the Beaufort ice stream that bisects the Canadian Arctic, here flowing towards the south east. The two ships were trapped without a winter harbour in the worst part of the ice stream, where it piles up onto the north-west shore of King William Island.

Sledge parties completed mapping of the North-West Passage in spring 1847, and again a scientific program was carried out. During this time Sir John Franklin died just after his sixty-first birthday. Captain Crozier took command but chose to remain aboard *Terror*, rather than move aboard *Erebus* as the expedition's orders specified. Undoubtedly, all hoped for a release in the summer of 1847 and a speedy return to England to report their successes.

However, summer 1847 proved very cold and the ships were not released. *Terror* was ice heaved onto her beam ends. The two crews wintered aboard *Erebus*, that became a hell ship with men on reduced rations and illness that resulted in a further twenty deaths (eight officers and twelve crewmen). The tinned food was probably condemned by the ships doctors, as unopened tins of meat were found by the Inuit in the abandoned ships. Scurvy, lead poisoning and possibly botulism from undercooked tinned meat (hastily produced in time for the sailing date) have been blamed for the high death rate.

Without the shelter of a winter harbour, there must have been great concern that the remaining ship could be crushed by the ice and rendered incapable of returning home. The first action after abandoning *Terror*, was for the crews to build a depot camp on King William Island that was likely called Terror Camp (today known as 'Crozier's Landing'). Many items salvaged from *Terror* were found there. Heavy coils of rope, including one with a diameter of five centimetres, may have been the contents of *Erebus*'s rope locker, emptied to make additional winter quarters for *Terror*'s crew.

In the cold and darkness of the polar winter of 1847-48, the crews did not take their dead the seventeen miles across the ice hummocks to hard frozen ground, but instead placed them in bunks in the abandoned *Terror*, which became a mortuary ship (a ship with many dead men as described in later Inuit testimony).

Captain Crozier after only two months of his first polar expedition command (he was a veteran of seven previous polar expeditions) decided, because of the poor health of the crew, to retreat as a single party of 105 men urgently to the south. Probably only four boats as well as a number of sledges were taken. One of the boats (a twenty-eight foot pinnace from *Erebus*) found eleven years later by Admiral Sir Leopold McClintock (mainly buried in snow), had been modified to lighten her and she was to be propelled by paddles made from cut down oars. She carried fifty fathoms of line for being towed up rivers.

The retreat set off to the south in April 1848 before the ice melted, hauling the boats on sledges. The object was to get to the southern shores of King William Island and the estuary of Back's Great Fish River, where an abundance of deer, musk oxen, birds and fish were reported in June, July and August by earlier explorers.

In 1869, some twenty-one years later, American Lieutenant Frederick Schwatka and party encountered thousands of deer on the south-western part of King William Island in June. The retreat could carry only short rations for forty days (lasting until the first week of June). Their target was to sledge haul for life, fresh food and home. They needed to make six miles a day to get to the estuary before the food ran out.

The desperate urgency was for fresh food, so the party could strengthen themselves, then with the summer thaw and the opening of the seaways, the boats could be used. The plan was probably not to ascend the 500 miles of Back's Great Fish River with its eighty-three rapids, falls and cascades, but perhaps to tackle the more navigable Mackenzie or Coppermine rivers, along the already-explored northern sea coast of the American continent.

Crozier had been forced into a premature departure by the ill-health of the crew, probably at the urging of the ships' doctors. It was a case of get out now, six weeks before the thaw began, or never get out. Survival chances would have been greater if smaller parties had set out at different times, but this would have left many aboard the ships too weak and ill to make the long trip of over 1,250 miles to the Hudson's Bay Company outposts.

Because of the illness of some of the crew, Crozier decided upon the convoy system of retreat – one large party travelling together with the strong supporting the weak. This had the major disadvantage that the speed of the convoy was the speed of the slowest. They abandoned the two ships, that had drifted only sixteen miles in the nineteen months while trapped in the ice stream. The men travelled seventeen miles or five leagues across the ice to their depot camp known today as Croziers Landing. From there they set off to the south, the remaining officers no doubt encouraging the men to haul for their lives, for fresh food and for home.

The retreat failed. Bad weather was probably a major factor. Lieutenant Hobson of the McClintock search expedition in 1859, traversed the line of retreat on the west coast of King William Island in May – the same month as the retreat - and barely saw the sun, encountering continuous snowfall and gales that prevented travel on many days (Hobson developed scurvy and was carried back to his ship by sledge). In addition, the men were weak and in particular the hard exercise of sledge hauling and illnesses, combined to incapacitate the crews.

According to the 1846 record, it had taken the boat party about three to four days to cross the well-used track across seventeen miles of ice to Croziers Landing at a rate of four to five miles a day. The retreat from Croziers Landing was slower. Instead of making the required six miles a day, they could barely make two miles. At Erebus Bay, only fifty miles from Croziers Landing, two large boats with about a half of the retreating men were halted. The method of the retreat was to follow the smoothest ice along the shore and to camp at night near clear ground, as the men carried no ground sheets.

Many would sleep inside the boats with the sails as wind protectors and the others in tents on ground free of snow and ice. The two boats halted in Erebus Bay never moved again and numerous skeletal remains (of twenty to twenty-eight men, Appendix 2) have been found associated with them. Modern forensic study of these remains found evidence of cannibalism.

Since leaving Crozier's Landing, the two boats had travelled only fifty miles in about forty days – an average of one and a quarter miles per day.

The advance part of the retreat with two remaining boats and sledges reached a further thirty miles to Terror Bay, where their retreat stopped. A hospital tent was set up and maybe as many as fifteen men died there. The retreat had failed and the crews could not escape by marching out.

About a half of the men, led by their two Captains, returned to the ships, where the last resort was to sail out if the ship was released by the ice later that year. Not all of the able bodied returned to the ships. Some men (including possibly *Erebus* Ice Master James Reid) remained to look after the sick. Some smaller parties continued south, one may have hauled a boat into Dougles Bay. The immobile sick died at the two boat places in Erebus Bay and the camp at Terror Bay in 1848. These three sites are now known as 'the death camps'.

An earlier interpretation suggested that the 1848 retreat was only a hunting trip and that almost all of the men returned to the ships. It was suggested that the camps were formed in 1850, when the ships had drifted as far south as Erebus Bay and the crews came ashore by boat in summer. This interpretation is not followed because the Erebus Bay remains are too insubstantial. The one boat found by the McClintock expedition in Erebus Bay had been extensively modified for river work with paddles and a long rope for hauling upriver, suggesting a serious planned escape to a Hudson's Bay outpost. The contents of the boat (including officers' silverware) suggest she was untouched since the 1848 retreat. The three death camps are here regarded as the furthest points reached by the 1848 retreat, halted when the immobile sick reached around fifty percent. The march had persisted to reach the summer hunting grounds.

Inuit testimony suggests that only *Erebus* was reoccupied, and *Terror* was still on her beam ends in Spring 1849. The two captains evidently worked *Erebus* south, in an attempt to rescue some of the sick men immobilised in tents in Erebus and Terror Bays. Although *Erebus* reached an area (south of Cape Crozier at Imnguyaaluk Island in the Royal Geographical Society Islands) where the hospital tent at Terror Bay could be seen, the Inuit descriptions of the three 'death camps' indicate that most men there had died. A paucity of animal bones suggests the hunting had failed.

The Imnguyaaluk area was much frequented by the Inuit for hunting and contact was made with them. There adjacent to the Royal Geographical Society Islands, she spent two years (1849 and 1850) with many visits and good relations with the Inuit, including a successful joint summer hunt when many caribou were killed. In Inuit testimony she was known as the ship at Imnguyaaluk Island and the Inuit gave descriptions of some of her crew.

Through 1849 and 1850, the two crews fed themselves poorly by hunting caribou, fish and birds in summer and seals in winter and learned the survival techniques of the Inuit out of necessity (the ships had only been supplied for three years). The winter hunters left a 'Fireplace Trail' of sites, where they cooked their seal meat over blubber fires. The oil sank into the ground where it remains today. On the southern end of Imnguyaaluk Island, adjacent to where *Erebus* was anchored, a campsite has been identified where the ground is saturated in seal oil. The two Captains kept the men away from the death camp in Terror Bay and warned the Inuit away from it.

Captain Crozier is believed to have died some time in 1849-1850. His military burial was witnessed by the Inuit along with the burial of paper expedition records (for which a search is suggested of south Imnguyaaluk Island).

In summer 1850, after the death of Captain Crozier and with *Erebus* still trapped in the ice, most of the remaining *Terror* crew set out to retreat overland to Repulse Bay. They were led by a senior officer (possibly Ice Master Thomas Blanky of *Terror*) and a marine officer (possibly Marine Sergeant Solomon Tozer also of *Terror*). The retreating party encountered Inuit in Washington Bay. The party next divided (probably to increase their hunting chances) and a boat party crossed to the mainland and reached a place named 'Starvation Cove' by the Schwatka search expedition. Here, many perished but a few continued into Chantrey Inlet.

The rest of the party followed the coast of King William Island and left a trail of graves and remains along the south-west coast. The senior officer (carrying a telescope and an unopened tin of pemmican) with four colleagues died on the Todd Islets. [Pemmican is a concentrated mixture of fat and protein used as a nutritious food. Historically, it was an important part of Native American cuisine in certain parts of North America, and is still prepared today.]

Later in 1848, four men arrived near the Boothian Peninsula and were befriended by Inuit. They were led by a man who may have been Marine Sergeant Tozer. They wintered with the Inuit and set off south for Fort Churchill in 1851 carrying a Halkett inflatable dinghy. Inuit testimony suggests they reached the Chesterfield Inlet area, where the last one or two survivors may have been mistaken for Indians, and were possibly killed by the fierce Kinnapatoo Inuit of the area, only some 350 miles from Fort Churchill.

Meanwhile, aboard *Erebus*, possibly as early as the summer thaw of 1850, a physically large officer, probably Captain Fitzjames, possibly Lieutenant Fairholme, took the intact *Erebus* with a small crew directly south. He headed for the summer open sea lane along the northern margin of the American continent. Fitzjames's writing from Greenland indicates that he had intended to get to the Bering Strait and Petro Paulowski [Petropavlovsk] in Kamchatka to where he had had his mail forwarded. In the 1850 or 1851 thaw, *Erebus* arrived in Wilmot and Compton Bay on the west side of the Adelaide Peninsula.

It appears that Fitzjames had died on or shortly after arrival, for the body of a very large man was left in the great cabin. After his death, with no surviving officers, the ship was turned towards the east side of the Adelaide Peninsula (away from the route to Bering Strait), probably for proximity to summer hunting. Camps were established on islands in the vicinity for hunting. There is some possibility that a boat left *Erebus* and travelled west, as there are several mentions of 'white men' in the vicinity of the Mackenzie River.

Possibly in summer 1851 or 1852, the last three survivors from *Erebus*, being a small group of accomplished hunters accompanied by a dog (possibly Neptune the ships dog brought from England, now used to locate seal holes in the ice), set out for the east where whaling ships might be encountered. Inuit testimony indicates that they arrived on the Melville Peninsula where their trail fades.

An abandoned *Erebus* was found by the Inuit completely intact with doors locked and with five boats in the davits. She was salvaged by the Inuit for at least eight years. During that time she became known to the Inuit as 'The Utjulik ship' and she drifted ashore, where her fore part probably became submerged. In 1859 the McClintock expedition was told that she had last been visited during the previous summer, when not much remained to be salvaged. This is consistent with the state of the recently discovered wreck where much of the stern, masts and bowsprit are missing. She was later ice rafted a short distance offshore, where she sank. The *Erebus* wreck was located in 2014, in the area described by the Inuit.

Sometime after *Erebus* sailed south from Imnguyaaluk Island, an abandoned ship with many dead bodies aboard, was ice rafted to an area south of Cape Crozier. She was found by the Inuit who salvaged some metal and wood. The Inuit found some tins of pemmican on board and ate the contents. They became ill and several died. This and the dead men aboard seem to tell a tale. The ship when found was securely locked up, so the Inuit cut a way through the damaged side near the waterline, so that she sank with only minor salvage having taken place. This ship is *Terror* abandoned in 1847, and was found and identified offshore of Terror Bay in summer 2016 still closed and locked up.

It seems a small number of men of the expedition, by adopting Inuit survival methods, lived for up to six years (1851) and died near Chesterfield Inlet only 350 miles from Fort Churchill. The successful group of hunters from *Erebus* appear have lived for a few years longer on *Erebus* and on the Melville Peninsula.

1: SEARCHES CARRIED OUT FOR THE LOST EXPEDITION

Numerous Admiralty, American and private search expeditions for the lost expedition during the nineteenth century only found the 1845 winter quarters of the expedition at Beechey Island. The first Europeans to reach the line of the Franklin expedition retreats of 1848 and 1850, were Lieutenant Hobson and Captain McClintock of the private *Fox* expedition in 1859. The only written records of the expedition found are two sheets of paper brought back by the *Fox* expedition. The logbooks and scientific records and specimens of the expedition have not yet been found and Sir John Franklin's grave has not been identified. However, with the support of the Canadian government and the advent of the internet, interest continues to grow, publications appear frequently and there is a slow but steady progress in understanding the history of the lost expedition.

Discoveries in the Canadian Arctic of three submerged shipwrecks (*Investigator* in 2010, *Erebus* in 2014 and *Terror* in 2016) are helping to clear up some of the mysteries of the lost 1845 expedition. Hopefully, the shipwrecks of *Erebus* and *Terror* will yield some written records and more details of the expedition's history.

Sir John Franklin was a decorated war hero, Arctic explorer and former Lieutenant Governor of Van Diemen's Land. The two ships *Erebus* and *Terror* were fitted out with the latest inventions for heating, steam engines to drive retractable propellers, a vast amount of food, much preserved by the new process of sealing in tins, as well as enough lemon juice to give every man a daily allowance of one ounce as a precaution against scurvy. The expedition's objective was thought to be a simple one – to complete an unmapped 100 mile long stretch of what proved to be Victoria Strait, to link the coastline mapped by James Clark Ross in 1830 with that mapped by Dease and Simpson and in 1839. The plan was to sail the ships through the North-West Passage and emerge in the Bering Strait.

Sir John Barrow, the Second Secretary of the Royal Navy was the man behind the polar exploration program of the Royal Navy following Admiral Horatio Lord Nelson's success at the Battle of Trafalgar and the subsequent paying off of the bulk of the navy. Barrow believed the expedition would return in triumph in a year. He proposed for leadership a young thirty-three-year-old commander with no polar experience but great expectations - Commander James Fitzjames. The latter was so confident of success that he had his mail forwarded to Petro Paulowski [Petropavlovsk] in Kamchatka and arranged that when the ships emerged, he would make a quick overland passage back to England to announce the success before the ships completed their lengthy route home.

Overconfidence was so great that no contingency plans were made should the ships become trapped in the ice, nor were they equipped with sufficient Arctic clothing and hunting equipment (especially hunting rifles) to make a retreat overland. The expedition with 129 men of the Royal Navy was last sighted by whalers on July 26 1845 and then vanished. The men were officially declared dead on March 1 1854.

In the Victorian era, polar exploration commanded great interest, rather as space exploration does today. Polar explorers became household names for the Victorians and most of the expedition leaders were eventually knighted. How the largest and best equipped of these expeditions could be entirely lost generated massive interest at the time and this continues to the present day. A vast outpouring of publications about the mystery continues undiminished and with the advent of the internet and rapid communications is now reaching new levels of interest.

The Royal Navy had evolved two separate methods for exploring the Arctic regions. One method was to send out small parties by land, travelling by foot and boat or canoe, usually supported by local hunters. In this manner, Sir John Franklin had led two such expeditions in 1820-1822 and 1825-1827 to the north-western shores of the American continent and mapped almost 600 miles of coastline. Similarly, George Back had descended and mapped Back's Great Fish River and Chantrey Inlet in 1834. Between 1836 and 1839, Dease and Simpson, using boats, mapped the north-eastern coastline of the American continent more or less from west of the Mackenzie River, past Backs Great Fish River to the Castor and Pollux River.

The Hudson's Bay Company employed Scotsman Dr. John Rae who adopted Inuit methods of dress and survival and proved extraordinarily successful mapping much of the coastline of the American continent, the south coast of Victoria Island and eventually demonstrated that King William Land was an island and not attached to the Isthmus of Boothia. Dr. Rae supported his small parties by hunting. He proved that Victorian men could adopt the Inuit style of survival including eating raw meat. The other method was to use pairs of large ships with large crews.

In 1818 John Ross (later Sir John Ross) mapped in Baffin Bay. William Parry (later Sir William) in 1819 had brilliant success by sailing 620 miles through Lancaster Sound and Barrow Strait and on, to become the first Royal Navy ship to winter in the Arctic at Melville Island.

Big ships have the disadvantage of deep drafts, so they could not get through shallow channels. They were also unfortunately extremely prone to becoming trapped in winter ice. Some years before the Franklin expedition, Sir John Ross on another expedition to explore for the North-West Passage, was also trapped in the Arctic ice and after four years, and considerable hardship, he and his crew abandoned their ships and sledged north, to reach an area frequented by whaling ships and were rescued. So if Sir John Ross, with most of his men, could escape after his ships became frozen in the ice and were abandoned, (on the 1829 to 1833 expedition) then why should the Franklin expedition not do the same thing after 1845?

In 1850 the British government offered £20,000 to anyone who assisted the Franklin Expedition, and £10,000 to anyone ascertaining the fate of the expedition. Twenty-five major rescue expeditions took place in the following decades as well as smaller ones. The many search expeditions produced only one result concerning the lost expedition. In 1850 Captain Erasmus Ommanney and some officers of *Assistance* (part of a search squadron under Captain Horatio Austin) discovered traces of the lost expedition and their winter quarters (1845 to 1846) on Beechey Island. Unfortunately no written record was found there, only three graves.

The first information about the fate of the lost expedition was brought to the Admiralty in 1854 by the very competent and accomplished Dr. John Rae from Orkney – a Chief Factor of the Hudson's Bay Company and Arctic explorer. While mapping the coastline of Boothia with a small party on foot, he learned of a disaster from Inuit from whom he purchased some relics. These included Sir John Franklin's Star of the Order of Hanover. The Inuit reported seeing men hauling a boat with a raised sail on a sledge some four years previously in 1850. They also spoke of cannibalism. Dr. Rae prepared two reports, one for the Admiralty, including Inuit testimony that the last survivors of the Franklin expedition had resorted to cannibalism and another for The Times newspaper in which the cannibalism was excluded. Very regrettably the Admiralty released their report to the press. It caused a sensation and a headline of 'Sir John Franklin a cannibal?'

It was a catastrophe for Dr. John Rae. Victorian Society, and Franklin's wife Lady Jane, in particular, were utterly horrified. Lady Jane considered Dr. Rae's crime had been to use the word 'cannibalism' in his writing.

She organised a campaign against Dr. Rae and the Inuit. This included a remarkable tirade by Charles Dickens.

British Arctic explorer Sir George Richardson agreed, stating that the cannibalism could not be the action of English men, but rather of the primitive Inuit. Modern forensic studies of skeletal remains have confirmed the cannibalism. Dr. Rae, as the bearer of the bad news, was never recognised for his remarkable achievements of mapping large areas of the Canadian Arctic, while supporting himself and his small party by hunting off the land (something the 105 men strong party that abandoned the Franklin ships could not do).

Dr. Rae's lack of recognition is still a concern in his native Orkney and Shetland Islands. There, the John Rae Society, the Friends of Orkney Boat Museum and the Rt. Hon. Alistair Carmichael, MP for Orkney and Shetland campaigned for over ten years for his recognition. On September 30 2014, a plaque to the memory of Dr. John Rae was finally unveiled and dedicated in the Chapel of St. John the Evangelist in Westminster Abbey, London. Dr. Rae intended to return to search the line of the retreat himself and had a boat built to do this. But the boat was destroyed in a fire and he did not return.

At the time when Dr. John Rae identified the location of the Franklin disaster, the Crimean war had begun (October 1853 to February 1856) and all Admiralty resources were directed to war. Three private expeditions, requiring considerable feats of endurance, went out to finally reach the line of retreat of the Franklin expedition. The first two of these reached the line of retreat when it was buried in winter snow, but the third arrived at the line in summer.

Lady Jane Franklin sponsored the *Fox* expedition. Captain (later Admiral Sir) Leopold McClintock in the steam yacht *Fox*, arrived at the line of retreat of the Franklin Expedition in 1859, some eleven years after the ships were abandoned. His two sledge parties travelled over 310 miles from the ship. Numerous relics, including a twenty-eight foot pinnace on a sledge, skeletons, guns, equipment and the only written records of the expedition (two sheets of paper) were found. The first brief record reported great success in exploration during the first year. The second reported the death of Sir John Franklin in June 1847 and that in April 1848 the 105 survivors had abandoned the ships and were setting out to the south where the nearest civilisation was at the outposts of the Hudson's Bay Company, some 1200 miles away.

From 1864 to 1869, some sixteen years after the abandonment of the ships, American, Charles Francis Hall, travelled alone to the Arctic and resided there for five years with the Inuit, and collected numerous eyewitness accounts of the lost expedition. He believed he was answering a call from God to find the survivors of the expedition. He briefly visited part of the line of retreat, found relics and returned what was weakly identified as the skeleton of Lieutenant Henry Thomas Dundas Le Vesconte for burial in Scotland. Hall was later poisoned by arsenic when leading an expedition to the North Pole, confirmed when his frozen body was exhumed and examined in 1970. His notes and notebooks were purchased from his widow by the American Congress and edited by Professor Nourse for publication.

From 1878 to 1880, thirty years after the ships were abandoned, American Lieutenant Frederick Schwatka of the Third United States Cavalry, led a five-man American expedition in search of lost records. The party made a remarkable achievement by sledging for eleven months and twenty days and covered a total distance of 2,819 miles for the first summer search of the line of retreat of the Franklin expedition. They failed to find any records, but buried bones and collected many relics and testimony. One skeleton was returned to Engkand that was weakly identified as that of Lieutenant John Irving.

Like Dr. John Rae's small parties, this small expedition lived almost entirely on food which they hunted and sometimes ate raw in Inuit fashion. The small expedition traversed the entire known line of retreat in summer. No records were found but much Inuit testimony was collected, including a report of finding and opening a box of books on the American continent in a boat at a place Schwatka named Starvation Cove. The books and papers were of no value to the Inuit, who gave them to their children to play with and they were destroyed.

For the Victorians the testimony of perhaps forty men hauling a boat on a sledge together with the discovery of about thirty bodies on the American mainland nearby and another five bodies on an small island provided the classical interpretation of the retreat. McClintock believed the twenty-eight foot pinnace he found to be from *Erebus* with portions of two skeletons inside and numerous relics. He confirmed the Inuit stories of the retreat trail marked by graves, bodies and relics including a large tent with many skeletons inside. This and the brief record were interpreted to mean that the 105 men who started the retreat on April 22 1848 (1848 Record), had all died in 1848 during the retreat.

More information on the lost expedition appeared when aircraft began landing on King William Island in summer. The first of these was Major L.T. Burwash who landed near Victory Point in September 1930 and found many relics and the remains of a camp site. In August 1949 Inspector H.A.

Larsen of the Royal Canadian Mounted Police searched the north-west coast of King William Island and also visited and searched the mainland area of Starvation Cove. He was followed by American Paul Fenimore Cooper who flew to the island three times.

Perhaps, not surprisingly, these early searchers did not gather all the Inuit testimony available. Roald Amundsen in the *Gjoa* (1903 to 1906), Knud Rasmussen in 1923 as well as Dorothy Harley Eber (between 1996 and 2008) were able to collect more Inuit testimony vital to understanding the history of the lost expedition.

Canadian Captain, harbour master, diver and writer David Woodman made major contributions to understanding the events of the lost expedition. He sifted carefully through the Inuit testimony (including Hall's original notebooks) recorded in the decades after the expedition was lost. Woodman followed Inuit testimony of a shipwreck that has become known as 'the Utjulik ship'.

Captain David Woodman played a major role over ten years in privately funded searches for the Utjulik ship, first by towing a side-scan sonar and next by using sledge-born geophysical surveys (with a magnetometer) on the ice of the frozen sea in the areas where the Inuit testimony pinpointed the location. The surveys, commencing in 1998, located magnetic anomalies of the kind that the ferrous metal on the lost ships might provide, but proved to be geological (iron-rich rocks) and the wreck was not found. His efforts had been preceded by a number of successful land searches by a group of Canadians in a project known as the Franklin Trail throughout the 1990s.

Unlike the Victorians, David Woodman took the Inuit testimony seriously as shown by the finding of *Erebus*. He also concluded that the retreat reported by Dr. Rae in 1850 was not the retreat of 1848 referred to in the brief written record found by the McClintock expedition. He concluded that the 1848 retreat had failed and that the crews had returned to the ships in 1848, so that there had been a second retreat in 1850. He was also able to reason that an officer's burial witnessed by the Inuit was probably not that of Sir John Franklin.

In a second book by Woodman, the Inuit testimony was further sifted to remove tales of whaling ships and other expeditions. Testimony remained reporting some small groups that almost made it back to civilization and only narrowly failed. Woodman's study of the original notebooks of Hall showed that portions of Hall's Inuit testimony that were not clear to Professor Nourse were omitted or compressed in his publication of Hall's diaries. Woodman was able to extract new information and further details that had not been published by Nourse. Woodman has since organised searches of north-west King William Island to relocate places found in the nineteenth century by the Inuit and reported in their testimony.

In 2008, the search for the missing ships was taken over by the Canadian Government in the form of Parks Canada. It was motivated in part as a result of global warming and the possibility of commercial use of several North-West Passages in the era of icebreaker ships. The submarine surveys of the sea floors in the passages are a necessary preliminary step. Additionally, the relics of the early British expeditions in what is now the Canadian Arctic are proving a strong basis for Canada's territorial claims. Great Britain transferred sovereignty of the arctic islands to Canada in 1880.

With the creation of the internet, information on the lost expedition began to circulate widely. A numbers of books and new ideas have appeared as well as websites and blog spots. In the field, searches continue to locate more bones and relics. The graves of three Franklin expedition crewmen on Beechey Island have been opened and post mortems carried out. Variable but high lead levels were found in the bodies and bones believed to be derived from early lead-soldered food tins. High lead levels were common in Victorian people and it is possible that some, but not all, of the crew may have suffered the effects of lead poisoning. Modern forensic examination of bone fragments along the line of retreat has also been carried out (Map II). Lately the value of the Inuit testimony (ignored by Victorian society) has been realised. Also today, after the events of the twentieth century, the subject of cannibalism (proved independently by modern forensic study on Franklin expedition remains) is no longer such a taboo subject.

Erebus was found on September 7 2014, after being missing for 166 years. The 2014 Victoria Strait Expedition was the biggest ever assemblage of experts and technology with seven vessels and underwater robotic craft. The Government of Canada's partners were Parks Canada, Fisheries and Oceans Canada, the Canadian Coast Guard, the Royal Canadian Navy, Defence Research and Development Canada, Environment Canada, the Canadian Space Agency, and the governments of Nunavut and Great Britain. In addition private and non-profit partners included the Arctic Research Foundation, and the Royal Canadian Geographical Society. The latter brought in the W. Garfield Weston Foundation, Shell Canada and the One Ocean Expeditions as partners.

The discovery was not announced until September 9, as the Canadian prime minister and then Downing Street and H.M. Queen Elizabeth had first to be informed. Prime Minister Stephen Harper of Canada announced on September 9 that the first of two ships lost with the entire 1845 expedition of Sir John Franklin in search of the North-West Passage, had been found. Both ships were abandoned on April 25 1848 and had been the subject of study and speculation ever since. There were no survivors of the 1845 expedition and over forty search expeditions went looking for them, which resulted in largely completing the exploration of the Canadian arctic.

The *Erebus* wreck was found in only eleven metres of water by side-scan sonar towed by Parks Canada research ship *Investigator* and was confirmed on September 7 by Parks Canada's remotely operated vehicle. The wreck is located in the same area described by the Inuit near O'Reilly Island on the west side of the Adelaide Peninsula within the southern search area of the Canadian Government's Parks Canada. The Canadian prime minister said; 'I am delighted to announce this year's Victoria Strait Expedition has solved one of Canada's greatest mysteries, with the discovery of one of the two ships belonging to the Franklin Expedition lost in 1846.'

Following two days of diving by archaeologists of Parks Canada a second announcement was made on October 1 again by Prime Minister Stephen Harper, that the ship was *Erebus* – the flagship of Sir John Franklin. The identification was based on measurements and details of the ship and artifacts photographed by the divers. Thus, considerable study and speculation based on the Inuit testimony was verified, even if some researchers had concluded that the Utjulik ship was likely to be *Terror* commanded by Captain F. R. M. Crozier. The position of *Erebus* off the coast of the American continent proves that she did in fact make the traverse through Victoria Strait to complete that part of the North-West Passage. In the words of Sir John Richardson (who had accompanied Sir John Franklin on two earlier explorations of part of the Arctic) 'they forged the last link of the North-West Passage with their lives'.

How the *Erebus* wreck was found is an interesting story, as it was more by accident than planning. Parks Canada had identified two areas to be searched. A northern area lies in Victoria Strait and a southern area in Queen Maud Gulf. Much exploration of the southern area had failed to locate the Utjulik ship, so the main target planned for the 2014 search was the northern area. This was believed to be more promising because of remains and artifacts found on the nearby shores. However, poor weather with early and heavy ice floes prevented the northern search.

The breakthrough occurred when two archaeologists decided to survey a small barren island near O'Reilly Island in the southern search area. They flew there by helicopter and while there, the helicopter pilot found a large heavy iron part of a ship rigging (thought to be a davit at first) marked with the Admiralty broad arrow. Nearby were the wooden remains of a ships hawse pipe stopper. The iron artefact was too heavy to have been carried far by the Inuit from the Utjulik ship. So an underwater search was initiated in the adjacent waters and the wreck soon found.

The discovery has confirmed what many modern people think today, that the Inuit testimony was both correct and reliable. This was not the case at the time of the loss because of reports of cannibalism by the some of the crews in their final desperate straits. This was not believed by the Victorians.

The discovery of *Terror* was also accidental and not a part of the planned survey area for 2016. It came about when the research vessel *Martin Bergmann* (a converted trawler) of the private Arctic Research Foundation funded by Jim Balsillie (former corporation leader of Research and Motion) was passing King William Island. Foundations Operation's Director Adrian Schimnowski was on the bridge with Inut Sammy Kogvit from Gjoa Haven, who was describing places along the west coast. When opposite Terror Bay, Kogvit reported that seven or eight years before he had been crossing Terror Bay on a hunting trip, and saw a ship's mast standing through the ice. Schimnowski turned the ship into Terror Bay and then turned away heading for Cambridge Bay. A short while later the *Terror* wreck was seen on the side-scan sonar.

The wreck was found on September 3 2016. She appeared to be intact in sixty feet of water with her bowsprit intact and her three masts still standing. *Terror* is in much better shape than *Erebus* as she is believed to have sunk rapidly, whereas *Erebus* was ashore for at least eight years being salvaged by the Inuit. On *Terror*, panes of glass still remain in the windows of the captain's cabin and the hatches are closed. There is a good chance of finding diaries, scientific books and charts preserved below decks. Parks Canada did not learn of the discovery of *Terror* for a week and spent that time searching for *Terror* in Victoria Strait. Parks Canada divers visited *Terror* on 16, 17 and 18 of September and confirmed her identity. News reports suggest that the Parks Canada budget for locating the two Franklin ships was C$ 2.8 million. Also that the five-year budget for exploring *Erebus* is C$16.9 million.

Another Franklin-era ship had been discovered in July 2010 by Parks Canada. She is *Investigator*, abandoned in 1853 in one of the search expeditions for the lost Franklin expedition. She had become trapped in ice in Mercy Bay on Banks Island. She was found after only fifteen minutes underwater search by sonar, in the position where she was abandoned.

The discovery of these three sunken ships eliminates a lot of earlier suggestions of what had happened to *Erebus* and *Terror*. For example Rear Admiral Wright had suggested that the wreck now known to be *Erebus* (the Utjulik ship of Inuit testimony) with a body with long teeth aboard, might have been *Investigator* with her figurehead. In 1851 two three-masted ships resembling *Erebus* and *Terror* were seen on an immense ice floe off the Newfoundland Banks.

The work of Woodman based on a detailed study of Hall's original notebooks of the Inuit testimony, as well as relics found on the line of retreat, came up with a more detailed and complex interpretation of the history in which the crews returned to the ships and that some lived on until as late as 1851 or 1852 and possibly later. It is now twenty-five years since Woodman presented his interpretation and during that time more Inuit testimony has been published, and more Franklin sites and relics found that have been subjected to modern forensic study and the two ships have also been discovered.

Between 1994 and 2008 Dorothy Harley Eber collected new testimony of a manned single ship and camp at Imnguyaaluk Island (the smaller of the two Royal Geographical Society Islands) lying between where the ships were abandoned in 1848, and where the two wrecks were recently found. This volume is a new independent reappraisal of the evidence and pays particular attention to Inuit testimony. It builds on the work of Woodman but contains new interpretations based on the latest information. Perhaps over the coming years of careful archaeological work on the wrecks, written records and even daguerreotypes may be recovered to give more detail of the events that happened to the lost expedition. There still remain to be found the buried records and scientific collections (including rock samples) of the expedition, also Sir John Franklin's grave. Some suggestions for future lines of search are given in Appendix 3.

2: THE RELIABILITY OF INUIT TESTIMONY

As much of the reconstruction in this book depends heavily on Inuit testimony, the question must be raised at once of how reliable is this testimony.

For the Victorians, the mentions of cannibalism were abhorrent and were regarded as impossible by Victorian gentlemen. Prominent Victorians such as Lady Jane Franklin, Charles Dickens and Sir George Richardson found the Inuit testimony completely unacceptable, but 'unacceptable' is not the same as 'unreliable'. This attitude has in some cases persisted to modern times, for example by Roderic Owen, a descendant of Sir John Franklin, who regards the Inuit testimony as 'nonsense'.

The bulk of the Inuit testimony was collected by American Charles Francis Hall who made two expeditions to the Arctic in search of survivors of the Franklin expedition. In his first expedition he spent from 1860 to 1863 on South Baffin Land. From Inuit testimony he learned of the actions of Martin Frobisher and five of his lost crewmen who had visited the area on a third voyage in 1578 and mined what proved to be fool's gold. Hall described this and his life with the Inuit. His second expedition lasted five years from 1864 to 1869. He visited King William Island and was successful in bringing back much testimony and relics of the lost Franklin expedition.

Charles Francis Hall died by arsenic poisoning by his crew aboard the ship Polaris on route to the North Pole on November the eighth 1871. The arsenic was identified when his frozen body was exhumed and examined in 1968. The crew were afraid of becoming trapped in the ice too far north to escape. In a similar manner, Henry Hudson and his son were likewise abandoned in a small boat in Hudson Bay when their crew decide to sail for home.

Dorothy Harley Eber collected Inuit testimony describing the arrival of an old man with a long white beard and a young boy in a small wooden boat. She suggests that these may have been Henry Hudson and his son John, set adrift in Hudson's Bay on June 23 1611 by a starving mutinous crew, while searching for the North-West Passage. The two were taken to the Inuit encampment and fed. The old man died and as the Inuit had never seen a white person before, the young boy was tethered to one of their houses so he could not run away. The Inuit tribal memory seems remarkable today.

When Hall died he had not had time to edit and write up his copious notes of his second Arctic expedition concerning Inuit testimony and Franklin relics collected over five years of living with the Inuit. It was his intention to do this and he had promised Lady Jane Franklin that on his return from the North Pole expedition, he would return to King William Island to try to recover the buried records of the expedition, believed to be in cemented vaults. After his death his manuscripts and notebooks were purchased from his widow by an Act of Congress approved on January 23 1874. The task of editing his notes for publication fell to Professor J.E. Nourse who was ordered to carry out the work by the United States Naval Observatory. The results were published as a 644 page long narrative by the United States Naval Observatory of the United States Navy Department.

Hall and the members of the later Schwatka expedition accepted the Inuit testimonies as the truth. Gilder, of the Schwatka expedition, wrote in 1881:

> It is but fair to state that we have reason to put great faith in the statements of these people, as truthfulness seems to be an inherent quality in them. They never attempted to deceive us in regard to relics, though perhaps it would seem easy and profitable. In many instances what appeared to us to be interesting relics they told us came from the natives of Repulse Bay and elsewhere.

A big step forward with the testimonies was made by David Woodman in two books, who separated the Franklin testimonies from those of other expeditions and whaling ships and re-examined Hall's original notebooks. Woodman led searches for the 'Utjulik ship' of Inuit testimony, that was eventually found by a Parks Canada led consortium in 2014.

Dr. John Rae in 1854 met the Inut In-nook-poo-zhe-jook who was wearing a gold officer cap band and who provided the first testimony of the lost Franklin expedition. Twenty-five years later Hall also met In-nook-poo-zhe-jook and rerecorded the same testimony. When Anne Keenleyside found cut marks on human remains and bones broken to extract marrow, she went back to Hall's notebooks for original descriptions of the finds.

The Inuit were living in isolation and had sharp eyes for detail, they retained stories of anything they encountered as their oral history. The arrival of large ships amongst them and the actions of the crews and the many new things they saw, and often did not understand, provided a rich oral history that was handed down through generations. The testimonies often give graphic details and today can be seen as eyewitness accounts by simple honest people. Throughout this account, the original testimonies are given, so they might be examined in this light. Some of the testimonies give so many details that they can be seen to be beyond the abilities of people to fabricate them.

With the intense interest today in the lost expedition and the rapid exchange of information on the internet, a case can now be made to reorganise, re-edit and publish Hall's notebooks in full, to bring out more of the Inuit testimony now seen as eyewitness accounts.

Throughout this reconstruction, all available Inuit testimonies are included that have enabled a somewhat detailed reconstruction to be made. There remain puzzles and problems, for example there are two additional testimonies of ships sinking and men dying that are here rejected, as they are not compatible with what is now known of the wrecks of *Erebus* and *Terror* (See Appendix 4). It is hoped that the recently discovered wrecks of *Erebus* and *Terror* will eventually yield written records of activities of the lost Franklin expedition.

3: KING WILLIAM ISLAND, ITS SEASONS AND THE ICE STREAM

The island (Map II) is the focus where the Franklin expedition, the pride of the Royal Navy with the latest Victorian technology, was lost. Yet the Inuit had lived there for generations.

The difference was that the naval expedition with the ships locked in the ice seventeen miles offshore, was bound by naval traditions with the crews comfortable and isolated within their ships. At first they failed to learn the basics of local survival from the Inuit, according to the seasonal changes of the island. The remains of the Franklin expedition, as well as Inuit testimony indicate that some of the ships crews survived long after the 1848 abandonment by adapting to the Inuit way of life.

The knowledge of the Inuit way of life and the changing seasons of the island were documented by Charles Fennimore Cooper in 1961, after he flew to the island three times and took a great liking to it. The Inuit had learned how to adapt to the seasons on King William Island and lived on a diet (often eaten raw) of fish, caribou, seals, bear, Arctic hare, foxes, lemmings and fish. In the winter they lived on the ice in ice houses or igloos, and in the summer on land in skin tents or tupics.

The island is known to the Inuit as Kirkerktak. The arrival and loss of a great two-ship expedition of 'white men' in this land of isolated people essentially still in the Stone Age and living a precarious hunter way of life, provided a rich history of Inuit testimony. Their observation of detail was remarkable, even when they did not understand everything they saw. Their oral tradition of preserving their history provides a remarkable testimony with graphic and minute detail of what happened to the Franklin expedition, in the absence of any Franklin expedition survivors.

The key to survival in the area had been discovered by the Inuit long before the Franklin Expedition. There is considerable seasonal variation in the area and the Inuit had adapted their lifestyle to it. Their many tales of the lost expedition are given without dates, but because of the profound changes between the seasons it is possible from the tales to identify the time of year. This is critical for the years after the ships became trapped in the ice about seventeen miles northwest of the northern tip of King William Island (Cape Felix).

King William Island has very distinct seasons which dictated the precarious but successful lifestyle of the Inuit (the Kikerktarmiut) inhabitants of the nineteenth century. In January the Inuit moved out onto the sea ice of the Utjulik area (defined below) to hunt seal at their blow holes, using specially trained dogs to locate the holes that are often snow covered. In June, the best month of the year when the snow starts to melt, the Inuit left their ice homes and returned onshore to collect at the points where the northern migration of the caribou occurs in their thousands. August is the time of fishing and all the Inuit moved to Lake Amitsoq in the centre of the island. Here, two lakes are linked by a stream where trout can be trapped in a never failing supply, so that the Inuit regard it as a holy place. By the end of August, winter begins to return with thin ice on the lakes and snow flurries. In September the caribou start gathering in small herds to migrate across Simpson Strait. At the crossing point (called on King William Island 'Malerualik') to the mainland, the Inuit ambushed the herds until they had sufficient kill for winter clothing and food. There followed a time of butchering and making meat caches and of preparing the skins and sewing them to make new clothes ready for the annual cycle to begin again.

In late June to early July salmon were commonly speared in thousands by the Inuit along the coasts, as the salmon return to the lakes of King William Island to spawn in the fall. The heads were given to the dogs for food and the fish split and sun dried on lines. The dried fish were then sewn into seal skins and cached under rocks for a winter food supply.

On August 4 1869, the Schwartka party reached Terror Bay. The sea was not entirely free of ice but Klutschak described the area as a true paradise compared to the northern part of the island. It possessed a great abundance of caribou. Klutschak also noted that in the summer the caribou occupy the north and west of the island. But in the fall the southeastern part of King William Island has hundreds of caribou visible. By October 1 the ice cover in Simpson Strait is strong enough to support caribou and herds stream back to the mainland.

The cycles of birthing of the wildlife sees April as the moon for the birth of young seal, May for the musk ox, June for the deer and walrus, and July for the eider ducks.

The northern half of King William Island is relatively barren compared to the central and southern areas, where meadows of summer flowers and lichen provided lush summer feed for the visiting herds of thousands of caribou, and the lakes in the southern half of the island abound with fish.

Where *Erebus* and *Terror* were trapped in the hummocky ice of the Beaufort ice stream, no seal fishing can be carried out, while ashore hunting is relatively poor as the ground is barren. The area where the ships were trapped was very infrequently visited by the Inuit.

Of great importance to the Inuit was the area known as Utjulik. This name came up repeatedly in Inuit testimony, as the site of the wreck of one of the Franklin ships. The ship was located in 2014 by a Canadian government search expedition and identified as *Erebus*. Captain McClintock was the first European to hear of the two wrecks. One sank in deep water and little was got out of her, but the other was driven ashore by ice and very much material was obtained by the Inuit. It was this second ship that was described as being at Utjulik and became known as the 'Utjulik ship'. McClintock unsuccessfully searched the west coast of King William Island for her remains.

In 2008, Dorothy Harley Eber reviewed the definitions of 'Utjulik'. She identified L.A. Learmouth - a HBC trader who spoke fluent Inuktitut - as describing 'Oot-loo-lik' as an area where the bearded seal is plentiful. Eber reported it to be an immense area where Inuit hunt over the ice in spring. It includes the Royal Geographical Society Islands and extends south along to south-west coast of King William Island, to the shores of the north American Continent and includes the Adelaide Peninsula and west as far as Jenny Lind Island off the south-east tip of Victoria Island – an area measuring ninety-seven miles east to west and ninety-one miles north to south.

Eber also described from within this area, some new discoveries by the present day Inuit population of Gjoa Haven. These are sites in the area where Europeans had cooked seal meat using seal blubber fires, so that the ground became impregnated with seal oil. This was something the Inuit would not do and indicated that a few of the longest living expedition members (of the reoccupied *Erebus*) had eked out their existence for at least two winters by seal hunting in the Utjulik area.

The first Europeans landed on the northern end of King William Island, led by James Clark Ross who sailed on board the '*Victory*' paddle steamer in May 1829 under the command of his uncle Captain John Ross. They arrived at Cape Felix at the northern tip of the island on May 28 1830, after sledging for thirteen days from their ship in Prince Regent Inlet. They pushed four hours south along the western coast and camped. Two of the party including Ross moved on south for another four hours arriving at a low spit of land at midnight. They named it 'Victory Point'. There they built a cairn six feet high and put a canister with a record inside in it. At one o'clock in the morning they started back to the camp and the whole party then returned to the ship.

The south-west corner of the island was sighted by Captain George Back in 1834. A search party led by Back was sent out to look for the missing Ross expedition. However the Ross party was rescued by whalers and Back's expedition ordered to continue with exploration. George Back led his men via the Hudson's Bay Fort Resolution on the Great Slave Lake, crossed several other lakes and descended the 500 mile long Back's Great Fish River in 1834. He then travelled along the estuary of the river (Chantrey Inlet). From its entrance, in bad weather he glimpsed two headlands to the north that were the south-western corner of King William Island. Back then returned north. However his journey and the abundance of wildlife that he reported would have a profound effect on the trapped Franklin expedition who in 1848, retreated south for Back's Great Fish River, rather than heading north as John Ross and his crew had done.

Back discovered on his return to England that while at the mouth to the estuary of Chantrey Inlet three of his men had surprised some Inuit who fired their bows at them. The men retaliated with gunfire and three Inuit fell dead and others were wounded. Repercussions of this incident may have played a role in the retreat of the Franklin survivors. After the Franklin disaster C.F. Hall heard of a small party of survivors who appeared in the east in Boothia. They reported encountering hostile Inuit and turning away probably from Back's Great Fish River.

In August 1839, Thomas Simpson with a boat party, travelled along sixty miles of the south-west coast of King William Island in what is now known as Simpson Strait. The party observed plenty of musk ox, and caribou, while overhead vast numbers of snow geese passed in triangular flights. Numerous old Inuit encampments were seen but no Inuit (who would have been summer fishing at Lake Amitsoq). Simpson landed on Cape Herschel on south-west King William Island and built a cairn there, only 100 miles from Ross's cairn at Victory Point, and then returned westward.

The islands of the Arctic are divided by a great ice stream up to seventy miles wide that originates in the Beaufort Sea (a part of the Polar Sea) and is carried by wind and current (see Map 1). The pack moves south-east between Banks and Melville Islands and then turns to the east along Viscount Melville Sound where it divides. Part of it continues east along Barrow Strait and Lancaster Sound and on into Baffin Bay. The other half continues to the south-east between Victoria and Prince of Wales Islands. The south-eastern branch of the ice stream, after travelling 700 miles from the Beaufort Sea, is blocked by the north-western shores of King William

Island. The stream forms a barrier impassible to wooden sailing ships for most years. It was in this ice stream, off the north-west coast of King William Island that the Franklin ships were trapped on September 12 1846 and abandoned on April 22 1848.

The stream was first seen by William Edward Parry in 1819-1820, after his remarkable voyage west through Lancaster Sound to Melville Island where he wintered. The ice stream blocked his further passage west.

This ice stream was encountered in 1830 by James Clark Ross with a sledge party out of the paddle ship *Victory*, captained by his uncle John Ross. James Clark Ross described it as they saw it on the north-west coast of King William Land in his uncle's book:

> The pack of ice which had in the autumn of the last year, been pressed against the shore, consisted of the heaviest masses that I had ever seen in such a situation, with others, the lighter flows had been thrown up on some parts of the coast, in a most extraordinary and inconceivable manner; turning up large quantities of shingle before them, and, in some places, having travelled as much as a half mile beyond the limits of the highest tide mark.

It was in this ice stream off the north-west coast of King William Island that both ships of Sir John Franklin's expedition were trapped and abandoned. It was known that in summer a sea route existed along the northern shores of the American continent. If the Franklin Expedition ships could cross the ice stream, they could then sail to Bering Strait and home.

With the knowledge that the Franklin expedition had at the time, this was the only possible route for the long sought after North-West Passage. The pity was that an open-water route existed down the east side of King William Island, but at the time Franklin arrived it was not yet known, and King William Land was believed to be a peninsula joining the Isthmus of Boothia. This channel is today known as the James Ross Strait.

Nearly sixty years later, between 1903 and 1906, Roald Amundsen in the small *Gjoa* (a former herring sloop of forty-five tonnes, sixty nine feet long, beam twenty three feet and draft nine feet), made the first voyage through the North-West Passage by this route. But even his small ship grounded and many stores had to be thrown overboard to lighten her on the reefs around Matty Island.

The Beaufort ice stream was observed by several of the search expeditions looking for the lost Franklin Expedition. In 1851 Captain Robert McClure in the *Investigator* sailed around the north-east corner of Banks Island and worked south along the coast with the ice stream on his port side. *Investigator* was worked along a narrow passage between the land-fast ice and the ice stream. Eventually the ship became trapped in the ice of a winter harbour and never escaped. In 1852 McClure and his crew abandoned *Investigator* and walked east across the sixty-mile wide ice steam to their rescue by *Resolute* of the Belcher Relief Expedition. They become the first men to complete a North-West Passage route and survive.

The Austin Relief Expedition of 1850-51, carried out an extensive winter sledging program from Cape Walker. Captain Erasmus Ommanney and Lieutenant Sherard Osborne of *Assistance* travelled down the west coast of Prince of Wales Land and observed the heavy unnavigable ice of the ice stream to the west.

Allen Young, Sailing Master of the *Fox*, under command of Captain Leopold McClintock in the spring of 1859, sledged across Peel Sound to examine the southern part of Prince of Wales Island. He reported on the heavy ice in McClintock Channel as making it certain that the missing Franklin Expedition had not sailed that way.

In 1865 Captain Sherard Osborn described the ice stream at night thus:

> Through the long dark night, the sullen grinding of the moving pack, and the loud report made by some huge mass of ice which burst under pressure, boomed through the solitude, and as starlight glimmered over the wild scene to seaward, the men could just detect the pack rearing up and rolling over, by the alternate reflected lights and shadows.

The pre-Franklin expedition reports of abundant summer life on southern King William Island and in the estuary of Back's Great Fish River had a profound effect on the officers of the Franklin expedition when it came to abandoning the ships. For instead of heading north to Fury Beach as expected, they headed south for Back's Great Fish River – a fact never discovered by the many Royal Navy search expeditions. Had Sir John Franklin been alive at the time of the retreat, he may have decided against a southern route, as it would have meant crossing hundreds of miles of 'the Barren Lands,' where more than a half of his 1820 to 1822 expedition had died of starvation and cannibalism had occurred. Sir John Franklin became famous from that expedition by narrowly escaping starvation to become known as 'the man who ate his boots'.

4: THE DREAM OF A NORTH-WEST PASSAGE

Two centuries after the 1616 voyage of William Baffin to the Arctic regions, interest in the possibility of a sea route linking the Pacific and Atlantic oceans north of the American continent, was revived by the British Admiralty. This followed the victory at the Battle of Trafalgar on October 21 1805, when 100 years of peace followed.

A series of naval expeditions by land and sea took place over the next twenty years that mapped a lot of what is now the Canadian Arctic. The leaders of these expeditions were Lieutenant John Franklin, Commander John Ross, Lieutenant Edward Parry, Captain George Back and Commander James Clark Ross (John Ross's nephew). The adventures of these men and their ships created enormous interest in Victorian society and the men and ships became household names, in much the same way as the NASA lunar exploration commanded interest in the twentieth century. The above named expedition leaders became distinguished explorers and were all knighted.

In 1818 the British Admiralty selected Captain John Ross to lead an expedition to seek a northern sea passage between the Atlantic and Pacific oceans. Ross was an experienced captain who had seen service in the Baltic and White Sea. The expedition was not a great success particularly as Ross missed the significance of Lancaster Sound which he thought was a bay. He thought he saw a distant range of mountains behind it, that he named the Croker Mountains after the Secretary of the Admiralty. Ross was accompanied by Lieutenant Edward Parry, a twenty-eight-year-old naval officer, who had doubts about Ross's interpretation and thought he had missed a great opportunity for exploration.

The next year Parry returned with two ships, *Hecla* and *Griper*, and sailed 500 miles westward through Lancaster Sound and beyond naming many islands and opening the way to the North-West Passage. Parry returned twice more to the Arctic in 1821 and 1824, each time learning more of the area north of the American continent.

The 1824 expedition proved an expensive disaster as during the winter of 1824-25, *Fury* was badly damaged by ice in Prince Regent Inlet. In an attempt to lighten her, provisions and stores were put ashore but the ship had to be abandoned. The stores and provisions were left and the site became known as Fury beach and proved a lifesaver for later crews also trapped in the Arctic. *Fury's* crew boarded *Hecla* and returned home.

Meanwhile, in 1820 the Admiralty sent Lieutenant John Franklin to map the northern shoreline of the American continent with the help of the Hudson's Bay Company. The party travelled overland and used sledges and canoes. They were gone for three and a half years and made a journey of 5,200 miles but suffered starvation and some cannibalism. Franklin returned a second time to continue the work. Other voyages were undertaken by Lieutenant Edward Parry and Captain George Back.

A lost expedition in 1719

The Franklin expedition was not the first to be entirely lost in the Arctic. In 1719, an Englishman, James Knight in his seventies, with vast Arctic experience and a governor of the Hudson's Bay Company, set out to find a North-West Passage.

He took forty men in a Hudson's Bay ship - the *Albany* - together with a sloop - the *Discovery*, commanded by Mr Barlow and Mr Knight. They entered Hudson's Bay, but were cast ashore on Marble Island.

Forty years later, in 1759, Samuel Hearne of the Hudson's Bay Company learned of their fate from the Inuit. Most of the men got ashore onto the island, where they built a wooden house for the winter. The Inuit returned the following spring and found the numbers of sailors much reduced and very unhealthy. Sickness and famine had reduced their numbers to around twenty by the start of the second winter. The Inuit camped nearby at this time and supplied the sailors with what blubber, seal meat and train oil they could spare.

Next spring the Inuit set off on their annual hunting trip and returned in the summer of 1721, when only five sailors remained alive. The sailors were so hungry that they devoured raw seal meat and blubber, as they purchased it from the Inuit. They were so weak that three of them died within a few days. The two survivors, although very weak, managed to bury them. They managed to live a few days longer. The last survivor died while digging a grave for his companion. The two ships were found by John Geiger and Owen Beattie, who carried out a full forensic investigation and wrote a book on their findings.

The precedent set by Sir John Ross

For a full decade after his first Arctic expedition, John Ross did not return to the Arctic, but submitted to the Admiralty a plan for further Arctic exploration for the North-West Passage. He considered that much could be achieved by smaller exploration parties. He did not get Admiralty approval. So he put up £3000 - about £300,000 at modern prices - of his own money and obtained the remainder required (£17,000) from Felix Booth, a distiller and Sheriff of London. Ross purchased the small eighty-five ton paddle ship *Victory* (150 tons loaded weight) which drew only nine feet of water.

Ross had the fixed paddles and engines replaced with an auxiliary engine and paddle wheels that could be hoisted up to avoid sea ice. She had three masts and had been used as a packet on the run between Liverpool and the Isle of Man. Her crew comprised four officers and nineteen men. Second in command was a nephew of John Ross, Commander James Clark Ross. It was to be the first time an engine would be used in Arctic exploration. However, the engine took up so much space in the ship that there was insufficient space to store all the stores and equipment. The overflow was put aboard a sixteen ton decked sloop - the *Krusenstern* - provided by the Admiralty.

The expedition sailed from Woolwich on the Thames, on May 23 1829. Almost immediately the engine developed piston problems and the boilers leaked, reducing the ship's speed to only three knots. Dung and potatoes were placed inside the boilers but they continued to leak and soon burst. However the brisk Atlantic winds gave the expedition a fast ten day passage to the southernmost point of Greenland. Then the engines let them down again with a speed of only one and a half knots. But on August 6 they entered Lancaster Sound, finding it ice free. They turned south between Somerset Island and Baffin Island and reached Fury Beach.

There they found the supplies left by Parry four years earlier to be intact and unspoiled, although there was no sign of Fury. They took aboard sufficient supplies and provisions including ten tons of coal to supply them for two and a half years. They proceeded south, but unfortunately missed Bellot Strait – the only channel leading west. Ross saw granite hills to the west and named the land Boothia Felix. They continued south until September, when the ships were frozen into a bay they named Felix Harbour on the eastern side of what is today known as the Isthmus of Boothia. Their first act was to dismantle the engine and put it ashore. With its tools, it had taken up two thirds of their tonnage and had let them down badly. They created valuable space for their winter quarters. Rigging and sails were taken down and the deck housed in with canvas. A good Christmas followed.

On January 9 1830, thirty-one Inuit appeared and camped a short distance from the ship. The carpenter made a wooden leg for one of them. From the Inuit, John Ross learned much about the geography to the west and that the land (named the Isthmus of Boothia by John Ross) was narrow and a great sea lay to the west. The Inuit also described the then undiscovered channel across the isthmus that later became known as Bellot Strait.

In May and June 1830, James Clark Ross made a sledge trip west across the isthmus with an Inuit guide. It was an exploring trip that had profound implications for future searches for the North-West Passage. He crossed over what is today called James Ross Strait to Matty Island and then Tennent Island, before discovering King William Land (then believed to be a part of the American continent). At Tennent Island he discovered an excellent harbour and wrote of it:

> A reef extending from this point north-westward, for two miles and a half, so as to meet the north point of Tennent Island, protects an excellent harbour, could such a harbour be of any use; and its entrance, which is two miles wide, is divided in the middle by an islet that would effectively cover it from the invasion of heavy ice. As the island was named after Mr. Emerson Tennent, so has this, by the title of Port Emerson.

Next, his party explored the northern part of King William Land, naming the northern tip Cape Felix. Port Emerson lies only thirty-one miles southeast of Point Felix. Ross continued for a further nineteen miles south-west from Cape Felix along the coast of King William Island to reach his furthest point from his base aboard the *Victory*. He named this Victory Point. About Victory Point he wrote:

> At Victory Point we erected a cairn six feet high, and we enclosed in it a container containing a brief account of the proceedings of the expedition since its departure from England.

Here, on the west coast of King William Land, he was only 100 miles from Cape Herschel (on the south-west coast) that would be revealed and mapped by Simpson in 1839. Simpson would demonstrate a North-West Passage with only 100 miles left to complete the mapping. At Victory Point Ross built a cairn before returning to their ship. The completion of the mapping of this short stretch of the North-West Passage between Cape Herschel and Victory Point became the main objective of the Franklin Expedition of 1845. Regrettably the cairn and record at Victory Point were never again found and a controversy of exactly where Ross's Victory Point was, continued with later explorers up until the mid-twentieth century.

In late 1830 the Ross expedition anxiously awaited the breakup of the ice. A trip was made to a nearby Inuit camp, where a ton of fish was purchased for a knife. Finally, on September 17 the ships were released but only progressed three miles up the coast before being frozen in again for a second winter.

During this winter, James Clark Ross studied the Earth's magnetic field and concluded that the North Magnetic Pole lay somewhere on the west coast of the Isthmus of Boothia and he decided to seek it. On May 19 1831, he and his party set out for the magnetic pole. They were accompanied by another party led by his uncle John Ross. They crossed the isthmus together and then split up. James Clark Ross located the magnetic pole, where his party built a cairn and claimed it for Great Britain and King William the Fourth. Meanwhile, his uncle and party proceeded to explore the coastline.

Back aboard the *Victory*, summer was an anxious time awaiting release of the ship. This happened on August 28 1831. But again the distance travelled was minor, before the ship was once again frozen in for another year. A third winter had not been planned. This time no Inuit came to visit or trade. Scurvy broke out and caused despondency. Captain John Ross dared not await another summer in case *Victory* might not be released. He planned that in the spring of 1832, the men would make their way on foot north to Fury beach to pick up food and three of Fury's boats. Then, in the boats they would proceed to Baffin Bay, where they might find whaling ships. During April and May advance depots were laid out along the coast of Boothia. On May 20 *Victory's* colors were raised and she was abandoned by her officers and crew.

A month later the entire party, after travelling 200 miles north, arrived at Fury Beach. The first requirement was shelter and they built a house thirty feet long, fifteen feet wide and seven feet high covered in canvas. They named it Somerset House. It was divided into two rooms, one for the men and the other was divided into four small cabins for the officers. The wooden frame took a day to erect, and after three days they moved in. The carpenters strengthened the three boats, which were equipped with sails. On August 1 they were ready to move. The boats were seaworthy and provisioned for two months. The twenty-one remaining men were divided into groups of seven for each boat. Behind them they would leave a base at Somerset House with ample supplies.

On August 27 they set out, but the weather proved atrocious. It took until September 2 to reach the north-east corner of Somerset Island. There from high land they could see Barrow Strait and Lancaster Sound - but both were solidly packed with ice. They waited for two and a half weeks. On September 25 they gave up hope and started the return to Somerset House. It proved impossible to get the boats all the way back. They were placed in a safe position and sledges made from empty bread boxes. On October 7 they were back in Somerset House.

Their fourth winter proved, not surprisingly, very hard, especially with terrible gales in October and November. They did not have enough clothing to work outside in the cold weather. All the same, they celebrated Christmas. The men had meat and the officers shared a fox.

Scurvy affected many. On February 22 the carpenter died. By spring, three of the group were too weak to get out of bed. The others could just manage to get about. In April and May they struggled to carry two months' supplies to the boats. On July 8 1833, they set out and reached the boats on July 12. Then they waited for the ice to break up. On August 15 a lane leading north opened and they set out following leads. Later that day they finally reached open water after four years in the ice.

A favourable wind took them seventy-two miles to the east. The next day, in calm weather, they rowed along the northern shore of Baffin Land. The next day they made only five miles against an easterly wind. Then for the next five days gales kept them landbound. On August 26 they reached a small harbour near the entrance to Lancaster Sound and after twelve hours of rowing the party rested. At four am the lookout saw a sail, confirmed by John Ross, with his telescope. They burned powder to make smoke and set out for the ship that was becalmed. They were making good progress in their boats, when wind suddenly filled the ships' sails and she sailed away to the south away from the boats. Throughout the morning the ship remained in sight and was pursued by the boats.

At ten o'clock a second sail was sighted, but she too turned downwind and sailed on again with the boats in pursuit. Then a calm fell and the boats approached her. At eleven o'clock she hove to and lowered a boat. When they met, Captain John Ross identified himself. He was informed that he was believed to have been dead long ago. However, by noon they were aboard the ship and safe after spending five summers in the Arctic. In England, Ross's return from the dead was widely celebrated. He was knighted and his crew, although not in the Royal Navy, was paid double wages for their time by the Admiralty.

The achievement of John Ross in extracting his party from the Arctic after abandoning his ships, required great leadership as well as prodigious amounts of good luck. The latter was the presence at Fury beach of the stores and boats of *Fury*, finding clear water in Lancaster Sound and locating a whaling ship. The achievement of Captain John Ross in extracting most of his men from the Arctic, after abandoning his ships and spending five summers in the ice, set a precedent. When the Franklin expedition disappeared, the example of John Ross was much cited. If Ross and his men could survive in the Arctic why couldn't Franklin and his crew?

Luck was indeed certainly a factor, but it was by no means the only one. Ultimately, Franklin and his large crew were simply not sufficiently well equipped for the conditions they would have to face after abandoning the ships. They were also unquestionably handicapped by imagining that their time in the Arctic desert would be considerably easier than it was to turn out to be.

5: THE SENIOR OFFICERS

By the early 1840s, while a great deal of the Arctic remained to be explored and mapped, there was a general belief that a North-West Passage existed.

The entrance was through Lancaster Sound to Barrow Strait, then through an unknown area to get to the summer open-water channel that had already been mapped along the northern edge of the American continent. What remained was a link between the two. One possibility was that if the shoreline between Victory Point and Cape Herschel on the west coast of what is now King William Island could be linked by sea – a distance of only about 100 miles – then a North-West Passage existed, although it was probably of limited commercial use because of short periods of open water.

The man behind much of the Arctic exploration was Second Secretary of the Admiralty Sir John Barrow, a man who did not like views that differed from his. He had written a book on the polar regions and was keen to see a British expedition sail through the North-West Passage.

Barrow was a highly-competent organiser who, during the long period of post-Napoleonic peace following the Battles of Trafalgar and Waterloo, decided to use the largely redundant Royal Navy (1000 ships, and 143,000 men) for exploration of the globe to increase the British prestige and empire. From 1816 until his retirement in 1845, Barrow dispatched a series of expeditions world-wide. Barrow persuaded the British government to offer a reward of £10,000 to the first ship to reach the Pacific via Arctic waters.

When it was suggested that *Erebus* and *Terror*, which had been used from 1839 to 1843 by Sir James Clark Ross for three summer Antarctic voyages, be fitted with engines and sent to explore the North Pole, Barrow opposed the suggestion. He proposed an alternative - the completion of the North-West Passage - using for the first time in the Arctic, ships with propellers. He suggested a course along Lancaster Sound and Barrow Strait as far as Cape Walker and then south west through a North-West Passage, if this proved not possible, then to ascend Wellington Channel in search of an open water polar ocean.

The proposals were examined by the Royal Society, Sir Edward Parry, Sir James Clark Ross and Sir John Franklin. Neither Ross nor Parry liked

Barrow's proposed course as they thought it would lead into the heavy ice stream they had both encountered on their voyages. Later Sir John Ross agreed and said that the expedition was likely to be lost without trace. Nonetheless the North-West Passage option of Sir John Barrow was approved.

The expedition was approved in January 1845. There was an immediate flurry of work as the two ships, *Erebus* and *Terror*, had recently returned from a lengthy expedition to the Antarctic led by James Clark Ross with Francis R. M. Crozier, second in command and Captain of the *Terror*. An appreciation of the working relationships of the officers commanding the Franklin Expedition can be gleaned by looking at the methods of selecting the officers and a valuable journal kept by Commander Fitzjames and mailed back to his sister-in-law before the ships left Greenland.

Leadership problems emerged immediately when Barrow proposed for expedition leader, a thirty-three-year-old promising commander and his protégé – James Fitzjames – who had no polar experience. Barrow had favoured Fitzjames because of his high birth, friends in high places, strong personality and leadership qualities. Barrow's patronage had speeded Fitzjames's advance within the navy. But the Admiralty favoured men of experience.

The most obvious choice of expedition leader was Sir James Clark Ross, who had stood at the North Magnetic Pole in 1831. He had just led a round-the-world expedition to study magnetism and natural sciences as well as to explore Antarctica and locate the South Magnetic Pole. He had mapped 500 miles of coastline, discovered the Antarctic ice shelf and sighted a smoking volcano that he named Mt. Erebus after his ship. A nearby crater was named Mt. Terror after the smaller of the two expedition vessels. He had come within 160 miles of the South Magnetic Pole.

However he declined the position despite being offered a baronetcy and a pension to take it. He argued that he had just married a lady who had already waited four yours for him when he led the three Antarctic expeditions. It is also possible that he favoured giving his friend Sir John Franklin the opportunity to regain his reputation after problems with his governorship of Van Diemen's Land. Ross was to reverse his decision when he led an expedition in search of the missing Franklin expedition in 1848 - 1849. The next two possible leaders considered were Sir John Franklin and Captain John Lort Stokes (who had captained *Beagle* on her third voyage of discovery to the Pacific).

Sir John Franklin

The position was offered and enthusiastically accepted by the aging Sir John Franklin, Kt., K.R.G., K.C.H., D.C.L., F.R.S., then fifty-eight years old (fifty-nine at the time of sailing). He would raise his flag aboard *Erebus* with second in command of *Erebus* being Commander Fitzjames – an outstanding officer but also a polar novice. Sir John was born in Spilsby in Lincolnshire on April 16 1786. He joined the Royal Navy at the age of fourteen. In 1845, he was portly, known to suffer from the cold and was beginning to stoop. Sir Edward Parry, also a contender, commented that Sir John was likely to die of disappointment if he did not go.

An excellent summary of Sir John's life was published by Wilson in 2001. Sir John Franklin had been with Nelson at Copenhagen at the age of fifteen (He was to distinguish himself again with Nelson as signal midshipman on board *Bellerophon* at Trafalgar in 1805). In 1801 he joined *Investigator* under the command of his uncle Captain Matthew Flinders, to survey the coastline of Australia. This first voyage of discovery established his life-long interest in exploration. He remained with Captain Flinders until the wreck of *Porpoise* on August 17 1803, off Australia on an uncharted reef. Franklin brought the survivors by small boat fifty miles to Sydney. He was next appointed to *Bellerophon*, and in 1805, was Signal Midshipman at the Battle of Trafalgar. In February 1808 he was promoted to Lieutenant and was appointed to Bedford, one of the escort ships assisting the Portugese royal family escape the French army by travelling from Lisbon to South America. He took part in the war with the United States and off New Orleans, in 1814, he commanded a division of small ships against superior American gunboats.

His first Arctic expedition was in 1818 when he joined *Trent* as second in command to Captain Buchan. With two ships, they reached Spitzbergen, but the ships were damaged by ice and the expedition, that had set out to explore the pole, returned to England. Franklin, at thirty-two years of age had acquired a reputation both for battle and exploration, so that he stood out among the many half pay officers redundant after the Battle of Trafalgar.

In 1820, Franklin led an overland expedition ordered by the Admiralty to map North America's unknown north coast. The party mapped 210 miles of coastline east of the Coppermine River, but got into difficulties on their return, crossing an area known as the 'barren ground'. Franklin almost died of starvation, ten of the party died and murder and cannibalism occurred. On his return to London, Franklin became known as 'the man who ate his boots'. He was promoted to Captain and elected a Fellow of the Royal Society.

In 1823 he married the poetess Miss Eleanor Porden. She died on February 22 1825, leaving a daughter, while Sir John was on his second land exploration of the Arctic. He had returned to mapping the North American coastline in 1825-27 in a better organised expedition. Another 200 miles of coastline were mapped and on his return Franklin was knighted and awarded the honorary degree of Doctor of Civil Law by the University of Oxford and received a gold medal from the French Geographical Society. On November 5 1828 he married Miss Jane Griffin, who later was to become world famous for her efforts to support the searches for the lost 1845 expedition. Sir John was next appointed to *Rainbow* on the Mediterranean Station, where he assisted the Greek Government. He was awarded the Cross of the Order of the Redeemer of Greece by King Otto of Greece. King William IV created him a Knight Commander of the Guelphic Order of Hanover.

Next, he was offered and accepted, the Lieutenant Governorship of Van Diemen's Land (now Tasmania) and arrived there with Lady Franklin in January 1837. They remained there for six years, but Sir John was recalled in 1843, after a catastrophic collision with the vindictive Colonial Secretary John Montagu. The issue was over the role played in the island administration by Lady Jane Franklin.

Both Sir John and Lady Jane were both very hurt and offended by Montagu's slander and vilification of them both that appeared in both Tasmanian and London newspapers and resulted in Sir John's dismissal and recall to London. For example Montagu wrote:

> It was necessary for someone to have the guidance of Sir John Franklin, as he is a perfect imbecile... unable to put two sentences together in correct English so as to be intelligible. Lady Franklin prepares all his despatches.

Montagu travelled twice to England to present his grievances to Edward Lord Stanley, Secretary of State for the Colonies. Lord Stanley took Montague's side and he was promoted, while Sir John was dismissed. Sir John was deeply offended and visited Lord Stanley on his return but failed to get his support. Finally Sir John wrote a 157 page justification of his actions in Van Diemen's Land that was published in 1845, shortly after the 1845 expedition sailed. Sir John wrote in the Preface to the report on May 15 1845:

> The work most reluctantly begun has occupied more time than I had anticipated. It was very far from being finished when the preparations for

the Arctic expedition called off my thoughts and time to other duties more congenial to my habits, and still more imperative; and thus it has happened that, to my extreme vexation and regret, I find the day of my departure at hand without the satisfaction I had expected of seeing my pamphlet out of the press. This delay has however given me the advantage of receiving from Van Diemen's Land the documents contained in the Postscript. I have had this part of the work printed off, and have enclosed a copy to the Secretary of State for the Colonies.

In 1845, both Sir John and his wife, saw the planned new Arctic expedition to complete the North-West Passage as an opportunity to vindicate their reputations, despite Sir John's health and age (the expedition was expected to last for only one or two years). For Lord Stanley, the removal of Sir John to the Arctic avoided further conflict over his dismissal as Governor of Van Diemen's Land.

The resulting loss of the entire expedition and both ships has given Sir John's name immortality and generated a vast literature on the lost expedition that shows no sign of abating. Lady Jane Franklin also won international fame for her strong support for the lost expedition and her husband, that involved much letter writing to prominent people including the President of the USA and the Czar of Russia, requesting support in the search for the lost expedition and her husband. She also used her own finances to send out a number of private search expeditions. The very many search expeditions almost completed the mapping of what is today the Canadian Arctic and forms the basis for territorial claims to the area.

Captain Crozier

Command of *Terror* and second in command of the expedition was Captain Francis Rawdon Moira Crozier aged forty-nine, who had immense experience in polar regions and had participated in seven polar expeditions before he joined the Franklin Expedition. Other than Sir James Clark Ross, he was the most experienced of the Royal Navy's polar explorers. An excellent summary of his life was published by Smith in 2014. Captain Crozier was about as opposite to Commander Fitzjames as it was possible to get. He was a quiet, somewhat shy, retiring person who did not seek personal glory. Smith described him as a modest, unassuming man. He was popular with his crews, good natured with a strict and fair discipline. Because he and his family originated in northern Ireland, he did not have the social standing of Fitzjames, nor the patronage, and was never considered for command of the expedition. He lacked the confident ability of Fitzjames to win the approval of his superior officers.

Captain Crozier was born in Bambridge, County Down, Ireland in September 1796. He joined the Royal Navy at the age of fourteen and served in various ships. His vast experience in polar regions, before the Franklin expedition, began when he sailed as midshipman on board *Fury*. The expedition was led by Edward Parry on his second Arctic venture in search of the North-West Passage from 1821-1823. In 1824 he again accompanied Parry as midshipman on board *Hecla*, on Parry's third voyage in search of the North-West Passage. In March 1826 he was promoted to Lieutenant. In 1827, Crozier, accompanied Edward Parry on a voyage towards the North Pole. In 1836, Crozier accompanied Captain John Ross in an Arctic search for missing whaling ships, after which he was promoted to commander (in January 1837).

From 1839 to 1843 Crozier accompanied Sir James Clark Ross with the two ships, *Erebus* and *Terror* to explore unknown territories of Antarctica. Crozier was promoted to the rank of Captain in August 1841 during the Antarctic expedition. He captained *Terror* and achieved a rare distinction by not losing a single man on that expedition. The expedition spent two winters in Van Diemen's Land, where the two commanders were the guests of Sir John and Lady Franklin. It was while he was a guest of Sir John Franklin, that he met Franklin's niece Sophia Cracroft, that led to an unhappy romance.

After returning from the Antarctic and having had two marriage proposals to Miss Cracroft turned down, Crozier took himself on leave. When he heard of the planned 1845 expedition, he was in Florence. He immediately wrote a short note to his friend Sir James Clark Ross:

> I hesitate not a moment to go second to Sir John Franklin, pray tell him so, if too late I cannot help it. Of course I am too late to volunteer to command but, in truth, I sincerely feel I am not equal to the leadership. I would not on any terms go second to any other, Captain Parry or yourself excepted. Act for me, my dear friend, in this as you see fit and I will carry it out in every particular. I will write you by tomorrow's post more fully but to the same purpose.

The next day he wrote again:

> If not too late I am quite ready to go second to our kind friend, Sir John, with none else, save and exempt yourself and Captain Parry would I go. I am, in truth, still of opinion as to my own qualities to lead. You, on that subject as well as all others, know my whole mind. Whatever you arrange

for me, I will hasten, on hearing from you, to carry out to the fullest of my ability. Now I leave all with you, and have only to say that whatever you settle I will be quite content with. If I hear from you that Sir John would accept my services, I would start from here immediately for London, if not, I propose accompanying my friends from here to Rome and Naples. Til I hear from you I will not leave my present abode. Your letter was ten days coming. I, therefore, cannot expect an answer from you before 19th or twentieth January so that I could not be in London before February but, as ships would not sail before May, there would be plenty of time.

Captain Crozier was appointed second-in-command of the expedition under Sir John Franklin and Captain of *Terror*. Crozier, sailing with James Clark Ross, had carried out a scientific program in magnetism, water sampling and astronomic observations. On his return he was elected a Fellow of the Royal Society for his work in terrestrial magnetism that included the invention of a dip needle, that was to be used on the 1845 expedition. But he was not in a happy frame of mind, because of the failure of his two proposals of marriage to Sir John Franklin's niece Miss Sophia Cracroft. The latter refused to be married to a sea captain. Lady Jane Franklin is reported to have said that Miss Cracroft 'liked the man but not the sailor.'

A return to polar exploration might have been an antidote, something to take the mind off a failed courtship, a return to a challenging physical world he understood and where he felt his great polar experience would be a valuable asset. However, this was not to be the case and when he found that officer selection had been assigned to Commander Fitzjames, after he had successfully selected the crews for the Antarctic expeditions, he would have felt snubbed. This was repeated when he learned that the magnetic work had also been assigned to Commander Fitzjames, despite the fact that he had just been elected to the Royal Society for his scientific work in Antarctica.

Commander James Fitzjames

The third senior officer was Commander James Fitzjames, who, at thirty-three years of age was appointed commander of *Erebus*, serving directly under Captain Sir John Franklin. Much information about Fitzjames has become available in an excellent book by Battersby published in 2010. Fitzjames was a large, personable and a strong leader with a good sense of humour. He had influence or friends in high places. He has been described as 'amongst the most promising officers in the navy at that time,' 'strong, self-reliant, enthusiastic,' 'a born leader of men,' 'the handsomest man in the navy,' 'a well-bred young gentleman.' His demeanour was 'an easy mix of self-effacing humour and firm command'. He spoke confidently with an upper class accent and a slight lisp. Perhaps the Admiralty felt that although Sir John was rather old, the young competent Fitzjames would make up for any deficiencies.

James Fitzjames joined the Royal Navy in August 1825, and served in various ships. In 1835 he joined an expedition led by Colonel Chesney to see if the River Euphrate was navigable by steamers and could be used for a route to India. This involved disassembling two steamers and transporting the sections across the Syrian desert to the river, to reassemble them and then descending the river. In February 1835, while preparing for the expedition in Liverpool, Fitzjames rescued a Customs official from drowning and was awarded silver medals by the Royal Humane Society and the London Shipwreck Society. The two steamers were assembled and set out. One was wrecked and the other, with Fitzjames as mate, completed the passage, providing him with a valuable experience in steam engines. He then served in *Ganges* on operations to bombard the coastal fortresses of Mehemet Ali in Lebanon and Syria. In May 1841 he went to China in Cornwallis to fight in the Chinese opium wars. He commanded a rocket brigade in several engagements. He was wounded during the capture of Ching-Kiang-Foo. In 1842 he was promoted to the rank of Commander and joined *Clio* until October 1844. He was promoted to Captain during his absence on the 1845 expedition.

In his book, Battersby uncovered a dark secret kept hidden by Fitzjames. The latter was the illegitimate son of Sir James Gambier with several admirals as ancestors. Sir James Gambier with his wife and six children had lived at one time in Rio de Janiero as a British diplomat working with the exiled Portuguese royal family. Fitzjames's mother is unknown but was of some social rank in Brazilian society. At the end of the Napoleanic wars, Sir James Gambier returned to England and brought his one-year-old illegitimate son with him. The baby was christened James Fitzjames and handed over to foster parents Louisa and Robert Coningham, along with his Portugese nurse, so that at fourteen years he spoke fluent Portuguese. The Coningham's only son to live to maturity, William, became Fitzjames best friend. An earlier son John had died and Fitzjames of similar age was adopted in his place. The boys were well educated.

At the age of twelve Fitzjames was enrolled into the Royal Navy, probably because he proved a large boisterous boy in an otherwise quiet family. His first ship's captain was his natural cousin Robert Gambier, who took him on as a volunteer, registering him on August 25 1825. He lived with the Gambier family in Portsmouth while the ship was readied. It was the start of an adventurous life.

Fitzjames was a large strong jovial leader and when appointed executive officer of Franklin's flagship, *Erebus*, was made responsible by the Admiralty for selecting the crews of both ships. Battersby states that a third of the officers selected by Fitzjames had previous polar experience (Franklin, Crozier, Gore, Reid, Blanky, Collins as well as Osmer, MacDonald and Stanley). This is a higher proportion than James Clark Ross took with him to the Antarctic. Many of the officers Fitzjames selected were his friends with whom he had sailed previously, and like him had distinguished records. This became an important factor in decision making in the future for the expedition. From his days on *Clio*, he selected his former First Lieutenant Henry Thomas Dundas Le Vesconte (Lieutenant, *Erebus*), Edwin Helpman (purser and paymaster, *Terror*) and Richard Aylmore (Fitzjames servant, *Erebus*). From his time on *Cornwallis*, Fitzjames selected Dr. Stephen Stanley (senior surgeon, *Erebus*), Lieutenant George Hodgson (Lieutenant *Terror*), and Charles Des Voeux (mate *Erebus*). His China Seas days led to the selection of George Hodgson (Lieutenant, *Terror*), and Edward Couch (mate *Erebus*). From his days on *Ganges* he selected James Fairholme (Lieutenant, *Erebus*).

Not all of Fitzjames's selections were approved by the Admiralty and Captain Crozier. Fitzjames's particular friend D'Arcy Wynward was turned down. Captain Crozier selected Thomas Jepson to be his servant. At Disko Island in Greenland Captain Crozier had two crewmen of *Terror*, who had been selected by Fitzjames, returned to England as being entirely useless at their professed trades. Amongst the 101 crewmen of the two ships were men who followed particular officers. Battersby estimated that almost 10% of the Franklin crews of *Erebus* and *Terror* had served on the two ships during James Clark Ross's Antarctic expeditions of 1839-43. A full list of the crews who went into the ice and were lost is given in Appendix 1.

Fitzjames was an ambitious man. For him the Franklin expedition, which appeared to be a rounding off work on a near completely mapped North-West Passage (only a 100 mile section left to be completed), offered a good chance to make his name. Fitzjames tried to arrange a visit by Queen Victoria to the ships but did not succeed. He also asked for his mail to be forwarded to Petro Paulowski [modern name 'Petropavlovsk'] in Kamchatka, Russia and asked his patron Barrow to arrange a speedy passage through Russia for him, so he could return to England with the news of the conquest of the North-West Passage, ahead of the ship on the long passage home via the Pacific.

This self-interest without any concern for assisting his ageing Commanding Officer get the expedition back home, shows him to be an unashamed glory hunter. Perhaps, not surprisingly, at a dinner on May 8 hosted by Lord Haddington (of the Admiralty) for the senior expedition officers to which all famous explorers attended, he met Parry and informed him that after the Franklin expedition he would like to attempt the North Pole (never having yet been to polar regions). It must have been galling to Captain Crozier to watch the friendship growing between his friend Sir John Franklin and this rather brash young officer without polar experience. Crozier was probably worried that Commander Fitzjames might influence the expedition leader with enthusiastic suggestions that because of his polar inexperience, and because Crozier was isolated on *Terror*, might place the expedition in danger.

Interaction of the three senior officers

The roles and interaction of the three senior officers eventually caused problems for the expedition as they each had different motivations.

Fifty-nine-year-old Sir John Franklin was the big name who brought confidence to the expedition. He was however injured by public slander and his abrupt dismissal and recall from his post of Lieutenant Governor of Van Diemen's Land. Although late in life for polar work, he badly wanted a last chance to re-establish himself and retire in glory, as it was eighteen years since he returned from his last polar expedition. The ignominious recall from the governorship of Van Dieman's Land and criticism of his wife Lady Jane deeply offended him. He badly wanted to make one last great achievement.

Captain Crozier on the other hand, had courted Miss Cracroft and had twice had his marriage proposals turned down. He was also recovering from the four arduous years of exploring around Antarctica with James Clark Ross. He was not a rich man, being the eleventh child, he did not own large estates and had spent the past year on half pay. By accepting the second in command position, he was probably escaping back into the familiar rugged world of shipboard life and polar exploration. He had volunteered as he felt his immense polar experience would be of great value to the expedition.

Commander Fitzjames aged thirty-three, was ambitious, personable, confident, a good leader of men and determined to rise to great heights. Without previous polar experience, like Sir John Barrow, he saw the expedition as the biggest and best equipped polar expedition ever mounted and fully expected the ships to return through the Bering Strait the following year. The Admiralty confidence was so great that there was no discussion of what might be done if the ships were trapped in the ice and failed to return as with Parry's *Fury* and John Ross's *Victory*. Fitzjames had made some arrangements to leave the ships at Petro Paulowski [Petropavlovsk] in Kamchatka and to travel overland through Russia to arrive in London ahead of the ships to announce the completion of the North-West Passage. He even had his mail forwarded to Petro Paulowski [Petropavlovsk]. He did not consider Franklin's age nor need for support on the long voyage back.

When Crozier returned to London, he soon found cause for dissatisfaction with the expedition. Instead of using his great experience, the Admiralty had already assigned responsibility both for recruiting the officers and men for the expedition as well as the magnetic work to polar novice Commander Fitzjames. This was a considerable snub to Crozier, as on the Antarctic expeditions with James Clark Ross these duties had been Crozier's responsibilities as second in command. He was very proud that of the crews he selected, there had been no deaths on the arduous voyages. As a result of his scientific work he had just been elected a Fellow of the Royal Society.

It did not help when he found that Commander Fitzjames had become a personal favourite of Sir John Franklin. Crozier was placed in a difficult position as the officers chosen by Fitzjames were not the more experienced polar men that Crozier might have favoured. It became obvious to the quiet retiring Crozier, that he was engaged in a very risky venture. Risky because his great expertise was not being utilised. Crozier ran a tight ship with a tight discipline. He began to view Sir John Franklin and Commander Fitzjames aboard *Erebus* as far too easy going. He wrote to his friend and former commanding officer James Clark Ross that the flagship with lax discipline had become a confused mess. He added a major criticism of Sir John Franklin, that he was very decided in his views and lacked good judgement.

Clearly Crozier's vast experience (like that of his Ice Master Thomas Blanky), had resulted in a lack of confidence in the senior officers of the flag ship. By the time the ships reached Greenland, Crozier and Blanky (the hugely experienced men of *Terror*) both held very grim views on the possible outcome of the expedition. The two ships were therefore run very differently. *Terror* was run on strict navy lines, whereas the flagship *Erebus* was a very sociable and happy ship with a somewhat relaxed discipline. This situation seems to have remained throughout the expedition, for when Sir John Franklin died on June 11 1847, Captain Crozier failed to carry out the Admiralty instruction that he transfer to command of *Erebus*, and put Fitzjames in charge of *Terror* (1848 Record).

Unfortunately, by the time Crozier gained command of the expedition, both ships were trapped in the ice stream on a lee shore of King William Island without the protection of a winter harbour. Perhaps the flagship had decided to take a major gamble on getting through to Bering Strait or nothing. Events proved it to be a situation that Crozier, despite his vast experience, was unable to resolve despite his well disciplined crew.

Crozier's last letter to his close friend Sir James Clark Ross (see later) is not a happy one and he is clearly depressed. His courtship of Miss Sophia Cracroft has failed. He deeply misses his friend, confident and former expedition leader James Clark Ross. It is difficult for him to accept the new role of the flagship *Erebus* under the leadership of Sir John Franklin and to see his junior, Commander Fitzjames, usurping his position in the expedition both as magnetics officer and playing the sociable role of the 'life and soul' at the heart of the flagship. His daily separation aboard *Terror* minimised his ability to influence the major decisions of the expedition. He was avoiding *Erebus* as he did not wish to see Sir John occupying the great cabin where he enjoyed the company of his friend Sir James Clark Ross. He is doing his duty, but he sees the expedition leader as not up to the standard of James Clark Ross. He fears the judgement of Franklin and that the ships will blunder into the ice and repeat the events of 1824.

The latter is a reference to Parry's third voyage to the Arctic in 1824-25 in which Crozier participated. Parry took two ships (*Hecla* and *Fury*) to explore Regent's Inlet. The ice proved heavy that year and Parry pushed them until both were driven ashore by the ice and *Fury* had to be abandoned. This was not a false fear because it is just what came about when *Erebus* and *Terror* under the command of Sir John Franklin became trapped in the ice two years later, and both ships and their crews were eventually lost. The letter also shows that Crozier is lacking the buoyant confidence of an expedition leader. Instead he is revealed as a man who has doubts and worries a lot. For this reason he was a superb second in command under James Clark Ross, but lacked the flair needed for expedition leadership. His letters to Sir James Clark Ross indicate that he knew of this weakness. His style was to play things by the book - navy fashion.

Roderic Owen is a descendant of Sir John Franklin and today is in possession of the final personal letter sent by Franklin to his wife Lady Jane from Greenland. In this Franklin is aware of the depressed state of Crozier. The Franklins had hosted James Clark Ross and Crozier when *Erebus* and *Terror* twice-wintered in Van Diemen's Land. He noted the effort that Crozier was making to be sociable. Franklin obviously thought the depression was because his niece Miss Sophia Cracroft had twice turned down his proposals of marriage. Franklin wrote to Lady Jane:

> entre nous – I do not think that he has had his former flow of spirits since we sailed – nor that he has been quite well. He seemed more cheerful and better today, and has always been very kind and attentive – I endeavour to encourage in him a close intimacy with me, which I think will soon come on. He has never mentioned Sophy – nor made the slightest allusion to her – and I sometimes question myself whether or not it would be agreeable or proper for me to speak of her to him.

Some of the other officers.

Lieutenant Graham Gore of *Erebus* was selected by Sir John Franklin to lead the party to map the final link in the North-West Pasage. Gore had entered the navy five years before Fitzjames, but lacked the patronage that saw Fitzjames rise rapidly to the rank of Commander. Gore had fought at Navarino. He was mate on *Terror* during Back's attempt at the North-West Passage. He had sailed aboard the *Beagle* on her third voyage under Captain Stokes. His father and grandfather both had distinguished naval careers.

Naval expeditions often took outstanding scientists with them. Captain Cook had taken Sir Joseph Banks with him. Charles Darwin had sailed aboard the *Beagle* on her second voyage to the Galapagos Islands. Captain Ross and Crozier had taken Joseph Hooker with them to the Antarctic. The appointment of Dr. Harry Goodsir as Assistant Surgeon aboard *Erebus* provided an outstanding medical and scientific researcher, who was friendly with Hooker and Darwin.

A particularly valuable man was Thomas Blanky, appointed Ice Master of *Terror*. He was a Yorkshireman with a vast Arctic experience. He had served on three earlier naval Arctic expeditions, the first two as an able seaman. He had been mate aboard *Victory* on John Ross's epic voyage and his experience there was not unlike the desperate situation that would arise for the Franklin expedition, when the ships were abandoned. He was regarded as a rough diamond and had at one time run a public house in Whitby.

James Reid was appointed Ice Master on *Erebus*. He was a former Greenland whaler and would advise the officers on ice conditions. Fitzjames liked him and made fun of his strong Scottish accent and thought him rough, intelligent, unpolished, good humoured and honest. The other officers did not like Reid. Le Vesconte described him as a queer fellow, meaning strange, and most thought they would be better off without him.

Part of his unpopularity stemmed from his not being of the same social level as the young officers.

The voyage out to Greenland

The ships left Woolwich for Greenhithe on May 12 1845. They carried three pets, a monkey (named Jacko) presented by Lady Jane Franklin, a Newfoundland dog called Neptune, and a cat. At Greenhithe, the crews were given a pay advance in order to provide for their families. The expedition with a complement of 134 men set out from Greenhithe on May 19 1845 and from Sheerness on May 26. The ships stopped at Stromness for water and to replace cattle that had died in a storm on route. Franklin wrote to his wife talking about the expedition. The two ships sailed very well together. He had taken a great liking to Graham Gore. Because of the weather, they had not seen much of Crozier aboard *Erebus*. They reached Disko Island in Greenland in early July.

This first part of the voyage, lasting six weeks, was the 'shakedown cruise' when relations were established between the officers and men and a number of events occurred that have implications for understanding the later events of the expedition. Details of the shakedown cruise are preserved in letters written home from Stromness, from Disko Island in the Whale Fish Islands of western Greenland and in a journal kept by Commander Fitzjames.

About half way to Greenland on a calm day, Lieutenants James Fairholme and Henry Le Vesconte took the infatable Halkett boat and visited *Terror*. Fairholme wrote:

> on a calm day, about a half way across in Peter Halkett's boat when the *Terror* was ¼ a mile from us and Le vesconte went with me and it carried us capitally. It holds just 3, and we got a board the *Terror*, paid our visit and got back again without the least wet or discomfort, altho of course sitting much below the level of the sea. The exertion of paddling is rather severe or rather it was so then from neither of us having paid much practice recently.

[This inflatable dinghy, carried aboard *Erebus*, was taken in the 1850 retreat and was described by the Inuit who had never seen such a thing before.]

On the shakedown cruise to Disko Island, a number of small events marked Crozier as being distant and somewhat aloof from the jollity on the flagship. One concerned discipline. At Stromness, Crozier would not let any of his crew ashore. Fitzjames was more humane and allowed two men with families nearby to go ashore, and when one overstayed he did not punish him. Crozier wrote to his friend and former commanding officer, James

Clark Ross and contrasted the disciplined way he ran *Terror* to the more relaxed discipline on *Erebus*. Crozier ran a tight ship and he considered Fitzjames' more relaxed style as resulting in everything aboard *Erebus* being in confusion.

A growing disharmony between Fitzjames and Crozier was demonstrated when the ships arrived at the Whale Fish Islands and approached the anchorage of Disko Island. Ice Master Reid lost his way and took the flagship thirty miles in the wrong direction. Franklin and Fitzjames went along with Reid as the expert. Crozier had been to the Whale Fish Islands before and realised the error. But along with Griffiths on *Barretto Junior*, they followed the flagship. When the error was discovered Fitzjames was very embarrassed and Ice Master Reid's reputation plummeted. Almost a day had been wasted.

Finally when the ships were correctly anchored, Fitzjames boarded *Terror* to discuss the matter. He was surprised to learn that Crozier knew of the error, but had not informed the flagship. Crozier argued that he thought the flagship had decided to anchor somewhere else. The incident demonstrates poor relations between Fitzjames and Crozier. It seems that Crozier let the ships wander off course, just to find how long it would take the overconfident jolly officers of the *Erebus* to discover their error and perhaps measure their overconfidence.

Another point of concern emerged during the passage to Greenland. Fitzjames was concerned that Sir John Franklin was recklessly crowding on too much sail and risking damage to the ship. These actions may have a bearing on how the ships came to be fatally entrapped in the ice stream, so that they had to be abandoned. Were both ships recklessly put into the ice stream in the hope of a short and speedy route home through the North-West Passage?

The relationship between Fitzjames and Sir John Franklin was excellent. Fitzjames greatly enjoyed the bonhomie of the dinners and the company of the famous man. Franklin evidently saw himself as a father figure to the younger officers, and regaled them with many tales. This included tales of his unhappy days as governor of Tasmania. He wrote a long justification for his actions there and Fitzjames assisted him in reading and commenting helpfully on it.

6: DESCRIPTIONS OF COLLEAGUES ON THE OUTWARD VOYAGE BY COMMANDER FITZJAMES

Commander Fitzjames kept a private journal on the outward journey to Disko Island. The journal was written only for his 'sister in law', Elizabeth Coningham, for whom he had a strong affection. The journal was sent to her from Disko Island and, after the loss of the expedition, was published. This is a valuable document for followers of the Franklin expedition, as it provides an important source of highly valuable insights of the men and their relationships developing on the shakedown part of the voyage. It was however written to entertain a lady, whom Fitzjames admired, and is therefore somewhat light hearted and entirely lacking in any mention of problems. His valuable comments are mainly on the crew of the flagship *Erebus* and are listed below by officer and date of the comment.

Re: Sir John Franklin, Expedition Leader
June 5th 1845: 'We drank Lady Franklin's health at the old gentleman's table, and, it being his daughter's birthday, hers too.'

6th June 1845: 'To-day Sir John Franklin showed me part of his instructions as related to the main purposes of our voyage, and the necessity of observing everything from a flea to a whale in the unknown regions we are to visit. He also told me I was especially charged with the magnetic observations. He then told all the officers that he was desired to claim all their remarks, journals, sketches, etc., on our return to England, and read us some part of his instructions to the officers of the *Trent*, the first vessel he commanded, in 1818, with Captain Buchan, on an attempt to reach the North Pole, pointing out how desirable it is to note everything, and give one's individual opinion on it. He spoke delightfully of the zealous co-operation he expected from all, and his desire to do full justice to the exertions of each.'

6th June: 'At dinner to-day Sir John gave us a pleasant account of his expectations of being able to get through the ice on the coast of America, and his disbelief in the idea that there is open sea to the northward. He also said he believed it to be possible to reach the Pole over the ice by wintering in Spitzbergen and heading north before the ice broke up and then drifting to the south, as it did with Parry on it.'

8th June: 'I like a man who is earnest. Sir John Franklin read the church service to-day and a sermon so very beautifully, that I defy any man not to feel the force of what he would convey. The first Sunday he read was a day or two before we sailed, when Lady Franklin, his daughter, and niece attended. Everyone was struck with his extreme earnestness of manner, evidently proceeding from real conviction.'

June 10th: 'I have been reading Sir John Franklin's vindication of his government of Van Diemen's Land, which was to come out a week or two after we sailed. He had ready all of the sheets, and cuts up Lord Stanley a few, and says he is haughty and imperious'.

10th June: 'We are very happy, and very fond of Sir John Franklin, who improves very much as we come to know more of him. He is anything but nervous and fidgety; in fact, I should say remarkable for energetic decision in sudden emergencies; but I think he might be easily persuaded where he has not already formed a strong opinion.'

19th June: 'Twelve o'clock at night. I suppose we are 140 or 150 miles from Cape Farewell. Blowing hard but not a rough sea, although there is a swell. When I say hard, I mean fresh; we can carry much sail, and do. I can scarcely manage to get Sir John to shorten sail at all.'

24th June: 'Sir John at dinner; most amusing with anecdotes of an Indian chief, whom he met in the journey in which he suffered so much – named, I think, Akatcho, who appears to have been a fine character.'

Re: Francis Rawdon Moira Crozier, Second in Command of the Expedition, and Captain of *Terror*
16th June: 'Calm day, sea glassy smooth, cloudy weather, no sun. After breakfast I went on board the *Terror* to see Captain Crozier about my 'Fox' observations.
[The 'Fox' was a dipping-needle invented by Captain Crozier].
Fairholme and Le Vescomte followed in the India-rubber boat, which was being tried when you came to Woolwich. Crozier and Little, first Lieutenant, and Lieutenant Griffiths, the agent for transport, dined on board with Sir John.'
26th June: 'Crozier dined on board, and Hodgson came, looking very ill.'

July 3rd: 'This morning, instead of going into Whale-fish Islands, by some mistake, Reid fancied we were wrong, and away we went up to the end of the bay, thirty miles, to the mouth of the Waigat Channel, looking for them – the bay full of the most glorious icebergs, packed close along the shore. At noon we found out our mistake, and had our sail for nothing, which would be good fun but for the delay. I went on board the TERROR in the evening, and found Captain Crozier knew the mistake, but fancied we had given up the idea of going there. Fortunately, the wind favoured us right round the bay, and we had a delightful sail. We are now running into the Whale-Fish Islands.'

Re: Henry Collins, Second Master, *Erebus*
5th June: 'The second master Collins is the very essence of good nature, and I may say good humour.'

Re: Graham Gore, Lieutenant, *Erebus*
10th June: 'Graham Gore, the first Lieutenant, a man of great stability of character, a very good officer, and the sweetest of tempers, is not so much a man of the world as Fairholme or Des Voeux, is more of Le Vescomte's style, without his shyness. He plays the flute dreadfully well, draws sometimes very well, sometimes very badly, but is altogether a capital fellow.'

Re: James Walter Fairholme, Lieutenant, *Erebus*
10th June: 'Fairholme, you know or have seen, is a smart, agreeable companion, and a well informed man'.

Re: Henry Thomas Dundas Le Vesconte, Lieutenant, *Erebus*
10th June: 'Le Vescomte you know. He improves, if possible, on closer acquaintance.'

6th July: (Whale Fish Islands): 'Le Vescomte and I on the island since six this morning, surveying. It is very satisfactory to me that he takes to surveying, as I said he would. Sir John is much pleased with him.'

[Note: The day before Fitzjames had spent on Boat Island with Lieutenant Fairholme, observing 'the little dipping needle' or 'Fox,' and got very wet and cold. They worked inside a magnetic observatory with copper fastenings described as 'a little square wooden house.' The expedition carried two of these and in spring 1853 a fragment of one of them was found on the shore of Victoria Strait on SE Victoria Land (opposite the line of retreat of the Franklin expedition) by Captain (later Admiral Sir Richard) Collinson of the search ship *Enterprise*. Unfortunately, at the time its significance was not recognised and the west coast of King William Island - the line of the

Franklin retreat - was not searched. The magnetic observations were an important part of the research program of the expedition. So as Fitzjames, Fairholm and Le Vesconte formed a team at the Whale Fish Islands, it is likely that later they were responsible for the remains of the magnetic camp found near Cape Felix at the northern tip of King William Island.]

Re: Stephen Samuel Stanley: Surgeon, *Erebus*

10th June: 'Stanley, the surgeon, I knew in China. He was in the *Cornwallis* a short time, where he worked very hard in his vocation. Is rather inclined to be good-looking, but fat, with jet black hair, very white hands, which are always abominably clean, and the shirt sleeves tucked up; giving one unpleasant ideas that he might not mind cutting one's leg off immediately – 'if not sooner.' He is thoroughly good-natured and obliging, and very attentive to our mess.'

Re: Harry D. S. Goodsir, Assistant Surgeon, *Erebus*

6th June: 'Towards midnight. – I can't make out why Scotsmen just caught always speak in a low, hesitating, monotonous tone of voice, which is not at all times to be understood – that is, I believe, called 'cannyness.' Mr. Goodsir is 'canny.' He is long and strait, and walks upright on his toes, with his hands tucked up in each jacket pocket. He is perfectly good humoured, very well informed on general points, in natural history learned, was Curator of Edinburgh Museum, appears to be about twenty-eight years of age, laughs delightfully, cannot be in a passion, is enthusiastic about all 'ologies, draws the insides of microscopic animals with an imaginary-pointed pencil, catches phenomena in a bucket, looks at the thermometer and every other meter, is a pleasant companion, and an aquisition to the mess. So much for Mr. Goodsir.'

10th June: 'A fine clear sunset at a quarter to ten, and Goodsir examining 'mollusc', in a microscope. He is in ecstasies about a bag full of blubber-like stuff, which he has just hauled up in a net, and which turns out to be whales' food and other animals.'

10th June: 'I meant to go to bed when I finished the other sheet; but went to look at some beautiful specimens of crustaceous animals in the microscope, one of which, about a quarter of an inch long, is an entirely new animal, and has a peacock's tail. Goodsir is drawing it. And now I must really say good night; it is past one o'clock.'

25th June: 'Goodsir is catching the most extraordinary animals in a net, and is in ecstasies. Gore and Des Voeux are over the side, poking with nets and long poles, with cigars in their mouths, and Osmar laughing; he is really an original, and a delightfully dry fellow.'

Re: James Reid, Ice Master *Erebus*

June 5th : 'The most original character of all – rough, intelligent, unpolished, with a broad north-country accent, but not vulgar, good humoured, and honest hearted – is Reid, a Greenland whaler, native of Aberdeen, who has commanded whaling vessels, and amuses us with his quaint remarks and descriptions of the ice, catching whales, etc. For instance, he just said to me, on my saying we should soon be off Cape Farewell, at this rate, and asking if one might not generally expect a gale off it (Cape Farewell being the southern Point of Greenland) 'Ah! Now, Mister Jems, we'll be having the weather fine, sir! Fine! No ice at arl about it, sir, unless it be the bergs – arl the ice'll be gone, sir, only the bergs, which I like to see. Let it come to a blow, look out for a big 'un. Get under his lee, and hold onto him fast, sir, fast. If he drifts near the land, why he grounds afore you do.'

[Note: Fitzjames was a novice to the polar regions, he followed this description with the comment – 'The idea of all the ice being gone, except the icebergs, is racy beyond description'. His first sightings of icebergs also reflected his lack of polar experience, as on June the twenty-nineh he wrote: 'I had fancied icebergs were large transparent lumps, or rocks of ice. They look like huge masses of pure snow, furrowed with caverns and dark ravines.']

June 14th: 'Reid still amuses us. He has just told me how to boil salt fish when it is very salt. He saw the steward towing it overboard, and roared out: - 'What are you making facers at there! That's not the way to get the sarlt oout'. It appears, that when it boils it is to be taken off the fire and kept just not boiling.'

June 17th: 'the 'crow's nest' is up – which is usually a cask lined with canvas – at the fore-top-mast-head, for a man to stand in and look for channels in the ice. With us, it is a sort of canvas cylinder, hooped, and is at the main-top-gallant-mast-head (if you know where that is). Reid, who will have the particular privilege of being perched up there, says it is a very expensive one.'

25th June: 'Reid says, 'We shall soon see the Huskimays', which he says are vulgarly called 'Yacks' by the whalers, and 'Huski's' for shortness.'

Re: Charles Hamilton Osmer, Purser, *Erebus*

June 5th: 'I have just had a game of chess with the purser Osmer, who is delightful. He was with Beechey in the *Blossom*, when they went to Bering Strait to look out for Franklin, at the time he surveyed the north coast of America, and got within 150 miles of him; he was at Petro Paulowski [Petropavlovsk], in Kamschatka, where I hope to go, and served since on the lakes of Canada. I was at first inclined to think he was a stupid old man, because he had a chin and took snuff; but he is as merry-hearted as any young man, full of quaint dry sayings, always good humoured, always laughing, never a bore, takes his 'pinch after dinner,' plays a 'rubber,' and beats me at chess – and he is a gentleman.'

[Note: Fitzjames' comment on hoping to go to Kamchatka is important and will be discussed later.]

July 2nd: 'Osmar has just come from on deck (midnight). And is dancing with an imaginary skipping-rope. I said to him, 'what a happy fellow you are, always in good humour.' His answer is, 'Well sir, if I am not happy here, I don't know where else I could be.'

Re: Edward Couch, Mate. *Erebus*

10th June 1845: 'Couch is a little, black-haired, smooth-faced fellow; good humoured in his own way; writes, reads, works, draws, all quietly. Is never in the way of anybody, and always ready when wanted; but I can find no remarkable point in his character, except, that he is, I should think, obstinate.'

Re: Robert Orme Sargent, Mate, *Erebus*

10th June: 'Sargent is a nice, pleasant looking lad, very good natured.'

Re: Charles Frederick Des Voeux, Mate, *Erebus*

10th June: 'Des Voeux I knew in *Cornwallis*. He went out in her to join the *Endymion*, and was then a mere boy. He is now a most unexceptionably, clever, agreeable, light-hearted, obliging young fellow, and a great favourite of Hodgson's, which is much in his favour besides.'

[Note: 'Hodgson' was *Terror*'s Lieutenant George Henry Hodgson.]

Re: The seamen aboard *Erebus*

10th June: 'Our men are all fine, hearty fellows, mostly north-countrymen, with a few man-of-war's men.'

6th July (at Disko Island): 'Every man nearly on shore, running about for a sort of holiday, getting eider ducks' eggs, etc., curious mosses and plants being collected, as also shells.'

Re: The ship's monkey, Jacko, *Erebus*
23rd June: 'The sea is beginning to get colder. The air still at 41 degrees, but today it felt delightfully cold. The monkey has, however, just put on a blanket, frock, and trowsers, which the sailors have made him (or rather her), so I suppose it is getting cold.'

7: SOME FINAL LETTERS SENT BY EXPEDITION MEMBERS

As one might expect, a major source of information concerning the fate of the expedition are the final letters and journal entries sent to families before the ships sailed from Disko Island.

The letters were likely to be the last heard by the families for some years. As things turned out, they were the last anyone heard of any of the expedition members.

The letters contain the hopes and fears of the men involved. Sir John Franklin wrote sixteen pages to his wife Lady Jane, full of hope for the expedition. The other officers were also optimistic. Fitzjames wrote that there was laughter from morning to night. Purser Osmer of *Erebus* wrote his wife that they would be home in 1846. Goodsir and Fairholme visited the Inuit and Goodsir began putting together a dictionary of Inuit words that would help the expedition communicate in their Arctic exploration. The very high moral of the expedition and jollity of the officers was enjoyed by Sir John Franklin, who did nothing to break the spell.

As it was his first visit to Greenland, this portly old gentleman ran off one day to climb the highest hill on the coast taking young Lieutenant Le Vesconte with him. The atmosphere on the flagship was one of extreme overconfidence. No possibility of failure or entrapment in the ice was even considered. Four letters are considered here. The first two are from the *Erebus* and the last two from the *Terror*. They are separated here because they show that very different atmospheres existed in either ship at the time of departure.

Letter from Sir John Franklin (the twelfth of July 1845 aboard *Erebus*)

Sir John Franklin sent back with the *Barretto Junior*, what was to be his last official letter.

Her Majesty's Ship *Erebus*,

Whale-Fish Islands, 12th of July, 1845.

I have the honor to aquaint you, for the information of the Lords Commissioners of the Admiralty, that her Majesty's ships *Erebus* and *Terror* with the transport, arrived at this anchorage on the 4th instant, having had a passage of one month from Stromness: the transport was immediately taken alongside this ship, that she might be the more readily cleared; and we have been constantly employed at that operation till last evening, the delay having been caused not so much in getting the stores transferred to either of the two ships, as in making the best stowage of them below, as well as on the upper deck: the ships are now complete with supplies of every kind for three years; they are therefore very deep; but, happily we have no reason to expect much sea as we proceed farther.

The magnetic instruments were landed the same morning; so also were the other instruments requisite for ascertaining the position of the observatory; and it is satisfactory to find that the results of the observations for latitude and longitude accord very nearly with those assigned to the same place by Sir Edward Parry; those for the dip and variation are equally satisfactory which were made by Captain Crozier with the instruments belonging to the *Terror*, and by Commander Fitzjames with those of the *Erebus*.

The ships are now being swung, for the purpose of ascertaining the dip and deviation of the needle on board, as was done at Greenhithe, which I trust will be completed this afternoon, and I hope to be able to sail in the night.

The governor and principal persons are at this time absent from Disko, so that I have not been able to receive any communication from head quarters as to the state of the ice to the north: I have, however, learnt from a Danish carpenter in charge of the Esquimaux at these islands, that though the winter was severe, the spring was not later than usual, nor was the ice later in breaking away hereabout; he supposes also that it is loose as far as 74 degrees latitude, and that our prospect is favourable of getting across the barrier, and as far as Lancaster Sound, without much obstruction.

The transport will sail to England this day. I shall instruct the agent, Lieutenant Griffiths, to proceed to Deptford, and report his arrival to the Secretary of the Admiralty. I have much satisfaction in bearing my testimony to the careful and zealous manner in which Lieutenant Griffiths has performed the service intrusted to him, and would beg to recommend him, as an officer who appears to have seen much service, to the favourable consideration of their Lordships.

It is unnecessary for me to assure their lordships of the energy and zeal of Captain Crozier, Commander Fitzjames, and of the officers and men with whom I have the happiness of being employed in this service.

I have, &c.,

(Signed) John Franklin, Captain.

Letter written by Commander Fitzjames (eleventh July 1845 aboard *Erebus*).

His final communication was a hastily written letter on the eleventh July 1845 - the day before they sailed for Lancaster Sound

TO WILLIAM CONINGHAM, ESQ

Whale-fish Islands, 11th July, 1845.

DEAR CONINGHAM, - E's bundle of yarns will show you that I am well and happy, and have not forgotten you yet. I have not much time, as the transport sails tomorrow evening, and we shall be all day at work. It was a heavy job, clearing the transport, and took us longer than we imagined it would have done, though we worked from four till six. We are now full – very – having three years' provisions and coals bedsides the engine.

The deck is covered with coals and sacks, leaving a small passage fore and aft, and we are very deep in the water. We sail, if possible, to-morrow night, and hope to get to Lancaster Sound by 1st August, which however is a lottery. It is now eleven o'clock, and the sun shines brightly above the snowy peaks of Disko. From the top of one of the islands, the other day, I counted 280 icebergs, and beautiful objects they are. Should you hear nothing till next June, send a letter, via Petersburg, to Petro Paulowski [Petropavlovsk], in Kamschatka, where Osmar was in the BLOSSOM, and had letters from England in three months. And now God bless you, and everything belonging to you.

Always your affectionate,

James Fitzjames.

[Note: E was Elizabeth Coningham, wife of William Coningham.]

Letter from Ice Master Thomas Blanky (twelfth of July 1845 aboard *Terror*)

Mrs Blenky [her spelling] copied the letter to the Morning Herald newspaper in 1852, when concern for the missing expedition was at its height over the food supply.

> SIR, - Knowing the interest which is now felt in the question of Sir John Franklin's long absence, I venture to offer you, for publication in the Morning Herald, an extract from the last letter I received from my husband, who is ice-master on board the *Terror* which will show that they looked forward to the possibility of being detained much longer than had generally supposed.
>
> I may state that my husband was previously out with Sir John Ross in the *Victory*, when they were so many years missing. The letter was written on board the *Terror*, at Disko Island, and is dated 12th July 1845. He says:
>
> The season is a very open one, much such a one as when we came out with Captain Ross. We are all in good health and spirits, one and all appearing to be of the same determination, that is, to persevere in making a passage to the north-west. Should we not be at home in the fall of 1848, or early spring of 1849, you may anticipate that we have made the passage, or likely to do so; and if so, it may be from five to six years, - it might be into the seventh, - ere we return; and should it be so, do not allow any person to dishearten you on the length of our absence, but look forward with hope that Providence will at length of time restore us safely to you.
>
> I am, etc.
>
> Esther Blenky.

Letter from Captain Crozier (the ninth of July 1845 aboard *Terror*)

Crozier's last letter was sent from Greenland aboard the supply ship *Barretto Junior* to his close friend and former commanding officer Sir James Clark Ross and his wife Anne. It is a very personal letter

> Whale Fish Islands
>
> 9th July 1845
>
> My Dear James: I cannot allow Transport to leave without writing you a line altho' I have little to say and our many details keep me in anything but a fit mood for letter writing. We got here on morning of the fourth and have been busily employed ever since clearing and stowing away from

Transport. 'Tis very tedious work from the small space we have to stow things. We have now a mean draft of 16 feet and all our provisions not yet on board. I send home our largest cutter (and fill launch with patent fuel) 2 anchors and cables. Iron Waist davits and various other things of weight as I think it better to have the provisions, come what may afterwards. But I do miss you. I cannot bear going on board *Erebus*. Sir John is very kind and would have me there dining every day if I would go. He has Fitzjames and two officers every day. [At this point the next part of the letter had been heavily obliterated with circular strokes of the pen].

All things are going on well and quietly but we are, I fear, sadly late. From what we can learn, the winter here has been very severe with much easterly wind, there was, however, an early breakup of the ice and the last amounts (accounts?) of whale(r)s is that fish were plenty and ships as high as the Woman Isles (73 deg.). What I fear is that, from our being so late, we shall have no time to look round and judge for ourselves, but blunder into the ice and make a second 1824 of it. James, I wish you were here, I would then have no doubt as to our pursuing a proper course.

I must have done with this croaking. I am not growling, mind, indeed I never was less disposed to do so. I am, I assure you, beginning to be a bit of a philosopher and hope that before the season is over to have so tutored myself that I will fret for nothing. [There follows a page of scientific details].

Why I should have gone so far and not said one word about dear 'Thot', who from my heart, I do hope has benefitted by change of air and getting away from comfortless Blackheath. I would have liked to have seen your place that I might often picture to myself your little employments. With God's blessing my Lady, I will not fail on my return to soon find my way down to see you to be condoled with peradventures, if, on the other hand, to rejoice with you, at all events one thing is certain, meet when we may it will be to me a source of heartfelt pleasure. I hope the little son is going on well, the mild weather of the interior must be, to him, beneficial. That Blackheath was a scorching place.

Goodsir in *Erebus* is a most intelligent fellow, a perfect enthusiast in Mollusca, he seems much in his habits like Hooker, never idle, making perfect sketches of all he collects very quickly and in the most extraordinarily rough way. He has the happy knack of engaging everyone around him in the same persuit. He certainly is a great acquisition. I find Irving (3rd Lieut.) will do all the chart work that I want quite well enough. He is a diligent hard working fellow.

All goes on smoothly, but, James dear, I am sadly alone, not a soul have I in either ship that I can go and talk to. 'No congenial spirit as it were'. I am generally busy but it is after all a very hermit like life. Except to kick up a row with the helmsman or abuse Jopson [the captain's steward] at times I would scarcely ever hear the sound of my voice. The Transport is nearly clear and my sugar and tea have not made their appearance. The sugar is a great loss to me but the tea I care not for. I cannot at all events say much for Fortnum and Mason's punctuality. They directed my things to Captain Fitzjames, *Terror*, but by some strange accident they discovered my name sufficiently accurate to send me the bill and I was fool enough to pay it from their declaring that the things were absolutely delivered on board. Growling again.

Well, my dear friends I know not what else I can say to you – I feel I am not in the spirits of writing but in truth I am sadly lonely and when I look to the last voyage I can see the cause and therefore no prospect of having a more joyous feeling.

Inferences

The above letters identify very different views of the expedition on each ship. So off they sailed – two ships with officers in opposite frames of mind. On the flagship Sir John Franklin was enjoying himself with guests to dinner nightly, and there was much jollity and good humour on board. Second in command, Commander Fitzjames with no knowledge of the Arctic, was hoping because of the nice weather that they would not be home for the end of 1845 because he would like to experience an Arctic winter. He was overconfident to the point of having his mail forwarded to Petro Paulowski [Petropavlovsk], Kamchatka, in Russia, to be collected when he made his dash for glory ahead of the ships to first report the conquest of the North-West Passage. On *Terror* the atmosphere was very different, perhaps gloomy with foreboding. Captain Crozier worried that the flagship might get them into a situation like that of the *Fury* that was trapped and abandoned (he was right as events proved). While Ice Master Thomas Blanky, who despite the good weather they found, remembered his experience with Sir John Ross when the *Victory* was abandoned and it took the men five Arctic summers to get back home. Blanky saw the great difficulties of crossing the entire Canadian Arctic with the possibility of being repeatedly frozen in, so that the trip might take up to seven years.

8: THE LAST SIGHTINGS OF *EREBUS* AND *TERROR*

The expedition topped up their stores from the supply ship *Barretto Junior* that had accompanied them. Lieutenant Griffiths, in command, would report on his return that all hands were well and in good spirits. The supply ship returned to England carrying letters, one officer, two invalided men and *Terror*'s sail maker and armourer who proved unskilled. One man had been returned when the ships were at Stromness. This left the expedition with 129 men.

The ships sailed on July 12 and *Erebus* was last spoken to on July 22 by Captain Martin, of the *Enterprise*, in lat. 75 deg. 10 min, long. 66 deg. West. They reached the ice at Lancaster Sound on July 26 where they met two whaling ships *Prince of Wales* and *Enterprise*. *Prince of Wales* was visited by a party of officers. Captain Robert Martin of *Enterprise* spoke to Sir John Franklin and reported the ships made fast to an iceberg on which they had set up an observatory. When *Enterprise* departed she had *Erebus* and *Terror* in sight for two days. The ships were comfortable, spirits excellent and they had their own newspaper. Captain Martin later reported:

> The *Enterprise* was alongside the *Erebus* in Melville Bay, and Sir John invited Captain Martin to dine with him, which the latter declined doing, as the wind was fair to go south. Sir John, while conversing with Capt. Martin, told him that he had five years provisions, which he could make last seven, and his people were busily engaged in salting down birds, of which they had several casks full already, and twelve men were out shooting more.

This remarkable boast by Sir John Franklin marked the extreme overconfidence of the officers of the Flagship *Erebus*. Indeed in retrospect with half of the expedition dead only three years later, this extreme overconfidence can only be regarded as extreme foolishness or utter irresponsibility.

The happy atmosphere of laughter, light heartedness and pleasure with the expectation of an easy passage that pervaded the flagship, did in fact divert thinking away from any disaster planning. Sir John and his officers on *Erebus* had no thoughts of failure. In modern terms, the planning was utterly devoid of any safety net. Even the Admiralty in London, had grown overconfident and evidently did not consider the possibility that the ships would become trapped or might be abandoned. It would have been possible in advance to select several places where the crews might head for in the event of an abandonment.

A last journal entry (Sunday July 6 1845 aboard *Erebus*) by Commander Fitzjames demonstrates this overconfidence:

> A man just come over from LIVELY, a Dane, who married an Esquimaux, says that they believe it to be one of the mildest seasons and earliest summers ever known, and that the ice is clear away from this to Lancaster Sound. Keep this to yourself, for Sir John is naturally very anxious that people in England should not be too sanguine about the season. Besides the papers would have all sorts of stories, not true. I do believe we have a good chance of getting through this year, if it is to be done at all; but I hope we shall not, as I want to have a winter for magnetic observations. And now here goes a new pen into the porcupine, to say that your journal is at an end, at least for the present. I do hope it has amused you, but I fear not; for what can there be in an old tub like this, with a parcel of sea bears, to amuse a 'lady fair'. This however, is a facon de parler, for I think, in reality, that you will have been amused in some parts, and interested in others, but I shall not read back, for fear of not liking it, and tearing it up.

Not everyone shared the optimism. Captain Crozier was one. He did not enjoy the light-hearted merry dinners aboard the flagship. In his own quiet way he had tried to demonstrate to the flagship their folly when Ice Master Reid got lost off Disko Island. He did not notify the flagship but followed quietly until they realised their mistake. One can imagine some rather grim conversations between him and his Ice Master Blanky. Undoubtedly Blanky would be repeatedly queried about his experience with Sir John Ross and how they escaped after four summers in the Arctic.

The overconfidence on the flagship led to a series of decisions that were not sufficiently weighted at the time, but which in retrospect were serious mistakes. One was when a possible grounding of one of the ships in Poctes/Poet's Bay and a large stack of boxed food was abandoned on an island when one of the ships was lightened. To have abandoned so much food might have been the act of men overconfident and still thinking they would soon be home shortly. The major decision, that was the fatal one, was to put both ships into the ice stream off the north-west coast of King William Land. The two senior officers aboard the flagship *Erebus* might have agreed on this as taking a chance to get through and achieve success.

Another result of overconfidence and lack of disaster planning was the complete failure of the expedition to build cairns and leave messages along their route to inform others following of their actions. Many ships searched in vain for such clues to the missing expedition. Sir John had not been ordered to leave messages on land, but he was ordered to frequently release brass cylinders with progress messages into the sea. Undoubtedly, this was done but only one of the cylinders was ever found. The expedition did build cairns on Beechey Island that led search ships to the expedition's first winter quarters, but no message was found. The main information gathered lay in three headboards on crew graves and the physical remains of the winter camp.

There was one last sighting of the expedition four days later. The *Prince of Wales*, a whaler, reported that on July 26 1845, Franklin's vessels were seen in Baffin Bay at lat. 74 deg 48 min, long 66 deg. 13 min. They were then moored to an iceberg, awaiting the opening of the middle ice to allow them to cross over to Lancaster Sound.

From July 26 1845 until August 23 1850 there was no news of the expedition. On the latter date the first traces were found on Cape Riley on Devon Island by Captain Erasmus Ommanney of the Austin Relief Expedition of 1850 – 1851. Four days later Captain William Penny (on the twenty-seventh) landed on Beechey Island and Franklin's winter quarters for 1845-46 were identified. Regrettably no records were found there, perhaps due to carelessness aboard the flagship. Many pondered the Admiralty's instructions to Sir John Franklin and speculated on what might have happened. The Admiralty sought advice and dispatched many search expeditions without finding the lost expedition. The wrecks of *Erebus* and *Terror* were not found until 2014 and 2016, following years of searching based on Inuit testimony and relics washed ashore. The searches grew bigger each year and were finally consortiums lead by Parks Canada.

9: SUMMER 1845 TO SUMMER 1846 – EXPLORATION AND WINTER QUARTERS ON BEECHEY ISLAND

After the last sightings of the *Erebus* and *Terror* of the lost Franklin expedition of 1845, there are only three sources that provide clues to what happened to them. These are:

1. The very brief records made in 1847 and 1848, recovered by the McClintock *Fox* expedition in 1859. Both records are written on a single sheet of Naval Message form.

2. Inuit testimony – mainly collected in the nineteenth century, by three expeditions under extremely difficult conditions. Perhaps not surprisingly additional information is still emerging with modern travel into the area.

3. The physical remains of the Franklin expedition. The first of these to be found were the remains of the 1845-46 winter camp on Beechey Island (Map 1). Later came the relics along the line of the retreat (Map II). Many relics were purchased from the Inuit by the search parties of the nineteenth century. Much has been found in modern searches on the ground, especially in Erebus Bay where the relics have been subjected to modern forensic study. Major finds were the sunken wrecks of *Erebus* in 2014 and *Terror* in 2016. However it is likely to be a decade or more before the contents of these ships, especially any papers or books, can be recovered, preserved and possibly read.

The brief 1847 and 1848 written records were recovered some eleven years after being deposited in a cairn near Victory Point in 1848. A duplicate of the 1847 record was found in another cairn nearby. They were found by Lieutenant (later Captain) William Robert Hobson leading a sledge party from the *Fox* – a private search expedition led by Captain (later Admiral Sir) Francis Leopold McClintock. Hobson's account has recently been published by Stenton, and contains more information than McClintock's book. Apart from the Inuit, the sledge parties from the *Fox* were the first western searchers to reach the Franklin line of retreat.

Captain McClintock found a skeleton on the south coast of King William Island (about 135 miles from the abandoned ships) carrying a notebook containing papers that were badly water-damaged. McClintock recognised the remains of the uniform as those of an officer's servant. The skeleton was incorrectly identified as that of Harry Peglar (Captain of the Foretop of *Terror*) as about a half of the papers appear to have belonged to him. The papers have become known as the 'Peglar Papers.'

In fact, the servant is most likely to have been Thomas Armitage (Gunroom Steward, *Terror*) who had served together with Harry Peglar on board *Gannet* from May 7 1834 to June 23 1837. The papers and many other Franklin relics, mainly brought back by the McClintock *Fox* expedition, are kept at the National Maritime Museum in Greenwich and can be seen on their website.

The Peglar papers have yielded only minor information about the Franklin expedition. One item is a cheerful naval song written by Peglar and dated April 21 1847. The opening line reads 'The C the C the open C it grew so fresh and Ever free.' It suggests that the men were happy at that time, as confirmed by the May 1847 record, written by Commander Fitzjames, that states 'All well.' On another water-damaged paper there is a mention off a 'Terror Camp.' One piece of paper may carry some information concerning preparation of new boots to be ready on the night before the ships were abandoned. Another is the sea service record of Harry Peglar. There are some London addresses. Another is a description of how a stranger enjoyed a friendly reception from a group of people singing and dancing in a tent at Cumanar, Venezuela. There are other fragments but nothing that gives information on the lost expedition. Presumably Harry Peglar had died and his friend the steward was carrying his papers along with others of his own.

Lieutenant Hobson found two tin message cylinders in cairns. One was at Crozier's Landing, and the other some eight miles further south (at a place now named Gore Point on the south side of Collinson Inlet). Each cylinder contained a blue paper naval message form with the 1847 Record and was deposited in May/June 1847. The cylinder near Victory point had been opened and the 1848 message added around the margins. These provide the only written communication from the crews of the expedition to date.

Captain Erasmus Ommanney and others located the Franklin expedition winter camp of 1845/46 on Beechey Island in 1850. Thirteen ships were searching the Arctic for the lost expedition that summer and many visited Beechey Island, but no written record was found there. That it was the site used by the Franklin expedition was confirmed by the grave boards of three men who died and were buried there.

Before proceeding with further interpretation of the Inuit testimony and the physical remains along the line of retreat, the two written reports will be considered next as they provide the basic outline of what happened. The single message form from Crozier's Landing with both the 1847 and 1848 messages is now in the National Maritime Museum, Greenwich. The other was kept by Lady Jane Franklin and is now in the Scott Polar Institute.

The 1847 record

The two records have been meticulously described by Franklin researcher Dr. Richard Cyriax. In 1847, the two cylinders were deposited by Lieutenant Gore when he led a six-man sledge party south to complete the mapping of the remaining 100 mile stretch of the North-West Passage. The two copies of the 1847 message are essentially the same, but for minor variations. The messages were written by Commander James Fitzjames, who left the date blank for it was unknown when the cylinders would be deposited. The cylinders were then sealed and taken by the sledging party. The 1847 message found at Crozier's Landing is given below. The other version is almost the same but has some minor differences. The words in brackets are printed on the forms and the rest is written by Fitzjames:

Ships *Erebus* and *Terror*

(of) May (184)7 Wintered in the Ice in (Lat.) 70 deg. 05 min. (Long. 98 deg. 23 min. W.

Having wintered in 1846-7 at Beechey Island, in lat. 74 deg. 43 min. 28 sec. N. Long. 91 deg. 39 min. 15 sec. W after having ascended Wellington Channel to lat. 77 deg., and returned by the West side of Cornwallis Island.

Sir John Franklin commanding the expedition.

All well.

Party consisting of 2 officers and 6 Men left the ships on Monday, 24th May, 1847.

Gm. Gore, Lieut. Chas. F. Des Voeux, Mate.

The position given for wintering in the ice is about fifteen miles north-west of Cape Felix. There is a very obvious error in the message as the expedition wintered at Beechey Island in the winter of 1845-6. A less obvious error is in the longitude given for the Beechey Island winter quarters. The longitude given lies some thirty-two miles east-northeast of Beechey Island. Interestingly, the report of the ships discovering and sailing through a sea passage on the west side of Cornwallis Island (now named after Crozier) was not confirmed until some ninety years after the Franklin passage. McClintock considered that the errors duplicated on the two forms suggested that they were not regarded at the time, as being of any great importance.

The words 'All Well' written by Commander Fitzjames surely speak volumes, indicating that the two ships were intact and the required mapping is going ahead. The problem of the two ships being locked in an ice stream that rides up onto the north-west shore of King William Island and the lack of a winter harbour to protect the ships from ice movements is ignored. If the ships could have escaped the ice in summer 1847 and returned home, then indeed all would have been well.

The 1848 record

This record provides the vital information of what happened in what proved to be a disastrous eleven month period between the times of the 1847 and 1848 records. The ships remained locked in the ice and drifted slowly southwards – a distance of only sixteen miles in nineteen months. Sir John Franklin died and Captain Crozier took over leadership of the expedition. The ships were abandoned and 105 men (fifteen officers and ninety men) set out on a retreat to the south to reach the southern part of King William Island and the estuary of Back's Great Fish River, where in summer deer, oxen, birds and fish were available in plenty according to previous explorers. The record does not say they intended to ascend Back's Great Fish River, with the aim of reaching the nearest Hudson's Bay Company outpost on the shores of the Great Slave Lake, some 1,250 miles to the south.

The 1848 message is written as marginal notes around the 1847 message form. When found the bottom right hand corner of the paper was rotted away. In the message below the parts in brackets are rotted away on the original:

> (25 April 1)848 – H.M. Ship(s) *Terror* and *Erebus* were deserted on 22 April, 5 leagues N.N.W. of this (hav)ing been beset since 12 Septr, 1846. The Officers and Crews, consisting of 105 souls, under the command (of Capt)ain F.R.M. Crozier, landed here in Lat. 69 deg. 37 min. 42 sec. Long. 98 deg. 41 min. (This p)aper was found by Lt. Irving under the

cairn supposed to have been built by Sir James Ross in 1831, 4 miles to the Northward – where it had been deposited by the late Commander Gore in June 1847. Sir James Ross' pillar has not however been found, and the paper has been transferred to this position which is that in which Sir J. Ross' pillar was erected - Sir John Franklin died on the 11 June 1847; and the total loss by deaths in the Expedition has been to this date 9 Officers and 15 Men.

James Fitzjames,

Captain, *Erebus*.

F.R.M. Crozier,

Captain and Senior Offr.

and start tomorrow 26th for Back's Fish River.

This second record briefly identifies the great crisis. The eleven-month period between the two records was catastrophic for the expedition. Not only had Sir John Franklin died prematurely, but the total number of deaths to the twenty-fifth of April 1848 was nine officers and fifteen men, and included the newly promoted Commander Gore. The expedition left Greenland with twenty-four officers and 105 men on July 12 1845. After great successes in the first two years the ships were not released by the ice and were abandoned on April 22 1848. The retreating party consisted of fifteen officers and ninety men. Had the ships been released in summer 1847, they could have returned home and avoided the heavy casualty rate of winter 1847 - 48. Three of the men died on Beechey Island. Their grave markers show them to be: John Torrington (Leading Stoker, *Terror*) died January 1 1846 aged twenty; William Braine (Private, Marine, *Erebus*) died April 3 1846, aged thirty-two; John Hartnell (Able Seaman, *Erebus*) died January 4 1846 aged twenty-five. As Captain Fitzjames recorded that Lieutenant Irving (*Terror*) had recovered the record deposited by the late Lieutenant Gore and Mate Charles Des Voeux in 1847, it seems probable that not only had Graham Gore died but Mate Des Voix might also have died or been disabled since then.

The record confirms that after the death of Sir John Franklin, Captain Crozier as senior officer, took command of the expedition. Commander Fitzjames of *Erebus* became Captain of the *Erebus* and second in command of the expedition after the death of Sir John Franklin. Lieutenant Graham Gore was promoted into his position as Commander of *Erebus* (replacing Fitzjames).

Fitzjames signs himself as Captain of the larger flagship *Erebus*. Captain Crozier should have moved aboard the flagship *Erebus* according to the Admiralty orders, and taken over the late Sir John Franklin quarters and transferred Fitzjames to *Terror* as second in command of the expedition. Instead the two Captains retained their ships, cabins and crews. This would in part be because they had each welded their crews into teams that were notably different. But also because the two captains were very different people and the command had become divided.

It is remarkable that a half of the 1848 record (sixty-eight words) deals with the problem of the location of Victory Point. In fact it is astonishing considering all that might have been reported, that the relatively minor matter of the location of James Clark Ross's Victory Point should occupy so much of the precious record. Indeed having written about it at length, Fitzjames omitted to mention where the retreat was heading - surely the most important point of the 1848 Record. It was left to Captain Crozier to add the destination as an eight word note after his signature.

The location of James Clark Ross's Victory Point with the six-foot pillar and record that he left there was a very real problem, not only as outlined by Fitzjames in the 1848 record, but also for later writers. First to encounter the problem would have been Lieutenant Gore and his party as they headed south to map the last 100 mile stretch of the North-West Passage. Close scrutiny of the 1848 record shows that it was also written by Fitzjames, except for the footnote added by Captain Crozier stating their destination.

An interesting point noted by McClintock from the colors of the inks used, was that Fitzjames had inserted into the 1847 record the date 'twenty-eight' in front of the line '(of) May (184)7'. This could mean that Gore had deposited the record on May 28 1847. However, this is contradicted by Fitzjames' statement that Gore deposited the cylinder at Victory Point in June 1847. Fitzjames first wrote 'May' then crossed it out and wrote 'June'. As he was aware of the error when he wrote 'May', it seems that the Victory Point cylinder was deposited in June. It seems likely that Gore and party left the ships on May 28 1847, not the 24 as stated on the record. This probably arose because the date May 24 was the planned date of departure, and after the cylinders were sealed, the departure date was delayed until the twenty-eighth. If Gore deposited the cylinder at Victory Point in June, then he would have done it on his return trip to the ships.

Exploration of Wellington Channel and Cornwallis Island (summer 1845)

The brief 1847 record recovered by the McClintock expedition in 1859 states that the expedition wintered at Beechey Island after ascending Wellington Channel to latitude 77 degrees and returning by the west side of Cornwallis Island (Map II). There is no more information, but from this it can be deduced that the ships had probably been blocked by ice at Cape Walker and followed the alternative route with great success. The entrance to Wellington Channel had been discovered by Sir Edward Parry in 1819 and 1820. The Franklin expedition was the first to explore and map the channel (they sailed about 150 miles along it). They must have discovered that the Polar Sea was ice-covered and not open water.

They returned by circumnavigating Cornwallis Island along the channel between it and Bathurst Island – now known as Crozier Strait. The ships then returned to the entrance to Wellington Channel and found their winter quarters at the eastern side of the entrance at Beechey Island. These quarters must have been selected when they first passed them before ascending Wellington Channel. The expedition had proved Wellington Channel and that Cornwallis was an island, and not a peninsula attached to Bathurst Island. They had also learned that there was no open-water Polar Sea. These expedition discoveries were not known until the brief 1847 and 1848 records was found by the McClintock search expedition of 1859.

Winter quarters at Beechey Island (winter 1845-summer 1846)

Beechey Island is triangular shaped with sides a little over two miles long. It lies south of Devon Island and east of the entrance to Wellington Channel. To its east is Cape Riley on Devon Island and between Beechey and Devon islands lies a sheltered bay ideal for wintering ships. This is now known as Erebus and Terror Bay. The Franklin winter quarters were not discovered until 1850 when the search for the lost expedition peaked.

There were thirteen ships searching for the lost expedition in the Arctic that summer. Captains Richard Collinson and Commander Robert McClure were approaching from the west via Bering Strait in *Enterprise* and *Investigator*. Eleven ships entered through Lancaster Sound in the east. There were two Admiralty fleets. Four ships were commanded by Captain Horatio Austin (*Resolute* bark), with second in command Captain Erasmus Ommanney (*Assistance* bark), with two steam tenders with Lieutenant Sherard Osborn (screw steamer *Pioneer*) and Lieutenant J. Bertie Cator (*Intrepid*). Another Admiralty group led by Whaling Master Captain William Penny (the brig *Lady Franklin*) and Captain Alexander Stewart (the brig *Sophia*) went north into Jones Sound. In addition, Lady Jane Franklin sent a ship to join the search. This was a 90-ton ex-pilot boat

(*Prince Albert*) commanded by Commander Charles Forsyth. The United States Navy assisted New York merchant Henry Grinnel who outfitted two ships led by U.S. Navy Lieutenant Edwin J. De Haven (*Advance*) with Dr. Elisha Kent Kane as surgeon, also *Rescue* commanded by U.S. Navy Lieutenant S.O. Griffin. Finally, a seventy-three-year-old Sir John Ross led an expedition with a small schooner and a yacht (*Felix* and *Mary*) funded by the Hudson's Bay Company and public subscription, in search of his old friend Sir John Franklin. The Hudson's Bay Company also sent Dr. John Rae overland and by boat to search Victoria Land.

They had no idea where the Franklin expedition might be, except for Franklin's orders. Peel Sound was checked and found to be closed by ice, then they searched Wellington Channel. On August 23 1850, Captain Erasmus Ommanney on board *Assistance*, landed with a party on the beach at Cape Riley to examine a cairn, and found scattered European relics of the lost expedition. There was a rake as used by botanists to collect seaweed, some rope, beef bones and some stone tent circles. Later that day another cairn was seen on Beechey Island and Ommanney landed there, but it failed to yield any message, but there were traces of the missing expedition. Soon ten vessels of the relief expeditions assembled at Beechey Island and searched for written records.

None were ever found, but there was ample evidence that the island was the 1845-1846 winter quarters of the lost Franklin Expedition. Most informative were the headboards on three graves of crewmen who had died in early 1846. These three graves were exhumed in 1984 and 1986 by Canadian forensic anthropologist Owen Beattie and colleagues. A surprising conclusion was the discovery of high, but not fatal lead levels, in the bodies. The search of the island revealed a campsite (where the ground had been levelled), washing places with tubs, the site of an observatory, a carpenters shop, an armourer's forge with an anvil and a large storehouse with a small garden nearby. The storehouse had been used for moving the ships stores ashore to make space for the winter quarters aboard the ships. A shooting range gallery was found in a gully at the east end of the island with stones marking ranges and a target of a large tin with many holes shot into it. Also, found on the north-east slope of the island were between 600 and 700 tins mostly for preserved meat. These had been filled with gravel and every one was searched. Two finger posts, each with a board painted with a black hand on a white background nailed onto eight foot long pikes, were found. One was near where the ships had been anchored and the other was on the shore of North Devon Island opposite Beechey Island. Their use was to direct the crews in snowstorms and fog.

The many empty tins caused some concern when Sir John Richardson suggested the numbers were excessive, implying that large quantities of the tins of meat were bad, as had been found with other tins supplied from the same source to the navy after the expedition sailed. However, Dr. Cyriax has argued that the number of tins is not excessive nor were the tins of meat of poor quality from the same source as supplied to the navy in the years immediately after the Franklin expedition.

Scattered about the area of the winter quarters were pieces of canvas, one marked '*Terror*', rope, empty coal bags, cinders, a key, old clothes, and pieces of paper. There were shreds of newspaper, some wrapping paper marked 'Immediate to Lieut. C.P...', a scrap with a few words written by Commander Fitzjames (a part of a memorandum on magnetic observations), another scrap with a row of figures and another on which calculations had been made.

There was also evidence that a program of scientific work and exploration had been carried out. Runner marks left by sledges were found by the searchers running in various directions. Some led to the valleys that lie to the north of Erebus and Terror Bay. Other tracks led to a large limestone mass named Creswell's Tower located a few miles from Beechey Island. Near the Tower, was a campsite with stones marking the tent sites, porter bottles, empty soup and meat tins, feathers and scraps of fur from Arctic hares. The site had been used as a hunting camp. Another party had travelled a short distance up Wellington Channel and camped about six miles north of Cape Spencer and nine miles from Beechey Island. There sledge tracks led to a circular wall about four feet high with a paved floor laid inside it. This was probably a tent site. Associated with it were some meat tins, bones of birds, a piece of paper with 'Mr. MacDonald' (the Assistant Surgeon of *Terror*) written upon it, and another piece with the words 'To be called' written on it.

At Cape Riley, in addition to the relics mentioned earlier, there were many sledge tracks. It had probably been a camp for magnetic measurements. The searching parties found that the furthest points where cairns had been built were at Cape Bowden in the Wellington Channel and at Creswell's Tower in Barrow Strait. These suggested limited sledging distances of fifty miles at the most. This was normal for the time and it was later that Captain McClintock refined the naval sledges and sledging techniques and achieved considerable distances. Following Admiralty orders, there is no doubt that many rock, plant and animal specimens were collected and detailed charts, maps and reports prepared.

Barrow Strait is usually navigable from July to September, so that the

Franklin expedition stayed on the island probably for nine months. There is some indication of a hasty departure as a pair of cashmere gloves were found on a stone held down by smaller stones, to dry. An abrupt departure due to an unexpected breakup of the ice might explain the lack of any written record.

The lack of any record presented many problems to the search vessels. No one realised that the Wellington Channel option had been completed in 1845 and that the ships had headed south in 1846. So search expeditions went north-west. In 1850 Peel Strait was found to be ice filled and the searchers formed the opinion that the Franklin Expedition could not get through that way.

10: SUMMER 1846 – EXPLORATION OF POCTES/POET'S BAY AND INTO THE ICE STREAM

The route to King William Island - summer 1846

The next information of the progress of the Franklin Expedition comes in the brief sentence in the 1847 record stating that the ships *Erebus* and *Terror* had been beset off King William Island since September 12 1846. From this it can be estimated that the ships were released from their winter harbour at Beechey Island, probably in July, and were trapped in the Beaufort ice stream on September 12, so that they had a summer season of exploration of only about two months.

There is no record of how the expedition got from Beechey Island to the location north-west of Cape Felix on northern King William Island, where the ships were both fatally beset in the Beaufort ice stream. There are two possibilities. First the ships sailed west towards Cape Walker (situated on the north-east corner of Russell Island off the north coast of Prince of Wales Island). But before reaching it, they saw that Peel Sound situated between Somerset Island and Prince of Wales Island was open. They proceeded south along Peel Sound and then continued south between the Isthmus of Boothia and Prince of Wales Island, along what is today named Franklin Strait. This would bring the ships out at a point north of Cape Felix on King William Island.

However there is an alternative route. For this the ships would proceed west past Cape Walker until opposite the entrance to what is today called McClintock Channel, that separates Prince of Wales Island from Stefansson and Victoria Islands. By proceeding south along this channel, the ships would arrive at the same point north of Cape Felix. However McClintock Channel is the route followed by the southern tongue of the Beaufort ice stream. For this reason most people today believe that the Franklin Expedition took the Peel Sound route.

In 1982 in order to check if there was any trace of the Franklin Expedition in McClintock Channel, Hickey and others carried out a helicopter survey of northern coastline of McClintock Channel, visiting areas that had not been visited by previous searchers. The results were negative and no traces of the Franklin Expedition were found. Thus today there remains no evidence to suggest which route the Franklin Expedition took.

Exploration of Poctes/Poet's Bay north-east of King William Island

A major disadvantage of using the two heavily-laden bomb vessels for Arctic exploration amongst islands, sounds, channels and reefs was in their great drafts. [A bomb vessel was a wooden naval sailing ship specially strengthened to mount mortars on deck that fired explosive shells or bombs at shore installations.] *Erebus* was the slightly larger ship of 350 tons and when fully loaded at the Whale Fish Islands in Greenland (according to Fitzjames journal) was 'fearfully deep drawing 17 feet and 4 inches forward with no false keel.' *Terror* was slightly smaller at 330 tons, and Crozier's last letter to his friend James Clark Ross (above) states that *Terror* was heavily laden with a draft of 16 feet, despite his sending excess equipment back to England in the transport. These drafts prevented the ships from making passage through shallow water and may well be a major factor contributing to why the two ships became trapped in the ice stream off the north-west coast of King William Island. They were also cumbersome and relatively slow sailers. Both had been equipped with early railway steam engines to provide some power to the ships. Illustrations showing the type of locomotives used, can be seen in Peter Carney's blog of July 30 2010. A diagram showing how the steam engines were inserted into the ships can be seen in Peter Carney's blog of February 19 2011.

Regardless of the route followed from Beechey Island, from the southern end of Prince of Wales Island, the expedition proceeded south along what is now Franklin Strait, between Prince of Wales Island and the Isthmus of Boothia. They arrived somewhere north of King William Island (then known as King William Land). This was an area previously visited and mapped by James Clark Ross in 1830. The latter had sledged from Prince Regent Inlet across Boothia and crossed a frozen sea (now James Ross Strait) to an island he named Matty Island and then on to Tennent Island (where he found an excellent winter harbour that he named Port Emerson). His party moved on to the northern tip of King William 'Land' at Cape Felix (both named by James Clark Ross). Ross then turned south west and traversed part of the north-west coast of King William 'Land' and observed the ice stream on the west side of Cape Felix. Ross named his furthest point Victory Point. Although he did not know it, his trip had crossed the navigable route of the North-West Passage lying to the east of King William 'Land'.

The sea area north of Matty and Tennent Islands was named 'Poctes Bay' on the map of Captain John Ross. Contemporary Arrowsmith maps of the area show the progress of mapping. Early maps name the Bay 'Poctes' but later maps show it as 'Poet's Bay' opposite 'Artists Bay" (see maps at Peter Carney's blog of August 28 2015).

When the two Franklin ships arrived off the north of King William 'Land' everything they could see had been visited, mapped and named by James Clark Ross in 1830, after he had sledged 200 miles from the paddleship *Victory* in Prince Regent Inlet. Immediately to the south was Cape Felix. To the west of King William Island, the hummocky surface of the Beaufort ice stream banked up against the north-west coast of King William Island. To the east were the open waters of Poctes/Poets Bay and lying only thirty-one miles south of Cape Felix, the excellent winter harbour of Port Emerson (described by Ross).

On the Ross expedition maps, Poctes/Poet's Bay was known only as far as Matty Island and the south side was shown as a dashed line. However, such 'bays' with dashed coastlines were infamous in Arctic exploration due to poor visibility. John Ross in particular, had in 1818 sailed into the entrance to Lancaster Sound but mapped it as bay with a dashed line. Behind the 'bay' he thought he could see a chain of mountains that he named the Croker Mountains after the then Secretary of the Admiralty. A year later Parry sailed through Lancaster Sound and the site of Ross's Croker Mountains for a spectacular 600 miles to the west and firmly opened the possibility of a North-West Passage. On his return to England he collected a £5000 award for passing the 110th meridian. Sir John Barrow, second secretary to the Admiralty, afterwards ensured that John Ross never got another naval ship. Ross continued his Arctic work on privately financed expeditions.

In 1854 Dr. John Rae completed the mapping of the west coast of Boothia linking the work of Simpson at Castor and Pollux River with the work of James Clark Ross near Matty Island. He recognised a viable North-West Passage and had proved that Poctes/Poet's Bay did not exist. He named the new channel James Ross Strait. This North-West Passage route was first traversed by boat by Roald Amundsen in the forty-five ton fishing vessel *Gjoa* with a crew of six between 1903 and 1906.

When fully loaded *Gjoa* had a draft of over ten feet. However, with this much shallower draft *Gjoa* ran aground on a reef described by Amundsen as extending west from Matty Island towards Boothia and branching in many directions. Amundsen managed to lighten *Gjoa* to a draft of only six feet, by throwing overboard twenty-five cases of dog pemmican each weighing four hundredweight. This was followed by cases of deck cargo from one side only to cause *Gjoa* to heel over. This did not work and next day the rest of the deck cargo went over the side too. This succeeded and the ship forced her way over the reef losing her false keel.

For the Franklin expedition, having reached the north end of King William Land, there would have been little choice of where to sail. The only open water was in Poctes/Poet's Bay to the east side of King William Island. The rugged ice of the Beaufort stream with its many ice hummocks to the west of King William Island presented a formidable barrier. The vastly experienced Captain Crozier and the two Ice Masters would have been vehemently opposed to putting the ships into the ice stream, with no safe winter harbour to protect them from movements of the large ice floes. Ross in 1830 had seen ice forty feet thick which drove floes a half mile inland onto north-west King William Island beyond the high water mark. At Victory Point he had climbed a flow forty feet high to obtain sights of the coastline extending to the south. Only ten years earlier in 1836-37, *Terror*, captained by George Back with a crew of sixty, was caught in a sea of ice floes in the Hudson Strait area. Ice pressure badly damaged *Terror* throughout the winter and when she was released the following spring, she was in a sinking condition and barely made it back to Ireland, where George Back beached her at the first available site. The Admiralty salvaged and repaired her.

It is possible that the Franklin Expedition arrived early in the season at the north of King William Island and had no immediate need of the excellent winter harbour described by James Clark Ross only thirty miles south of Cape Felix in Poctes/Poet's Bay. The ships were not trapped in the ice stream until September 12 1846 (1848 Record). Inuit testimony indicates a surprising amount of European activity in Poctes/Poet's Bay that is best explained by an attempt by the Franklin Expedition to penetrate Poctes/Poet's Bay in summer 1846. This would be the logical choice on arriving north of King William 'Land'.

The Ross' maps show this bay as twenty-eight miles wide with small islands near the entrance (the Clarence Islands). Further south at Tennent Island was Emerson Harbour, which could provide an excellent winter harbour for the Franklin ships. Ross's guide had told him that Poctes/Poet's Bay was open water throughout the summer and the winter ice in it broke up very early. Today, the strait is known as James Ross Strait. If the Clarence island cluster is safely passed, the next obstacle in the James Ross

Strait is the large Matty Island and its reefs. McClintock having sledged around King William Island in 1859 recommended this route as the only practical one for the North-West Passage as it passes south of the ice stream. The route was successfully sailed forty-three years later by Roald Amundsen in his small vessel the *Gjoa*.

A second major scientific attraction for the Franklin Expedition in the Poctes/Poet's Bay area was the North Magnetic Pole, located on the eastern shore at the entrance to Poctes/Poet's Bay by James Clark Ross in 1830. There was no real choice facing the Franklin expedition. It was either to explore Poctes/Poet's Bay or to head north again, back the way they had come. This latter option was not possible until the last 100 mile section of the North-West Passage between Victory Point and Cape Herschel on the west side of King William Island had been mapped. The Franklin officers are likely to have carefully considered James Clark Ross's report (in his uncle's John Ross's book). Inuit testimony of activity in Poctes/Poets Bay suggests that the Franklin Expedition may have attempted to explore the bay in case it proved a strait.

Sailing to the east of King William Island through Poctes/Poet's Bay with the heavily laden *Erebus* and *Terror* with their deep drafts would however require extreme caution and was best carried out by boats. Being so far from home without any support lines, only one ship could be risked in support of the boats. The slightly smaller *Terror* is likely to have been ordered to carry out the exploration, leaving the larger *Erebus* behind for the safe return of the Expedition. There is Inuit testimony of sighting a ship near Cape Victoria on the east side of Poctes/Poet's Bay on the west coast of Boothia and of sledge parties heading south from it.

A ship and sledge parties sighted in Poctes/Poet's Bay

Hall in March 1866 set out from Repulse Bay for King William Island. In April his party, in the Coleville Bay area, encountered a group of Inuit led by Kok-lee-arng-nun. He and his group provided Hall with much testimony and some Franklin relics. Two unnamed men in the group had travelled to King William Island two years previously.

Two of these Pelly Bay men told of their own visit, two years before, to Ki-ki-tung (King William's Land), on which they had remained a short time. They pointed out on Rae's chart exactly the course they took in going and returning direct from the upper part of Pelly Bay overland to Spence Bay, and thence across the ice to Ki-ki-tung, passing the south point of Matty Island, and thence northwest - for sealing. When Hall questioned these two men as to any ships having been seen on the north or west of Ki-ki-tung, they pointed again on Rae's chart to Cape Victoria, and said that, a few years before, many Inuits had seen a ship near there from which Kob-lu-nas and sledges had come down from the south.

A shipwreck reported off the north-eastern tip of Matty Island

Terror with her sixteen foot draft may have sailed past the Clarence Islands only to ground on a rock ledge near Matty Island. Inuit testimony collected by Major L.T. Burwash in 1929 told by the Inuit of the Netchelu Tribe of eastern King William Island that:

a) A large wrecked ship was known to lie off the north-eastern tip of Matty Island.

b) A large vessel lay submerged off an islet off the north-western extremity of Matty Island.

This testimony might describe *Terror* on the reef, where she may have remained for some time before the crews lightened her sufficiently to get her off.

Enukshakak and Nowya's testimony of stacked wooden cases on an islet north-east of Matty Island.

More testimony was provided by two old men who lived on the east coast of Boothia. In April 1929 Major Burwash met these two men in Gjoa Haven and took down the following testimony. He estimated the ages of the old men to be probably over 60 years. A slightly condensed version is given in Woodman.

> When they were both young men, possibly twenty years of age, they were hunting on the ice in the area immediately northeast of Matty Island. When crossing a low flat island they came across a cache of wooden cases carefully piled near the centre of the island and about three hundred feet from the water. As described by them this cache covered an area twenty feet long and five feet broad and was taller than they were (more than five feet). The cache consisted of wooden cases which contained materials unknown to them, all of which were enclosed in tin canisters, some of which were painted red. To them and one other native with whom they shared the find, the wood in the outer casings formed the only prize. They said that on the outside of the pile of boxes the wood appeared old but the parts sheltered from the weather were still quite new. All of the boxes were opened by the natives and

the wooden cases divided between them as the lumber was much desired for the manufacture of arrows. Enukshakak's share was eleven cases, Nowya's nine and their friend two, making twenty two cases in all. After the wood had been divided they opened the tin containers but found them to contain materials of which they then had no knowledge. In a number they found a white powder which they called 'white man's snow' which they and their families threw up into the air to watch it blow away. Since learning more about the white man's supplies they have come to the conclusion that some of the cases contained flour, some ship's biscuits, and some preserved meat, probably pemmican, but they were still uncertain as to the contents of a part of the cache. All of the tin containers were cut open but none of the contents eaten as they did not think they were good. The empty tin containers were left scattered on the ground.

They also secured at this time a number of planks which they described as being approximately ten inches wide and three inches thick and more than fifteen feet long. These they found washed up on the shore of the island upon which they had found the cache and on the shore of a larger island nearby. Before the time of the finding of the cache on the island the natives had frequently found wood (which from their description consisted of barrel staves) and thin iron (apparently barrel hoops) at various points along the coastlines in this area.

The wreck itself, which had long been known to the natives, lay beneath the water about three quarters of a mile off the coast of the island upon which the cache was found. At the time they found the cache no cases had been opened and all were still piled together, indicating that whoever had put the cache in position had not returned.

Enukshakak and Nowya gave it as their opinion that the boxes had been put on the island by white men who had come on the ship which lay on the reef offshore…

This report caused some confusion, as Amundsen's *Gjoa* went aground in 1903 in the same area. Amundsen jettisoned twenty-five cases of dog pemmican and when this failed to free the ship, the deck cargo of four hundred weight cases was also thrown overboard. This enabled the *Gjoa* to cross over the reef, although she lost her false keel. The jettisoned cargo was not taken ashore to be neatly stacked, nor was flour jettisoned. If the two Inuit who made their report to Burwash were aged around 60 years in 1929 and had found their cache when aged around 20 years, their discovery took place around 1889 well before the *Gjoa* grounding. The canned meat tins of the Franklin Expedition were painted red.

The problem of the sunken ship was resolved nicely by Woodman, who pointed out that the 1848 Record recovered from the Franklin expedition states that both *Erebus* and *Terror* survived in the ice in spring 1848. Therefore the sunken ship is most likely to be one of the ship's thirty-foot whale boats, which by Inuit kayak standards would be a large vessel.

Tommy Anguttitauruq's testimony of a food cache on Blenky Island

Lately a third piece of Inuit testimony has emerged. This was collected by Dorothy Harley Eber between 1994 and 2008. Eber interviewed Tommy Anguttitauruq whose grandmother as a child was with a group of Inuit who discovered a supply depot also in the Matty Islands - reportedly on Blenky Island. This small island lies immediately east of Matty Island, where the channel between Matty Island and the Boothia Peninsula is narrowest. There were cans and burlap and cotton bags filled with flour and sugar and perhaps oatmeal.

The depot was covered with a cotton sail with stones on top and then a covering of sand. The Inuit did not know at that time what the materials were and discarded them keeping the sacks. They opened the tins but found the contents rotted and smelling bad. So they dumped the contents and kept the tins. Strips of tin were cut and attached to their knives and weapons with bone rivets. The Inuit remembered that the cache was found in the year Amundsen arrived in the *Gjoa* – 1903. They believed the cache was made by Amundsen. However this is most unlikely if the tinned food had already rotted and is more likely to have be cached by the Franklin expedition in 1846 as a food depot for sledging parties following the channel in later sledge exploration planned for spring 1847.

Interpretation of Franklin Expedition Activities in Poctes/Poet's Bay

The above testimonies suggest that the Franklin Expedition likely attempted to explore Poctes/Poet's Bay in a similar manner to that of Parry sailing through John Ross's Lancaster Bay and the Crocker mountains, to find another route for a North-West Passage. Perhaps things went well at first, but the presence of extensive reefs around Matty Island resulted in the decision to leave a cache of food on Blenky Island in the narrow channel between Matty Island and the Boothia Peninsula. This may be as far south as *Terror* reached. It would mean that sledge parties could return from the winter quarters next spring, to continue the mapping and exploration, where big ships could not go.

After the cache had been made, perhaps *Terror* was sailing north to join *Erebus*, and in bad weather went aground on one of the reefs of the north-east corner of Matty Island (in much the same place as *Gjoa* some fifty-seven years later). The ship may have remained on the reef for some time and was observed by some Inuit. There she lost some of the extra planking that had been added as sheathing to her hull. The boats took off food stores and neatly cached them on a nearby islet off the north-east corner of Matty Island.

Many water barrels were thrown overboard. Finally *Terror* escaped. But somehow one of the large whaleboats was lost to the north-west of Matty Island, and the double accident resulted in abandoning the two food caches. Because the two food caches were both found intact, it is evident that no sledging parties from the wintering ships ever returned to the area. Perhaps Sir John Franklin came within a whisker of sailing through the North-West Passage via the open water of Poctes/Poet's Bay and what would become known as Ross Strait. But his ships with draughts of around seventeen feet, failed to clear the reefs near Matty Island that also caught Amundsen's *Gjoa* with her much smaller draft of ten feet.

Summer 1846, Sir John Franklin's fatal decision – both ships caught in the ice stream

The major single factor leading to the loss of the expedition and its ships was their both being caught in the ice stream about which little was known at the time. However Captain Crozier on *Terror* had immense experience in sailing in polar ice. The Ice Masters on each ship (James Reid on *Erebus* and Thomas Blanky on *Terror*) were there to assist in navigating through the pack and reduce as much as possible the chances of the ships becoming trapped and crushed in the ice. These senior experienced men would have been vehemently opposed to entering the Beaufort ice stream and wintering there without the protection of a sheltered winter harbour. So how was it possible that both ships became trapped in the ice stream and the expedition perished?

Food caches and Inuit testimony suggest that on arriving at the north end of King William Land, the Franklin Expedition commenced a program of exploration in the Poctes/Poet's Bay area. This might have included the North Magnetic Pole located nearby by James Clark Ross in 1830. The exploration of Poctes/Poet's Bay failed because of the deep drafts of the two ships, and one was almost lost. While in Poctes/Poet's Bay it would have been possible to establish an expedition base where *Erebus* and *Terror* could winter at Emerson Harbour on the east side of King Willian Island. From this base, exploration could continue by sledge. This was probably not done, as McClintock found no evidence of the Franklin Expedition on the eastern shores of King William Island. Instead both ships became trapped in the ice stream to the north-west of King William Island.

The possibility must be considered that the divided leadership of the expedition had much to do with this. The two senior officers on *Erebus* could have made the fatal decision to put both ships into the Beaufort ice stream in an all or nothing gamble to get through the North-West Passage.

Both officers had a reason for justifying such a huge risk. Sir John after his humiliating clash and dismissal as Lieutenant Governor of Van Diemen's Land, was very badly in need of regaining some honours for both himself and Lady Jane. Polar novice Commander Fitzjames was an ambitious gambler and hoping to win great fame by being the first man back in London to announce the success of the expedition. Both had their reasons to justify putting the ships into the ice stream. The group of younger and happy officers on *Erebus*, who were friends of Fitzjames, would have followed Fitzjames in his confident talk. The officers of *Erebus* would have supported any decision of the ailing Sir John Franklin to make a bold attempt to force the ice stream in order to reach the open waters along the American continental margin. Was it an all or nothing glory attempt, an all or nothing throw of the dice? It would have been a simple matter to override the warnings of Ice Master James Reid, especially as the two most experienced polar men - Captain Crozier and Ice Master Thomas Blanky - were absent from informal daily discussions, and isolated aboard *Terror*. It might have been possible to put one ship into the ice stream and keep the other in Emerson Harbour in Poctes/Poet's Bay, for a possible retreat by the route by which they had arrived.

Did Sir John Franklin boldly order both ships into the ice stream and ignore the warnings of Captain Crozier and the two Ice Masters? Alternatively was it an accidental event, say when the two ships were threading their way through pack on the edge of the stream and a sudden change of wind shifted the ice to lock them in and they evidently never escaped? Or were the ships becalmed and carried by a current into the ice stream despite having locomotive engines.

The 1848 Record does give an overly brief statement of what happened:

H.M. Ships *Terror* and *Erebus* were deserted on 22nd April… having been beset since 12 Septr, 1846

So both ships were beset in the ice stream, on September 12 1846. This date is when winter starts to freeze the ice pack and sea. The ships were both inside the ice stream. Why did they not go into winter quarters in Emerson Harbour in Poctes/Poet's Bay? They were not working their way back north to Lancaster Sound. It seems they were intent on forcing both ships through the North-West Passage including the remaining unknown 100 mile stretch between Victory Point and Cape Herschel. The idea of putting the ships into a winter harbour in Poctes/Poet's Bay and sledging from there, as well as completing the mapping of Poctes/Poet's Bay seems to have been abandoned.

One concludes that Sir John Franklin ordered both ships into the ice stream knowing there would be no safe harbours available and gambled on getting the ships through the ice stream in a year or two, to complete the North-West Passage. This seems to be exactly the type of decision made by the flagship that Crozier most feared, when he wrote to James Clark Ross from Greenland. He missed his friend and former commanding officer and wrote that if Ross were leading the expedition he would have no doubts about their persuing the proper course. He feared their blundering into the ice and losing the ships, as had happened to *Fury* in 1824. His Greenland fears seem to have become reality when Sir John Franklin commanding the expedition, put both ships into the ice stream without a safe winter harbour, north of King William Island. The decision was probably not seen as suicidal at the time. Nor was it realized as late as the April 1847 Record, when Commander Fitzjames summarised the situation with a cheery 'All Well'. One suspects that such a decision would have raised considerable doubt and fears in the experienced polar veterans of Captain Crozier and the two Ice Masters. But it was a Naval expedition and there would have been no questioning of orders. No doubt, that aboard the flagship the confident 'All Well' lasted until the late summer thaw of 1847, when the ships were not released and able to sail home for Christmas.

11: WINTER 1846 TO SPRING 1847 – MAPPING OF A NORTH-WEST PASSAGE AND THE DEATH OF SIR JOHN FRANKLIN

When the ships were inexorably set in the ice to the north-west of Cape Felix, one of the first things the expedition did was to build a camp on land to be used for hunting and magnetic observations near Cape Felix. This would have been in the autumn of 1846 or the spring of 1847. What happened at the camp is not known for certain, but some conclusions can be reasonably deduced from the descriptions of the camp by the search parties that found it.

Captain McClintock's 1859 report of the hunting-observatory camp near Cape Felix

This camp was found by Lieutenant Hobson of the McClintock-led *Fox* Expedition in 1859 and his report is summarised in McClintock's book:

> It was at a short distance westward of Cape Felix that Hobson first came across the traces of the Franklin expedition; he found a large cairn, and close beside it three small tents, with blankets, old clothes, and other vestiges of a shooting, or a magnetic station; but although the cairn was dug under, and a trench dug all around at a distance of ten feet, no record was discovered. A sheet of white paper folded up was found in the cairn, but even under the microscope no traces of writing appears.
>
> Two broken bottles (corked) lay amongst the loose stones which had fallen off the cairn, and these may perhaps have contained records. The most interesting of the relics, including a small English ensign and the iron heads of two boarding pikes, were brought away.
>
> The tents lay prostrate, and without tent poles; it seems highly probable that the pikes had been used for that purpose and were subsequently burnt for fuel.

Two miles further to the south-west a small cairn was found, but neither record nor relics; and about three miles northward of Point Victory a third cairn was examined, but only a broken pickaxe and empty tin canister were found.

The report continued:

> The camp was situated on the west coast of King William Land near Cape Felix; it had apparently been occupied for some time by a party consisting of about 12 officers and men. Three small tents were used; they were lying flat when found by Lieutenant Hobson, and beneath them lay bear skins and blankets. Boarding pikes had apparently served as tent poles. Three fireplaces were near the tents. Under one tent, which was smaller than the others, and had presumably been occupied by officers, lay the remains of an ensign, a parcel which contained some packets of needles (perhaps intended as presents for Eskimos), some shot, fragments of clothing, etc. Other relics found by Lieutenant Hobson at the camp included matches; scraps of wood, partially burnt ptarmigan feathers; broken pipes; some tobacco; a copper cooking-stove apparently made on board; pieces of broken china; a badge from a marine's shako; old clothing; two pike heads, etc. No article was marked with a name or initials. The pike heads had been twisted off the poles, and since the poles could not be found, Lieutenant Hobson concluded that they had been used for fuel. The party had apparently abandoned the camp hurriedly and Lieutenant Hobson believed that it had intended to return to the ships, since it had left the greater part of its equipment behind.

Gilder's 1881 description of the camp near Cape Felix

Schwartka's group revisited this camp in 1879 and Gilder wrote:

> Where we encamped, which was about three miles south of Cape Felix, was what appeared to be a torn-down cairn, and a quantity of canvas and coarse red woollen stuff, pieces of blue cloth, broken bottles, and other similar stuff, showing that there had been a permanent camping place here from the vessels, while a piece of ornamented china tea-cup, and cans of preserved potatoes showed that it was in charge of an officer.

Gilder also wrote:

> The minuteness of our search will appear in the number of exploded percussion caps, shot, and other small articles that were found in various places.

An indication of graves in the Cape Felix area

The Schwatka party carried out the first summer search of the north part of the island especially between Crozier's Landing and Cape Felix for graves including that of Sir John Franklin. They considered the ground here suitable for digging graves. Their search was without success. However Dr. Cyriax reports that in summer 1949, Inspector Henry Asbjorn Larsen of the Royal Canadian Mounted Police (famous for making the first west to east voyage through the North-West Passage in RCMP ship *St. Roch*, and repeating the feat in the opposite direction some years later) carried out a survey on foot along the coast from Cape Felix to Cape Franklin. At Cape Felix he found a skull between some rocks on a ridge about a half mile from the sea. The skull was identified in Ottawa as that of a twenty-five year old white male. This is the only indication to date of graves in the Cape Felix area. Potter states that today Larsen's report and the Franklin relics he collected cannot be found. However Potter obtained a photograph of the Franklin bones collected by Larsen from his daughter Doreen Larsen Riedel and included it in his book. The photograph appears to show the recognisable remains of three crania, a jawbone, part of a limb long bone and an isolated tooth. The remains would be from the coastline searched between Collinson Inlet and Cape Felix.

Interpretation of the camp near Cape Felix

The Franklin camp, about three miles south of Cape Felix, was likely established in late 1846 or Spring 1847 for magnetic and meteorologic observations. It was occupied for a considerable period of time. It was then the nearest land to the two ice bound ships and a suitable place for a jumping off point for sledge parties moving south. In summer it evidently served a recreational role. The magnetic work was the responsibility of Commander James Fitzjames of *Erebus* and it is most likely the camp was manned by the crew of *Erebus* for this work.

As Fitzjames had worked the Whale Fish Islands of Greenland training *Erebus* Lieutenants Le Vesconte and Fairholme in magnetic work, it is not difficult to see the three friends sharing the officers' tent with a glass of wine or Willow Pattern tea cups [Willow Pattern crockery was found on the wreck of *Erebus* in April 2015]. Other parties travelling south would also have visited the camp and some beer drinking took place. It is likely that *Erebus* officers Commander Graham Gore, mate Frederick Des Voeux and their six seamen of the North-West Passage team (1846 record) spent a night there before tracing the footsteps of James Clark Ross to Victory

Point. It is possible that this camp was known as 'Erebus Camp' for the Peglar Papers identify another as 'Terror Camp.'

The case that the camp had been hastily abandoned, leaving much equipment behind, is particularly interesting, as this event can probably be dated, in this reconstruction, to the onset of the summer ice break up in Autumn 1847, when the ships were not freed, but when *Terror* was heaved over onto her beam ends by the ice. This event marked the end of the normal routine and the scientific program of the expedition and the abrupt beginning of a desperate fight for survival by all members. Very regrettably, despite superb efforts they ultimately failed.

Kok-lee-arng-nun's testimony – a possible description of Sir John Franklin

In 1866 Hall on route to King William Island encountered a group of Inuit:

> Kok-lee-arng-nun, their head man, showed two spoons which had been given him by Ag-loo-ka (Crozier), one of them having the initials F.R.M.C. (Francis R. M. Crozier) stamped upon it. His wife Koo-narng, had a silver watch-case. This opened up the way for immediate enquires. Through Too-koo-li-too who as usual soon proved a good interpreter, it was learned that these Inuit had been at one time on board of the ships of Too-loo-ark, (the great Esh-e-mut-ta, Sir John Franklin), and had their tupiks (tents) on the ice alongside of him during the spring and summer. They spoke of one ship not far from Ook-kee-bee-jee-Iua (Pelly Bay), and two to the westward of Net-tee-lik, near Ook-goo-lik. Kok-lee-arng-nun was 'a big boy when very many men from the ships hunted took-too [caribou]. They had guns and knives with long handles, and some of their party hunted took-too on the ice, killing so many that they made a line across the whole bay of Ook-goo-lik.
>
> The Pelly Bay men described the Esh-e-mut-ta as an old man with broad shoulders, thick and heavier set than Hall, with grey hair, full face and bald head. He was always wearing something over his eyes (spectacles, as Too-koo-li-too interpreted it), was quite lame, and appeared sick when they last saw him. He was kind to the Inuit; - always wanting them to eat something. Ag-loo-ka (Crozier) and another man would go and do everything that Too-loo-ark told them, just like boys; he was a very cheerful man, always laughing; everybody liked him – all the kob-lu-nas (white men) and all the Inuits. Kok-lee-arng-nun showed how Too-loo-ark and Aglooka used to meet him. They would take hold of his hand, giving it a few warm and friendly shakes and Too-loo-ark would say, 'Ma-my-too-mig-tay-ma.'

Aglooka's hand shaking was short and jerky, and he would only say 'Mun-nig-too-ne.' After the first summer and winter, they saw no more of Too-loo-ark; then Ag-loo-ka (Crozier) was the Esh-e-mut-ta.

This delightful piece of testimony has caused considerable headaches for Franklin researchers. It appears (as Hall believed) to be a detailed description of Sir John Franklin as we would expect it. His physical appearance and baldness are quite distinct and there are no other Arctic explorers with these features. His demeanor is what we would expect of him – a man in the last year of his life, not in good health, possibly with gout and possibly like modern stressed career men, some heart ailment.

He was probably aware that his life would end soon, but he was happy. He was with his men, had led the ships into the North-West Passage and if he died there before they broke out, then he was assured of great honor and the immortality of fame. Robert Falcon Scott would be the next polar explorer to also achieve these honours in this manner. It is a happy picture suggesting that the happy atmosphere aboard *Erebus* known from the voyage out had continued. An independent confirmation of this is given by Captain Fitzjames' message of 'All well' in the 1847 Record.

However, Woodman has suggested that the Franklin expedition had no contact with the Inuit until the 1848 retreat, so that the above testimony is likely to refer to the years 1849 and 1850, rather than 1847 and 1848. The testimony continues and describes how the Esh-e-mut-ta's ship was later crushed and sank rapidly. Hall believed that the description was of Sir John Franklin, so that it relates to a time before he died on June 11 1847. Followers of Hall therefore assumed that it was *Erebus* that was crushed and rapidly sank. The discovery of *Erebus* as the Utjulik ship in 2016 was therefore a surprise. Woodman argued that as neither ship sank before the 1848 retreat, the testimony of the sinking occurred after the ships were reoccupied – a conclusion followed here.

There is a clue in the report of the successful joint summer hunt with the Inuit for caribou. This is most likely to have occurred when the reoccupied *Erebus* was moved south to the south side of the Royal Geographical Society Islands to an area much used for hunting by the Inuit. The description of Inuit tents or tupics alongside the ship for two seasons further suggests that the testimony is describing events in 1849 and 1850 when the ship had moved further south. At this time for the expedition, the great Esh-e-muta was Captain Crozier. Although portraits show Captain Crozier to be partly bald, the details of the testimony do not fit Crozier.

After the death of Sir John Franklin, Captain Crozier of the *Terror* became senior officer in charge of the expedition, but (as the 1848 Record tells) he did not immediately transfer to *Erebus*, as he should have done according to the Admiralty instructions, but remained aboard *Terror*. In 1849 and 1850 the Esh-e-mut-ta who died would have been Crozier, then with the remaining survivors living aboard the reoccupied *Erebus*.

The terms 'Esh-e-mut-ta' and 'Aglooka' were not only applied to the Franklin-Crozier leadership, but also to other pairs of leaders of other ships. The name 'Aglooka' means only 'one who walks with long strides'. This, the Woodman interpretation, does not explain why the detail of the testimony fits so well with the unique appearance and behaviour of Sir John Franklin. Potter considers Kok-lee-arng-nun's testimony to be a mixture of memories of different times. Kok-lee-arng-nun's testimony of the sinking of a ship taking some of the crew with her, has been rejected in this review in Appendix 4.

A closer scrutiny of the testimony reveals some other discrepancies. Kon-lee-arng-nun is described as an old man in 1866 when Hall met him, but he was a boy when the Franklin crew joined with the Inuit for a successful caribou hunt (See above). If he was aged around fifty or sixty in 1866, then as a boy of around fifteen years, he would be recalling events of some thirty-five to forty-five years earlier or around 1821 to 1831 – well before the Franklin expedition. This was the time of the visit of Sir John Ross and his nephew Sir James Clark Ross on the 1829 to 1833 *Victory* expedition. The yacht *Krusenstern* sank but was raised and left on shore. However, neither of the Rosses were bald, Sir John Ross was not a happy laughing man and his nephew Sir James Clark Ross was not on speaking terms with him. There were only a few deaths on the Ross expedition. The Inuit did not see the Ross party retreat north to Fury beach nor their eventual rescue by a whaling ship in Baffin Bay. They did find the abandoned ships that provided the local Inuit with a great wealth of wood and metal for many decades. The simplest conclusion the Inuit might have drawn on finding *Victory* abandoned, might be that the crews had died.

For the present the best explanation is that suggested by Potter that the Kok-lee-arng-nun testimony is of mixed origins, being a mix of memories of perhaps the Ross and Franklin expeditions. This does leave the door open for a meeting of Inuit with the Franklin expedition before the 1848 retreat. Kok-lee-arng-nun was old, blind and partly crippled when he met Hall and shortly afterwards he requested his son to hang him and his wife to end their suffering. This was the custom in those days of precarious life, and this was duly carried out.

Woodman's case for there being no meeting between the Inuit and the

Franklin expedition before the 1848 retreat is a good one. In 1859 two sledge parties from the McClintock search expedition travelled from Prince Regent Inlet to King William Island. They arrived on the north-east part of the island where they found a village of Netsilingmiut Inuit. These people had many items from the Franklin expedition that they reported came from the wreck of a ship at Utjulik (now known to be *Erebus*). She had gone aground on a small island and been salvaged for years. The last visit to her had been in 1848.

When the McClintock sledge parties searched the west coast of King William Island, they found that the remains of the retreat from Crozier's Landing to Terror Bay had not been disturbed. From this Woodman reasoned that the Netsilingmiut had no knowledge that the ships had spent two years off the north-west coast of King William Island. The Netsilingmiut did learn from the McClintock expedition of the great treasure of wood and metal on the north-west coastline and some small parties set off to search there and found many things. Hall estimated that one of them reached Erebus Bay in 1862.

North-west King William Island is a barren and hostile area without lakes of fish, seal hunting grounds and lush areas of summer vegetation to attract summer caribou herds. Terror Bay on the south side of Cape Crozier (the westernmost point on King William Island), marks the northern end of the area with good hunting and is frequented by the Inuit. Lieutenant Hobson, of the McClintock search expedition, noted this in 1859:

> That the Esquimaux have not visited the cairns found by my party to the North is, I think, placed beyond doubt by the many articles that would have been of great value to them, being left there. For the same reason I conclude they have never been to the boat found on our return journey. Added to this we saw no traces of winter huts or summer encampments to the North of the boats position. Inside the islands along the southern coast, the ice is so smooth that no one could doubt its being one season old.

Lieutenant Hobson also reported:

> On the north end of the island, I saw no traces, however old, of Esquimaux, until we had passed the boat at Lat. 68 deg. 56 min. N. A little to the south of this, some circles of stones were seen indicating the summer tent places, and to the South the traces of caches and summer encampments became numerous. I doubt much if they have any knowledge of the North shore of the island. They certainly have not been as far North on the shore as the abandoned boat, since she was left there: if they go up that way at all, it must be on the sea ice.

However, there is another possible explanation for the apparent lack of contact between the Inuit and the Franklin expedition before the 1848 retreat. This is that at the time McClintock, Hall and Schwatka visited the Franklin area, it was occupied by the fierce Netsilingmiut.

This was not the case in the time of Franklin. Possibly following the great wealth of wood and metal recovered from the abandoned *Erebus* (the Utjulik ship) by the Utjulingmiut (who had occupied the Adelaide Peninsula - Queen Maud Gulf area at the time the Franklin ships were frozen in the ice), the Netsilingmiut had invaded the area and displaced and killed many of their predecessors. It was the Netsilingmiut who had no knowledge of the Franklin ships trapped in the ice for two years before the 1848 retreat. Klutschak of the Schwatka expedition in 1879 met an old man and his family who told them they were the last survivors of the formerly numerous Utjulingmiut. The old man explained how his tribe had been driven out by a later invasion by the hostile Netsilingmiut:

> The natives of the Netsilingmiut group today occupy the entire coast of the Adelaide Peninsula, but this was certainly not the case in Franklin's day. Their old hunting grounds are located on Boothia Isthmus (east of King William's Land) and only occasionally would the odd family, responding to the nomadic urge, undertake a journey to the area they now inhabit and to King William's Island. Even now they visit the latter only in the fall, and even then only the southeasternmost part. The northwestern coast of the island first became known to them through the loss of Franklin's crews, and their attention was drawn to this part of the island by McClintock's visit.

An alternative explanation is that the Franklin ships may have been visited by the friendly Utjulingmiut before they were displaced and largely died out. It was the Netsilingmiut who learned much later of the two ships and the retreat. The Utjulingmiut are unlikely to have given away the secret of their source of precious wood and metal to a hostile enemy tribe invading their territory in search of those very items. Interestingly, this different interpretation to that of Woodward was given by Russell Potter on his blog of November 30 2011. This problem of when the first contact between the Franklin expedition and the Inuit occurred will reappear with other testimonies.

There is more testimony about the displacement of Inuit by the Netsilingmiut. Kok-lee-arng-nun's group proved hostile to Hall and his companions and prevented them from proceeding west to King William Island. Hall retreated to Colville Bay and decided to return next year with some white men from the whaling ships. Kok-lee-arng-nun and his band were at the time in the process of retreating away from a more hostile group. Hall wrote:

> But other news received from these strangers was anything but gratifying. It effectively barred further progress to King William's Land for the year 1866. The first words to Nu-ker-zhoo, Mammark, and Ar-mou told the loss of their friends and relatives some years before by starvation, murder, and cannibalism. This was followed by such accounts of the dangers awaiting them if they went on to Pelly Bay and Ook-goo-lik, as to throw a damper on the whole party except Hall himself. The old chief said that a very old and infirm man on removing to Oot-goo-lik had been immediately murdered with his whole family, that very recently there had been fights among the Neit-tee-lik Innuits for a woman, and one of them had been killed to get his wife; while some of the Pelly Bay natives who were without wives, and who were being aided by the friends in their attempts to steal wives from their husbands, would certainly carry off Mam-mark; and that he himself was leaving his own country for Repulse Bay through fear especially of See-nee-mee-utes.

The North-West Passage sledge party heads south and the Victory Point problem (May 1847)

The top priority objective of the Franklin expedition was to complete mapping of the North-West Passage and ideally to sail through it to emerge into Bering Strait and return home via the Pacific Ocean. A stretch of the coastline on what was then known as King William Land remained to be mapped. This was the stretch between James Clark Ross's Victory Point that he had reached in 1830, and Simpson's Cape Herschel reached in 1839. Both explorers had built cairns and left records at these points (Map II).

Selection for the sledge party for the great honour of being the first to complete the closure of the North-West Passage was given to Lieutenant Graham Gore of Franklin's flagship *Erebus* – a man thought highly of by Sir John Franklin. Second in command of the party was Mate Charles Frederick Des Voeux, also of *Erebus*. The 1847 record shows that the sledge party comprised two officers and six men, who remain unidentified. It is probable that Gore's party was ordered to leave their own prepared records at each of these cairns. The challenge did not look very great and aboard *Erebus* and back at the Admiralty, there were great expectations for a short and successful expedition – an opinion unlikely to be shared by the hugely experienced polar explorer Captain Crozier and his Ice Master Thomas Blanky.

A study of King William Island on Google Earth reveals that the unmapped section of coast from Victory Point meant traversing first the coastline to the south-southwest as far as Cape Crozier. The straight line distance is fifty-three miles. Then, turning and following the coast to the southeast for a straight line distance of forty-four miles to reach Cape Herschel. So the total straight line distance of unknown coastline to be mapped was ninety-seven miles. The mapping team would also have had to travel seventeen miles from the ships across the frozen sea to Cape Felix. From there to Victory Point there is a straight line distance of nineteen miles. So the total journey one way was about 130 miles. As the sledges followed the smooth near shore ice, the actual distances travelled might be considerably greater.

The matter was urgent because the ships were provisioned for only three years – until July 1848. So it would be ideal to complete the mapping of the North-West Passage in the spring of 1847 and sail home with the mission completed in time for Christmas 1847. They had explored and mapped the new areas of Wellington Channel and the west side of Cornwallis Island and probably also Peel Sound and Franklin Strait. To complete the mapping of the North-West Passage, although blocked by the ice stream would also be an honourable success. Home for the winter of 1847-48 would have been the hope of the expedition.

It is probable that other sledge parties of similar size were also sent out at this time. One group established a camp and magnetic station near Cape Felix at the north end of King William Island under the direction of Captain Fitzjames. But nothing else is known of the spring 1848 exploration program of *Erebus* and *Terror* as no records have been found in cairns in surrounding areas.

So in May 1847 there would have been a mood of high optimism, at least aboard the flagship. Message forms were completed bearing the 'All well' by Commander Fitzjames and sealed inside tin cylinders. The planned date of departure of the North-West Passage party was stated to be on May 24 1847 (1847 Record). However, in the 1848 record Captain Fitzjames inserted the date of May 28 for the 1847 trip, where it had been left blank the previous year. This was concluded by McClintock from a study of the inks on the single sheet of paper showing both 1847 and 1848 records recovered from Crozier's Landing. This insert is interpreted here to mean that the North-West Passage team was delayed and did not leave the ships until May 28 1847.

Fitzjames also wrote in the 1848 record that Gore's Victory Point cylinder was deposited in June 1847. He first wrote 'May' and immediately crossed it out and wrote 'June.' Dr. Cyriax considered this to be a mistake. However, there is a much more probable explanation followed in this reconstruction. The Gore-Des Voeux party were travelling south along the west coast of King William Island carrying sealed cylinders with the 1847 message inside. They failed to find Ross's pillar on their way south and deposited the cylinder (that was re-used in 1848) on the way north and back to the ships in June.

One can imagine the enthusiasm of the party as they headed south. The ships were then situated about seventeen miles north-west of King William Island and Gore's party may have landed at Cape Felix (or even accompanied the Cape Felix magnetic party). They would then follow in the footsteps of Sir James Clark Ross and would have closely studied his account published in his uncle John Ross's book on the *Victory* expedition and saga of 1829 to 1833.

In 1830 Commander James Clark Ross was second in command aboard the paddle ship *Victory*. The expedition led by his uncle Captain (later Sir) John Ross, was in search of the fabled North-West Passage. In April, 1830 James Clark Ross made a number of exploration trips from their ship in Prince Regent Inlet using small parties and sledges pulled by dogs. In one of these Mate Thomas Blanky (later Ice Master on *Terror* on the lost Franklin expedition) had driven a dog sledge. On May 17 James Clark Ross set off looking for the western sea reported by the Inuit. On May 23 the party camped on an island that they named Matty Island, in what they named Poetess or Poet's Bay, which became, through poor handwriting, Poctes Bay.

They reached and named Cape Felix at the northern tip of King William Land (as it was then) at six pm on May 29, having lightened the sledge to four days rations only. They started down the north-west coast at two am on May 30 and halted at six am having covered twenty miles. They determined the position of their camp (which they named Point Culgruff) at Lat.: 69 deg. 46 min. 19 sec. N., Long. 98 deg. 32 min. 49 sec. W. Here James Clark Ross left the men to rest, and accompanied only by Second Mate Thomas Abernathy, set off on foot to go as far as possible before turning back to the ship, as they had already consumed more than a half of their provisions.

They started at eight o'clock in the evening and walked until midnight. They named their furthest south as Victory Point, where they erected a pillar six feet tall and left a message with a brief account of their expedition to date. They saw and named a headland to the south-west as Cape Franklin. At one am they started their return to their camp at Point Culgruff. There they estimated, from the distance travelled, that the position of Victory

Point was Lat.: 69 deg. 37 min. 49 sec. N., Long.: 98 deg. 40 min. 89 sec. W. From the estimated distance to Cape Franklin, they estimated its position at Lat.: 69 deg. 31 min. 13 sec. N., Long.: 99 deg. 17 min. 58 sec. W. At seven pm they started for their ship estimated to be 200 miles away, and arrived back there on June 30 1830. So the 400 mile round journey took twenty-seven days, with an average of almost fifteen miles per day, but assisted by dogs.

So Gore and party moved down the coast, no doubt closely following the description given by James Clark Ross in his uncle's book on the *Victory* expedition. At first they would have located Point Culgruff from the Ross coordinates. Next, they would have looked for Ross's six foot tall pillar with its message at the site he had named Victory Point. The pillar and message have never been found and must have been opened by Inuit in the fifteen years between Ross's 1830 visit and Gore's 1845 arrival. At the time of Gore's trip the winter snow still lay on the ground and a partially dismantled cairn might have been buried in the snow. Without finding the cairn, Gore's party would have continued another four miles south to arrive at the point given by Ross's estimated coordinates. Again this would have yielded no sign of Ross's cairn or pillar.

They proceed on for another four miles, passing Cape Jane Franklin (where they also could check Ross's estimated coordinates for Ross seems to have underestimated the distance he and Abernathy had walked that night) and crossed Collinson Inlet (called Back's Bay at the time). There they knew they had not found Ross's Victory Point. So on the south side of Collinson Inlet, they built a compromise cairn and deposited a cylinder with the 1847 message. The latter was also found by Lieutenant Hobson of the *Fox* expedition some eleven years later. Today this place is called Gore Point. It is situated eight miles south of where Gore eventually decided on the return trip north, was the correct position for Ross's Victory Point

Gore's party would have continued south mapping the coastline until they reached Cape Herschel. This was more easily identified on the south side of Washington Bay. There they either found Simpsons cairn and message or built a replacement cairn and deposited another cylinder with the 1847 message. What exactly they found there, if they reached that far south, is unknown because when McClintock's sledge party arrived at Cape Herschel, eleven years later the cairn was opened and much broken down. McClintock wrote:

...I ascended the slope which is crowned by Simpson's conspicuous cairn. The summit of Cape Herschel is perhaps 150 feet high, and about a quarter of a mile within the low stony point which projects from it, and on which there was considerable ice pressure and a few hummocks heaped up, the first we had seen for three weeks. Close round this Point, or by cutting across it as we did, the retreating parties must have passed; and the opportunity afforded by the cairn of depositing in a known position – and that too, where their own discoveries terminated, including the discovery of the North-West Passage – some record of their own proceedings, or, it might be, a portion of their scientific journals, would scarcely have been disregarded.

Simpson makes no mention of having left a record in this cairn, and nothing was found at what remained of the once 'ponderous cairn' was only four feet high; the south side had been pulled down and the central stones removed, as if by persons seeking for something deposited beneath.

McClintock shows a drawing of Simpson's cairn as he found it. His men dug down into the cairn and with a pick axe into the frozen ground beneath, but found nothing from either Simpson or the Franklin expedition. So it would seem that the Inuit had broken into the cairn sometime in the eleven years since the Gore party visit.

On the return journey to the ships in June, the Gore Party would have made a meticulous search for Ross's Victory Point. They resolved their problem by deciding that Victory Point was four miles north of the estimated coordinated position of Ross. However, the problem of locating Ross's Victory Point did not finish there. It was to rumble on for the next 105 years.

It is difficult to understand how Gore's work was overruled on his return. This is known from the lengthy note making up part of the 1848 record. He had closely examined the coastline including two possible positions for Ross's Victory Point and made his interpretation. No doubt the problem generated interest. Yet, why did Captain Crozier decide not to agree with his officer who had twice-examined the critical coastal section. On what justification did he disagree and decide to go along with the position given by Ross's estimated coordinates. This position is known today as Crozier's Landing for it is where a depot camp was built and where the retreating crews assembled after abandoning the ships for the start of the 1848 retreat to the south.

The return of the North-West Passage party and Gore's 'mistake' (June 1847)

The North-West Passage party had to complete the mapping of only a ninety-seven mile long stretch of the west coast of King William Land (as it was then known) to demonstrate a route for the passage, although it was crowded with ice and unnavigable to wooden sailing ships for most of the year. However it would mean that the expedition had completed its assigned task, with only one winter spent in the Arctic, and could return home in triumph for Christmas 1847. So when the North-West Passage party returned to the ships in June 1847 after sledging a total round journey distance of at least 260 miles and reported completing the unmapped section, there would have been joy and relief that the major objective had been accomplished. Unfortunately, Sir John Franklin died on June 11.

Just when in June the party reached the ships can be estimated. The departure of the Gore party was likely delayed and they did not leave *Erebus* until the twenty-eighth of May (Fitzjames's 1848 correction to 1847 Record). It is likely that the party was ordered to leave message cylinders at both James Clark Ross's 1830 cairn at Victory Point and Simpson's 1839 cairn at Cape Herschel to prove that the passage had been completed. For a fit party of men pulling perhaps two smaller sledges a distance of about twelve miles a day might be reasonable, so that the return trip of 260 miles, might take twenty two days.

James Clark Ross's party travelled twenty miles a day on northern King William Island, but he used dogs with his sledges. His 400 miles trip to Victory Point and back averaged just under fifteen miles per day. Maybe Gore and party pushed themselves hard to complete the main mission of the trip and matched James Clark Ross's distances. If so they would have made the trip in seventeen days (averaging fifteen miles per day). The two estimates get the party departing on May 28 (rather than May 24) back aboard *Erebus* on either June 13 or 18. However, it seems they were delayed on the way back because of the failure to locate the Ross pillar and Victory Point on the way south. So a return before the death of Sir John Franklin on June 11 is highly improbable.

Lady Jane Franklin worked, after the loss of the expedition, to ensure her husband's fame. She had two copies of a larger-than-life bronze statue made of Sir John, with one mounted in Waterloo Place in London and the other in Hobart, Tasmania. She hired the sculptor Matthew Noble to make the statue and had the pose described as Sir John Franklin addressing his men to inform them that the North-West Passage had been completed. This event is unlikely to have occurred, as Sir John, at the time of the return of the North-West Passage party had either died or was very ill and close to death.

With the death of Sir John Franklin, Captain Crozier became the leader of the expedition. The 1848 record indicates that Commander Fitzjames and Lieutenant Gore on board *Erebus* took the ranks of Acting Captain and Acting Commander. After the shock of losing their well-loved leader, the completion of the mapping of a North-West Passage would have raised morale, as the crews of both ships could now look forward to Christmas at home in England, when the ships were released from the ice in the August-September thaw. Christmas 1847 at home with the objectives of the expedition successfully met was now the main hope.

Meanwhile, back in England in 1847, hopes were very high as the population awaited news of the successful conquest of the North-West Passage. Lord Francis Egerton wrote anonymously in the Quarterly Review that on their return *Erebus* and *Terror* should be permanently moored on either side of *Victory*, as monuments to the Nelsons of discovery in the service of their country and the world.

However, all was not roses for Lieutenant Graham Gore on his return. After the death of Sir John Franklin on June 11, Captain Crozier took over as leader of the expedition. He countermanded the Admiralty orders to move aboard *Erebus* and transfer Fitzjames to his ship *Terror*. Evidently, he still disliked the air of light hearted jollity and lax discipline that characterised the flagship, as compared to his running of *Terror*. Aboard the latter he may have shared his vast experience of polar ice with his Ice Master Thomas Blanky of similar experience. Both men are likely to have been deeply worried at the crisis in which they saw the ships, both trapped in the ice stream without a harbour on a lee shore. Maybe they bitterly resented orders from the flagship that had ordered both ships into the ice stream, without leaving one in Poctes/Poet's Bay as an escape vehicle. Their mood was evidently quite different to that of Acting Captain Fitzjames, who saw the situation as without crisis and wrote in the 1847 Record that all was well.

Blanky had been with John Ross on his remarkable escape after four summers in the ice (1829 to 1833). Perhaps Crozier felt that the best hope of extracting the expedition lay with himself and Ice Master Blanky. Perhaps at the time Crozier had become very intolerant at the light hearted approach to the Arctic of the flagship. This appears to have had an unfortunate outcome for the newly promoted Commander Gore. Gore's report on the problem of locating Ross's Victory Point seems to have incurred the displeasure and even wrath of Captain Crozier. The latter did not agree with

Gore's deduction of the location and exact position of James Clark Ross's Victory point (It was a problem that would not be resolved for the next 105 years). Crozier differed completely with Gore's position and decided that Ross's Victory Point was not where Gore had located it, four miles north of Ross's estimated coordinates. Crozier evidently decided that the correct position was that given by Ross's estimated coordinated position. This view was supported later by McClintock. The difference of opinion is known because almost a half of the 1848 Record, written by Fitzjames around the margins of the 1847 message form concerns the location of Victory Point and that Gore made a mistake in its identification. The part of the 1848 Record concerning Gore's location of Victory Point states:

> This paper was found by Lt. Irving under the cairn supposed to have been built by Sir James Ross in 1831, 4 miles northward, where it had been deposited by the late Commander Gore in June, 1847. Sir James Ross' pillar has not, however, been found, and the paper has been transferred to this position, which is that in which Sir James Ross' pillar was erected.

After Acting Captain Fitzjames had squeezed the 1848 message including the above into the margin space of the message form, he signed it. Then Captain Crozier signed it and added the note 'and start tomorrow for Back's Great Fish River'.

It seems Fitzjames might have been exasperated at the trouble concerning the location of Victory Point. Perhaps he resented his late friend and shipmate Gore being accused of making a mistake. He was so occupied with the Victory Point problem that he omitted to state the intentions of the party - one of the main parts of the message in case any search expedition found it. Such a message left at Beechey Island stating intentions might have saved the expedition. It was Crozier who added the destination as a footnote. It appears that neither Gore and his party nor subsequent searchers ever found James Clark Ross's six-foot tall cairn with its message concerning the *Victory* expedition deposited in 1830. In the seventeen years that had elapsed before the Gore party searched for it, the Inuit must have opened it and removed the valuable (to them) metal cylinder. This also suggests that Inuit did infrequently visit the north-west coast of King William Island.

When the Gore party set out to return to the ships they must have very carefully searched for Victory Point. They must have carefully considered Ross's description and his sketch of the low lying Victory Point. It was this sketch that helped clear up the mystery when it was studied by Dr. Cyriax in 1952. Ross's coordinates gave a location where there was no indication of a cairn or pillar, and so the Gore party identified Victory Point (correctly as posterity has shown) about four miles north of the position given by Ross's coordinates. There they may have found the remains of a broken down cairn in the snow, which they rebuilt and deposited in it a record cylinder.

Crozier (1848 Record) gave the position (of what is today known as Crozier's Landing) of his Victory Point as being at 69 deg. 37 min. 42 sec. N., Long.: 98 deg. 41 min. W. These are almost identical coordinates to those estimated by James Clark Ross. Crozier's difference of opinion played a significant role when in September 1847, *Terror* was ice-heaved onto her side. Crozier ordered a depot camp to be built at the position of the estimated coordinates. The depot and camp were used by sledge parties ferrying equipment from the ships to shore and it became the start point for the 1848 retreat, where Crozier and the 105 survivors landed.

Today, at the suggestion of David Woodman, it is known as Crozier's Landing, to distinguish it from Ross's Victory Point. Its purpose was to have enough supplies there in case both ships were too badly damaged by the ice stream to sail home. The work was completed and when the retreat began in April 1848, Captain Fitzjames, possibly in a mood of exasperation, wrote the lengthy report (relative to the length of the 1848 record) about moving the cylinder deposited by Gore the previous year.

So for the Franklin expedition, Gore's position of Victory Point was regarded as a mistake. No doubt much discussion took place aboard the ships and it is possible that there were two groups – the *Erebus* group agreeing with Gore, and the other – the *Terror* group with Crozier. Sadly Gore for the short period that he survived after the North-West Passage trip had to put up with Captain Crozier's decision that he had made a mistake. However, the matter did not end there but rumbled on for the next 105 years. Interestingly, posterity has shown that Gore was correct and Crozier wrong about the position of Ross's Victory Point.

The first summer search of western King William Island was by an American expedition led by Lieutenant Frederick Schwatka. The party searched Croziers Landing for records in June and July 1879. They found Crozier's Landing to be about a mile and a half north of Cape Jane Franklin. A map from the Schwatka expedition places Victory Point at the north end of the five and a half mile long Irving Bay (named by Schwatka who collected the bones of what he believed to be Lieutenant Irving there and returned them to England). McClintock disagreed with Schwatka's location of Victory Point and favoured Crozier's version.

There the matter rested unquestioned for a long time. Even the meticulous researcher Dr. Cyriax in his 1939 book followed Crozier's identification of Ross's Victory Point and referred to Gore's 'mistake'. However he must have been puzzled, for in 1952 he published a full discussion on the problem of identifying Ross's Victory Point. Interestingly, he concluded that Gore's position was the correct one and that then-current maps were in error. Dr. Cyriax included a map to show the problem. Briefly, there are several critical positions. Northernmost is Culgruff Point, near where Ross left his men to rest. About five miles to its south is a small low promontory (the Victory Point of both Ross and Gore). To its south is a coastal indentation named 'Irving Bay'. Near the south end of this indent and three miles south of Gore's position is Crozier's Landing within Irving Bay. About four miles further south is Cape Jane Franklin, which marks the eastern mouth of a forteen mile sea arm named Collinson Inlet (originally Back's Bay). The opposite side of the entrance of Collinson Inlet is Franklin Point. Near this Gore deposited a message cylinder, on his southward march.

Major Burwash landed by aircraft at Crozier's Landing on the fifth of September 1930. The next visitor by aircraft was Inspector Larsen in August 1949. He was seeking unburied human remains for the Royal Canadian Mounted Police. Both these later visitors agreed that Victory Point was at the north end of Irving Bay. Dr. Cyriax corresponded with Inspector Larsen and also concluded that Ross's Victory Point was correctly identified by Gore in 1847. So the problem first encountered by Gore and no doubt much discussed aboard *Erebus* and *Terror*, was finally laid to rest some 105 years later by Dr. Cyriax. The many recent search expeditions have confirmed Dr. Cyriax's 1952 findings and today Crozier's Landing is regarded as lying about four miles south of Ross's Victory Point and about three miles north of Cape Jane Franklin, as first resolved by the Gore party of 1847.

Sir John Franklin dies and Captain Crozier takes command (June 1847)

The first of a series of closely spaced disasters overtook the expedition beginning with the premature death at the age of sixty-one of its highly respected and much admired leader, Sir John Franklin, on June 11 1847. He had been very popular with his officers and never dined alone, but always encouraged his senior staff to join him. The Fitzjames journal records how his tales of his many adventures around the world thrilled the expedition. He was also their religious leader and led the Sunday services. Woodman believes that there was no contact between the Franklin expedition and the Inuit before the 1848 retreat, so that the burial of Sir John Franklin was not witnessed by the Inuit. The latter did witness one military officer's burial, but it was accompanied by the burial of papers in vaults nearby. This is likely to be a very late event in the history of the expedition and Woodman believes it records the burial of Captain Crozier after the failed 1848 retreat. The burial was in the ground and many guns were fired.

The location of Sir John Franklin's grave remains one of the outstanding mysteries of the lost expedition and has not yet been identified. At the time he died it was June - a month of early summer when birds return to King William Island and there is much daylight. Because of this, it seems likely that Sir John was buried on land.

When Owen Beattie and his group exhumed the graves of the three Franklin seamen buried on Beechey Island in 1984 and 1986, they found very ordinary but well-made graves. Each had a wooden headboard with the name of the deceased, his details and on two a bible verse. The bodies were wrapped in shrouds and placed inside wooden coffins with metal plates on the lids repeating the details of the deceased. *Terror*'s Leading Stoker John Torrington had died on January 1 1846, aged twenty. *Erebus*'s Able Seaman John Hartnell had died on January 4 1846, aged twenty-five. *Erebus*'s Marine Private William Braine had died on April 3 1846, aged thirty-six. Despite the frozen winter ground on Beechey Island the graves had been dug, but Hartnell's grave was only half as deep as Torrington's.

Along the north-west coast of King William Island, officers' graves have been found and identified by the nature and quality of the uniform remnants. Some of these graves are very different to those on Beechey Island. Two are vaulted graves built of large stone slabs with a cyst for the body. The work required for the stone slab graves was very great, as the stones had to be transported to the grave site and then be fitted together, which required time and effort. Four of these graves from the north-west coast will be considered and compared with one from the south coast at Tulloch Point.

a) The deepest and most impressive grave was found by Su-pung-er and his uncle sometime in the early 1860's. They summer searched north-western King William Island after learning from the 1859 McClintock expedition that there were many 'treasures' left there. The location is 'above Back Bay, not far from Victory Point' and their search is described by Potter.

b) The second was found at Crozier's Landing and described by the Schwatka expedition. The latter on June 27 1879 searched the area of Crozier's Landing in summer. There they found a very well constructed vaulted grave.

c) The third example was also found by the Schwatka expedition. It lies near Franklin Point. Few details of its construction are given.

d) A fourth officer's grave was found by the Schwatka expedition near Point Le Vesconte. It was dug into a small hillock of sand and gravel.

e) A grave from the south for comparison - Tulloch Point.

The grave found by Su-pung-er and his uncle in the early 1860s

David Woodman set up a 'Project Su-pun-ger' after finding more detailed testimony in Hall's unpublished notebooks, than was included in Professor Nourse's summary volume of 1879. When the Inuit learned from the McClintock visit in 1859 that there were abandoned wood and metal objects on the north-west coast of King William Island, two men ('Su-pung-er' - modern spelling, but 'See-pung-er' of Hall and Nourse - and his uncle) set out to retrieve such valuable materials. At a coastal location 'above Back Bay, not far from Victory Point' (near Cape Jane Franklin and Crozier's Landing), they found a large collapsed tent on the shore and nearby the deepest and most elaborate grave known on King William Island. Hall's unpublished notebook is quoted in Potter and reproduced here with permission:

> They came to a place where they found a skeleton of a Kob-lu-na (white man) some parts of it having clothing on while other parts were without any it having been torn off by wolves or foxes. Near this skeleton they saw a stick standing erect wh. had been broken off – the part broken off lying close by. From the appearance both he & his uncle thought the stick, or rather small pillar or post, had been broken off by a Ni-poo (polar bear). On taking hold of that part of the wooden pillar which was erect they found it firmly fixed – could not move it a bit. But what attracted their attentions the most on arriving at this pillar was a stone – or rather several large flat stones lying flat on the sandy ground & tight together. After much labour one of these stones was loosened from its carefully fixed position & by great exertion of both nephew and uncle the stone was lifted up a little at one edge just sufficient that they could see that another tier of large flat stones firmly & tightly fitted together underneath.

Hall's account continued:

> The pillar of wood stood to one side of it – not at the end but on one side. The part of the stick or pillar standing about 4 feet high as indicated by

Su-pung-er on my person & the whole height on replacing the part broken off, about six feet from the ground. As nephew & uncle were in want of wood they spent a good deal of time in digging the part erect loose. It was deeply set in the sand. The shape of this stick or pillar was a peculiar one to these natives. The part in the ground was square. Next to the ground was a big ball & above this to within a foot or so of the top the stick was round. The top part was about 3 or 4 inches square. No part of it was painted – all natural wood colour.

The post was identified as a topgallant mast and may have carried a flag for signalling the ships, or possibly raising or lowering the wooden ball.

Hall's account continues:

After a while they concluded to go & make other attempts to raise some of the stones where the pillar was found. At last they were successful in raising enough of the stones to see what they covered up. They found a hole of the depth from the feet up to the navel & of a length more than a man's height & wider than the width of a man's shoulders & this was all nicely walled with flat stones placed one above another, flatwise. In this vault they found a clasp knife, a skeleton bone of a man's leg & a human head (skull). There was much water, mud and sand at the bottom of the vault. The sand had been carried in by water, as they thought, running in at the hole that had been made by the wild animal on one side of the vault. Near this vault they saw parts of a human skeleton with fragments of clothing on the limbs. There was no head about these skeleton bones & Su-pung-er & his uncle concluded that the same wild animal that had made the hole in the vault had taken these skeleton bones out of the vault & dragged them where he & his uncle saw them.

The vault was about four feet deep. This is interesting because 'Lieutenant Irving's' grave at Crozier's Landing, of similar but cruder stone slabbing is only a foot deep and the length of a body, but raised above the ground (a photograph is shown in Potter's book). Inside the grave opened by Su-pung-er and his uncle was a human skull, a leg bone and a clasp knife. As the grave was at ground level and left open it would soon have filled with washed material. This was not the case with the Irving grave that was built above ground. Woodman led a team for Project Su-pun-ger in 1994 and 1995 without success in relocating this grave. They concluded that the grave lies somewhere between Cape Felix and Collinson Inlet (perhaps near Cape Maria Louisa or at Wall Bay). According to Potter, the search continues to the present day by Tom Gross.

An officer's grave ('Lieutenant Irving') at Crozier's Landing

The appearance of 'Irving's' grave is readily seen in Potter where Klutschak's 1887 drawing of the grave is put alongside a modern photograph of the grave by David Woodman, who relocated it during his Project Su-pung-er. The grave is made of large slabs of rock, with a lining at the bottom and a boulder used as a 'pillow stone'. It was roofed by large slabs of stone. It was described by Gilder as:

> ...an open grave, wherein was found a quantity of blue cloth, part of which seemed to have been a heavy overcoat, and a part probably wrapped around the body. There was also a large quantity of canvas in and around the grave, with coarse stitching through it and the cloth, as though the body had been incased as if for burial at sea. Several gilt buttons were found among the rotting cloth and mould in the bottom of the grave, and a lens, apparently the object-glass of a marine telescope. Upon one of the stones at the foot of the grave Henry found a medal, which was thickly covered in grime, and was so much the color of the clay stone on which it rested as to nearly escape detection. It proved to be a silver medal, two, and a half inches in diameter, with a bass-relief portrait of George IV., surrounded by the words 'GEORGIUS IIII., D. G. BRITTANNIARUM REX, 1820', on the obverse, and on the reverse a laurel wreath surrounded by 'SECOND MATHEMATICAL PRIZE, ROYAL NAVAL COLLEGE' and enclosing 'AWARDED TO JOHN IRVING. MID-SUMMER, 1830'. This at once identified the grave as that of Lieutenant John Irving, third officer of the *Terror*. Under the head was found a figured silk pocket handkerchief, neatly folded, the colors and pattern in a remarkable state of preservation. The skull and a few other bones only were found in and near the grave. They were carefully gathered together, with a few pieces of the cloth and the other articles, to be brought away for internment where they may hereafter rest undisturbed.

The remains were taken back to America and sent to Scotland where they were buried with full military honours in Edinburgh's Dean Cemetery.

Klutschak's description of the grave at Crozier's Landing

Heinrich Klutschak, also of the Schwatka expedition, reported the find independently and gave better details of this very fine stone slab cyst grave, as well as publishing a drawing of the grave with the skull alongside it:

> ...on the 27th, Franz Melms and I were walking along the coast towards Victory Point, where Sir James Ross had erected a stone cairn on one of his

journeys. Near the waterline Melms found a strip of canvas (such as used for hauling a sledge), with the marking T.11. While he was making a more thorough inspection of the area I spotted a cairn and near it a human skull. It was a grave made of flat slabs of sandstone, with a grave-vault but built above ground. It had once been covered but had obviously been subjected to a search. The skull (indisputably that of a white man) lay outside, along with other human bones. Inside the grave a luxuriant growth of moss was flourishing on some remnants of blue cloth which, judging by the buttons and the fine texture, had once belonged to an English officer's uniform. A silk handkerchief in a remarkably good state of preservation lay at the head end and above it on a rock a silver medal measuring 2.5 – 2.75 inches in diameter lay openly exposed. The fact that this medal had escaped the eyes of the Inuit I can only ascribe to the fact that it had either been hidden away by snow, or that the natives' loot was already quite considerable and that they overlooked this piece of silver in their joy. Even I did not notice it at first glance since it was the same colour as the rock. The solid silver medal bore on one side a bas-relief of the British King with the inscription 'Georgius IIII D.G.Britain. Rex 1820'. On the other side was a laurel wreath and around the outside of it was engraved the inscription 'Second Mathematical Prize, Royal Naval College', and inside it 'Awarded to John Irving, Midsummer 1830'. The medal had been placed in the grave along with the dead man (lieutenant on board *Terror*) about thirty years earlier. During this long period it had even left a mark on the rock, and it provided definite proof as to the identity of the person buried here.

Less than a hundred paces from the shore lay the remains of an artificial heap of rocks which had been thrown together, a pile of old clothes, and a large number of objects which clearly belonged to the equipment of an arctic expedition. They included four stoves with pots and other accessories. Along a short stretch of coast lay items of clothing, stockings, and mittens sewed from woollen blankets, razors, etc. as well as a surgeon's tourniquet. An earthenware jug bore the imprint 'R. Wheatley, Wine and Spirit Merchant, Greenhithe, Kent', while a brush carried the name 'H. Wilks' carved into the wood.

Ockarnawole's testimony – a visit to Crozier's Landing before the Schwatka party

Gilder of the Schwatka expedition wrote:

An old Netchillik, named Ockarnawole, stated that five years ago he and his son, who was also present in the igloo, made an excursion along the north-western coast of King William Land. Between Victory Point and Cape Felix they found some things in a small cask near the salt water. In a monument that he did not take down, he found between the stones five jack-knives and a pair of scissors, also a small flat piece of tin, now lost; saw no graves at this place, but found what, from his description of the way the handle was put on, was either an adze or a pickaxe. A little north of this place found a tent place and three tin cups. About Victory Point found a grave, with a skeleton, clothes, and a jack-knife with one blade broken. Saw no books. In a little bay on the north side of Collinson Inlet saw a quantity of clothes. There was plenty of snow on the ground at the time they were there.

Viewing this statement in the light of our subsequent search upon this ground, I am inclined to believe that the grave they found was not at Victory Point, but was Irving's grave, about three miles below there.

The grave on Franklin point

This was discovered by the Schwatka expedition in 1879 and is described briefly by Klutschak:

> In a cairn on Franklin Point which had the appearance of a grave built above ground, we found the skull which Lieutenant Schwatka immediately identified as that of a white man. After a thorough search of the grave the skull was buried and the spot marked by a small monument.

It was further described by Gilder:

> The point marked (on the Schwatka map) as the grave of an officer between Franklin Point and Erebus Bay, is one of especial interest. The care with which the grave had originally been made seems to indicate the popularity of the individual and that the survivors had not yet exhausted their strength to such a degree as to be the cause of neglect.

The grave near Point Le Vesconte

Pointe Le Vesconte is a small peninsula separating Grover Bay to the immediate south of Point Franklin from Erebus Bay to the south. A grave there was discovered during the summer search of 1879 by the Schwatka expedition. It was described by Gilder:

> Near Point Le Vesconte some scattered human bones led to the discovery of the tomb of an officer who had received most careful sepulture at the hands of his surviving friends. A little hillock of sand and gravel – a most rare occurrence upon that forbidding island of clay-stones – afforded an opportunity for Christian-like interment. The dirt had been neatly rounded up, as could be plainly seen, though it had been torn open and robbed by the sacrilegious hands of the savages; and everywhere, amid the debris and mould of the grave, the little wild flowers were thickly spread as if to hide the desecration of unfriendly hands. The fine texture of the cloth and linen and several gilt buttons showed the deceased to have been an officer, but there was nothing to be seen anywhere that would identify the remains to a stranger. Every stone that marked the outline of the tomb was closely scrutinised for a name or initials, but nothing was found. After reinterring the remains, which were gathered together from an area of a quarter of a mile and erecting a monument, Lieutenant Schwatka plucked a handful of flowers...

Klutschak, also of the Schwatka expedition also wrote of this grave:

> On the point named after Le Vesconte (one of the officers of the expedition) another grave was located, and just as in the case of Lieutenant Irving's grave, the bones from the grave, which had since been disturbed by the natives. But the builders of this grave no longer had the strength to build an above-ground grave out of large rocks. A few stones were all that they had used to cover the corpse and there was nothing to indicate any chance of learning the name of the man buried there.

An example of a grave on the south coast for comparison – Tulloch point

Gilder wrote:

> ... it is probable that all who died on the march were decently interred. A very significant fact in this connection is recognisable in the appearance of a grave which had been opened by Esquimaux near Tulloch Point. It was made of small stones, while larger and more appropriate abounded in the vicinity, showing the reduced physical conditioned the party at the time...
> The graves east of this point presented the same general appearance.

An estimate of the location of Sir John Franklin's grave

The two ships from the time of besetment to the time of abandonment in 1848 remained about seventeen miles offshore but drifted slowly southwards in the Beaufort ice stream. Sir John may have been buried at some place of special significance, such as the site of the magnetic pole located by James Clark Ross in 1830, or at the site of where it was located in 1847 (as it moves about). If he was buried on the nearest piece of adjacent shore of King William Island, an estimate can be made of a possible area of the gravesite. This is because it is know that the two ships slowly drifted in the ice southwards down Victoria Channel.

When first trapped in the ice on September 12 1846, the nearest land was near Cape Felix, where a camp was built about three miles south of the cape. When the ships were abandoned nineteen months later on April 22 1848, the ships had drifted sixteen miles to the south. The nearest land was then Crozier's Landing (seventeen miles from the campsite near Cape Felix on Google Earth). When Sir John Franklin died in June 1847, nine months after entrapment, assuming a steady drift (which is not likely to be correct), about forty-seven percent of the drift distance would have occurred. This would approximate Sir John Franklin's burial site in an area about eight miles north of Crozier's Landing, four miles north of Culgruff Point and just to the south of Cape Marie Louisa or centred on about latitude 69 deg. 45.28 min. N., and 98 deg. 14.95 min. E.(Google Earth). Interestingly this is the same area where Woodman and colleagues concluded, after Project Su-pung-er, that the missing vault grave might lie.

The significance of the different types of graves

The graves left by the Franklin Expedition show a remarkable variety in styles that reflect the varying fortunes of the expedition. The three on Beechey Island are the most normal and are similar to modern Christian graves. The Torrington and Hartnell graves were constructed in January in the coldest and darkest time of the year. Marine Braine's grave is similar, but was constructed in late March to early April. The condition of his body suggests he may have died while away on a sledging trip and the body was brought back to the ships. In January the crews were in winter quarters nearby with not a lot to do, so they were able to find the time and effort to dig the graves in the frozen ground, prepare wooden coffins from the carpenter's wood stores, as well as metal plaques and wooden head boards. The three graves are something of 'make work' projects, as well as allowing the men's mess mates to express their sorrow.

In contrast, the grave at Tulloch Point, on the south coast, like the others there, was prepared by the retreating crews in 1850, when the men were weak and retreating without the support of the ships. The south coast graves were made by laying the body on the ground and then covering it with small stones. Larger stones in the area were not used, which reflected the illness and physical weakness of the retreating crews.

Of the four officers' graves on the north-west coast, the one at Point Le Vesconte is different being dug into sand and gravel with only a few rocks covering it. This is most likely to be a grave built during the 1848 retreat where the crews were discovering the very slow rate of progress and great effort needed to move the boats and sledges. Little time and effort could have been spared for grave construction.

It is perhaps the most northerly pair of graves that are the most interesting. Both are vault graves built of slabs of rock some of considerable weight and have been described in detail. They differ because the most northerly one, four feet deep, was built below and up to ground level, whereas the grave at Crozier's Landing was built as a vault but above ground. The overly brief description of the grave at Point Le Vesconte suggests that although disturbed it was also probably an above-ground vault grave like that at Crozier's Landing. Because of the poor description, this grave is not further considered.

Large blocks of rock are scattered on the surface of the limestone gravel beach ridges, where they were dropped by the melting ice sheets. Both sandstone and granite blocks can be found. The northernmost grave was dug into the ground and lined with flat lying stone slabs (dry stone walling) and a roof was fitted that was level with the ground surface. This one took the most effort to build. The grave at Crozier's Landing was above surface, consisting of large rock slabs laid on the surface and roofed over. There does not appear to have been a wooden coffin, but instead the body was sewn into canvas and prepared in the manner for burial at sea, but laid on stone slabs with a boulder or 'pillow stone'. Both northern graves required much time and effort by the crews for their preparation. This suggests that both were prepared before the retreat began on April 22 1848. Using the argument in the above section, it seems the northern grave is the older. The spare topgallant mast not only marked the northern grave but might have been used to signal the ships. It might have had a flag or the round wooden ball described might have been raised or lowered.

The grave at Crozier's Landing might have been prepared when some of the men were staying at the camp there. It is not accepted that the stone cyst grave at Crozier's Landing is that of Lieutenant Irving, who was alive and well at the time of the 1848 retreat. It must be the grave of another officer who died before the ships were abandoned in 1848. The presence of Lieutenant Irving's silver medal on a stone at the margin of the grave is probably fortuitous and dates to after the grave was despoiled. It was probably accidentally left there by someone salvaging wood and metal at Crozier's Landing, when there was an overabundance of wood and metal to be sledged away. It is possible that this grave situated at the start of the section of the North-West Passage mapped by the Graham Gore party is that of Lieutenant Graham Gore placed there by colleagues to commemorate his feat.

Interestingly both of the early cyst graves may have lacked wooden coffins with the bodies sewn into canvas shrouds as if for burial at sea. The absence of wooden coffins may have been a deliberate attempt to protect the graves as the Inuit placed a very high value on wood.

From the argument presented above, the most northerly cyst grave that had the topgallant mast must be considered a strong contender for Sir John Franklin's grave. Justification for this is the considerable amount of effort taken to prepare the grave. It is the most elaborate grave known to date. The coincidence between Woodman's view of its location with the position calculated here is suggestive.

12: SUMMER 1847 TO SPRING 1848 - NO RELEASE OF THE SHIPS, *TERROR* THROWN ONTO HER BEAM ENDS & PREPARATIONS FOR ABANDONMENT

After the return of the North-West Passage party, despite the death of Sir John Franklin, morale was doubtless raised by the expectations of returning home with great honour. 'Home by Christmas' might have been the toast of the wardroom table. The newly appointed commander of the Expedition, Captain F.R.M. Crozier would need to keep morale high in the expedition. The best way he could have done this was probably to keep the men busy, especially with preparations for going home. For this there was an immense amount of work to be done. The ships had been converted to large camps for winter quarters with the hulls encased in snow for insulation. The sails, spars, upper and top masts and the miles of rigging had been taken down. Spars had been re-rigged along the length of the ships as ridge poles to support canvas awnings set up to encase the decks, so that through the dark days of winter the crew could exercise. The snow that had been dug to encase the hulls had to be removed. The awnings had to be taken down, then the upper and top masts had to be raised up, along with the spars and the rigging put up again. Then the sails had be raised and then bent onto the spars until the ships were ready to be sailed away.

There is no information about whether sledge parties were sent out in the spring to continue the exploration. The most obvious target would be to send two teams east together back to Matty Island, retracing the footsteps of the James Clark Ross team of 1830. A food cache had already been left on Blenky Island in readiness for a team exploring probably the continuation of Poctes/Poet's Bay southwards. A considerable depot of food had also been left on Matty Island when one of the ships grounded there. Matty Island was therefore an ideal target to send two parties together. One could split off and head south and the other (under the ships magnetic program) could return to the North Magnetic Pole and relocate it. It should have migrated some distance since it was first located by James Clark Ross in 1830. A team from each ship might have set out. An *Erebus* team might again be led by Lieutenant, now Commander, Graham Gore with mate Charles Des Voeux. However the graphic testimony of the Inuit clearly indicates that the two food caches in the Matty Islands were never reached by members of the expedition and remained untouched until found by the Inuit. Was the exploration program cancelled by Captain Crozier?

Captain Crozier may have had good reason to cancel the exploration program. This would depend on when ice pressures started to affect the two ships. Because the ships were not protected in a winter harbour they would be subjected to ice pressures by local movements, long before the summer breakup of the ice field occurred. A good example of a ship trapped in similar circumstances was that of Sir Ernest Shackleton's later experience in his ship *Endurance*, trapped in the ice of the Weddell Sea in January 1915.

Endurance was trapped in the ice of the Weddell Sea, some 200 miles from her destination at Vahsel Bay, when a northerly gale compressed and compacted the ice around her. The ice in the Weddell Sea drifts in a clockwise circular motion that brought the ship within sixty miles of her destination, but across impossible hummocky ice. It wasn't until July 21 that the ice began working and producing noises. On August the first, the ice lifted *Endurance* and tilted her to port with scraping, grinding noises before dropping her back into the water. Thus began a long period of ice movement with heavy shocks to the ship and noises like thunder. These increased in intensity as the summer-autumn melt advanced. Massive deck beams bent and uprights buckled.

By early October the ice showed signs of opening, and steam was raised for the first time on October 16. On October 24 the ship was squeezed in the most powerful pressure yet. The stern post was partly torn off so that a wooden cofferdam had to be built across the ship ten feet forward of the stern. The crew pumped as hard as was possible, but the water gained. Next evening the pressure returned and ice floes gouged along the port side producing loud screaming sounds. The crew pumped continuously. Next day, at four o'clock, the pressure returned with new intensities. The decks buckled, the beams broke and the stern was lifted up twenty feet. The water drained forward and the bows sank down. At five pm the order was given to abandon ship.

The crew moved onto the ice with the dogs, the ships boats, camping gear and food. Since being beset, the ship had been rafted by the ice for 600 miles. Ice penetrated the sides of the ship, but she did not slip under the ice for another 150 miles. Attempts to drag the boats and equipment over the hummocky pressure-ridged ice did not really succeed and so the party remained on the ice and were rafted a further 400 miles north. Here, Shackleton and his men took to the boats and reached Elephant Island. From there Shackleton took a party totalling six men in a single boat on one of the epic small boat passages of all time, 850 miles through the Southern Ocean to the whaling station on South Georgia, from where he organized the rescue the twenty-two men remaining on Elephant Island, arriving on May 10 1916.

Erebus and *Terror* probably began to experience the early onset of ice pressure long before the hoped for summer breakup of the ice (as did *Endurance*), then Captain Crozier would have had to keep all his men together in case one of the ships was crushed or thrown over and every man would be needed to save the ship and if necessary, salvage the basics of survival in the Arctic. The American Schwatka expedition observed the breakup of the sea ice in Erebus Bay and Victoria Strait on July 24 1879. Roald Amundsen observed the ice in Simpson Strait to break up on July 31 1905.

There is a second possibility that could cause Captain Crozier to have cancelled the exploration program. This would be an outbreak of serious illness aboard both ships. The 1848 record states that at the time the ships were abandoned on April 22 1848, some ten months after the death of Sir John Franklin, the total number of deaths in the expedition was nine officers and fifteen men. As three men died on Beechey Island and Sir John Franklin next, this meant that eight other officers and twelve men died during this ten month period.

It is here that the research of Scott Cookman, published in 2000, gives a possible explanation. Cookman considered the role of Stephen Goldner – a Hungarian immigrant and the man who provided newly-invented tinned food – meats, vegetables, soups, gravy and milk. The Admiralty contract for the tinned food for the Franklin expedition was awarded to Goldner on April 1 1845, only a month and a half before the expedition sailed. Goldner's bid was the lowest and he promised immediate delivery. The contract was to supply forty-five tons of tinned food in one, two, three, four, six and eight pound tins. Fifteen tons of this were of seven kinds of meat: boiled mutton, roast mutton, roast beef, seasoned beef, veal, ox cheeks, and beef with vegetables. Vegetable soup, meat soup and concentrated gravy made up another twelve tons. There were nine tons of tinned potatoes, carrots, parsnips and mixed vegetables. The tins had also to be produced, including hand soldering each one with lead-based solder.

Goldner delivered nothing for the first month and persuaded the Admiralty that to meet the deadline he needed to deliver a portion of the order in larger tins. Nine and twelve pound tins were produced, but these required longer cooking time to sterilise the contents. This was not done in the rush to meet the departure deadline. Cookman suggested that some of the larger tins of undercooked meat contained botulism bacteria (Clostridium botulinum) in the core of the tin, where Goldner's cooking was lightest. For normal use aboard the ships and in the winter quarters on Beechey Island, the normal cooking procedure of giving the food a good boil on the Frazer's Patent coal stoves would have sterilised the food.

Cookman argued that a problem may have arisen for the sledging parties. A typical party of two officers and six men could be fed from a single twelve pound tin, as each would get a daily allowance of a pound and a half each. The problem arose because of the big demand to melt drinking water as well as to boil the food. The sledge parties carried limited fuel in the form of one pint bottles of ether (a light flammable liquid) used in a spirit stove. Because of the great need for drinking water by the sledge parties, it is likely that the tinned food was not thoroughly boiled, but just heated up and eaten. The light cooking would not destroy the botulism bacteria in either tinned meat or vegetables and poisoning could result.

Cookman described the symptoms of botulism poisoning as appearing twelve to thirty-six hours after consumption. Rarely the poisoning can occur up to ten days after consumption. The first symptoms are gastrointestinal problems of nausea, vomiting, abdominal cramps and diarrhoea. This stage is followed by neurological symptoms – a dry mouth, blurred and double vision. Next the vocal chords are affected producing a distorted voice and difficulty in swallowing. The poison in effect short circuits the nervous system and paralysis begins in the body's upper extremities. Finally, the respiratory muscles become paralysed and the victim suffocates. However this was not understood at the time of the Franklin expedition, and the doctors would have recorded such deaths as due to a poisoning leading to a suffocating death.

Perhaps two sledge parties consisting of four officers and twelve men did set out for Matty Island. Included in the two parties would have been most of the men from the successful but short exploration of the North-West Passage. One of these parties was probably led by Acting Commander Gore and the parties may well have also included mate Charles Des Voeux. If one of the sledges carried a twelve pound tin of contaminated food then a sledge party could become seriously ill. It is probable with the wide variety of labels on the tins that each sledge crew might select different choices.

Disaster is likely to have occurred soon after leaving the ships. There is a strong hint that one sledge party was affected. Inuit testimony recorded by Major Burwash in 1931 describes sick men being brought to a campsite likely to be near Cape Felix, where they died and were buried on a ridge behind the camp. This might well be one of the sledge parties rapidly got back by the second sledge party. In a map drawn by Captain Bayne their six graves are shown. The single skull of a twenty-five-year-old man found in the area by Inspector Larsen, might be one of these. So in this reconstruction, six or seven deaths are considered to have occurred after the death of Sir John Franklin and before the summer thaw and ice break up occurred.

So a failure of the exploring sledge teams to get back to Matty Island might be accounted for in this manner. Sadly, the 1848 Record states that Acting Commander Graham Gore was deceased by that time. Also Mate Charles Des Voeux was not available to recover the 1847 Record they had deposited at Victory Point and Lieutenant Irving was sent to locate it and bring it to Crozier's Landing. The implication is that Des Voeux had also died. Perhaps these two men were victims of one of Goldner's undercooked twelve pound tins and the suffocating death.

If a sudden high death rate in a single sledging party occurred, it would have alerted the doctors of the expedition to the possibility of food poisoning. From this time onward the tinned food would be suspect. Clearly something was known by the expedition members because along the line of retreat McClintock reported that there were almost no empty tin cans. On the Todd Islets a group of five bodies were found, one of which was carrying an unopened tin of meat. This was enjoyed by the Inuit. Eber reports that in 1905 Roald Amundsen was told about Inuit who boarded an abandoned ship and found full tins of meat. These were opened and eaten and the Inuit became ill and some died.

The drift measuring pillar

In early July 1879 Lieutenant Schwatka and his team made the first summer search of the Cape Felix area. Gilder reports:

> Lieutenant Schwatka found a well built cairn or pillar seven feet high, on a hill about two miles back from the coast, and took it down very carefully without meeting any record or mark whatsoever. It was on a very prominent hill, from which could plainly be seen the trend of the coast on both the eastern and western shores, and would most certainly have attracted the attention of any vessels following the route of the *Erebus* and *Terror*, though hidden by the intervening hills from those walking along the coast. The next day Frank, Toolooah, and I went with Lieutenant Schwatka to take another look in the vicinity of the cairn, and to see if, with a spyglass we

could discover any other cairn looking from that hill, but without success. It seemed unfortunate that probably the only cairn left standing on King William Land, built by the hands of white men, should have had no record left in it, as there it might have been well preserved. When satisfied that no document had been left there, the inference was that it had been erected in the pursuit of the scientific work of the expedition, or that it had been used in alignment with some other object to watch the drift of the ships. Before leaving we rebuilt the cairn, and deposited in it a record of the work of the Franklin search party to date.

The Gore - des Voeux party returned to the ships in late June probably after the death of Sir John Franklin. They would have completed the top priority objective of the expedition to map the coastline of western King William Island between the cairns at Victory Point and Cape Herschel. A North-West Passage had been identified and the two ships were in it, although they were trapped in the ice stream moving slowly south along Victoria Strait. Summer 1847 would be the ideal time for the ships to break free and return to England to announce their discoveries. It is not difficult to image how intently they studied the rate of drift of the ice stream.

By building a tall pillar on a prominent hill in the Cape Felix area it would be possible to daily take compass bearings on the pillar and calculate the rate of drift. This would be a much simpler method of measuring the drift than using a sextant and calculating from sun and star sightings. This is almost certainly the reason for the pillar being constructed. At first the pillar would lie southeast of the ships, then later it would lie to the east and finally to the north-east. In winter there was probably no drift and the bearing would remain unchanged. The drift of the ships towards the south-south west along Victoria Strait and hopefully to release from the Beaufort ice stream, was fast becoming a matter of life or death to the trapped crews. No doubt the officer on watch recorded the daily compass bearing on the pillar, and the result was the talk of each ship.

The 1847 and 1848 records report that the ships were trapped in the ice on September 12 1846 and wintered at lat. 70 deg. 05 min. N., long. 98 deg. 23 min. W. The ships were abandoned on April 22 1848, five leagues (seventeen geographic miles) NNW of Croziers Landing. In the nineteen and a half months that they were beset they had drifted with the ice for a distance of only sixteen miles, corresponding to an average rate of around seven tenths of nautical mile per month.

The unusually cold summer of 1847

The summer breakup of the ice and the release of the ships in 1847 would have been much anticipated by the crews who might have reasonably hoped to return to England to report their great successes by Christmas 1847. How anxiously they must have watched the drift pillar and looked out for a breakup of the ice!

But unfortunately for the Franklin expedition, according to Inuit testimony, the two winters of 1846-47 and 1847-48 were exceptionally cold without summers. These unbroken winters badly affected hunting in the area. Summer 1847 was not really a summer at all but an exceptionally cold period and the ships were not released. The longer cold periods and poor hunting of this unusually cold spell sealed the fate of the Franklin Expedition.

Too-koo-li-too's testimony – two abnormally cold winters

Hall wrote:

> ...the two winters the two ships were at Neitch-ille were very cold. The Inuit never knew such cold weather – there was no summer between the two winters – could catch no seals or kill any reindeer at most of the usual places where they were most accustomed to find them.

This is an interesting comment because it appears to describe 1846-1848 when the ships were trapped. There is a second period of two years (1848 to 1850) when the remanned *Erebus* was trapped in the ice at Imnguyaaluk Island. At this time there was contact between the Inuit and the ship including a successful joint caribou hunt. The implication of the above testimony is that there may well have been some contact between the ships and some Inuit before the 1848 retreat.

Ook-bar-loo's testimony – poor hunting in the area of the ships

Hall wrote:

> 'two annatkos (conjurors) of Neitchille conjured so much, that no animal, no game whatsoever would go near the locality of the two ships, which were in the ice near the Neitchille many years ago. The Innuits wished to live near that place (where the ships were) but could not kill anything for food. They (the Innuits) really believed that the presence of the Koblunas (whites) in that part of the country was the cause of all their (the Innuits') trouble.'

The two cold years without summers and without good hunting must refer to the first two years - 1847 and 1848 - before the retreat. After the reoccupied *Erebus* was worked south to Imnguyaaluk Island, there were two years that included good hunting of both caribou in summer and seals in winter. Again this testimony implies that some Inuit were aware of the ships before the 1848 retreat.

When spring and summer 1847 finally arrived, movement of the ice stream would have occurred and masses of it followed the usual pattern of being crushed and heaved up onto the shores of north-west King William Island. Without the protection of a land-locked winter harbour, *Erebus* and *Terror* would have been strained with the ice pressures and noises and tremors of the moving ice blocks would have been experienced by all. It would have been similar to Sir Ernest Shackleton's later experience in his ship *Endurance* trapped in the ice of the open Weddell Sea in January 1915.

Report of the Master of the whaling ship *Chieftain* – four ships in the ice, one on her side

There was no release for the ships in the summer of 1847. Instead, ice movements are believed to have thrown *Terror* over onto her beam ends, so that she lay port side down. This major event is best known from the *Chieftain* report described by Woodman.

> In the late summer of 1849 the Master of the whaler *Chieftain*, then lying in Pond's Bay, was visited by a strange Eskimo, who of his own volition and without previous questioning, handed him a remarkable drawing. It depicted a long narrow strip of land. On the right were shown two three-masted ships, on the left two more three-masted ships, one of which was on her beam ends. The Eskimo then explained, mainly by signs, for no interpreter was present, that two of the ships had been frozen up for four years on the west side of Prince Regents Inlet, and the other two on the eastern side for one year. That second pair was probably the *Enterprise* and the *Investigator*, then on their first relief expedition under the command of Sir James Ross; they had been ice-bound for nearly a year at Leopold Island off the western entrance to Prince Regent Inlet.......The Inuit and some companions had been aboard all four ships the previous spring and they were safe.

When Sir James Clark Ross returned home with *Enterprise* and *Investigator*, after unsuccessfully searching for the Franklin expedition, he reported that he had not met any Inuit. Because of this the *Chieftain* report was discarded. The drawing is reproduced in Woodman who reanalysed it. The whalers thought the drawing showed a pair of ships on either side of Prince Regent Inlet. However Woodman points out the narrow Isthmus of Boothia can be seen down the middle of the drawing. This account today suggests that the two ships on the west of Boothia were *Erebus* and *Terror*, with one ship lying on her side. The overturned ship is likely to be *Terror* and the season of her turning over would be the time of breakup of the ice in the Victoria Strait. The Shwatka expedition witnessed this breakup on July 24 1869.

Sir James Clark Ross in the *Enterprise* and Captain Bird in the *Investigator* had set sail in spring 1848 for Lancaster Sound. Both ships were locked in the ice for winter 1848-1849 on September 11 1848 at Port Leopold in Prince Regent Inlet. It is possible for the Inut to have visited all four ships in spring 1849, before the 1849 summer meeting with the whaler *Chieftain* occurred. This is after the 1848 retreat and supports the idea that some returned to the ships and were seen if not visited by Inuit.

It is thought in this reconstruction that *Terror* was thrown over onto her port side (as shown in the *Chieftain* sketch) and rendered unseaworthy in summer 1847 – an event that helped to precipitate the 1848 retreat. The Inut's sketch also suggests that both *Terror* and *Erebus* had their top masts, and spars re-rigged ready for a summer escape (after taking them down for the winter).

With one ship damaged and uninhabitable, Admiralty order Article twenty-one originally issued to Sir John Franklin now became operable:

> In the event of any irreparable accident happening to either of the ships, you are to cause the officers and crew of the disabled ship to be removed into the other, and with her singly to proceed in prosecution of the voyage, or return to England, according as circumstances shall appear to require, understanding that the officers and crew of both ships are hereby authorised and required to continue to perform the duties according to their respective ranks and stations on board either ship to which they may be removed, in the event of an occurrence of this nature. Should, unfortunately, your own ship be the one disabled, you are in that case to take command of '*Terror*,' and in the event of any fatal accident happening to yourself, Captain Crozier is hereby authorised to take command of the '*Erebus*,' placing the officer of the expedition who may then be next in seniority to him in command of the '*Terror*.' Also, in the event of your own inability, by sickness or otherwise, of any period of service, to continue to carry the instructions into execution, you are to transfer them then to the officer next in command to you employed on the expedition, who is hereby required

to execute them in the best manner he can for the attainment of the several objects herein set forth.

Depot camp or Crozier's Landing (Autumn 1847 to Spring 1848)

In summer 1847, *Erebus* and *Terror* were not released from the ice stream, and *Terror* was turned onto her side by the ice. This would have caused great concern for the two Captains, as it was possible that their sole remaining seaworthy ship - *Erebus* - might also be rendered unseaworthy. Immediately, the crew of *Terror* were moved ashore and a depot camp was built there for stores and equipment from both *Terror* and *Erebus*. The latter were taken ashore to make additional living space aboard *Erebus* to house both crews through winter 1847-1848. It seems that Captain Crozier selected the camp site to be built at the coordinated position of Ross's Victory Point, some four miles south of Ross's cairn at Victory Point. This site was named 'Crozier's Landing' by David Woodman to distinguish it from Victory Point because of the confusion of these two places described earlier.

Crozier's Landing described by McClintock in 1859

> A great quantity and variety of things lay strewn about the cairn, such as even in their three days march from the ships [17 miles] the retreating crews found impossible to carry further. Amongst these were four heavy sets of boats cooking stoves, pickaxes, shovels, iron hoops, old canvas, a large single block, about four feet of copper lightening conductor, long pieces of hollow brass curtain rods, a small case of selected medicines containing about 24 phials, the contents in a wonderful state of preservation; a deep (i.e. dip) circle by Robinson, with two needles, bar magnets, and light horizontal needle all complete – the whole weighing only nine pounds; and even a small sextant engraved with the name of 'Frederick Hornby' lying beside the cairn without its case...

> The clothing left by the retreating crews... formed a huge heap four feet high; every article was searched, but the pockets were empty, and not one of all these articles were marked, - indeed sailor's warm clothing seldom is. Two canteens, the property of marines were found, one marked '88 Co. Wm. Hodges' (William Hodges, Corp. Royal Marines, *Terror*), and the other '89 W. Mark' (William Mark, Able Seaman, *Erebus*).'

The first party to reach Crozier's Landing in summer, was the American expedition led by Lieutenant Schwatka. The party in summer 1879 identified a camp site near the depot some thirty-one years after it was abandoned. Gilder writes:

> 'There were several cooking stoves, with their accompanying copper kettles, besides clothing, blankets, canvas, iron and brass implements, and an open grave, wherein was found a quantity of blue cloth, part of which seemed to have been a heavy overcoat, and a part probably wrapped around the body...
>
> Among the various articles found was a brush with the name 'H. Wilks' cut in the side, a two gallon stone jug stamped 'R. Wheatley, wine and spirit merchant, Greenhithe, Kent', several tin cans, a pickle bottle, and a canvas pulling strap, a sledge harness marked with a stencil plate 'T 11', showing it to have belonged to the *Terror*. We also found a stocking, rudely made of a piece of blanket, showing that they were in need of good stockings.'

Crozier's Landing described by Major Burwash in 1930

On September 5 1930, Major Burwash landed there by aircraft. He found a scatter of relics over about 100 yards on a shingle ridge (seventy yards from the sea and at an elevation of ten feet). Lower down he found signs of a fairly large camp. This was presumably the camp set up for the crews building the depot in September 1847, and for the retreating crews in 1848. Major Burwash produced a map of Crozier's Landing. It is interesting to note that the relics he found suggest that the stores of the depot were stacked above the campsite along a ten foot raised beach. They may have been in stacks along a 400 foot length of the ridge. From north to south the depot contained one inch rope, a tent, barrel stave, iron and coal, scattered canvas and small rope, and naval broadcloth.

Crozier's Landing described by Inspector Larsen in 1949

The next visitor was Royal Canadian Mounted Police Inspector Henry Asbjom Larsen, famous for taking the R.C.M.P. vessel *St. Roch* through the North-West Passage in both directions. With two RCMP men he flew to North-West King William Island in August 1949 and was joined there by his former engineer on the *St. Roch*. The party searched the north-west coast on foot. At Cape Jane Franklin they found wood chips and part of the sole of a shoe. At Crozier's Landing they found two iron brackets (boat knees), some canvas, blue cloth, and rope. Near Cape Felix the party made their most significant discovery – a human skull, that was later identified as that of a fairly young white man. Unfortunately, today Inspector Larsen's report cannot be found, but some of his information is available from correspondence he had with Dr. R.J. Cyriax.

Dr. Cyriax following his correspondence with Inspector Larsen, describes the camp site as flat but rising from the sea in a series of gravel terraces to thirty feet in height composed of limestone fragments with some granite boulders. These are raised beach deposits which encircle the island, which is rising after the melting of the ice cap of the last glaciation. Locally, the gravels have been pushed up into heaps by ice advances from the sea. The campsite is on one of the lower terraces. Dr. Cyriax quotes Major Burwash as reporting that 'an army of men might work without exhausting the possibilities of finding relics or records.'

Beattie and Geiger's discovery in 1982

In summer 1982, Canadian forensic anthropologist Owen Beattie and his team visited Crozier's Landing and made a new important observation. On the shore in an area of mud his group found coils of rope of various sizes. Unlike the organic remains on land, the ropes in the mud were well preserved by the anaerobic conditions and long periods of freezing. One of the coils was of rope about five centimetres in diameter, likely to be used for heavy ship work.

Beattie and Geiger made other valuable observations. They reported a series of at least thirteen stone circles marking the campsite. They also saw other stone circles that they attributed to visits by later searchers – mainly Hobson and McClintock in 1859, and Schwatka and party in 1879. The main result of the Beattie party work was the discovery of elevated levels of lead in bone fragments that are described later.

Significance of the heavy coils of rope

In this reappraisal the presence of these coils of rope, especially the very thick and heavy coil, are seen as critical data that can be used to date the time of crushing and overturning of *Terror*. To get the heavy coils of rope ashore, would require three days of very hard sledge hauling across the seventeen miles of hummocky ice of the Beaufort ice stream. The decision by Captain Crozier would not have been taken lightly. The heavy rope coils ashore confirm that Crozier's Landing was not a temporary camp for both crews as they came ashore in April 1848, but rather an older depot camp to be used as a land base in case both ships were crushed. With *Terror* on her side and winter coming, Crozier would need to double the living space aboard *Erebus* to accommodate both crews.

Aboard the sailing ships of the Victorian era, rope was immensely important for anchoring, and making both standing and running rigging. Each naval dockyard would have its own ropewalk, where the various types of rope were manufactured. One of these is still operating in England and is open for business and tourism. This is the 'Historic Dockyard' - a preserved Royal Naval dockyard - at Chatham, Kent where the original Victorian ropery is operated as 'Master Ropemakers'. The original quarter mile long rope walk is used with the original machinery (plus some modern equipment) to make Chatham hemp (from flax), tarred muslin, sisal and manila, coir and poly propylene ropes that are sold to sailing ships as well as to the public for garden and ornamental purposed. The Chatham ropewalk has now been in use for 400 years.

Crozier could not dump equipment alongside the ships on the ice, because it would become embedded and frozen into the ice. Dark objects absorb heat and sink their way down into ice. Clearly Crozier wanted to preserve some of his best ropes, so he ordered them sledged ashore. It must have been a terrible task for the seamen and they must have been exhausted when they arrived at Crozier's Landing. Instead of hauling the heavy coils up onto the beach ridges above the sea ice, they left them on the smooth ice adjacent to the shore, thereby defeating the purpose of bringing them ashore. It was most likely done because the crews were too exhausted to haul the sledges further, or because the summer thaw had removed the snow cover from the stony beach ridges and the sledges could no longer be used.

The coils of rope were probably the contents of *Erebus*'s rope store, emptied to make extra winter accommodation for both crews after *Terror* was crushed and turned over. Their presence indicates that up to the time of turning over of *Terror*, normal naval discipline and conditions existed aboard the ships and the objectives of the expedition were in good order. Captain Crozier would not have ordered the crews to sledge haul excess material ashore unless the expedition was facing a life threatening situation. Rather he had an emergency and plenty of men to deal with it. So he was able to put ashore much equipment salvaged from both ships, including the contents of *Erebus*'s rope store.

The rope collection found by the Beattie party provides a critical piece a dating evidence by which a very different reconstruction of the history of the Franklin expedition has been made here. The two ships once trapped in the ice were drifting slowly down Victoria Strait. At first the nearest land was Cape Felix, near where a magnetic and hunting camp were first established.

In April 1848 when the retreat came ashore, the ships had drifted sixteen miles further south and the crews landed at Crozier's Landing.

Woodman believes because of the *Chieftain* report that the two ships, when reoccupied after the 1848 retreat, drifted down to the vicinity of Erebus Bay where one ship was crushed. The evidence of the contents of a ship's rope locker are cited here that *Terror* was turned over when offshore of Crozier's Landing, as stores and equipment were brought ashore here before the retreat began in 1848. To abandon the ships ropes was a serious matter and could only be justified if the space was needed to winter both crews. This would have been for the winter of 1847-48. The turning over of *Terror* in summer 1847, helped trigger the urgent need for the retreat in case *Erebus* suffered a similar fate. The presence of the heavy coil and other ropes is therefore taken as new evidence that *Terror* was crushed in the summer of 1847, when offshore of Crozier's Landing. The Woodman model with the ship turned over off Erebus Bay should have resulted in the ropes being brought ashore in Erebus Bay. Over the winter of 1847-48 with both crews crowded aboard *Erebus*, the unseaworthy *Terror* was used as a mausoleum ship owing to the impossibility of burials in the long Arctic winter.

The Admiralty orders (article twenty-one) stated what was to be done in the event of one ship being damaged. The two crews would live and work together on the undamaged ship (*Erebus*) throughout the winter of 1847-48. There was much to be accomplished as soon as possible before winter set in. First would have been to salvage as much equipment and stores as possible. A temporary camp could be established on a large ice floe near *Terror*. This was probably the Terror Camp mentioned in one of the 'Peglar' Papers. There was no point in putting everything aboard *Erebus*, as it would have been evident that she would have to be abandoned next spring as there were insufficient stores to stay on and wait beyond summer 1848. There was also the problem of fitting both crews into the space available aboard *Erebus* for the coming winter.

So abruptly the fortunes of the expedition had changed. Hope of release in 1847 and Christmas at home in England after reporting great successes, was no longer an option. Suddenly, the entire effort of every man was needed to work on the new problem of survival. The men at the magnetic camp near Cape Felix must have been urgently recalled.

A great deal of new activity must have occurred. It is likely that until space was cleared aboard *Erebus*, some of the *Terror* crew would have to camp on a large slab of ice alongside the overturned *Terror* as well as at Crozier's Landing. For the coming winter accommodation, space could be created aboard *Erebus* by removing stores and equipment. This situation had similarities to that of Sir Ernest Shackleton with his ship *Endurance* on his 1914 Trans-Antarctic expedition.

Like Shackleton and his expedition, members found that as the disaster approached, the ship was increasingly subjected to months of creaking and groaning as the ice floes moved. Concern by all members of the Franklin expedition would have been great as the fear was that both ships might be crushed in the ice and unable to return home. So very hectic days followed and the ice continued to move.

Crozier must have ordered a depot camp to be established on the nearest land. He selected the site as given by James Clark Ross's estimated coordinates for Victory Point. Dr. Cyriax refers to the site as 'Croziers Encampment' but today David Woodman has promoted the name 'Crozier's Landing' to avoid confusion with James Clark Ross's Victory Point, four miles to the north.

Interpretation of Crozier's Landing

The excess of materials found at Crozier's Landing, has caused Franklin researchers many problems as it was suggested that the crews when they abandoned the two ships in April 1848, took with them vast amounts of unnecessary gear. Because of the Beattie party's discovery of the contents of a rope store, including the heaviest cable in the mud at Crozier's Landing, one can now confidently say that the materials were a depot established from September 1847 onwards, in part to create space aboard *Erebus* for the two crews to winter there. It was also to be a base and possible repair facility in case both ships were crushed in the ice stream and the start point for the 1848 retreat to the south.

Before winter set in there would have been time to build up the depot with most things needed to support the two crews in the event of disaster overtaking both ships. These were tents, cooking gear, food, clothing, coal, wood, tools and possibly two of *Terror*'s boats ready for the long retreat back to civilisation. There was much preparation work needed for the planned spring 1848 retreat. Some of the carpentry needed to lighten the boats and the preparation of sledges was carried out both aboard *Erebus* and at Crozier's Landing. This is indicated by Lieutenant Hobson's 1859 report. Hobson observed when he found the pinnace at Erebus Bay, that heavy metal fittings had been removed. At Crozier's Landing he found the missing metal fittings. Some of them were still there in 1949, when Inspector Larson visited Crozier's Landing. The fittings show that the camp at Crozier's Landing was used to lighten and prepare some of the boats for the 1848 retreat.

As materials were made ready, they could be moved to Crozier's Landing until the long Arctic night closed down. This is likely to have been the role of the depot at Crozier's Landing. The fact that no food was found at Crozier's Landing, suggests that some was taken south by retreating crews. When the men returned to the ships after the 1848 retreat failed, any food and coal remaining at the depot at Crozier's Landing would have been moved back aboard *Erebus*.

Terror Camp

There was a Camp Terror. Its existence is known from one of the poorly preserved letters on the steward's skeleton found by McClintock near the Peffer River known as 'The Peglar Papers' as they contain a certificate of service for Harry Peglar – Captain of the Foretop of *Terror*. The letter is described by Battersby and may read:

Erebus
tell the Captain
you and Peglar
on bord onn hay
The Terror Camp
is clear

Battersby thought the document might be a note to the Captain of *Erebus*. The *Terror* crew may have then been living ashore at Crozier's Landing. Until the 2014 discovery of the Utjulik ship and her identification as *Erebus*, a Terror Camp was difficult to explain. For example, the camp site found near Cape Felix was used for magnetic and meteorologic observations. It would have been set up and manned by officers of *Erebus* under the direction of Commander Fitzjames. Maybe this was known as 'Erebus Camp'. With *Erebus* now located in 2014, with much Inuit testimony suggesting she was reoccupied and worked south towards the American continent in an attempt to reach the summer open water along the coast, it has to be concluded that the ship ice heaved over and damaged must have been *Terror*.

In the emergency of a ship lying on her beam ends, a top priority would be to get as many stores, fuel, equipment, tools and wood out of her in case she sank. Captain Crozier would have given the order to 'Abandon ship' with the uncertainty that their second ship – *Erebus* - might suffer the same fate. A very temporary camp would have to be formed on a large raft of ice nearby, although at the time of the disaster this ice might still be in motion. This temporary camp is likely to be the 'Terror Camp' mentioned in the 'Peglar Papers'. Some of *Terror*'s crew might have been accommodated there in tents, until better accommodation was available in *Erebus* or ashore, where the salvaged materials were more safely stored in a land depot, now known as Crozier's Landing.

Some insights might be gleaned from further consideration of the fate of Sir Ernest Shackleton and his twenty-seven man-crew after they had to abruptly abandon their ship *Endurance* when she was crushed and sunk by ice pressures in the Weddell Sea, during the British Trans-Antarctic Expedition in 1915. The ship had been increasingly subjected to pressure for months before she was finally abandoned. Shackleton and his crew established a camp on an ice flow nearby. Shackleton made a disastrous decision to sledge haul the boats to the ice edge to escape across the Antarctic Peninsula. They set out (having abandoned much food and equipment, including wooden boards used to floor the tents to keep dry) man-hauling their boats on sledges, but progress was so slow over the hummocky ice that they abandoned the effort after traversing only nine miles in five days.

Just before they halted, there was a major confrontation between the ships carpenter 'Chippy McNeish' and Shackleton, as the carpenter saw the boats being damaged by the ice and thought the small distances achieved to be pointless. The group shortly settled into a more permanent camp on the ice that was named 'Ocean Camp'. They then drifted only, to finally be released and reach Elephant Island in the boats. Shackleton then made one of the most perilous small boat voyages with a small crew including Chippy McNeish, over 850 miles in the Southern Ocean to South Georgia. From there he returned several times before finding an ice free route to Elephant Island and rescuing his men. The crew were then 'black men', bearded, with pinched faces, wearing oil-soaked clothing coated in blubber soot. They had been living on seals and birds, using blubber to cook and seal oil for light, under two overturned boats for four months, and before that almost six months drifting on the ice.

Preparations for abandoning the ships

The summer 1847 throwing over of *Terror*, together with the failure of release of the ships, would have precipitated a number of very serious crisis meetings between the two captains and their officers. Presumably these meetings were held in the great cabin of *Erebus*, chaired by Captain Crozier.

There were a number of vital issues that had to be considered. The expedition had been supplied with three years food. If they waited for release in 1848, then the food supply would be largely gone and there was no guarantee of a release. Therefore a retreat would be necessary before the food supplies were exhausted. All scientific work should cease immediately and all efforts made to save the trapped men of the expedition. Before winter set in there were many things to be accomplished before the daylight ceased. Throughout the darkness of winter there were many jobs that could be done aboard *Erebus*, but the extreme crowding and lack of a work space would be the main problem. Some of the tasks accomplished can be deduced from the observations of relics found along the line of retreat.

The Admiralty lack of emergency plans

The expedition was not at all prepared for disaster and abandoning the ships. Disaster had not been considered by the Admiralty nor by most of the officers of the Franklin expedition. If only some simple forethought had gone into the matter of possible abandonment of *Erebus* and *Terror*, a considerable amount of searching in the wrong places might have been reduced. The failure to leave a message at Beechey Island resulted in the entire Arctic region having to be searched. All that could be said was that their position and plight would be unknown at home, and they were very much on their own. It they were to survive, it would be only by their own unaided efforts.

Although the Admiralty did send out a very large number of relief expeditions, the complete lack of communication and failure to leave messages at Beechey Island, resulted in the expedition not being located until long after everyone had died. There had been no planning in the equipping of the expedition for a retreat. There would be insufficient camping equipment, no outdoor clothing for the men to travel in the Arctic, insufficient cooking apparatus, insufficient tents and insufficient sledges for a large number of men. The ships had not been supplied with hunting rifles and had only muskets and shotguns, so that hunting would have been less successful than it might have been. Battersby records how a polar bear killed at Beechey Island by a search expedition, was found to have a Franklin musket ball embedded in its fur that had failed to penetrate the hide. In 1850 Captain Saunders of the *North Star*, deposited food and equipment for 100 men for one year as well as a steam launch for the expedition in the Wollaston Islands. However, this was not known to the Franklin expedition and the stores were eventually destroyed by the Inuit.

Accommodation of two crews aboard *Erebus*

In order to fit the two crews aboard *Erebus* before winter set in and darkness arrived, space had to be created aboard ship. The only information available is the discovery by the Beattie party in 1982 of the contents of a rope store probably from *Erebus* in the shore mud at the depot camp at Crozier's Landing.

The land depot

The decision was taken to move as much material as possible to a land camp and obviously Captain Crozier selected the site with a camp for overnight stays to be built at the coordinated position of Victory Point – known as Crozier's Landing today. This would have been around seventeen miles from the ships across difficult hummocky ice.

Some of the items transported to the land depot had their owner's names on them. McClintock collected a number of these from Crozier's Landing:

A brass plate from a gun case engraved 'C.H. Osmer R.N.' (Purser Charles Hamilton Osmer, *Erebus*); A double framed sextant with the name 'Fredrick Hornby R.N.' (Mate Fredrick John Hornby, *Terror*); A canteen marked '88 Co. Wm. Hedges' (William Hedges, Corporal Royal Marines, *Terror*); A canteen marked '89 Co. Wm. Heather' (William Heather private, Royal Marines, *Terror*); A stocking marked 'W. Green' (not a member of the Franklin expedition).

The Schwatka party collected a single item with a name on it. It was a brush marked 'H. Wilks' (Henry Wilkes, Private, Royal Marines, *Terror*).

So for five items with Franklin Expedition names found abandoned at Crozier's Landing, four were owned by crewmen of *Terror* and one from *Erebus*. This hints at the possibility that most of the material stored at Crozier's Landing came from *Terror*, but some also came from *Erebus*. The first was probably salvaged from the ship lying on her beam ends and the rest removed to make space on *Erebus* for the two crews to winter aboard her. It is possible that some of *Terror*'s crew were accommodated on land before winter set in to carry out work in preparation for the retreat. The rest of *Terror*'s crew might have lived at Terror Camp alongside *Terror* to salvage materials needed.

Food and fuel

Dr. Cyriax made a detailed study of the provisions provided to the two ships by the Comptroller of Victualling. When the ships sailed, they carried enough preserved meat, salt meat, pemmican, and preserved soups to last 137 men for 1,150 days. 129 officers and men sailed from Greenland and three died at Beechey Island. Dr. Cyriax has calculated that when the ships were abandoned in April 1848 there were sufficient provisions left for 126 officers and men for at least three months. This is a theoretical calculation. It is known from the last whaling ships that the expedition encountered, that the crews were shooting birds and salting them down in barrels. A considerable amount of food stores appear to have been lost in Poctes/Poet's Bay, both in a sledging depot that was never revisited and in a stack of wooden cases placed on an islet to lighten a ship aground on one of the reefs.

This meant that as the ships were not freed from the ice in summer 1847, they would have to be abandoned at the end of the third winter (spring 1848 – which is what happened).

The failure of the two ships to be released in summer 1847 was the major disaster that turned the expedition from a major success, ultimately into a total failure. On the actual date of abandoning the ships, the crews had been aboard them for two years and nine months. The high death rate over winter 1847 – 1848 may have been attributed by the ship's doctors to contaminated tinned food. They may have condemned the tinned food, as unopened tins were found aboard both abandoned ships by the Inuit. Also, one of the five dead men found on the Todd Islets was carrying an unopened tin of pemmican. If this is correct then food may have been rationed in the year before the 1848 retreat. There is some indication of this in the 'Peglar Papers,' one of which states:

'briefest [breakfast] to be short rations.'

The ships had been provided with 9,554 lbs. of lemon juice, that was enough to provide every expedition member with one ounce a day for three years and two months. McClintock thought that the high mortality rate was caused in part by a major outbreak of scurvy, probably because the lime juice after more than two years in storage had lost its antiscorbutic properties when the vitamin C broke down. Alternatively, Cookman made a case that the largest tins of preserved food had been undercooked in the rush before the sailing date, and were not all sterile so that botulism occurred to account for the high mortality rate. Dr. Cyriax also pointed out that the expedition had been supplied with enough rum for only two years and five months.

Fuel was an important factor. Each ship had been supplied with only ninety tons of coal needed for using the steam engines and for cooking on the ships Fraser's Patent coal stoves. For sledging parties, there was ether for the spirit stoves. There was unlikely to be sufficient ether for the whole ships' company to cook on the retreat. The alternative was fire wood that could be prepared from spare timber or drift wood found along the island shoreline. Firewood had the disadvantage of being bulky and heavy, so that large amounts could not be carried on the retreat.

Boats and sledges

According to Scott Cookman, both *Erebus* and *Terror* each carried seven boats:

> One Pinnace twenty-eight feet long.
> One Jolly boat thirty feet long.
> Two Whale boats thirty feet long with six oars and double bowed.
> Two cutters twenty-five feet long with eight oars and a square stern.
> One dinghy twelve feet long.

In order to confirm this, the author wrote to the National Maritime Museum and received the following information from Mr. Jeremy Michell, Historic Photographs and Ships Plans Curator and Manager.

> Object I.D.: ZAZ5673
> Description: 1:48 Plan showing the inboard profile with fittings for *Terror* (1813) and *Erebus* (1826).
> One Pinnace twenty-eight feet.
> One Galley thirty feet.
> Two whale boats thirty feet.
> Two cutters twenty-five feet.
> One cutter twenty-three feet.
> One gig twenty-two feet.
> One dinghy twelve feet.

Jeremy Michell wrote on December 20 2016:

This is the boat compliment for the 1839 expedition to the Antarctic and I have no evidence on the plans to confirm that the same number was taken on the 1845 Arctic expedition. None of the other plans of the two ships contains a list of ship's boats.

Captain Crozier in a letter states that in order to lighten *Terror* at Disko Island in Greenland, he returned a thirty-foot whaleboat to the escort supply ship *Barretto Junior*. It is likely the ships did not carry thirty-foot galleys, so that *Erebus* may have carried eight boats and *Terror* seven.

McClintock gives a very detailed description for the twenty-eight foot pinnace that he found on a sledge in Erebus Bay. This is the pinnace, that he believed from the contents, to be from *Erebus*. His description is reproduced here and provides much insight. He recorded considerable modification of the boat to lighten it for travel up a river. The ships carpenters had planed down the stem and stern posts and keel to lighten the boat. Because of this the dockyard details carved into the stem post had been partly removed. The seven upper planks on either side had been removed and replaced by very thin fir planks. Heavy iron fittings had been removed. A nine inch canvas weather cloth had been fitted around the hull to keep out spray and snow. Perhaps most significantly the rudder and oars were missing, but had been replaced by paddles – more suitable for a rocky river.

The ships carpenters had also been busy constructing sledges on which the boats and survival gear would be hauled. McClintock described the *Erebus* twenty-eight foot pinnace and its sledge that his expedition found in Erebus Bay in 1859:

> The weight of the boat alone was about 700 or 800 lbs. only, but she was mounted on a sledge of unusual weight and strength. It was constructed of two oak planks twenty three feet four inches in length, eight inches in width with an average thickness of two and a half inches. These planks formed the sides or runners of the sledge; they were connected by five cross bars of oak, each four feet long, and four inches by three and a half inches thick, and bolted down to the runners; the underneath parts of the latter were shod with iron. Upon the cross bars five saddles or supporting chocks for the boat were lashed, and the drag ropes by which the crew moved this massive sledge, and the weights upon it, consisted of two and three quarters inch whale-line.
>
> I calculated the weight of this sledge to be 650 pounds; it could not have been less, and may have been considerably more. The total weight of the boat and sledge may be taken at 1,400 lbs., which amounts to a heavy load for even seven strong healthy men.

Clothing

Perhaps the greatest problem viewed from today was the clothing. The men marched out on the retreat wearing their best uniforms for they had no fur clothing. The officers wore blue woollen coats. These were completely unsuitable for Arctic travel as they trapped ice particles. In snowstorms such clothing would soon become encased in ice so that travel had to cease. Snowstorms and unsuitable clothing and footwear were probably a major factor in the failure of the 1848 retreat where frostbite would have been a common occurrence. McClintock described the clothing worn by the solitary body of a steward that he found, as being his best clothes for going ashore, to be worn on the day the ship returned home.

Boots

Another problem viewed from today was the leather boots and shoes that were worn on the retreat. These are most unsuitable footwear for marching over snow and ice because they lacked insulation, leading to early cases of frostbitten feet.

In contrast the several layers of fur booties worn by the Inuit did not. An attempt was made to provide warm booties like the Inuit by cutting up and sewing blankets. McClintock found many pairs of boots of various kinds in the pinnace in Erebus Bay. There were cloth winter boots, sea boots, heavy ankle boots and strong shoes. He also found a pair of worked slippers lined with calf skin.

European footwear with smooth soles was unsuitable or hauling heavy loads on snow and ice. So the crew's smooth-soled leather boots had been modified by putting screws through the soles to protrude, so they could grip the ice. This method was used in the Scott and Shackleton expeditions to Antarctica in the early twentieth century. Today steel spikes or crampons are strapped onto boot shod feet by climbers and ice walkers. A group of seven skeletons found at Thunder Bay on the Adelaide Peninsula had 'nails in the boots' suggesting the method worked well and got these men and a boat onto the American continent.

A hint of these preparations on the night before the first abandonment of the ships is found in some lower-deck doggerel written on a personal paper belonging to Captain of the Foretop (*Terror*) Harry Peglar. It was found with other papers by McClintock with the clothed skeleton of a ship's steward. The partially legible writing states:

> We will have his new boots in middle watch has we have got some very had ground to heave (illegible) shall want some grog to wet hour issel. All my art Tom for I to do think (illegible) time (illegible) I closes (illegible) should lay (illegible) and (illegible) the 21st night a gread.

This might be read as:

> We will have new boots in the middle watch [midnight to four am] as we have some very hard ground to heave [the sledges over]. We shall want some

grog to wet our whistle. All my heart Tom for I do think it is time to leave now. I close and should lay aft and ready for the twenty-first night agreed.

The twenty-first night might refer to the night before the ships were abandoned as the 1848 record states that both the *Erebus* and *Terror* were abandoned on Saturday 22 of April 1848 – the day before Easter.

The above message is from Harry Peglar. However the clothing of the skeleton carrying the papers and found by McClintock is that of a steward, but has been commonly missidentified as Peglar. The skeleton was of a slightly built young man and not that of an older stronger experienced seaman like Peglar. The papers were probably carried by Steward Tom of the *Terror*, for whom the above was written. There are only two candidates - the two stewards of *Terror* (Thomas Jopson – Captain's Steward or Thomas Armitage – Gun Room Steward). Thomas Jopson was a boy when the expedition left in 1845 and he is a most likely candidate. Sadly, the solitary skeleton probably records a part of the 1850 retreat that occurred after Captain Crozier died. Captain of the Foretop Harry Peglar is presumed to have died earlier, so that his steward friend Tom carried his papers including letters.

Camping equipment

For normal exploration only a small part of the crews would be engaged in outside exploration work and hunting and there would be insufficient camping equipment for the entire expedition to make a retreat. There was a major problem with clothing as Inuit-style clothing of animal skins was not possible, as a very large number of skins would be required and much work needed to be performed by Inuit ladies in chewing the skins to soften them. The crews therefore retreated wearing their uniforms with officers wearing their short coats ('Lieutenant Irving' was buried in his naval coat). Their passage and graves were marked by remnants of blue cloth from their uniforms.

Considerable saving of effort in tent making and weight was achieved by having many men sleep inside the boats with shelter provided by canvas awnings over them. The canvas awning would be the boat sails. The latter were raised when sledging in favourable winds, as described by the Inuit testimony of the famous encounter near Washington Bay in 1850. For a retreat by both crews, it would be necessary to make up more canvas tents, sleeping bags, and cooking stoves. It was also necessary to lighten the sledge loads as much as possible. From the very detailed description of the meeting near Washington Bay, it is known that many of the men on the retreat slept in the boat on the sledge. This was hauled and left on the smooth ice nearest the shore. The remaining men camped nearby on ground free of ice in a tent. This tells us that they did not carry heavy ground sheets to lie on. Bear skins had been abandoned in the camp near Cape Felix, but these were too heavy for the retreat.

Survival equipment was also made. A hunting knife was found that had been made by attaching the blade of a kitchen knife to a wooden handle. A scabbard with it had been made by cutting down the sheath of a marine's bayonet. Small cartridges were made from the fingers of gloves.

Snow goggles, stockings and mittens

In the original plan, the ships were to be sailed home, so that only selected parties of officers and men would venture out for scientific and exploration trips. To abandon both ships required equipment and clothing for 105 men. Snow goggles also had to be manufactured aboard the ships. These were made with wire mesh as several pairs were found and some returned to the National Maritime Museum in Greenwich, where they are displayed today. High on the list would be the preparation of woollen stockings and mittens made from ship's blankets. Examples were found by the Schwatka party.

The scientific collections - specimens, records, maps, charts, logs and diaries

After three years, the expedition would have accumulated a vast amount of new data and scientific specimens. Only a small fraction of this could be taken with the boats and sledges on the retreat. Most important would be the two ships log books and the charts showing the ships' tracks especially into the previously unknown regions (in particular the Wellington Channel and Peel Sound-Franklin Strait routes). Each officer would have produced a diary of his observations that he was expected to turn over to the Admiralty at the end of the voyage. There would be volumes of the magnetic readings, which had been a major part of the scientific work (the responsibility of Acting Captain Fitzjames). Maps of new lands would have been prepared. There would be marine creatures preserved and described by Assistant Surgeon Harry Goodsir, plant and lichen specimens, bird skins and bones, and a geological collection of rocks, fossils and minerals.

Most of this could not be taken on the retreat. So the questions would be raised of how to protect it, for it was known that the Inuit would tear down any cairn to get the message cylinder and discard any paper. Some expeditions had overcome this by burying their records ten feet north of a cairn. Inuit testimony describes a box one foot square and two feet long that was found full of books and papers with the boat at what Schwatka afterwards called Starvation Cove. These were probably core records being taken for return to the Admiralty. Inuit testimony also describes books and papers in a second boat found in Erebus Bay. These may have been the officer's diaries. What happened to the rest of the scientific results? One possibility would have been to bury these records (up to 1848) at Crozier's Landing. There is also Inuit testimony that later in 1849 or 1850, paper records were buried at the time of the burial of Captain Crozier, when the reoccupied *Erebus* was in the Royal Geographical Society Islands.

The boat teams

Another major task before abandoning the ships was to assign the officers and men to the various boats and their sledges. Cookman reports that the two ships carried a total of fourteen boats: cutters; pinnaces; whaleboats; jolly boats; dinghies; and ships boats. But one whale boat was sent back from Greenland to make deck space. Another boat, possibly a whaler, seems to have been lost at the Matty Islands. Largest were the whaleboats, double bowed, thirty feet long, light built with six pulling oars, no rudder but a steering oar. The cutters were smaller at twenty-five feet, deeper keeled, square sterned and with rudders. They were pulled by eight oars. The two jolly boats were each thirty feet long. The two pinnaces were each twenty-eight feet long. The four ships boats were each twenty-two feet long and the two dinghies each twelve feet long. The boat found by McClintock at twenty-eight feet long was a pinnace believe to be from *Erebus*.

Rear Admiral Noel Wright, from the detailed description of the boat on the sledge found by McClintock in 1849, concluded that each boat carried twenty-four paddles, so that only four large boats needed to be prepared. Presumably each ship would provide two teams and two large boats. The carpenters of each ship would be responsible for building the sledges for the boats, lightening the boats and cutting down the oars to make paddles. In addition, smaller sledges would be used to carry extra equipment (as reported at the famous meeting near Washington Bay).

With four large boats required for the 1848 retreat, only three are accounted for, two in Erebus Bay, and another in Douglas Bay. No boats were found by the Inuit at Terror Bay. The one boat at Starvation Cove is believed to be the one witnessed by the Inuit in Washington Bay during the 1850 retreat. It is possible that the fourth boat of the 1848 retreat is represented by enigmatic remains cached by the Inuit in Chantrey Inlet and on Montreal Island inside the estuary of Back's Great Fish River (described later). One of the cached items found there was a pair of snowshoes with Dr Stanley's name (surgeon, *Erebus*) on them.

13: SUMMER 1847 TO SPRING 1848 – HEALTH PROBLEMS

Despite the return of the successful North-West Passage team led by Lieutenant Graham Gore, the premature death of expedition leader Sir John Franklin in June 1847 marked the beginning of a serious decline in the fortunes of the expedition. The deaths of both officers and men continued. By the time the ships were abandoned in April 1848, the total number of deaths for the expedition had reached nine officers and fifteen men, leaving 105 men to make the retreat (1848 Record). Without the protection of a winter harbour, the two ships were subjected to great pressures by movement of the Beaufort ice stream (Map 1), but were not released in summer 1847 but instead *Terror* was heaved her onto her beam ends. This major event marked an abrupt change in the activities of the expedition.

Prior to *Terror* being rendered uninhabitable on her beam ends, the expedition was proceeding normally. From that time (June to July 1847) on, the expedition lost its objectives of scientific observation, collection and recording. They had been a scientific and exploration expedition from May 1845 – a total of two years and five months. Suddenly a great crisis was upon them. Every man and all effort was needed in a fight for survival. That the ships had to be abandoned was obvious, as the food supply was likely to run out before the winter of 1848 – 49. Also their survival in the conveyor belt of the ice stream and release, was not at all certain.

Erebus with two crews wintering aboard became a hell ship where conditions were so bad with frequent deaths, that Captain Crozier elected to retreat in April 1848, before the ice melted. He did not wait until August when the seas would have been open and the boats could be sailed away. Instead he chose retreat across the winter snow and ice hauling the boats. At best perhaps only one boat reached the estuary of Back's Great Fish River. Crozier's early departure can only have been caused by a very rapid deterioration in the health of the crews. He probably acted on the advice of the ships doctors. An epidemic of some sort of food poisoning was probably in progress and many men were affected. If the men could get to the south part of King William Land or into Chantrey Inlet (the estuary of Back's Great Fish River) then fresh food could be hunted and the health of the crews restored. When the thaw came the boats could then be used to get the men to some outpost of the Hudson's Bay Company. It must have been a case of getting everyone moving now, as another few weeks would be too late. Much has emerged concerning the health of the crews as they prepared to abandon the two ships.

Lead Poisoning

The forensic work of Beattie and Geiger on three bodies of the Franklin Expedition that they exhumed from graves on Beechey Island, as well as on bone fragments collected on King William Island, showed abnormal levels of lead. Some levels were spectacular. Such as the 600 ppm lead in the hair of *Terror*'s Leading Stoker John Torrington and between 110 to 151 ppm in his bones. Beattie's work also revealed high lead levels in the frozen soft tissues of the three exhumed bodies. This is important because whereas bone retains lead for a long time, the soft tissues do not. High lead in bone might have accumulated in early life in Victorian times, when lead water pipes were widely used. The soft tissue evidence indicated ingestion of lead during the expedition. The high lead levels identified by the forensic work of Beattie were not themselves fatal.

A further study of 400 bones and bone fragments from Erebus Bay by Keenleyside and others, revealed elevated lead levels between 49 and 204 ppm. Lead levels in fifty-two bones suggest the equivalent of 600 to 1500 micrograms of lead per decilitre of blood. These levels are three to ten times the recommended upper limit of forty to sixty ppm for occupational exposure. Although there is considerable variation between individuals, symptoms for lead levels of over eighty ppm include vomiting, constipation, colic and weakness in the extensor muscles. At levels of over 200 ppm, symptoms include colic, extensor muscle paralysis and coma. So some of the retreating crews were likely to be very weak. The effect of strenuous exercise in boat hauling would reduce body weight which has the effect of increasing the lead levels in the blood, so that the symptoms would become worse as the retreat advanced.

Beattie and others interpreted the source of the lead to have come from the solder used to make the cans for the food. Battersby observed that the firm of Goldner supplied 33,289 pounds of canned meat to the Franklin Expedition. Discarded Goldner's Patent meat cans from Beechey Island have been found with long stalactites of lead seal extending into the cans. Beattie and others have matched the chemistry of the lead solder to that found in the human remains. Goldner provided 2,741,988 pounds of canned meat to the Royal Navy between 1845 and 1851 without catastrophic poisoning.

Battersby argued that lead-tainted meat could not be the major factor resulting in the failure of the Franklin Expedition because it was widely used throughout of the Royal Navy, where it proved successful. Battersby found an alternative explanation for the source of the lead in a hot water system installed in both ships, as a new invention unique to this expedition. There was a demand for large amounts of fresh water to run the steam locomotive engine they each carried. Illustrations of the Fraser's patent fire hearth and coppers and similar stoves are shown in Peter Carney's blog of Monday March 30 2015. Steam from the fire hearth was led by a pipe into two overhead tanks or coppers in which ice was placed to be melted. The lead contamination is believed to originate in the lead pipe carrying the steam, well illustrated in a diagram in Peter Carney's blog of May 7 2011.

The lead study is a little bit weakened at present, as there is no data on the lead levels in the British Victorian population, where lead water pipes were in use. The presence of lead in the soft tissues of the bodies exhumed for autopsy on Beechey Island, does support lead ingestion at the time of death. The presence of high and variable lead levels in bone samples demonstrate that some of the Franklin Expedition suffered from severe lead poisoning. All samples tested were over levels where symptoms might affect brain function producing dullness, irritability, poor attention span, lethargy, headache, fatigue, gastric pain, constipation, vomiting, convulsions, coma and death. However, a re-examination of the problem by Millar and others concluded that a portion of the crew may have experienced few or no adverse effects, while others may have suffered some debility, so that lead alone may not have caused the disaster.

There is some Inuit testimony recently collected by Eber that suggests that aberrant behaviour, possibly induced by lead poisoning, was observed in the retreating crews.

Tommy Anguttitauruq's testimony

Tommy has heard the stories of cannibalism and says, 'Even before this, some of them already didn't seem to be right. Some of the Inuit would try to help some of these white people who seemed not quite right, but they wouldn't want to receive help. They would grab and burst out screaming. So something didn't seem right to the Inuit, though of course we couldn't understand what they were saying.

For the two crews squeezed aboard *Erebus* for the winter of 1847-48, the occurrence of symptoms of lead poisoning in both officers and crew would have created extremely difficult living conditions. Widespread loss of appetite, fatigue, dullness, lethargy, poor attention span combined with irritability, headache, gastric pain, vomiting, constipation and in some cases convulsions, coma and death would have created a hell ship and a nightmare for the ships' doctors looking for an explanation and a cure.

Scurvy

This disease was the scourge of nineteenth century voyages. It was caused by a lack of vitamin C (ascorbic acid) found in fresh meat and vegetables. Polar voyages were particularly prone. The onset of symptoms became apparent about three months after a person stopped getting sufficient vitamin C, such as switching to all-salt provisions. The symptoms begin with blood vessels rupturing so that hair follicles bled. Then red blotches appear all over the body. Gums become swollen, bleed and blacken and then teeth loosen and fall out. Previously healed wounds open again. Limbs become swollen and joints extremely painful. The body becomes bloated and misshapen and covered with ulcers. Within weeks the person is incapacitated and within months dies.

In 1774 it was discovered that a rapid cure for scurvy was achieved by eating two oranges and a lemon daily. This led to the Royal Navy issuing an ounce of lemon juice sweetened by an ounce of sugar in the daily ration of each seaman. The Franklin expedition was issued with 9,000 gallons of lemon juice enough for each member to have one ounce daily for three years and two months. However, the lemon juice was stored in five gallon barrels and it was known that after some years it would lose its antiscorbutic properties.

Scurvy was a well-known disease and would have been recognised by the ships' doctors. However, their main weapon against the disease – lemon juice – once it lost its effectiveness after about two or three years, left them with few alternatives except fresh meat. Inuit testimony of men seen with dry blackened lips and gums in 1850 (two years after the lemon juice had run out) as well as modern forensic recognition of scaling on bones, indicate that scurvy was present in the retreating crew in 1850. Previously this had been regarded as the major factor in the loss of the expedition, but the work of Beattie and his team and Cookman have provided alternative explanations for contributing factors, so that scurvy is unlikely to be the major failing.

A reappraisal of the effects of scurvy in the Franklin Expedition has been made by Mays and others. The work included a study of bone fragments for pathological changes and lesions potentially consistent with scurvy. The conclusion was that there was little evidence for scurvy, which could not have been a major factor in the loss of the expedition.

The tinned food problem

For long-term followers of the Franklin saga there has always been a puzzle about the tins of meat. The expedition ordered forty-five tons of tinned food in one, two, three, four, six and eight pound capacities. Fifteen tons of this were of seven kinds of meat: boiled mutton, roast mutton, roast beef, seasoned beef, veal, ox cheeks, and beef with vegetables. Vegetable soup, meat soup and concentrated gravy made up another twelve tons. There were nine tons of canned potatoes, carrots, parsnips and mixed vegetables. McClintock noted that at the magnetic camp near Cape Felix, there were no empty food tins only bones from salted meat. He also observed that there was a paucity of empty tins along the line of retreat of the crews.

These observations suggest that canned food was not a major part of the diet for the retreat, despite the convenience of the cans. On the Todd Islets, Inuit testimony describes the body of an officer with a telescope and shotgun (found in a group of five bodies) who carried an unopened tin of pemmican. The Inuit who found them opened the tin and ate the meat with relish. Perhaps most surprising is testimony collected by the Schwatka expedition, that when the abandoned *Erebus* as found near O'Reilly Island, many empty red food cans were found on board, along with four full tins of pemmican.

Amundsen's 1905 report – Inuit discover an unmanned ship off Cape Crozier with tins of poisonous meat on board

In 1905, Roald Amundsen met Inuit who told him of an unmanned ship found off Cape Crozier opposite the Royal Geographic Society Islands. The Inuit boarded her and found tins of food which made them ill and some of them died. In this reconstruction, the ship is identified as *Terror* and that she was ice-rafted into the area (where her wreck was found in 2016), after the reoccupied *Erebus* was finally freed and worked south to Utjulik.

The testimony suggests that the tinned meat was left aboard the ships and not taken on the retreat. The officer who died on the Todd islets carried one tin that he would not open. The probable explanation is that the various illnesses that broke out aboard *Erebus* with the two crews crowded aboard, were attributed by the doctors to the canned food. Some form of poisoning would have been recognised. The avoidance of the canned meat suggests that the ships doctors banned the use of the tinned food and put the crews on short rations to eke out the remaining food supplies.

The doctors would have strongly urged Captain Crozier to abandon the ships as soon as possible in order to get the crews to south King William Island and the estuary of Back's Great Fish River for a supply of fresh food to try to improve the health of the men. Previous explorers had reported an abundance of game and fish in these areas. However, the premature departure from the ships prevented the crews from taking best advantage of the summer hunting. It seems likely that a few of the last survivors carried a few tins of meat, but they were loath to eat it. During the final winters aboard the reoccupied *Erebus*, the last survivors had no choice but to eat some of the canned food, when seal hunting failed to provide an adequate supply. By then the crew of the reoccupied *Erebus* had adapted to some extent to hunting and no doubt kept the empty tins aboard *Erebus* for possible trade with the Inuit.

Interest in the health of the lost crews was shown when Beattie and Geiger exhumed the frozen body of Able Seaman John Hartnell of *Erebus*, who was the second expedition member to die and was buried on Beechey Island. The body was found to have already been autopsied in September 1852. Savours describes how this was carried out by Captain E.A. Inglefield of the *Isabel*, together with the ship's surgeon Dr. Sutherland. The *Isabel* was a screw schooner sent out privately by Lady Jane Franklin.

Ikinnelikpatolok's testimony – Inuit discover a ship near O'Reilly Island with the body of a large man and four tins of meat on board

This testimony was collected by the Schwatka expedition and recorded by Gilder.

> The next white man he saw was dead in a bunk of a big ship which was frozen in the ice near an island near about five miles west of Grant Point, on Adelaide Peninsula. They had to walk out about three miles on smooth ice to reach the ship. He said that his son, who was present, a man about thirty-five years old was then about like a child he pointed out – probably seven or eight years old. About this time he saw the tracks of white men on the main-land. When he first saw them there were four, and afterwards only three. This was when the spring snows were falling. When his people saw the ship so long without anyone around, they used to go on board and steal pieces of wood and iron. They did not know how to get inside by the doors, and cut a hole in the side of the ship, on a level with the

ice, so that when the ice broke up during the following summer the ship filled and sank. No tracks were seen in the salt-water ice or on the ship, which also was covered with snow, but they saw scrapings and sweepings alongside, which seemed to have been brushed off by people who had been living on board. They found some red cans of fresh meat, with plenty of what looked like tallow mixed with it. A great many had been opened, and four were still unopened. They saw no bread. They found plenty of knives, forks, spoons, pans, cups and plates on board, and afterwards found a few such things on shore after the vessel had gone down. They also saw books on board, and left them there. They only took knives, forks, spoons, and pans; the other things they had no use for. He never saw or heard of the white men's cairn on Adelaide Peninsula.

This report of the finding of the 'Utjulik ship', now known to be *Erebus*, also indicates that unopened tins of meat were still aboard when she was finally abandoned in 1850. It appears to be clear that the tinned meat was shunned by the starving men.

Botulism

New light on the problem of the tinned meat has been shown lately by an excellent piece of detective work by Scott Cookman in his book Ice Blink. Cookman described how the Admiralty contract for the tinned food was awarded to Stephan Goldner - a Hungarian immigrant - on April the first 1845, only a month and a half before the expedition sailed. Goldner's bid was the lowest and he promised immediately delivery. The story of the last minute rush to produce the tinned food for the expedition has already been described.

Reduced rations and emaciated men

A major factor leading to the premature abandonment of the ships might have been the doctor's advice that the illness and deaths in the crews might have been caused by the tinned food. They may have condemned the tinned food or suggested that it not be eaten except in emergencies. This would have put the crew on to short rations well before the retreat began. There is some evidence that this might be the case from a line written in the 'Peglar' papers:

> brekfest to be short rations

Another contributing factor to a food shortage before the retreat of 1848, could be the result of the large depot of food abandoned during the crisis of the grounding of one of the ships in Poctes/Poet's Bay, as well the food cache left on Blenky Island for an exploration team that never arrived. If the doctors stopped the issue of tinned food, then suddenly there would be a shortage of food requiring rationing. Major cuts in food were made by Captain McClure, when his ship *Investigator* was trapped in ice in 1851 and finally abandoned in 1853.

Tuberculosis

Tuberculosis was present amongst the expedition members, and was common in the nineteenth century. Five men – fortunate men, as it turned out - were sent back to England before the expedition departed from Greenland. Two of these were ill and may have had tuberculosis. Autopsies carried out on the frozen bodies of the three expedition members buried at the 1845-46 winter quarters on Beechey Island by Beattie and Geiger, revealed that all had symptoms of tuberculosis.

Dental problems.

The forensic work of Keenleyside and others has revealed that the men of the expedition had poor teeth. Examination of teeth and jawbone fragments found at site NgLj-2 in Erebus Bay, revealed evidence of periodontal disease in thirty-eight out of 123 tooth sockets (30.9%), dental caries in seven of seventy teeth, and dental abscesses in four out of 180 teeth. The men are believed to have died during the 1848 retreat at one of the death camps. Dentistry in the mid-nineteenth century was not yet a science. It was practiced by untrained persons. The objective was to stop pain by extraction. So the men developed cavities until they became painful and then the tooth would be extracted.

Another possible reason for the high death rate

There is a hint in the Inuit testimony that the high death rate aboard the ships before abandonment might be due to another factor not yet considered. The clue is provided because the overturned and abandoned *Terror* was used as a mausoleum ship. It is known from the 1848 Record that a lot of the deaths occurred during winter of 1847-48 when it was too dark and cold to dig graves, either through the ice or in the frozen land. When the ship was found by the Inuit many years later Rasmussen reported that the Inuit testimony recorded that the Inuit could see from the bodies inside that the men had died of a sickness. An unforeseen illness might have occurred on the very overcrowded *Erebus* with over 100 men confined aboard. It might have been something like an outbreak of cholera due to overcrowded conditions with poor hygiene.

Terror becomes a mausoleum ship

By the time the ships were abandoned on April 22, 1848, almost twenty percent of the original crews had died. Three men died on Beechey Island followed by Sir John Franklin on June 11 1847. Following the death of Sir John, eight officers and another twelve men died before the 1848 retreat.

With the 1847 record reporting 'All well', the majority of these deaths occurred during late 1847 and early 1848. Elaborate stone cyst graves, built by men with plenty of time, suggest that at first Sir John and some other officers were buried on north-west King William Island. It was seventeen miles across the rugged Beaufort ice stream to King William Island and the crews must have become familiar with the route as they set up the depot camp at what would become Crozier's Landing. However, in the bitterly cold long Arctic night burial ashore or even in the sea alongside the ships where the ice might be seven to fourteen feet thick was not possible. In the desperate situation, Crozier came up with a novel solution to avoid the terrible labour of taking the dead ashore and burying them. Inuit testimony described a ship they found out in the ice of Victoria Strait as filled with dead men. It seems the solution found was to place the dead in the bunks aboard the overturned *Terror* lying on her beam ends, so she became a mausoleum ship.

The forty days' calculation

The large libraries carried by both *Erebus* and *Terror* included accounts of other polar explorers. There the officers of the Franklin expedition could study at their leisure the sledging achievements of their predecessors. While the idea of expedition members enjoying reading in the libraries while their ships headed to an icy doom may seem incongruous and even surreal, in fact the ships were extremely well equipped and but for the disastrous frozen 'summer of 1847' that the expedition encountered, there was no necessary reason why the two ships and their crews could have returned home in triumph. Instead they entered an icy netherworld of gradual starvation, and never returned home.

In the ships' libraries were two publications critical to the planned retreat. First was Captain John Ross's 1835 book 'Narrative of a second voyage in search of a North-West Passage.' This was the story of the *Victory* paddle ship that became trapped in ice in Prince Regent Inlet and was abandoned. Ross marched and boated his crew north to Lancaster Sound and then to Baffin Bay, where the party was eventually rescued by a whaling ship after five summers in the Arctic. Thomas Blanky who had been on the *Victory* expedition served as Ice Master on board *Terror* for the Franklin expedition. The book described the retreat to the north after *Victory* was abandoned.

The other publication was Sir George Back's 1836 volume 'Narrative of the Arctic Land Expedition to the Mouth of the Great Fish Fiver, and along the shores of the Arctic Ocean, in the years 1833, 1834, and 1835.' It's a cumbersome title, but the kind of book that was immensely popular in the nineteenth century, when geographical exploration was often infused with a kind of religious fervour and sense of destiny. Back sailed in February 1833 in search of Captain John Ross and his party missing since 1829. He was accompanied by Dr. Richard King as surgeon-naturalist and three men, two of whom were carpenters to build the boats. Dr. Richard King also wrote an account of the expedition criticising his commanding officer. Back's instructions were to go to Montreal and then to the eastern end of the Great Slave Lake and winter there. In summer 1834 he was to follow the Great Fish River to the Arctic Ocean. However, locating the source took longer than anticipated and he had to return to their winter quarters for a second time.

The following April, in 1835, news that John Ross and party had returned to England arrived along with instructions to continue the mapping of the north-eastern shore of the American continent. He then decided to travel with a smaller party and use only the bigger of the two boats that had been built. The party left on June 7 and had to haul the boat on a sledge to Musk Ox Lake where Back's Great Fish River became navigable. The descent started on July 4. Back was ordered to start back no later than August 20 – only six weeks ahead.

They descended 530 miles through iron-ribbed country with no trees and passed through eighty-three falls, cascades and rapids to arrive at the mouth of the river on July 29 after twenty-nine days travel. They mapped their way to the entrance to the estuary (Chantrey Inlet), saw parts of King William Island in the distance and named Montreal Island within the estuary. They found their way to the west barred by ice. On August 14 they started the return. This proved easier than expected as the river was ice free in late summer. The party arrived at their winter quarters on

September 27 and from there they returned home. The resulting volume considered the merits of a retreat to the south.

The details of both journeys would have been studied carefully by the officers of the Franklin expedition, when they planned their retreat to the estuary of the Back's Great Fish River. Apart from information on food resources in the estuary of the Back's Great Fish River, the boat used to descend and ascend the river, had been built in what is now Canada and the wood was considered inferior and weakened the boat. It was double bowed (pointed at both ends) like a whale boat with a good beam and plenty of floor for stowage. It was thirty feet long and twenty-four feet on the keel. Extra oars, masts and a tiller were provided. The bottom was coated in tar. The lower part of the hull was carvel built (smooth) and the upper part clinker built (overlapping planks). The boat was similar to the pinnace found and described in detail by McClintock in Erebus Bay.

In 1848 at the time of the retreat, polar sledging by naval officers was in its infancy. An excellent account of its development is given by Dr. Cyriax. It was Lieutenant (later Rear Admiral Sir) William Edward Parry, who pioneered sledging by officers of the Royal Navy. On his first expedition seeking the North-West Passage in the winter of 1819-20, he used sledges to gather ballast stones, but for his spring journey took a two-wheeled wooden cart carrying a load of 800 pounds, but no sledges. He marched a distance of 180 miles and achieved a rate of twelve miles a day.

It was on his second expedition, in search of the North-West Passage (1821-23) that Parry and his second in command Captain G.F. Lyon, studied the Inuit method of sledging and purchased some dogs from them. Captain Lyon made the first long naval sledge journey accompanied by one officer and seven men. Each man pulled his own sledge and slept on them. The two officers each hauled a load of ninety to ninety-five pounds and the men 120 pounds. The party marched about 180 miles, averaging sixteen miles a day outbound and eighteen miles a day inbound.

In winter 1822-23 the crews of the two ships *Hecla* and *Fury* built sledges and provided them with dogs purchased from the Inuit. Parry and Lyon made trips with the dogs pulling the sledges and also carrying loads in panniers. In 1823 Lyon travelled with two men and a sledge with ten dogs. The sledge weighed 191 pounds and the load started at twelve hundredweight. The party travelled 130 miles averaging a distance of eight and a half miles on days when it was possible to travel.

It was not until 1827 that boats entered the equation. Parry was then on an expedition to reach the North Pole from Spitzbergen. Woolwich Dockyard had constructed for the expedition two identical 'sledge boats'.

That is boats that had steel lined runners on them, so they could be dragged like sledges. On June 27 1827, Parry began his journey northwards with two boats travelling at first through open water and then through ice-choked seas. The boats weighed 1,539 and 1,542 pounds, but when loaded weighed 3,753 pounds. Each boat was assigned two officers, ten seamen and two marines. On ice, the pulling load was therefore about 268 pounds per man. In addition, they took four sledges.

The party slept in the boats with the sails providing shelter as awnings. They carried no tents nor ground sheets and carried seventy-one days provisions. Their trip took them 172 miles from the ship and lasted sixty-one days. Parry calculated that the distance covered was 569 miles, but because of times they returned to move up their baggage, the real distance covered was 978 geographical miles. About 220 miles were travelled in the boats and the remainder over ice often broken by lanes of water.

The next expedition to use sledges and boats was Captain John Ross's famous *Victory* expedition of 1829 to 1833. Second in command was his nephew Commander (later Rear-Admiral Sir) James Clark Ross who had served in John Ross's 1818 expedition as well as all of Parry's expeditions. He had been in command of one of the sledge boats in the North Pole trip. On the seventeenth of May 1830, James Clark Ross along with Second Mate Thomas Abernathy and three men set out from the *Victory* to locate the western sea reported by the Inuit. The party started in Prince Regent Inlet, crossed Boothia to Cape Felix on the northern tip of King William Land and then down the north-west coast to their furthest south that they named Victory Point. They returned to the ship after sledging a round trip distance of 400 miles covered in twenty-seven days or an average of fifteen miles per day, but using dogs.

Sir John Ross in 1832 abandoned his ship the *Victory* and had marched his men from Victoria Harbour (where the ship was frozen in) a distance of 200 miles to Fury Beach in thirty days. The expedition had dogs that were used with the sledges and also carried two lightweight boats for carrying on the sledges. One was called a 'skin' boat and was canoe shaped, made of skins stretched over a wooden frame. The other was called a pontoon boat having a flat bottom and square ends and made of strong painted canvas stretched over a frame.

It was Lieutenant (later Admiral Sir) Leopold McClintock who in 1850 (in the search expeditions for the lost Franklin men) perfected the sledging technique by using depots laid in advance and lightening the sledges and equipment as well as using dogs. Several of the early explorers learned from the Inuit how to harness and use dogs with their sledges and some very long trips resulted. The Franklin expedition officers would of course be unaware of the McClintock developments as they occurred during the unsuccessful search expeditions. However they would have been aware of the achievements of James Clark Ross who got to and named Victory Point. The search carried out in 1859 by McClintock, independent of Lieutenant Hobson, was a sledge journey of around 1000 miles, completed in seventy-nine days and averaging twelve point six miles per day. Although travelling at the same time of year as the 1848 Franklin retreat, McClintock's party were able to kill for food only two reindeer, one hare, seventeen willow grouse and one seagull.

Neither Captains Crozier nor Fitzjames had any great experience with sledging. Fitzjames was a novice in polar regions and the Franklin expedition was his first polar venture.

The objective of the retreat was to get to the southern half of King William Island and to the Chantrey Inlet - estuary of the Back's Great Fish River - where fresh food should be obtainable in summer 1848. The mouth of the estuary was about 210 miles from Crozier's Landing and the distance to Back's Great Fish River was 250 miles. So the question was how long would it take the retreating crews to get to the estuary of Back's Great Fish River.

McClintock wrote:

> The retreating crews could not have carried with them more than forty days provisions at a very short allowance.

A healthy crew hauling a boat, with a load of about 200 pounds per man, might accomplish a distance of ten miles a day. In order to get the 210 miles from Crozier's Landing to the mouth of the estuary in forty days would require hauling the boats on sledges as well as camping equipment at a minimum rate of over five miles per day. In view of the achievements of their predecessors who were healthy men this would not seem unreasonable. However the men were in poor health. It is probable that the weather was bad with many snowstorms.

The retreat was to be one large party of 105 men man hauling four boats together with a number of sledges. Only three boats can be accounted for. Two were in Erebus Bay, and probably a third one in Douglas Bay. The enigmatic remains found on Montreal Island by the Anderson expedition may represent the fourth.

The health of the men on the retreat proved to be poor, and also the weather in April-May has gales, fog and snowstorms, so that the above calculations all proved hopelessly wrong. It took most of the forty days to get two of the boats only as far as Erebus Bay, where they halted with at least a half of the men immobile – only some sixty-five miles south of Crozier's Landing. This was an average of only one point six miles a day at best. For those who reached Terror Bay some eighty miles from Crozier's Landing (averaging two miles per day), again about a half of the men had become immobile. The immobile men, amounting to about a half of the retreating men, never left Erebus and Terror Bays. These very small distances and high casualty rates indicate why Crozier was in haste to abandon the hell ship. The results show that his too early departure as already too late for about a half of his men. The reason for the unexpected failure was most likely bad weather with many snow storms – a major factor in the later loss of Scott and his polar party in the Antarctic.

The 1848 record and Captain Crozier's decision

The 1848 record was written around the margins of the 1847 record and stated:

> 25th April 1848. - H.M. ships '*Terror*' and '*Erebus*' were deserted on 22nd April, 5 leagues NNW of this, having been beset since 12th September, 1846. The officers and crews, consisting of 105 souls, under the command of Captain F.R.M. Crozier, landed here in lat. 69 deg 37 min 42 sec N., long. 98 deg. 41 min W. Sir John Franklin died on the 11th June, 1847; and the total loss by deaths in the expedition has been to this date 9 officers and 15 men.
>
> (Signed) F.R.M Crozier, Captain and Senior Officer, and start (on) tomorrow, 26th for Back's Fish River.
>
> (Signed) James FitzJames Captain *Erebus*
>
> This paper was found by Lt. Irving under the cairn supposed to have been built by Sir James Ross in 1831, 4 miles to the northward, where it had been deposited by the late Commander Gore in June, 1847. Sir James Ross' pillar has not, however, been found, and the paper has been transferred to this position, which is that in which Sir James Ross' pillar was erected.

So Captain Crozier had made his decision. Both crews would retreat to the south in one large group with the strong supporting the weak. It was a navy type decision and raised the problem of feeding so many men in one party. It was a terrible decision as the lives of the crews of both ships were in great danger, so that whichever line of retreat was selected, there was likely to be a high mortality. It was probably the hardest decision by far that he or any man could make. An option had to be found that would maximise the chances of survival for as many men as possible.

This rather shy and sensitive man had never had command of a polar expedition before and the catastrophe he was facing had never happened on this scale before. He lacked the jovial confidence of Commander Fitzjames with his patronage of Sir John Barrow (second secretary to the Admiralty and the man behind the Admiralty's program of Polar Exploration). Crozier was a loyal second in command and great friend of Sir James Clark Ross and had stayed at his house in London with him, while the ships were being fitted out. He became expedition leader because of the premature death of Sir John Franklin on June 11 1847. Against standing orders, he did not switch to the flagship *Erebus* and did not assign Fitzjames to command *Terror*.

Once in charge, he probably had less than a month of normal expedition scientific work before disaster hit the expedition with the start up of movement of the ice stream conveyor belt. The ships lacked the protection of a winter harbour. One ship was thrown onto her beam ends. Neither ship was released by the ice, so there was no return to England that year. His life and those crowded for the 1847-48 winter on board one ship faced many problems. *Erebus* had become a hell ship.

Starting with the death of Sir John Franklin on June 11 1847, until the day the ships were abandoned on April 22 1848, a total of nine officers and twelve men died. Cookman has come up with an explanation for this abnormally high death rate. He has made an excellent case that it was due to selective botulism poisoning of the sledge teams sent out in spring and summer 1847. It is likely that the deaths increased as the year passed, particularly for the eight months of the hell ship period from August/ September 1947 to April 1848, when the death rate may have averaged two to three men per month. Additionally, the overall health deterioration due to developing scurvy and lead poisoning was a general weakening of the men. Crozier had the unenviable task of getting out of the ships before the illness became so widespread that the ships could not be abandoned. His ideal time for abandoning the ships would have been July/ August 1848, when the birds and caribou were returning to King William Island and the boats could have been sailed in the melted seas, rather than been hauled over frozen seas.

As we've seen, McClintock estimated that the retreating crews could carry no more than forty days' limited rations. However, so great was the need to break out of the hell ship, while there was a chance of moving everyone, that Crozier left at the remarkably early date of April 22. This was far too early because the seas would not begin to thaw for another six weeks – the same amount of time for which the retreat carried reduced rations was forty days. By early June the food would be exhausted. The condition of some of the men was probably so poor that it was a case of now or never.

So what would have been Crozier's reasoning? He had only two choices for the retreat. Either north to Fury Beach and follow John Ross's route through Lancaster Sound, or to go south to the southern half of King William Island and then on to Chantrey Inlet, where an abundant supply of fresh food was reported in summer. He had only forty days in which to find a fresh food supply for his men including those with scurvy. The tinned food at Fury Beach was unlikely to relieve scurvy being years older than that carried by the expedition. Worse was that there was a possibility that the food dump was no longer there. This was because before the expedition departed from England, it was learned that whalers were planning to remove the stores from Fury Beach and bring them back to England to sell them. However after the expedition sailed, the plan fell through.

It was also known from Commander Sherard Osborn (in McClure's book), and could be confirmed by *Terror*'s Ice Master Thomas Blanky, that Sir John Ross on his way south along Regents Inlet had partly provisioned his ship *Victory* from the Fury Beach depot. He had then retreated to the same beach and wintered there again living on the stores. Therefore the case to go north looked very risky and unlikely to provide the fresh food needed to revive the crews.

Captain Sir James Clark Ross set out to seek his lost friends, Sir John and Captain Crozier, and sent men to Fury Beach who arrived there in summer 1849, but found no traces of the Franklin expedition. This rescue attempt would have been a year too late had Crozier decided to retreat north.

Sir George Back's book about Back's Great Fish River (that would have been carried by the libraries of *Erebus* and *Terror*), as well as King's book, both had lengthy descriptions of the abundant wildlife along the river. Sir George Back had seen large numbers of caribou (up to 20,000 in a single day) and musk oxen there in July 1834. Birds, including geese, were seen to be plentiful and some Inuit they met in the estuary of Back's Great Fish River had caught thousands of small fish. Dease and Simpson also reported many deer and musk oxen on the south coast of King William Island in August 1839.

This source of fresh food, could cure scurvy, and replace the suspected tinned food. It was only 100 to 300 miles away from the trapped ships. Sir John Richardson suggested that Crozier departed early for the river because of a rapidly growing problem with scurvy, and because he wanted a supply of fresh food for his men so that they could recover in time to spend the summer travelling by boat and ascending the Coppermine or Mackenzie rivers (rather than the 530 miles of Back's Great Fish River with its eighty-three falls, cascades and rapids). There was also another reason why Crozier chose the southern retreat. Three months before the expedition departed, Dr. Richard King had proposed a joint expedition in which he would lead a party down Back's Great Fish River to assist the Franklin expedition. This had not been approved. However, the original expedition by Back and King down this same river had been a relief expedition to look for the missing Ross Victory expedition. Crozier might have thought a relief expedition for the Franklin expedition might also be sent down Back's Great Fish River.

It is reasonable to wonder if Crozier was trying to ascend Back's Great Fish River. The 1848 Record states only that the retreating party were heading for Back's Great Fish River. Sir George Back (1836) had described Back's Great Fish River as very difficult to navigate with a violent and tortuous course of 530 miles containing eighty three falls, cascades and rapids. The distance via the Great Fish River to the nearest Hudson's Bay outpost of Fort Providence on the Great Slave Lake, involved not only ascending Back's Great Fish River but also crossing the headwaters of the Coppermine and Mackenzie Rivers and then crossing several lakes for a total distance of 1,250 miles.

It was for this reason that the Admiralty would not send any search expedition to the estuary of Back's Great Fish River. Perhaps Crozier had a better plan, to strengthen the men by summer hunting and fishing and then to proceed west by boat along the mapped coastline. There they would encounter the more accessible Mackenzie and Coppermine Rivers or perhaps even go on to the Bering Strait. Back in 1834 ascended the Great Fish River, by having two teams of men alternating in hauling the boats upstream, in only six weeks. The distance from Crozier's Landing to Chantrey Inlet - the estuary of Back's Great Fish River - is about 210 miles and to the river 250 miles. However because the boats were hauled on smooth ice close to the irregular shoreline, the distance would have been greatly increased.

Dr. Cyriax made a careful review of the food stores supplied to the expedition. The supply was for 137 officers and men for three years and ten weeks from the day they left Greenhithe. But as only 129 men sailed from Greenland, the supply should have lasted longer. Dr. Cyriax estimated that on the day the ships were abandoned, there should have been enough food left for 129 men for another three months. Dr. Cyriax concluded that it was not starvation that forced Crozier to start the march so early.

There is some indication that Crozier's decision to retreat south and also to man haul the boats over the April ice rather than await the summer thaw, was not popular with all of the men. Hall was told that:

> there were a good many men together starving some started off from the main body of starving ones & never came back again. Every once in a while a part of the great many would go away & not return again.

Presumably these men could see, only too well, the hopelessness of hauling boats at less than two miles a day. By breaking away and carrying guns and ammunition they would make better speed and increase their chances of either meeting parties of Inuit or sharing the results of their hunting between a much smaller number of men.

14: THE FAILED RETREAT OF 1848

The 1848 retreat failed dismally.

It is possible that only one of the boat teams got further south than Terror Bay – a distance of only eighty miles from Crozier's Landing. There were several factors that produced this poor result. One of the major factors may have been poor weather. Gales and snowstorms produced days when no sledge hauling could be carried out. Lieutenant Hobson of the McClintock expedition of 1859 spent May sledging across the north coast of King William Island and then followed the west coast as far south as Cape Herschel. The 1948 retreat left Crozier's Landing on April 26, so that they were hauling the boats south through the month of May. Hobson wrote of the May weather:

> We left King William Island on the 31st May, after having been a month on its most inhospitable coast. In no part of the world have I ever experienced such a continuation of bad weather. From the 8th, the day we left Cape Franklin, to this date I scarcely saw the sun. It snowed almost incessantly. The wind held almost continuously from the NW varying in force from a strong breeze to a hard gale. The force of the wind was generally sufficient to raise snow drift.

Poor health of the crews and weakness due to reduced rations, as well as the great weight of the boats on heavy sledges with sick men inside proved too much for the retreating crews. This is shown by the abysmal distances covered by the retreating crews and the fact that none of the boats reached the estuary of Back's Great Fish River. All 105 men made the seventeen miles to Crozier's Landing (1848 Record) but as will be shown only about a half were able to walk by the time they had travelled the next eighty miles to Terror Bay. The immobile ones were left with two abandoned boats in Erebus Bay where the remains of twenty to twenty-eight men were found in 1859, 1982 and 1992 (Appendix 2). Another fifteen or so immobile men were left in the hospital tent at Terror Bay. Some small parties continued south, one perhaps hauling a boat into Douglas Bay. Other small parties of stragglers were recorded in Inuit testimony. Probably only around a half of the crews returned to *Erebus*. At best the remains show that most men did not get further than eighty miles from Crozier's Landing.

Rear half of the retreat halted at Erebus Bay

It has taken a long time for sufficient data to be collected, so that an interpretation of what happened at Erebus Bay can be made. Basically, two large boats were found during the nineteenth century. The boat found and meticulously described by the McClintock expedition of 1859 contained only two partial skeletons. However the other nearby (hidden by winter snow at the time of the McClintock expedition) was found by the Inut In-nook-poo-zhe-jook in 1862. It contained a mummified cannibal with a heap of cannibalised bones.

It was not until 1982 that Beattie found the remains of six to fourteen individuals on a small islet in Erebus Bay – the site now designated NgLj-1 (approximating to McClintock's boat place). A similar find was made in 1992 when amateur historian Barry Ranford located another islet site in Erebus Bay about a half mile from McClintock's boat place (designated Site NgLj-2) (approximating to In-nook-poo-zhe-jook's find). Here, human remains and relics were scattered over about 300 square yards on the north-western end of a small islet measuring about 150 feet east-west by seventy-five feet north-south. A map of this islet and an aerial photograph of it are shown in Potter.

The remains were studied by modern forensic methods by a team led by Anne Keenleyside. The remains of a minimum of eleven European men were identified. This would appear to be the site found by In-nook-poo-zhe-jook in 1862. A third site exists in Erebus Bay that has been designated NgLj-3. This site has the remains of three individuals (including three crania) that were located in summer by the Schwatka Expedition in 1879, at the boat place described by McClintock. The contents of the burial matched the description of the bones described by Gilder. Two of the skeletal sets correspond to the two partial skeletons found in the boat by McClintock in 1859, although at that time the skulls were missing. They must have lain hidden in the snow nearby and were not seen until the summer search by the Schwatka expedition in 1879.

Members of the Schwatka expedition had accidentally included in the burial four animal bones, two seal and two caribou and their identification of the remains as four individuals is not correct. Facial reconstructions were recently made on two of the skulls. The reconstruction for the large boned man in the stern of the boat found by the McClintock expedition, resembles Ice Master James Reid of *Erebus*. McClintock believed this boat was from *Erebus* because of the relics inside. The other facial reconstruction resembles Commander Graham Gore. However this cannot be correct for the 1848 record refers to the 'late' Commander Gore. The next step in the forensic work on the skeletal remains will be DNA matching with living relatives.

The McClintock find was made first, but in 1861 both boats were found on sledges about a quarter of a mile apart on the shores of Erebus Bay by In-nook-poo-zhe-jook (described in Nourse). One of the boats found in 1861 had been emptied by the McClintock expedition in 1859. The two boats found in Erebus Bay were only fifty miles from Crozier's Landing and sixty-five miles from the ships. Obviously, something momentous had happened here for the two largest boats were likely manned by almost 50% of the retreating crews. Before drawing any conclusions the data will be reviewed.

The first of the boats was found by Lieutenant (later Captain) William Hobson leading one of two search parties from the private yacht *Fox*. Captain (later Admiral Sir) Leopold McClintock leading the other search party from the *Fox* expedition arrived soon afterwards. The remains of the other boat were first found by the Inuit three years after the visit of McClintock. They were found again by Lieutenant Schwatka's American expedition in 1879.

McClintock's 1859 description of the boat in Erebus Bay

McClintock gave a meticulous description the boat that was barely visible under a thick snow cover as he found it in Erebus Bay on the morning of May 30 1859 (The site is now known as 'McClintock's boat place', sites NgLj-1 and NgLj-3):

> A vast quantity of tattered clothing was lying in her, and this we first examined. Not a single article bore the name of its former owner. The boat was cleared out and carefully swept that nothing might escape us. The snow was then removed from about her, but nothing whatsoever was found.
> This boat measured 28 feet long, and 7 feet 3 inches wide; she was built with a view to lightness and light draught of water, and evidently equipped with the utmost care for the ascent of the Great Fish River; she had neither oars nor rudder, paddles supplying their place; and as a large remnant of light canvas, commonly known as No. 8, was found, and also a small block for reeving a sheet through, I suppose she had been provided with a sail. A sloping canvas roof or rain awning had also formed part of her equipment. She was fitted with a weather cloth 9 inches high, battened down all round the gunwale, and supported by 24 iron stanchions, so placed as to serve likewise for rowing thowells. There was a deep-sea sounding line, fifty fathoms long, near her, as well as an ice grapnel; this line must have

been intended for river work as a track line. She had been originally 'carvel' built; but for the purpose of reducing weight, very thin fir planks had been substituted for her seven upper strakes, and put on 'clincher' fashion.

The only markings about the boat were those cut in upon her stem; besides giving her length, they indicated that she was built by contract, numbered 61; and received into Woolwich Dockyard in April 184-; the fourth figure to the right hand was lost, as the stem had been reduced as much as possible in order to lessen her weight; from this cause part of the Roman numerals indicating her length were also lost.

The weight of the boat alone was about 700 or 800 lbs. only, but she was mounted upon a sledge of unusual weight and strength. It was constructed of two oak planks 23 feet 4 inches in length, 8 inches in width, and with an average thickness of 2.5 inches. These planks formed the sides or runners of the sledge; they were connected by five cross bars of oak, each 4 feet long and 4 inches by 3.5 inches thick, and bolted down to the runners; the underneath parts of the latter were shod with iron. Upon the cross bars five saddles or supporting chocks for the boat were lashed, and the drag ropes by which the crew moved the massive sledge, and the weights upon it, consisted of 2.75 inch whale line.

I have calculated the weight of this sledge to be 650 lbs.; it could not have been less, and may have been considerably more. The total weight of boat and sledge may be taken at 1400 lbs., which amounts to a heavy load for seven strong healthy men.

The ground the sledge rested upon was the usual limestone shingle, perfectly flat and probably overflowed at times every summer, as the stones were embedded in ice.

The boat was partially out of her cradle upon the sledge, and lying in such a position as to lead me to suppose it the effect of a violent north-west gale. She was barely, if at all, above the reach of occasional tides.

One hundred yards from her, upon the land side, lay the stump of a fir tree 12 feet long, and 16 inches in diameter at 3 feet above the roots. Although the ice had used it very roughly during its drift to this shore, and rubbed off every vestige of bark, yet the wood was perfectly sound. It may have been and probably has been lying there for twenty or thirty years, and during such a period would suffer less decay in this region of frost than in one sixth of the time at home. Within two yards of it I noticed a few scanty tufts of grass.

But all of these were after observations; there was in the boat that which transfixed us with awe, viz., portions of two human skeletons! One was that of a slight young person; the other of a large, strongly-made middle-aged man. The former was found in the bow of the boat; but in too much disturbed a state to enable Hobson to judge whether the sufferer had died there; large and powerful animals, probably wolves, had destroyed much of this skeleton, which may have been that of an officer. Near it we found the fragment of a pair of worked slippers, of which I give the pattern, as they may possibly be identified. The lines were white, with a black margin, the spaces white, red and yellow. They had originally been 11 inches long, lined with calf skin with the hair left on, and the edges bound with red silk ribbon. Besides these slippers there were a pair of small strong shooting half boots.

The other skeleton was in a somewhat more perfect state; it lay across the boat, under the after thwart, and was enveloped with cloths and furs. This would seem to have been the survivor of the two men whose remains were lying in the boat. Close beside it were found five watches; and there were two double-barrelled guns – one barrel in each loaded and cocked – standing muzzle upwards against the boats side. It may be imagined with what deep interest these sad relics were scrutinised, and how anxiously every fragment of clothing was turned over in search of pockets and pocket books, journals, or even names. Five or six small books were found, all of them scriptural or devotional works, except the 'Vicar of Wakefield.' One little book, 'Christian Melodies,' bore an inscription upon the title page from the donor to G.G. (Graham Gore? Lieutenant *Erebus*). Another small book, 'A Manual of Private Devotion, by C.J. Blomfield, D.D.,' bore on its title page, 'G. Back, to Graham Gore. May, 1845.' A small Bible contained numerous marginal notes, and whole passages underlined. Besides these books, the covers of a New Testament and Church of England prayer book were found.

Amongst an amazing quantity of clothing there were seven or eight pairs of boots of various kinds – cloth winter boots, sea boots, heavy ankle boots, and strong shoes. I noted that there were silk handkerchiefs - black, white, and figured – towels, soap, sponge, tooth brushes, and hair combs; mackintosh gun cover, marked outside with paint A 12, and lined with black cloth. Besides these articles we found twine, nails, saws, files, bristles, wax ends, sail makers' palms, powder, bullets, shot, cartridges, wads, leather cartridge case, knives – clasp and dinner ones, needle and thread cases, slow match, several bayonet scabbards cut down into knife sheaths, two rolls of sheet lead, and in short, a quantity of articles of one description or another truly astonishing in variety, and such as, for the most part, modern sledge travellers in these regions would consider a mere accumulation of dead weight, of little use, and very likely to break down the strength of the sledge crews.

The only provisions we could find were tea and chocolate; of the former very little remained, but there were nearly 40 pounds of the latter. These articles alone could never support life in such a climate, and we found neither biscuit nor meat of any kind. A portion of tobacco and an empty pemmican tin capable of containing 22 pounds weight were discovered. The tin was marked with an E; it had probably belonged to the '*Erebus*'. None of the fuel originally brought from the ships remained in or about the boat, but there was no lack of it, for a drift tree was lying on the beach close at hand, and had the party been in need of fuel, they could have used the paddles and bottom boards of the boat.

In the after part of the boat we found eleven large spoons, eleven forks, and four tea spoons, all of silver. Of these twenty-six pieces of plate, eight bore Sir John Franklin's crest, the remainder had the crests or initials of nine different officers, with the exception of a single fork which was not marked; of these nine officers, five belonged to the '*Erebus*' – Gore, Le Vesconte, Fairholm, Couch, and Goodsir. Three others belonged to the *Terror* – Crozier (a teaspoon only), Hornby, and Thomas. I do not know to whom the three articles with an owl engraved on them belonged, nor who was the owner of the unmarked fork, but of the owners of those we can identify, the majority belonged to the '*Erebus*'. One of the watches bore the crest of Mr. Couch, of the '*Erebus*' and as the pemmican tin also came from that ship, I am inclined to think the boat did also. One of the pocket chronometres found in the boat was marked, 'Parkinson and Frodsham 980', the other, 'Arnold 2020'; these had been supplied one to each ship. Sir John Franklin's plate perhaps was issued to the men for their use, as the only means of saving it; and it seems probable that the officers generally did the same, as not a single iron spoon, such as sailors always use, has been found. Of the many men, probably twenty or thirty, who were attached to this boat, it seems most strange that the remains of only two individuals were found, nor were there any graves upon the neighbouring flat land; indeed, bearing in mind the season at which these poor fellows left their ships, it should be remembered that the soil was then frozen hard as rock, and the labour of quarrying a grave very great indeed.

I was astonished to find that the sledge was directed to the N.E., exactly for the next point of land for which we ourselves were travelling!

The position of this abandoned boat is about 50 miles – as a sledge would travel – from Point Victory, and therefore 65 miles from the position of the ships; also it is 70 miles from the skeleton of the steward, and 150 miles from Montreal Island: it is moreover in the depth of a wide bay, where, by crossing over 10 or 12 miles of very low land, a great saving of distance would be effected, the route by the coast line being about 40 miles.

A little reflection led me to satisfy my own mind at least that this boat was returning to the ships. In no other way can I account for two men having been left in her, than by supposing the party were unable to drag the boat further, and that these two men, not being able to keep pace with their shipmates, were therefore left by them supplied with such provisions as could be spared, to last them until the return of the others from the ship with fresh stock.

Much has been written about this boat and McClintock's conclusion that it was facing the wrong way and appeared to be on the way back to the abandoned ships. As McClintock points out, it was found deep inside Erebus Bay close to the shore where grass grew in summer. The presence of a large fir tree root inland of it is important as is the fact the boat was half off the sledge. Another critical fact is that everything described was inside the boat and nothing outside. A better explanation is not that the weakened men were dragging the boat back to the ships and taking the long way around the shoreline, but that the boat was halted during the retreat southwards, when about a half of the crew became too sick to drag the heavy load. She was more likely left alongside a small island where the crew encamped (site NgLj-1). Most men would have slept in the boat, but the others would find some land free of snow and ice on which to lie as evidently ground sheets were not carried. In the eleven years that elapsed before being found by McClintock, the boat and tree trunk were moved at times of high water. The boat almost floated off the sled which was turned around.

McClintock missed many remains lying nearby because of the thick snow cover, but these were seen during the summer Schwatka search. It is extremely unlikely that a few weakened men would try to drag the boat back to the ships and there was little purpose as many boats remained with the ships. Inuit testimony describes the Utjulik ship (in 2014 located and identified as *Erebus*) off the Adelaide Peninsula with five of her boats intact aboard her. In fact she may have carried some of *Terror*'s boats aboard.

It is interesting that new light can be shed on this boat by modern forensic study. Stenton and others have suggested that the facial reconstruction of the large-boned man in the stern, resembles Ice Master James Reid of *Erebus*. So it seems likely that the boat from *Erebus* was probably under his charge and he remained with the boat and the immobile sick men. He was also carrying some of the personal effects of the late Lieutenant Graham Gore of *Erebus*, presumably to return them to the family.

In-nook-poo-zhee-jook's testimony of two boats in Erebus Bay

Hall wrote:

> In-nook-poo-zhee-jook said that he had found a boat (a little way westward of the one found by Hobson), the planks, ribs, and all complete, and copper fastened. In the boat were a great many skeletons, the skulls with them. He gave me a double bladed knife, with a white bone handle, very rusty. It came from this boat. The boat had not been touched, and a great many papers and books and written stuff were in it. (These were all trash to the Innuits; the winds and the weather had made destructive work of them. The Innuits would trample them under feet as grass.)

More information was obtained from In-nook-poo-zhee-jook in a series of questions from Hall (published by Nourse):

> Question.   Who were with you when you found those two boats?
>
> Answer.   His brother's son Oo-ar-zhoo, now dead; Ook-pik, Ek-ke-pe-re-a, and his son, Neer-kood-loo. The party of men numbered five, and their families were with them. They were making a tour on purpose to search after such things as they could find that belonged to the white men that had died on King William's Land.
>
> Question: What particular time of the year was it?
>
> Answer.   I think the time of the year about when we returned to this bay encampment, - June 20. Water had begun to make on the ice, and water is a little late making there than here. Snow and ice were inside the boats, and all around.
>
> Question: Did the boats look as if anybody had visited them within two or three years?
>
> Answer.   Somebody had been to one of them, for everything was gone out of it. [This would have been McClintock in August 1859]
>
> Question.   What did you find in the other boat – the one that the white men [McClintock's party] from Ik-ke-hi-suk (Bellot Strait) did not find?
>
> Answer.   Six paddles; many table-knives, white handles; one watch; a spy-glass that his son has, a little longer than Joe's – something like my compass, but no glass about it; tobacco that had been wet and was in flakes

or thin pieces; very many tin dishes; one whole skeleton with clothes on, - the flesh all on, but dried; many skeleton bones; three skulls. Alongside of the boat a big pile of skeleton bone that had been broken up for the marrow in them; they were near a fire place; skulls among these. The number of them ama-su-ad-loo (a great many) – cannot tell how many. It is certain that some of the men lived on human flesh, for alongside the boat were some large boots with cooked human flesh in them.

The Schwatka expedition 1879 description of the McClintock boat

The remains of the boat first found by McClintock in 1859 were found again, thirty-one years after the ships were abandoned, by an American expedition in 1879 led by Lieutenant Schwatka, who reported:

> We found the coast on the south side of Erebus Bay cut into long narrow points, separated by deep inlets, that made the work of searching much greater. All along the shore at the bottom of the inlets we found pieces of navy blue cloth, which seemed to have been washed up by high tides. Quantities of driftwood were also seen. At the bottom of one of the deepest inlets or bays, the men found the wreck of a ships boat strewn along the beach, together with pieces of cloth, iron, canvas and human bones. We gathered together portions of four skeletons, a number of buttons, some fish lines, copper and iron bolts and rivets, the drag rope of a sledge, some sheet lead, some shot, bullets and wire cartridges; pieces of clothing, broken medicine bottles, the charger of a powder flask, an iron lantern and a quantity of miscellaneous articles that would naturally form part of the outfit of such an expedition. The bones were prepared for burial, and the relics gathered together in a pile...

The fact that this boat was the one described in detail by McClintock is demonstrated because Schwatka brought back the stem post of the boat which remains today in the National Maritime Museum in Greenwich (NMM). Unfortunately Woodman was informed by the curator of the NMM that the stem post lacked the numbers described and illustrated by McClintock. He therefore postulated a third boat abandoned in Erebus Bay. However communication with the NMM by this author (September 10 2016) has confirmed that the stem post does show the numbering described by McClintock and it is not necessary to postulate a third boat. The communication from the NMM states:

> The statement in David Woodman's 'Unravelling the Franklin Mystery' p.301 that the boat stem is unmarked, is incorrect. It is marked 'XXIV (24

foot) W (Woolwich) CON (Contract) N61 Apr 184'. This corresponds with the description and diagram in F.L. McClintock's 'The Voyage of the *Fox* in Arctic Seas' p. 292. She may have been *Erebus*'s pinnace as her 28 foot length would accord. In the years between the two search expeditions the Inuit had broken the boat up. They reported to Hall and Schwatka, that they had found a second boat at Erebus Bay and 14 skeletons. Although Schwatka could not find the other boat, he discovered the bones of four Europeans in the area. Barry Ranford found a boat site on a small island in Erebus Bay in 1993. An excavation revealed the remains of eleven more individuals.

Best Wishes, Nick Ball, Assistant Curator of Ship Models.

The boat stem post with the numbers carved on it was on display at a Franklin exhibit at the National Maritime Museum, in 2017.

Remains found on an islet in Erebus Bay by Beattie in 1982

In 1982, Canadian Forensic Anthropologist Dr. Owen Beattie investigating the catastrophic failure of the Franklin expedition, relocated McClintock's boat place in Erebus Bay. An area measuring ninety by 120 feet was littered with wood fragments. A barrel stave, a wooden paddle handle, a cherry wood pipe stem and boot parts (including the sole of a boot penetrated by three holes where screws had been inserted for hauling the boats) were found. This is now designated site NgLj-1. Additionally, scattered along the coast for a half mile to the north a collection of human bones and bone fragments was made. The bones represented between six and fourteen individuals. Several of the bones collected by Beattie showed the scarring due to scurvy. Laboratory analysis of the bones showed them to have elevated lead levels, indicating the retreating crews were suffering from lead poisoning.

The Schwatka expedition had visited the site in 1879 and collected and buried the bones of at least four individuals. This burial was relocated and the bones subjected to modern forensic study as mentioned above.

Keenleyside's description of remains found on a second islet in Erebus Bay by Ranford in 1992 (site NgLj-2).

In summer 1992, Canadian amateur historian and Franklin enthusiast Barry Ranford located a previously undiscovered Franklin site in Erebus Bay. It was within a kilometre of McClintock's Boat Place and occurs on a small island just over three hectares in size now designated Site NgLj-2. Human remains and other relics occur over an area of around 300 square yards on the north-western end of the island. Over 200 relics were collected – iron and copper nails, copper percussion caps, glass, wire gauze, a clay pipe fragment, pieces of shoe leather and fabric, buttons, a buckle and a comb. A scatter of mainly oak fragments over an area measuring thirty by forty-five feet represented the remains of a boat or sledge. In addition, nearly 400 human bones and bone fragments were also collected and subjected to modern forensic study. Perhaps, significantly, only twenty-five faunal bones were found including four seal bones.

The skeleton remains were identified as from a group of European males, all under fifty years in age with heights of between 63.8 and 69.7 inches (162 and 177 cm). The remains, including fragments of five crania, represent at least eleven individuals. Oxygen isotope study of the enamel of two teeth indicated lower values as found in Europe rather than the higher values of the Arctic regions. One individual estimated at only twelve to fifteen years old was likely one of the four cabin boys who accompanied the expedition (believed to be eighteen years old at the time of sailing).

As with the bones studied by Beattie, nine bone samples from this site all showed elevated lead levels of 49 to 204 ppm, compared to the range of 87 to 223 ppm found in twenty-seven bone samples collected earlier by Beattie and others. The new data further supports Beattie's conclusion that lead poisoning had greatly debilitated the men.

The major finding was that ninety-two of the bone fragments or roughly a quarter, show evidence of cut marks made by metal blades with straight edges. Most types of bones were affected. The cut marks indicate that systematic defleshing of the bodies had occurred, which is consistent with the ninteenth century reports of cannibalism first reported by Dr. John Rae and later explorers who visited King William Island. The exception was Captain McClintock whose book lacks the word 'cannibalism' as his sponsor Lady Jane Franklin was incensed by Dr. John Rae's report and insisted that nothing about cannibalism should ever have been put into writing. The closest McClintock got to admitting cannibalism and yet not offending Lady Franklin and Victorian Society was the statement in his book:

> The information we obtained bears out the principal statements of Dr. Rae, and also accounts for the disappearance of one of the ships.

Indications of a second leader.

As we've seen, the two surviving senior officers on the Franklin retreat were Captain Crozier – the senior officer – and Captain Fitzjames. The 1848 record tells us that the next officer in command - Commander Gore - had died along with eight other officers (including the expedition leader Sir John Franklin) before the retreat began. In a reconstruction of this kind it is therefore possible to trace the actions of the leader of the retreat - Captain Crozier. He was known to the Inuit and his legacy is a series of Inuit testimonies that Charles Francis Hall recognised as his 'trail of footprints' amongst the Inuit testimony. He was known as 'Aglooka' to the Inuit but the name was also applied to several different leaders of groups of Franklin survivors as it meant only 'he who walks with long strides'.

At this point in the reconstruction an interesting point has been reached where the actions or 'footprints' of a second leader begin to emerge both from the physical remains in Erebus Bay and Inuit testimony of another and independent attempt at a breakout using the reoccupied *Erebus* in 1850.

The trail of this second leader begins with the fact that the two large boats were drawn up adjacent to islets in Erebus Bay, only about a half mile apart. This is probably not a coincidence, rather it looks like naval discipline and order prevailed. It would have been obvious to the officers in charge of the two boats in Erebus Bay that the retreat had accomplished only sixty-five miles from the ships and there was no hope that the majority would make the 1250 mile journey to the Hudson's Bay Fort Providence on the Great Slave Lake.

Had the boats been under the command of junior officers and were lagging behind the retreat, the decision of a junior officer should have been to follow Captain Crozier's orders. This would have meant forming a camp for the sick men of both boats in Erebus Bay at one of the islet-boat camps, and then hastening on with one boat and the remaining able bodied men. Perhaps it was this realisation that caused the senior officer with the boats to call a halt and to have the two boats positioned near each other. This senior officer took the decision to halt both boats and leave the sick men in the two camps. Perhaps he next hurried on to catch up with the front part of the retreat which had halted at Terror Bay. To halt the two boats was an enormous decision to take for it meant that two boats were out of the retreat and would not continue. Obviously, the senior officer had an alternative plan in mind. He was prepared to stand up to Captain Crozier and present his views.

This senior officer is believed to have returned to *Erebus* with Captain Crozier and the able bodied of the 1848 retreat. After Captain Crozier died the same second leader emerges by working *Erebus* south to the American mainland, where he died. A description of this officer's dead body is available from the Inuit who found and entered *Erebus* when she was abandoned at Utjulik. He was a very big man requiring five Inuit to lift his body, that still proved too much for them. He also had long teeth. It seems that his body was in the great cabin aboard *Erebus*, as there was room also for five Inuit, which would not be the case in the very small officer's cabins. When the flagship *Erebus* was finally deserted, as a mark of respect, his body was left locked in the great cabin that had formally been used by Sir John Franklin some years before. It was an honour that showed the respect of the few surviving crew men who had gained a further two years of life and hope, after what proved to be a death march led by Captain Crozier.

There are three lines of reasoning that suggest that this senior officer was most likely to be Captain Fitzjames. First he was the only officer senior enough to countermand Captain Crozier's orders. Second is that Fitzjames was a polar novice and his experience in the Arctic to date, especially a long sledge journey, may not have been to his taste. Third, *Erebus* was intact and his ship. If they returned it was still possible that she might be released later in summer 1848. Fitzjames had plans to exit the Arctic via Bering Strait to Petro Paulowski [Petropavlovsk] in Kamchatka and then travel overland to England in advance of the ship.

There is a second officer other than Fitzjames who might have played the same role. This was Lieutenant James Walter Fairholme also of *Erebus* and a close friend of Fitzjames. Fairholme physically was bigger than Fitzjames. His independence of mind and action was reflected in his past experiences. Fairholme joined the Navy in 1874. Battersby described how when he was despatched with a prize of a captured slave ship, he was shipwrecked on the coast of Africa and captured by Moors. Within a few days he was rescued by some French Africans. He had served with Fitzjames on *Ganges* during the Syrian War in 1840. In 1841 he accompanied Captain Trotter in a perilous expedition up the River Niger. He obtained his Lieutenancy in 1841 and was in continuous service until his appointment to *Erebus* in 1845. It is not possible to identify the mystery second leader with certainty, but for the purpose of this reconstruction, the most obvious choice is Captain Fitzjames.

The front of the retreat halts at Terror Bay

With a half of the retreating party halted at Erebus Bay, because the immobile sick had reached proportions where boat and sledge hauling were no longer feasible, the head of the retreat was in little better shape. Presumably led by Captain Crozier, they were thirty miles ahead (at least ten days of sledge hauling) of the two boats at Erebus Bay. There is a long thin finger of sea ice cutting through the headland of Cape Crozier. This should have been found and mapped in 1847 by the North-West Passage party. This finger of ice leads directly from Erebus Bay towards Terror Bay. It would have saved considerable time and effort for the retreating crews, rather than following the longer tortuous route around the coast.

Captain Crozier, as the driving force behind the southern retreat, would have found himself at Terror Bay with a similar problem to the senior officer in charge of the rear two boats. The immobile sick had reached proportions where it was no longer possible to man haul the boats and sledges further. So the retreat also halted in Terror Bay and put up two large tents side by side. One was the hospital tent for the sick men and the other was for the able bodied men not sleeping in the boats.

The expedition was now in major crisis as it would have been obvious to the two captains that a 1,250 mile retreat up Back's Great Fish River to Fort Providence on the Great Slave Lake was impossible. Also the very early departure from the ships that required hauling the boats across the frozen sea so early in the year, could now be seen for most the men to be only a death march. At Terror Bay the men had retreated only 100 miles from the ship and eighty miles from Crozier's Landing. Casualties in the form of immobile sick might have been as high as 50%.

Presumably Fitzjames was angry with this Arctic venture, for he had recruited many of his friends and was watching them die. His ship *Erebus* was still intact and he had made arrangements for his mail to be delivered to Petro Paulowski [Petropavlovsk] in Kamchatka and then a swift overland passage to England. To abandon an intact ship (*Erebus*) which still had the potential to get through the ice during summer thaws, would not have been to his liking. At only thirty miles apart the two ends of the retreat might have been in communication.

It is not difficult to imagine an angry senior officer (believed here to be Captain Fitzjames) marching thirty miles to catch up with the advance party of the retreat. When he joined Captain Crozier, in the lead at Terror Bay, it was to find a repeat of the situation at Erebus Bay. It is unlikely that there was any angry dispute as it would have been obvious to the two senior officers that the retreat of the whole party had largely failed and the expedition's position was now dire in the extreme. The performance of the men on the retreat was now known to result in around a half of the men incapacitated by illness. The march had demonstrated a progress at around two miles a day. Their food supply had been for only forty days, and was largely exhausted.

However, those at Terror Bay, had reached the northern limit of the summer hunting areas. A distance of only 100 miles had been achieved from Crozier's Landing and only about a half of the distance along the west side of King William Island covered.

The Hospital Tent at Terror Bay.

Hall recorded In-nook-poo-zhee-jook's testimony of a tent at Terror Bay:

> A tent was near this boat, it was on the top of some rising ground on a small sandy hill. The place, as pointed out on the chart, was near the bottom of Terror Bay, a little way northerly of the point adjacent to Fitz James Inlet. The tent was large, and made of a ridge pole resting on a perpendicular pole at either end; small ropes extended from top of the tent at each end to the ground.
>
> Three men, one of whom was Tee-kee-ta, first saw the tent. It had in it blankets and bedding, a great many skeleton bones and skulls, the flesh all off, nothing except sinews attached to them; the appearance as though foxes and wolves had gnawed the flesh, some bones had been sawed with a saw, some skulls had holes in them. Besides the blankets, were tin cups, spoons, forks, knives, two double barrel-guns, pistols, lead balls, a great many powder-flasks, and both books and papers written upon. As the last were good for nothing for Innuits, the men threw them away, except one book, which Tee-ka-ta brought home and gave to the children, after a while it got torn to pieces.

In-nook-poo-zhee-jook's additional testimony of a tent at Terror Bay

> Question: What was the size of the tent?
>
> Answer: Never saw the tent itself, but only the tenting place, judging from the appearances, the tent must have been as long as to the further end of Ar-mou's tent from where he was sitting (Hall measured this distance to be 22 feet). The tent was on some rising ground, trou-puk (sandy), overlooking the sea, about as far off as an islet pointed out – half a mile. Three graves were near the tenting place.
>
> On showing In-nook-poo-zhe-jook the large Admiralty chart, he pointed out the place of the tent on Terror Bay.

In-nook-poo-zhe-jook's mother-in-law's testimony of the tent at Terror Bay, as given by Ook-bar-loo

> This mother of In-nook-poo-zhe-jook told her all about where and how she got the watch. She and her husband went to a big tent not very far from Neitchille, and among the frozen mass of human bones and bodies that

were lying around in it she saw one Kob-lu-na's body that had a bright white (probably silver) chain around the neck. She knew at once what the chain was for, as some other Neitchille Innuits had just come into possession of several watches and chains, which she saw.

The body of this man was lying on one side, and was half imbedded in solid ice from head to feet. The way the chain was about the neck and running down one side of the body indicated that the watch was beneath it; and therefore, to get at the watch, she found a difficult and disagreeable task before her. Neither she nor her husband had any instrument with them that they would use for any such purpose as was derived; therefore, while her husband was seeking around, in and about the tent, collecting such things as he fancied would best suit him, she procured a heavy sharp stone, and with this chipped away the ice from all round the body until it was released. Continued old mother Ook-bar-loo, in a truly sorrowful tone of voice. This woman told her that she could never forget the dreadful, fearful feelings she had all the time while engaged doing this. For, besides the tent being filled with frozen corpses – some entire and others, mutilated by some of the starving companions, who had cut off much of the flesh with their knives and hatchets and eaten it – this man who had the watch she sought seemed to her to have been the last that died, and his face was just as though he was only asleep. All the while she was at work breaking the ice near the head, especially the ice about the face, she felt very, very bad, and for this reason had to stop several times. She was very careful not to touch any part of the body while pounding with the sharp stone. At last, after having pounded away the ice from around and under the body, her husband helped her lift it out of its icy bed. Still she was troubled to get the watch from the frozen garments with which the body was completely dressed. Finally, the watch and key and chain were obtained entire, and the woman now keeps them very choice, in commemoration of the terrible feelings she had when getting them from the dead Kob-lu-na, whom she dug out of the ice with nothing but a heavy, sharp stone.

Ahlangyah's testimony of a tent at Terror Bay

Twenty years after the Hall expedition, the Schwatka expedition in 1879 met an old woman who provided more testimony of the tent at Terror Bay.

The following spring, when there was little snow on the ground, she saw a tent standing on the shore at the head of Terror Bay. There were dead bodies in the tent, and outside were some covered over with sand. There was no flesh on them – nothing but the bones and clothes. There were a great many; she had forgotten how many. Indeed, Inuits have little idea of numbers beyond 'ten'. She saw nothing to indicate any of the party she met before (in Washington Bay). The bones had the chords or sinews still attached to them. One of the bodies had the flesh on, but this one's stomach all gone. There were one or two graves outside. They did not open the graves at this time; saw a great many things lying around. There were knives, forks, spoons, watches, many books, clothing, blankets, and such things. The books were not taken notice of. This was the same party of Esquimaux who had met the white men the year before, and they were the first who saw the tent and graves. They had been in King William Land ever since they saw the white men until they found the tent place.

Three hospital tents

Ahlangyah's testimony conflicts with the previous ones as it suggests the hospital tent was found in 1849. That a hospital tent was found intact after McClintock's visit in 1859 is known from the testimony of In-nook-poo-zhe-jook. The year was calculated by Hall as 1861, and confirmed because In-nook-poo-zhe-jook found at the same time two boats nearby in Erebus Bay. One was intact with crew remains, but the other was entirely empty having been cleaned out by Captain McClintock in 1859. It is not possible that the same tent discovered by the Inuit in 1849 would still have the contents intact in 1861. The metal and wood contents were immensely valuable to the Inuit for making tools, weapons and jewellery. Yet such a tent was discovered before 1854, because Dr. John Rae collected testimony describing it in 1854. There is a simple explanation. That is, that there were three hospital tents, two on islets in Erebus Bay where the two large boats on sledges were halted, and a third one in Terror Bay. These were all hospital tents where the sick and immobile were left. It seems that one was found by Inuit in 1849, the Terror Bay tent in 1861 and the third tent site with many artifacts as well as bones with cut marks, not until 1992 by Barry Ranford and was described by Keenleyside and others.

The significance and ages of the three death camps

The three main sites where many men died are the two boat places in Erebus Bay (sites NgLj-1 and NgL-2) and the hospital tent at Terror Bay (known only from graphic Inuit testimony). According to the Inuit testimony as well as archaeological remains, perhaps twenty to twenty-eight men died at the two Erebus Bay sites and another fifteen at Terror Bay (Appendix 2.). Woodman has suggested that the boat place on the mainland (named Starvation Cove by the Schwatka expedition) may have had around only six to ten men die, not the forty as was at first believed by the Rea report of 1854. The Starvation Cove site is believed to have formed during the 1850 retreat.

Woodman has interpreted the three death camps at Erebus and Terror Bays as forming in 1850. He suggests that the 1848 retreat proved abortive very soon, when distances of only three miles a day could be made. He suggests that most of the 105 men who retreated in 1848 returned to the two ships within a month. He believes the camps were set up much later when the two ships were carried by the ice to the vicinity of Erebus Bay and that boats could reach the shores in the summers. They were therefore camps of some duration with repeated visits by groups from the reoccupied ships. Following the Woodman interpretation of the crushing and sinking of *Terror* in 1850, the last able bodied men made a last attempt at retreat and were met by Inuit in Washington Bay in 1850. The last men were left in the 'death camps' where they died in late 1850.

This interpretation is not followed here. Rather the three death camps are believe to mark the furthest points reached by the 1848 retreat. They mark the sites where the immobile sick reached about fifty percent of the men, so they could no longer be transported on the sledges. Their fate was sealed by the unusually cold summer where the hunting was very poor and not the usual abundance. The reasons for this difference of interpretation are as follows.

The Inuit testimony of the meeting in Washington Bay in 1850 of a party of men hauling a boat on a sledge describes the manner of a retreat. The method of travel was for the party to be led by an officer carrying a telescope and shotgun (on the lookout for birds) and an armed marine. The rest of the men were man hauling a boat mounted on a sledge together with another sledge or two with camping gear and sick men. The party moved along the smoothest ice close to the island's shores. Birds shot on route were hung on the sides of the boat to keep them frozen. Each night a campsite would be made adjacent to some land lacking snow cover, probably because the men were not carrying thick, bulky and heavy ground sheets, so that lying on ice was to be avoided as it would cause melting. Many of the men slept in the boat protected by a canvas awning.

A tent and kitchen camp would be set up on land free of ice and snow. Offshore islets provided ideal places for pitching camp with the boat still on the ice but near the tent. Such islets helped because the men hauling the boats could save time and effort by cutting across bays, rather than taking the longer route by following the shoreline smooth ice around bays and inlets.

In Erebus Bay, two large boats (one from *Erebus* described by McClintock) were left close together, each adjacent to a small island. One of these boats was described by McClintock who found the remains of two skeletons inside. The remains of at least four skeletons were later found in the same area by the Schwatka expedition in 1879, who buried the remains (sites NgLj-1 and 3). The second boat was found by In-nook-poo-zhee-jook in 1861. It contained one complete mummified skeleton with the cannibalised remains of several others alongside. These remains are likely to be those rediscovered by Barry Ranford in 1992. A forensic study was made by Keenleyside and others (Site NgLj-2).

The latter site is particularly well studied and is described by Potter with a map and aerial photograph. The small offshore islet can be seen to be composed of arcuate beach ridges. The site of the boat can be identified by a scatter of wood fragments. Nearby, other remains probably mark the camp site on a beach ridge. Of particular interest is the forensic report that described nearly 400 human bones and fragments (many with knife scars from defleshing) and only twenty-five animal bones including four seal bones. Although the site has been disturbed and much removed by the Inuit, it remained remarkably well preserved.

The camp is insubstantial as is particularly well shown by the map and aerial photograph in Potter. It does not have the characteristics of a camp that was repeatedly visited - like that on Beechey Island or Cape Felix. There were no buildings, no waste, no tins. The associated faunal remains are so sparse that life cannot have existed there for very long. A substantial camp repeatedly visited would be larger with more remains. Further the contents of the boats, as described above are time capsules of the 1848 retreat including the officers silver. It is a very barren site typical of a place where a boat was halted and an overnight camp made. Men were abandoned here and when the hunting failed and no rescuers returned, a few resorted to cannibalism. The site therefore has the appearance of a temporary overnight stop on the 1848 retreat and not a well-established camp that was in use for months or even years. Little details such as Ice master Reid carrying the personal possessions of Lieutenant Graham Gore home to his family speak of the 1848 retreat not of immobile men abandoned in 1850. Likewise, the paddles, the long line for hauling a boat upriver, tell of the crews' hopes for the retreat.

A few days into the retreat, it would have been realised that it was likely to fail. However, there was no point in turning back to the 'hell ship' where insufficient food remained to last out the next winter. Captain Crozier's decision was made to give as many of the crew as possible the chance to reach the hunting grounds of the Inuit further south. For that reason the retreat could not be abandoned until either the forty days rations were expended or until the sick became too much of a burden to be transported. Crozier evidently got a half of the men to Terror Bay and maybe Douglas Bay where the summer hunting should have been good.

The McClintock-Schwatka description of the second boat place also suggests that it was similar, but much more disturbed by high tide effects. The boat minutely described by McClintock had been considerably modified for river work with twenty-four metal fittings for the paddles and the long tow rope. McClintock's suggestion that the boat he described was half lying off its sledge was being hauled back to the ships is not accepted. Instead it is believed that in the years after abandonment, high tides disturbed this site by turning the boat and partly floating it off its sledge. The site was further disturbed by high tides before it was next found by the Schwatka expedition.

Although the remains of the hospital tent in Terror Bay have not been found by western searchers, and there is only the excruciatingly graphic detail of the Inuit accounts, the interpretation followed here is that it too marks a furthest point of the 1848 retreat. The Terror Bay camp may have been first set up in late 1846 or spring 1847 as a hunting camp after the return of the North-West Passage team led by Lieutenant Graham Gore.

There is a second case that can be made that the retreat did not return virtually intact within a month of setting out. This is because the retreat was a Royal Navy decision and Royal Navy discipline was enforced, so there may have been grumbling, but the decision of the senior Captain was law. Captain Crozier evidently knew he was committed to succeed in the retreat as the alternative was the probable deaths of everyone. In the military, especially that of the Victorian era, and also in the modern military, the quality of leadership is paramount. Officers were promoted for showing good leadership. When it became obvious in the first week or two of the retreat that the distances covered were hopelessly inadequate, there would have been no discussion nor questioning of orders. The men would follow good leadership and were trained to obedience without questioning their orders.

It seems likely that Captain Crozier led the retreat to Terror Bay because once there he entered the different geographical area reported by earlier explorers of summer lakes, abundant summer vegetation with caribou, migratory birds and fish. Southern King William Island in summer greatly contrasts with the north-west coast of the island, that is relatively barren without lakes and a poor hunting ground. It is concluded here that Captain Crozier exerted all his leadership abilities to get his men to the better hunting ground at Terror Bay. But only about a half of the men reached Terror Bay.

Captain Fitzjames probably countermanded the orders only some thirty miles to the south, when in Erebus Bay. Everything then hinged on the hunting as the forty days rations carried were probably nearly exhausted. But it was still early in the year and birds had begun to arrive. But the needs of 105 men were very great. The paucity of faunal remains at site NgLj-2 suggests that the summer hunting failed probably because of poor weather conditions. The three death camps resulted where the immobile sick were left with volunteers to look after them (e.g. Ice Master James Reid with the *Erebus* boat/camp in Erebus Bay) while the able bodied returned to reoccupy *Erebus* and to try to work her south in the summer thaw to assist the sick.

The interpretation presented here suggests that the 1848 retreat did not halt until about fifty percent of the men were immobilised by sickness. Only about a half of the crews got back to reoccupy *Erebus*. A measure of the great efforts made by individuals during the retreat, was a find made by Beattie and Geiger (1987). They found a leather sole of a boot at the site of one of the abandoned boats in Erebus Bay. Through the sole of the boot, three sturdy brass screws had been driven to give the boots a grip on the ice. However all three screws were broken off flush with the bottom of the boot (drawing on p. 82, Beattie and Geiger's book), preserving a record that the men hauled as hard as they could to move the heavy sledge loads.

15: SUMMER 1848 - THE CAPTAINS FACE DEFEAT

The two boats at the front of the 1848 retreat are believed to have halted in Terror Bay, after only around eighty miles of sledge hauling from Crozier's Landing and 100 miles from the ships. The other two boats were halted in Erebus Bay some thirty miles behind the others. Captains Crozier and Fitzjames would have met in Terror Bay to compare notes. Presumably, Captain Fitzjames would not have been as exhausted as his men, as he would not have been hauling sledges, and would have marched on to Terror Bay for a critical meeting. It is not too difficult to imagine the conversation between Captain Crozier and an angry (at first) Captain Fitzjames when they met. But each had a similar report to make and the seriousness of the situation would have been realised very quickly.

Captain Fitzjames must have been dismayed to find that the advance party was also halted for similar reasons. There still remained another 1150 miles to Fort Providence on the Great Slave Lake. It was the man-hauling of the boats over ice (rather than sailing them), the poor health of the crews after three years in the Arctic, and almost certainly extremely bad weather in what proved to be a poor summer that defeated them. However, at Terror Bay they had reached the edge of the target area reputed to have good hunting.

When the two captains met, they would have realized that there was now little hope of saving most of the crew, because the option to march out had failed. In fact the chances of survival for the entire expedition were now very small. They had only three options. To stay where they were, when all would soon die of starvation. To abandon the sick and with the remaining able bodied haul two boats further south – perhaps achieving another fifty miles only. Or to leave the sick in care and march back lightweight to the depot at Croziers Landing to resupply *Erebus* and await the 1848 thaw in July which might free the ship.

Crozier would have been very much aware of the limited food supply left on *Erebus* and at Depot Camp (*Terror* had been abandoned and was now a mortuary ship). Dr. Cyriax made a detailed study of the stores supplied to the ships and concluded that at the time they were abandoned, there would still be enough food left to supply 129 men for two months or about 260 man months. Unfortunately, much food had been left on the Matty Islands and much of what remained was tinned food that after winter 1847-48 was probably condemned by the surgeons as probably the cause of the illness and deaths. The presence of some scurvy indicated that the lime juice was beginning to lose its antiscorbutic properties. Clearly if they returned to the ships, their continued survival would depend heavily on hunting additional food. But by reaching Terror Bay the men had reached an area of relatively good hunting in summer, although their arrival at the end of May to early June, was early for success. Their situation was dire as their food supplies were near exhausted.

Klutschak noted that the barren gravel ridges of the north-west part of King William Island, are replaced at Terror Bay and to the south in summer with meadows of flowering plants that attract caribou and summer birds and lakes with fish:

> During the crossing from the north side to the south side of the large Graham Gore Peninsula a significant difference became discernible. The sharp mudstones ceased, to be replaced as we penetrated further by meadow areas and numerous lakes. The immediate vicinity of Terror Bay is a true paradise compared to the northern part of King William's Land and possesses a great abundance of caribou.

The strongest parties had advanced to Terror Bay. This would have occurred around early June, when the forty-day food supply ran out. This was a time when the first birds were arriving

Regarding which course should be taken, it would have been here that the different views of the two captains came into play. Captain Crozier liked to play by the rules of the Admiralty and ran a 'tight ship' and would do things 'the Navy way' or 'by the book'. He had ordered the retreat to the south but had not expected such a poor performance for the forty day short food supply that they carried with them. In contrast, Fitzjames was a gambler and an adventurer wanting glory. A death march so that a few only might survive, would be unacceptable to him. He would very strongly make a case that *Erebus* was intact and the summer melt only weeks away. By returning to *Erebus* there would be a chance to break the ship free and even to work her south, so that some of the immobile sick might be rescued. Evidently, Fitzjames's views won the day.

Unfortunately, the remains of the camp at Terror Bay, described in graphic detail by the Inuit, have never been found by western searchers and are believed to be buried by seasonal melt wash or were washed away by a high tide. It is therefore not known from animal bone debris how successful the hunting there might have been. What is known however is that the forensic study of Keenleyside and others of a site in Erebus Bay, located nearly 400 human bones and bone fragments and only twenty-five animal bone fragments including four seal bones. The reburied bones by the Schwatka expedition contained two seal and two caribou bones. The paucity of animal bones suggests that the hunting was not successful, probably because it was still too early in the year. Probably some hunters and carers were left at the three places (two in Erebus Bay and the hospital tent in Terror Bay) and the able bodied returned to the ships as fast as possible to reman one and see if the summer thaw might release them. It seems likely that from the numbers of bodies found at the death camps, that about a half of the retreating crews were well enough to return to the ships. About fifteen men would be left at each boat place in Erebus Bay and perhaps another fifteen men at the hospital tent in Terror Bay. Another ten or so men may have continued the retreat to the south and reached Douglas Bay with a boat. In addition testimony will next be presented describing another dozen stragglers who went on alone and encountered the Inuit. This would suggest that only around a half of the men returned to reoccupy *Erebus* in summer 1848 (Appendix 2).

The reversal of the retreat plan and a return to the ships would have been welcome to most of the crew. The Franklin expedition was very much a Victorian naval expedition, where the crews behaved as seamen aboard ship and did their best to maintain the ship and service the sledging trips of the scientific parties led by some of the officers. For the majority of the crew this might have meant never leaving the ship except to walk on the ice nearby and play a game of football. The crew were there at the command of the officers. All responsibilities lay with the officers. The mind of the crew was occupied with typical shipboard trivia. This is demonstrated by the Peglar Papers most of which have verses of naval doggerel, some written backwards. One of the papers is dated April 21 1847 (two years after the expedition set out) and is a sea poem written in Peglar's hand. At this time the ships had been beset in the ice off King William Island for seven months.

> The C the C the open C
> it grew so fresh the Ever free

It finishes:

> When I was On Old England Shore
> I like the young C more and more

and ofte times flew to a Shelltering Plase
like a bird that Seek its mother's Case
and a H She wos and Oft to me
for I love I love a young and Hopen C.

The Peglar papers especially this one dated example, clearly show how the crew and in particular Captain of the Foretop Harry Peglar of *Terror* was spending his spare time. All was well below decks and all decisions were in the hands of the officers. Clearly, at this time, the crew were not being trained nor thinking about retreating across more than 1000 miles of Arctic territory.

The breakup of the 1848 retreat appears to have been followed by some disorder. There is testimony of two small groups of stragglers moving as independent parties and encountering Inuit. They were ill prepared for the encounters. They may have been the men left behind as hunters with the immobile sick and when no help arrived and cannibalism broke out, they left the camps and set out independently. In addition, remains of seven bodies found in Douglas Bay, fifty-six miles south east of Terror Bay, suggest that a small party continued either hauling a boat on a sledge or just a sledge to reach that point.

Iggiararsuk's testimony – Inuit encounter a three-man sledge party on the western shore of King William Island (1848)

In 1923 Knud Rasmussen met an old man named Iggiararjuk at Pelly Bay whose father Mangaq had met three men from the Franklin expedition. His father along with two friends Tatqatsaq and Qublut were hunting seals to the west of King William Island when they heard shouts. They saw three white men on the shore waving to them. It was spring with open water along the coast and the Inuit could not get ashore until low water. They found the men to be very thin, hollow-cheeked and ill looking. They wore European clothes had no dogs and were hauling sledges. They exchanged a knife for seal meat and blubber which they cooked immediately using the blubber. Later the strangers went to Mangaq's tent and spent the night there before returning to their small tent. At the time there were already caribou on the island but the strangers seemed to hunt only wildfowl as there were many eider ducks and ptarmigan about. But summer had not yet fully arrived and there were no swans yet. They communicated by signs only and the strangers indicated that they had once been many of them together, but there were now few left and they had abandoned their ship in the ice. They pointed to the south towards Back's Great Fish River indicating that they were going home that way. They were never seen again.

This is an important encounter as the season identifies the month as early June before the swans arrive in late June, most likely June 1848. The three men would have been on King William Island since the retreat began on April 25 1848 or only a little over forty days – the duration of the sledging rations. This is the time when the retreat was halted at Erebus and Terror Bays and the two captains had had their big meeting. The three men with only a sledge were probably left to look after the immobile sick. When the food ran out and cannibalism broke out they probably preferred to take their chances alone.

Tommy Anguttitauruq's testimony - the crewmen who refused to eat seal

This piece of testimony was collected from two sources by Dorothy Harley Eber between 1996 and 2008. It is particularly interesting as it is given from the Inuit point of view. One of the versions is repeated here. The source is Nicholas Qayutinuaq told by Tommy Anguttitauruq:

> At this time there were four or five families with four or five separate igloos on the west side of King William Island to the south side of Terror Bay. The men were out seal hunting, and the women and children, and one elder too old to keep up with the younger men, were left in camp. At that time eight or nine white people came to the camp.
>
> When the white men entered the camp, all the Inuit were inside one of the igloos; they started hearing people outside. One of the women says, 'The hunters are here – they're back already'. They did not expect them back so soon. Then a woman went out to see them. She comes back very shaky and says, 'They're not Inuit; they're not human'. Everyone got scared, very, very scared and no one wanted to go outside the igloo. But the old man, when he hears something outside the igloo, he goes out to investigate – to see what's going on. When he sees what's outside, he says to himself, 'No, I have never seen anything like this'.
>
> He'd seen a shaman but he wasn't a shaman himself. He says to himself, 'I've never in all my life seen a devil or a spirit. These things are not human; so if they are not human I cannot see them. I have never in all my life seen any kind of spirit – I've heard the sounds they make, but I've never seen them with my own eyes; these are not spirits.

Then the old man goes over to touch one, to feel if it's cold or warm. He touched a cheek with his hand; cool but not as cold as a fish! They were beings but not Inuit. They were beings but he did not know what they were.

He had always thought to himself, 'If they are human I can feel them. If they are human, they will be warm. If devils or spirits, they will have no heat. So he touched one and the being was cold – but not as cold as a fish! You know the fish is cold blooded.

These beings seemed disoriented – not too interested in the Inuit, more aware of the igloo building; touching it. The Inuit invited them inside and the women tried to give them something to eat – seal meat that was cooked already, and they gave them water to drink. They drank the water. But when they tried to give them seal meat, they'd take a bite and some of them swallowed; some of them wouldn't swallow, they'd spit it out. They gave them soup. Some drank a little; some didn't want to take any.

Before the men came back, the old man instructed one of the women to bring these beings to one of the igloos – the biggest one. Then he walked to meet the hunters and told them what had been encountered; that there were strange beings in one of the igloos. They did not seem dangerous but were 'palakhonguliqtut' - getting weak, weak from hunger. The old man guided the hunters to the igloo where all the women and children were, so they could discuss.

They had to be qallunaat, people thought – they had iron; guns and knives. In those days, iron was valuable and rare; you could sharpen it and make tools out of it for hunting equipment. These strange people had iron; they were probably qallunaat.

The men decided to go and see them. These qallunaat were quite frightened when they saw the Inuit come in. But the men didn't harm them. They tried again to feed them with the cooked meat, but the qallunaat did the same thing as before – ate a little but not all.

You hear people say sometimes that all Inuit eat raw meat. In the west when they're in their igloos, they like it cooked. So the Inuit started talking among themselves, saying if they come from the east they probably eat raw meat; we'd better try and see if they eat raw meat. So they gave them three whole seals. They built them an igloo and built a fire.

Then the Inuit got together and talked to each other. 'We have heard that Indians kill Inuit. These could be Indians… or white people. And we have also heard that qallunaat kill Inuit people sometimes. We'd better be going before they wake up.

That night they got all their belongings together and took off towards the southwest. They never encountered those qallunaat again. But because they were in a hurry, they must have left a few of their belongings behind. Later that winter, two or three of them decided to go back to their old camp to gather up their possessions; they saw four dead bodies in that igloo. Originally there had been nine or ten white men. The seals were never touched; but two of the men were partly eaten; the other two must have been the last survivors,

Here is a sad story. It probably deals with some of the seamen who had lived and worked 'navy style' without any thoughts of a retreat. A few weeks boat hauling was followed by starvation. They set out without an officer, encountered the Inuit, but were unable to communicate or eat seal. When abandoned, four remained in the igloo and the rest carried on to the south. When two died, they preferred cannibalism to eating seal.

The boat party at Douglas Bay

William 'Paddy' Gibson in summer 1931 searched this bay following a report from the Inuit of skeletal remains and a boat on one of the islets within the bay. Islets in the entrance to the bay revealed no remains. The largest islet encountered was near the head of the bay off the eastern shore. It was 500 yards long by 150 yards wide and rose to thirty feet.

On the island and its shores Gibson found seven skulls and many bones, both on the shores and highest parts of the islet. A search revealed small roughly chopped oak and wood shavings of oak and pine. Two small pieces of pine were also found. Gibson believed these were the remains of a boat reported by the Inuit that they had broken up but might also have been a sledge. The Inuit reported the boat at the Todd Islets but as no wooden remains were found there despite a careful search, Gibson conclude that this was most likely the boat site.

The location of the remains deep inside the bay speaks of a tragedy where the boat party became lost. They were following the coast of King William Island towards the south east and rounded Tulloch Point. But on reaching Douglas Bay, they did not cross the bay but turned along the coast into the bay heading almost north. They proceeded about four miles in the wrong direction to the head of the bay. It cost the lives of seven men.

Such an error can be easily made. First because the magnetic compass is unreliable or does not work in such close proximity to the magnetic pole as described by Amundsen of the *Gjoa* voyage. Second because of the common occurrence in the Arctic of thick fogs where visibility is reduced to a few yards. The party is unlikely to have hauled their boat and sledge during a snow storm. The position of the remains can only be accounted for if the party were following the coastline on the smoother ice near the shore in thick fog and their compass was not working. They unknowingly turned into Douglas Bay and reached the head of the bay.

What a great disappointment it must have been when they discovered in their weakened state that they had hauled their boat four miles in the wrong direction. Gibson interred the remains on the highest point of the island and built a large cairn there.

A brief description of what might be the same boat was given by Rasmussen:

> But in the same year, later on in the spring, three men were on their way from Qequertak (King William Island) to the southward, going to hunt caribou calves. And they found a boat with the bodies of six men. There were knives and guns in the boat, and much food also, so the men must have died of disease. There are many places in our country here where bones of these white men may still be found. I myself have been to Qavdlunarsiorfik (a spit of land on Adelaide Peninsula, nearly opposite the site where Amundsen wintered); we used to go there to dig for lead and bits of iron. And then there is Kangerfigdluk, quite close here, a little way along the coast to the west.

The fate of the immobile sick at Erebus and Terror Bays

In this reconstruction, three groups of immobile sick men remained trapped in Erebus and Terror Bays. In all three places in the final extreme and hoping to prolong their lives until *Erebus* showed up, a few resorted to cannibalism. Since 1854 when Dr. John Rae returned to England with reports of the lost Franklin expedition that included references to cannibalism, the objectivity of trying to understand what happened to the expedition has been compromised by sensationalism such as newspaper headlines of 'Sir John Franklin a cannibal?'

Dr. Rae prepared a confidential report for The Admiralty describing the reported cannibalism and another account for The Times newspaper omitting the subject. Without his approval, the Admiralty report was immediately released to the press and caused a sensation and public outcry. Lady Jane Franklin was appalled and when she met Dr. Rae was livid and insisted that Dr. Rae should never have put the mention of cannibalism in writing. Lady Jane sponsored the *Fox* expedition led by Captain McClintock and of course the word cannibalism, does not appear in the excellent book that McClintock wrote of his successful search for Franklin remains.

Lady Jane organised a campaign against Dr. Rae that included the support of Charles Dickens. Dr. Rae was expected to be knighted for his very successful small team mapping of extensive coastline of the Arctic regions, but never received the honor. A plaque commemorating him and his achievements was finally erected in Westminster Abbey in 2014.

The report of cannibalism was offensive (and still is for many) and incompatible with the Victorian ideal of the English gentleman and the concept of a civilised technologically-advanced Christian England bringing civilization, Christianity and technology to the world. The outrage in London over the report of cannibalism was based on fairly brief material. However the later lengthy detailed descriptions of Inuit testimony recorded by Charles Francis Hall in his five years (1864 to 1869) with the Inuit provided graphic detail. The minutae in these reports does not support the Victorian charge of fabrications by savages. Rather they can be seen to be descriptions with the child-like innocence, simplicity and honesty, of a native people, most of whom had not encountered white men before and did not understand a lot of what they saw and described. Although they too were familiar with cannibalism in their precarious existence in the ice.

Today there is no doubt about the cannibalism, and it is of course understandable enough that starving and desperate men resorted to breaking this most ancient of human taboos. Modern forensic studies have revealed knife cuts on human bones consistent with defleshing. In a study of bone fragments from the Franklin expedition by Mays and Beattie, evidence was found of 'pot boiling' or the rounding of broken bone ends due to boiling in a cook pot. This was interpreted as 'end stage cannibalism' where the bones are broken and boiled to extract marrow from them. The Inuit testimony describing the gruesome contents of the hospital tent in Terror Bay and the second boat in Erebus Bay have already been given. In both places the last cannibal was recognisable as being the only intact body and wearing the gold chains of his fellows.

Cannibalism occurred in 1848 in places where immobile sick men found themselves with no hope of escape (The boat sites in Erebus Bay, and the hospital tent at Terror Bay). The reason would have been that the men who returned to the ships had told them that if *Erebus* were freed that summer, they would come back for them, so there was reason to stay alive and wait.

The gruesome findings of the Inuit make it clear that return parties did not get back in time to save anyone.

16: SUMMER 1848 TO SUMMER 1850 – AN OCCUPIED SHIP AND CAMP AT IMNGUYAALUK ISLAND AND THE DEATH OF CAPTAIN CROZIER

It seems likely that around fifty-eight men returned to Crozier's Landing and set about remanning *Erebus*. There is considerable Inuit testimony describing three different scenarios for the sinking of the two ships. Two different accounts of sinking occur in the vicinity of Cape Crozier – the westernmost point on King William Island. A third describes the sinking of the 'Utjulik' ship in Wilmot and Compton Bay, fifty-six miles further south, on the west side of the Adelaide Peninsula. The 2014 discovery of *Erebus* in Wilmot and Compton Bay and the 2016 discovery of the sunken *Terror* off Terror Bay can clear up the confusion. The *Chieftain* report suggests that both ships were intact in the ice in spring 1849 with *Terror* still on her beam ends. A case will be made that the damaged *Terror* was never reoccupied. Only *Erebus* was reoccupied.

Admiral Wright has noted that in 1848 there was an abnormally large movement of the Beaufort ice stream. Barrow Strait was filled with ice. The Franklin search expedition led by Sir James Clark Ross in his ships *Enterprise* and *Investigator* were carried with it into Baffin Bay. This expedition then returned to England without reaching its goal.

With the two captains aboard *Erebus* once more, the first priority would have been to get the ship south to relieve the immobile sick men stranded in Erebus and Terror Bays. It seems likely that they achieved this, probably in late 1848, because the Inuit report a ship south of Cape Crozier in the Royal Geographical Society Islands for two years (1849 and 1850). However, the Inuit testimony of the three 'death camps' indicates that the hunting by the three parties of immobile sick and their carers had failed and most men were dead or perhaps with a cannibal or two just surviving when men returned. The two captains evidently kept the men away from the horrors of the death camps and as recorded in the testimony of 'the black men' (see later), warned the Inuit away from such places.

The two captains evidently managed to work *Erebus* south through the leads and along the shore of King William Island, into the Alexandra Strait, past Cape Crozier (the most westerly extension of the island) and into the shelter (from the ice stream) on the south side of the smaller of the Royal Geographical Society Islands (Map II). Inuit testimony describes an occupied ship anchored just offshore of Imnguyaaluk Island, outside Terror Bay. There were Inuit encounters and much testimony including descriptions of some of the crew members.

The discovery of the wreck of *Terror* in the area in 2016 corresponds with other Inuit testimony of the arrival of a second but deserted ship with bodies aboard. The conflict between two accounts, one of an occupied ship and the other of an unoccupied ship in the same area can be resolved. The solution adopted in this reconstruction is that the remanned *Erebus* arrived in summer 1848, and remained there until freed in 1850 and then was worked south to Utjulik. After *Erebus* had left the area, *Terror*, now upright again but locked up with her cargo of frozen bodies in bunks, was later ice rafted into the area. She was found by the Inuit who made a hole in her side, so she sank before much salvage could take place. What is not resolved is the third account of an occupied ship in the Cape Crozier area being overwhelmed by ice and taking some of her crew down with her when she sank (See Appendix 4).

Inuit testimony describes the occupied ship as remaining at Imnguyaaluk Island for two years. Then in 1850, after the death of Captain Crozier, between seventeen and forty-five men (dominated by *Terror* men), made a last attempt to break out to reach Repulse Bay. It was this group that was encountered near Washington Bay by the Inuit and provides most of the eyewitness description of the manner of the retreat. Only around a dozen men believed to be led by Captain Fitzjames remained aboard *Erebus* and worked the ship south to Utjulik after the summer of 1850.

Patsy Topilikton's testimony – an occupied ship at Imnguyaaluk, 1848 - 1850

Recently collected testimony from the Gjoa Haven Inuit by Dorothy Harley Eber, provides details of an occupied ship wintering in the narrow strait between Cape Crozier (the westernmost point on King William Island) and the Royal Geographical Society Islands. In particular, the ship was on the south end of Imnguyaaluk Island – the smaller of the two Royal Geographical Society Islands. This would place the ship within sight of the hospital tent at Terror Bay.

Discovery of the Royal Geographical Society Islands is credited to

Amundsen who mapped and named them. However, it seems the islands were well known to the crew of the reoccupied *Erebus* long before.

Imnguyaaluk is the Royal Geographical Society Island nearest to Cape Crozier and the location of the ship is given as the south end of the island. The record states that a ship with white men wintered here. During their stay they had a camp where they made use of seal oil and blubber, as the ground there is impregnated with oil from blubber fires. The Inuit do not waste blubber in this manner. This is a critical observation for it means that if the reoccupied *Erebus* with very short supplies, wintered there from 1848-1849, then the crew considerably aided their survival by adopting the Inuit way of life and spent the winter hunting seals.

An area on Imnguyaaluk Island much contaminated by seal oil from blubber cooking fires would have been a central camp to which the seals were brought for butchering and eating. It is interesting to note that the crew did not adopt the Inuit method of eating the seal meat raw, but clung to their western method of cooking using blubber fires, presumably out of fear of getting parasites - probably on the advice of the ships doctors.

The Inuit say the ship was iced in and unable to move. They met with the white men and remembered some of the names they had given them. One white man was known as 'meetik' or 'duck' and another as 'Qoitoyok' or 'one who pees in his bed at night', or 'the great pisser' because he was sick. The white men showed the Inuit some papers – perhaps maps.

Frank Analok's testimony - a camp on Imnguyaaluk Island, 1849-1850

Testimony about an occupied ship within sight of the tent at Terror Bay has been strengthened by several recently collected Inuit testimonies gathered by Dorothy Harley Eber from the Inuit of Gjoa Haven - the small modern settlement on south-east coast of King William Island. Some testimony has identified a campsite on Imnguyaaluk Island - the nearer of the two Royal Society Islands to Cape Crozier:

> These people stayed on the island: that is proved by the fact that the ground is soiled by the rendered seal oil blubber. These people who stayed on the island used the seal oil for heat.

Frank Analok, the source of this information puts the location on the south coast of Imnguyaaluk (the smaller and more northerly of the two Royal Geographical Society Islands) at a distance of only twenty-three miles from Terror Bay.

The site is identified because the ground there is saturated with oil produced by burning seal blubber for cooking and heat. After the first three years of the expedition, the ships supplies and coal were largely exhausted, the hot water system on *Erebus* could barely be used. Also candles and lamp oil might have been largely used up. So the men cooked ashore using seal blubber stoves and may have had to use blubber lamps below decks on *Erebus*. They and their clothing would have become black and filthy with 'blubber soot'. This problem will be further discussed later in the testimony of the 'black men'.

A summer hunt with the Inuit in Utjulik Bay, 1848 or 1849

The summer of 1847was very cold and the Inuit reported very poor hunting and the ships were not released from the Beaufort ice stream. However, in 1848 or 1849 their fortunes changed and the remanned *Erebus* was released and worked south. When she arrived south of the Royal Geographical Society Islands, she entered the hunting grounds of the Inuit. With the improvement of the weather, summer hunting became successful once more. There is testimony to suggest cooperation and joint hunting with the Inuit. Because of the short food supplies in the ships, survival now depended on learning to hunt Inuit style.

Inuit testimony describes a joint hunting expedition that took place one summer and that the guns of the expedition hunters made a very big difference to the result. This joint hunting trip probably took place in summer 1848 or 1849 after the two disasterously cold years. With *Erebus* south of Cape Crozier for the winter of 1848-9, the ship was in the area known as Utjulik, famous for seal hunting in winter. This led to the reoccupation crew successfully summer hunting caribou and winter hunting seals and making friends with the Inuit. Testimony also describes a non-Inuit type dog that was probably 'Neptune' a Newfoundland brought aboard the expedition ships from England. This dog was used by the *Erebus* hunters to locate seal's breathing holes. Testimony of a joint hunt was obtained by Hall in his 1866 meeting with Kok-lee-arng-nun. The validity of this testimony in terms of referring to the Franklin expedition is discussed by Woodman:

> Kok-lee-arng-nun was a 'big boy' when very many men from the ships hunted Took-too (caribou). They had guns, and knives with long handles, and some of the party hunted the caribou on the ice; killing so many that they made a line across the whole bay of Ook-goo-lik.

Utjulik (Ootgoolik) is a large area where the bearded seal lives and was hunted by the Inuit in winter. It extends from the Royal Geographical

Society Islands, along south-west coast of King William Island, includes the Adelaide Peninsula and extends westwards to include Jenny Lind Island. This tale can be placed in early July or August 1848, 1849 or 1850, when the caribou arrive.

Tommy Anguttitauruq's testimony – a small crew who permitted looting of the ship, 1849-1850

There is also testimony collected by Dorothy Harley Eber from Tommy Anguttitauruq that may relate to the ship at Imnguyaaluk:

> In the later winter when the days were getting longer, the Inuit were seal hunting and they found people on a ship. This was way before Inuit in this region knew anything about white people. They did not know who these people were, what race they were – they only knew they were human. These Inuit people started taking stuff out of the ship – taking out metal and wood, anything they could put their hands on – while the ship was unable to leave. The white men didn't do anything, just watched. Maybe there were too many of these Inuit people – or maybe they were aggressive. We don't know who these people were – whether they were Netsilikmiut from Boothia or King William Island, Keelenikmiut from Victoria Island, or Iluiliqmiut from Queen Maud Gulf mainland.

This is an interesting story. It seems that most of the able-bodied crew were away from the ship (probably seal hunting) when the Inuit visited. Perhaps it was only a small watch crew of the weakest and sick left aboard at the time. It would have been possible to fire a few shots to warn off the Inuit. However this did not happen. The story is therefore likely to have occurred late in the visit of the ship, long after it was realised that she would probably never be released by the ice. By this time the crew would be feeding themselves mainly by hunting. The moral of the few crew may not have been high and they did not want to antagonise the Inuit, wanting only friendly relations. So they permitted them to take things from the ship. A ship going nowhere didn't need all of its equipment

Was a boat sent north for help?

With the reoccupied *Erebus* once more frozen into the ice, Captain Crozier would have been anxious to increase the chances of survival of the remaining crew. A call might be made for volunteers to take a boat during the summer thaw and try to return to Lancaster Sound and Baffin Bay, where whaling ships might be found and word got out about the trapped men. The Admiralty could then organise a rescue expedition.

There is some indication that such an attempt to send a boat back along the route the expedition had followed did take place, but failed. In 1993, a private expedition 'Lady Franklin Memorial Expedition' discovered the remains of what appeared to be a Franklin era whaleboat at Back Bay on Prince of Wales Island. Most of the wood and any contents had been removed, presumably by the Inuit. But the keel and stem post were intact and of similar dimensions and form to the boats supplied to the Franklin expedition. The site has not been examined by archaeologists and no bones or other artefacts are known, so that a provenance of the Franklin expedition cannot be proved. However, the position of the boat is where it might be expected, if a boat was following in reverse the route of the expedition. This would be north along Franklin Strait and through Peel Sound. The bid, if it occurred, probably failed when Peel Sound was found to be filled with ice.

Michael Angottitauruq's testimony - The 'Fireplace Trail' (Note: surname spelled differently to his brother Tommy)

Another piece of evidence for a ship wintering in the Royal Society Islands is described by Dorothy Harley Eber as 'The Fireplace Trail'. Eber records how today the population of Gjoa Haven is very well aware of the loss of the Franklin expedition and with their sharp eyes have since the 1980s been identifying the sites of blubber fires. Eber has named it 'The Fireplace Trail'. The Inuit do not waste blubber in fires and believe them to have been made by the Franklin expedition.

At the end of July and early August when the ground is snow-free, the sites of blubber fires are distinct because of the presence of 'oil slicks' in the sand. This is a place where the sand has been impregnated with hot oil from a blubber fire. The oil congeals in the ground to form a patch about two feet in diameter with the form of an inverted cone. [Note the author has seen similar structures in the Rub Al Khali Desert of Arabia, where Bedouin have carried out oil changes on their Toyotas. The waste oil sinks into the sand and then wind erosion exhumes oil-bound sand 'sculptures'].

Eber shows a map of the locations of the presently known structures. They are well developed on the Royal Geographical Society Island where the ship wintered, on two small islands on the north-west margin of the Adelaide Peninsula (Aveomavik and Enogeiaqtuq) and a third on the sand spit at Ogle Point at the entrance to the estuary of Back's Great Fish River.

The remains on Aveomavik were associated with the skeletal remains of three men. The area of the blubber fires is also the best Inuit hunting area for the bearded seal in spring time.

The distribution of the Fireplace Trail suggests that seal hunting and cooking with blubber was not only carried out on Imnguyaaluk Island but also later when the reoccupied *Erebus* was near O'Reilly Island in Wilmot and Compton Bay on the east side of the Adelaide Peninsula. Associated human skulls, if non-Inuit, suggest that life was very precarious and not everyone survived.

Emergence of 'The Hunter'

The 'Fireplace Trail' provides heartening evidence that some of the crew of the reoccupied *Erebus* spent much of their winters hunting the bearded seal in the vicinity of the ship. This area was a favourite for the Inuit who would spend from January to June on the ice. In order to succeed, the Franklin expedition hunters must have befriended the Inuit who taught them how to winter hunt for seals with a dog. A dog was essential to find the air holes, where the seals rose to breath and which could be covered with snow. It seems the reoccupied *Erebus* was visited many times by the Inuit including Ook-bar-loo's family and Kok-lee-arng-nun and family. Perhaps friendly cooperation and joint hunting began with the joint summer hunt of caribou and continued into winter seal hunting. Captain Crozier with his knowledge of Inuktituk, probably played a major role in this.

In any small group of men in difficult and challenging circumstances, one or two will emerge as the leader of a group as having the best skills. So 'The Fireplace Trail' can be argued as providing evidence of the emergence of a chief hunter, one who would lead a team of men willing to face the rigours of the outdoors. He will be referred to here as 'The Hunter.' His distinctive trail can be found in other Inuit testimony described shortly.

One such hunter had emerged on a previous Arctic expedition. This was Graham Gore, then mate, who accompanied Sir George Back on the 1836 Arctic expedition of *Terror*. He proved to be an excellent hunter, who provided the officers with a haunch of venison for their 1836 Christmas dinner. Unfortunately, the 1848 record refers to him as 'the late'. So it is likely that another member of the crew became the leading hunter.

The death and military burial of Captain Crozier (spring 1850)

Testimony of an expedition leader's death was given to Hall in April 1866 by an old Inut named Kok-le-arng-nun. Confusion exists about the death of this officer. Charles Francis Hall believed it referred to Sir John Franklin and his second in command 'Aglooka' or Captain Crozier. However, Woodman believes that there was no contact between the Franklin Expedition and the Inuit until after the 1848 retreat. He believes the testimony of Kok-lee-arng-nun is describing the two years that *Erebus* lay at anchor near Cape Crozier. In this reconstruction new testimony gathered by Eber, places the ship as anchored at the Royal Geographical Society Island of Imnguyaaluk. The great Esh-e-mut-ta died in the spring of the second year – spring 1850. Woodman made an excellent case that the great Captain or Esh-e-mut-ta of Kok-lee-arng-nun's testimony was Captain Crozier, and Aglooka (long strider) was another officer.

Kok-lee-arng-nun's testimony by Hall

In 1866 Hall on route to King William Island encountered a group of Inuit led by Kok-lee-arng-nun. Hall believed that he was hearing of Franklin and Crozier before the 1848 retreat rather than Crozier and Fitzjames after the 1848 retreat

> ... it was learned that these Inuits had been at onetime on board of the ships of too-loo-ark (the great Esh-e-mut-ta, Sir John Franklin), and had their tupiks on the ice alongside of him during the spring and summer... After the first summer and the first winter, they saw no more of Too-loo-ark, then Ag-loo-ka (Crozier) was the Esh-e-mut-ta.

Major Laughlin Taylor Burwash's record

There is further Inuit testimony that describes the military burial of an officer of the Franklin Expedition, with the simultaneous burial of paper records in adjacent vaults. It is the only testimony of an officer's burial with a military salute being fired.

Major Burwash (1873 to 1940) was a well-known Canadian Arctic explorer. He graduated in Mining Engineering from the University of Toronto and had his first career as Administrator of the Yukon Territory during the Yukon gold rush. In 1915 he joined the Canadian Overseas Expeditionary Force for the First World War. Returning as Major Burwash, he spent from 1925 to 1930 working for the Canadian and Territorial Government making three trips to the Canadian Arctic. The purpose of these trips was first to see what could be discovered of the lost Franklin expedition in particular the ship wrecks, second to record Inuit life and third mineral exploration.

He photographed over 2000 miles of Arctic coastline including the area of the North Magnetic Pole. He searched King William Island and brought back Franklin relics mainly from the camp site at Crozier's Landing. These included fragments of a linen tent, rope of various sizes, a small barrel stave, a fragment of Welsh coal and a rusty knife blade. A photograph of Major Burwash with his Franklin relics is shown in Potter's recent book.

Major Burwash paid particular attention to the Jamme Report (based on information supplied by whaling Captain Peter Bayne). The testimony did not come to light until 1930 in the 'Jamme document' that was sold to the United States Government. A Mr George Jamme had met an old man called Captain Peter Bayne who, long before with a colleague Pat Coleman and three others, were hired for 1867 to 1868 by Charles Francis Hall, from a whaling ship as hunters. Bayne had learned from Inuit friends of a story of a Franklin officer's burial. Hall was informed but in a dispute with his hunters, shot and killed Pat Coleman, so that Bayne and the others returned to the whaling ships. Bayne's story, including a map of a camp and the burial area, were written up as the Jamme document. The latter was of great interest to Major Laughlin Taylor Burwash who cited large parts of it. The report included the testimony, describes the burial of a great captain in a fissure sealed with cement (believed by Bayne to be Sir John Franklin's burial) along with cement vaults containing the missing expedition records at Victory Point (named on the Jamme map).

Burwash included in his lengthy report 'Canada's Western Arctic,' extracts from the Jamme Report including a summary of Inuit testimony. A single paragraph appears to report on three different incidents that occurred at what Burwash believed to be the campsite and grave area. The paragraph has been broken to separate the three events:

> Many of the white men came ashore and camped there during the summer; that the camp had one big tent and several smaller ones; that Crozier (Aglooka) came here some times, and he had seen and talked with him; that seal were plentiful the first year, and sometimes the white men went with the natives and shot seal with their guns; that ducks and geese were also plentiful, and the white men shot many;
>
> that some of the white men were sick in the big tent; and died there, and were buried on the hill back of the camp;
>
> that one man died on the ships and was brought ashore and buried on the hill near where the others were buried; that this man was not buried

in the ground like the others, but in an opening in the rock, and his body covered over with something that, 'after a while was all same stone'; that he was out hunting seal when this man was buried, but other natives were there, and saw, and told him about it, and the other natives said that 'many guns were fired.

The above testimony was interpreted by Woodman to refer to the years 1849 and 1850 when *Terror* was anchored off Erebus Bay. In this interpretation it is *Erebus*, anchored off Imnguyaalik Island west of Terror Bay, because of Eber's new testimony. The timing is probably 1848 to 1850 because the description of joint hunting with the Inuit when seals and birds were plentiful was not the case in 1847 – the year with no summer.

Bayne figured the camp to have been about a fourth of a mile back from the beach, and about the same distance south of where the ship's boats usually landed; that it was situated on a flat-topped mound near the base of a low ridge; that the crest of the ridge was not very wide and was formed of projecting rocks; and that the slope on the other side faced south-east. The Jamme Report continued:

> ...here were several cemented vaults – one large one, and a number of small ones; that the natives thought that these latter contained only papers, for many papers were brought ashore – some blew away in the wind, but others were buried. These natives had seen a number of the dead white men since that time, whose bodies lay as they had died, now frozen in the snow. Bayne and Spearman drew maps and got the natives to try and locate the camp and the graves and the ridge with respect to the beach. The sketch attached is made by the writer (Jamme) from memory from a map Captain Bayne had amongst his papers, but which cannot be located now.

Burwash in 1930 with colleagues, examined Victory Point carefully and failed to find any cairns or graves. He concluded that the area mapped as Victory Point in the Jamme Report and map was incorrect. The death of Sir John Franklin occurred at a time when 'all was well' with the expedition and the date is known from the 1848 record. As Woodman has pointed out, the Inuit did not witness early burials of officers. The military burial and associated vaults with paper records, is likely to be much later and is believed today to be the funeral of Captain Crozier in 1849-1850.

The sketch map of the camp site including the graves, shown in the Jamme report, was reproduced by both Burwash and Woodman. It shows a ridge oriented east-west. However a glance at the Google Earth images of the area shows all the ridges on north-west King William Island are oriented

NW-SE. Cooper noted that Victory Point is named on the Jamme map, but the morphology of the map is quite unlike it, where raised limestone beach ridges rise inland parallel to the coast. Cooper noted that the map could also fit the campsite near Cape Felix. To date however neither Sir John Franklin's nor Captain Crozier's graves have yet been identified. However, the reinterpretation of Woodman that the Jamme Report military burial is of Captain Crozier along with vaults of records suggest to him that the location might be in the Erebus Bay area, offshore of which he believes the two ships had drifted by that time. However, under the present reconstruction using the later testimony of Eber, the camp is believed to be situated on the south part of Imnguyaalik Island. Interestingly, Google Earth images show that the beach ridges here run east to west.

Shortly before Sir John Frankin died, the expedition was in a state described by Commander Fitzjames (1847 Record) as 'All well'. There would have been no reason to bury the expedition records at that time, as there would be every expectation of getting them back to England when the ships were released. However in 1850 after five years in the ice with the reoccupied *Erebus* at anchor for two years off Imnguyaalik Island awaiting help, and at least a half of the crew dead nearby, the death of Captain Crozier would have been a final blow. The hopes of rescue were all but abandoned and burial of the expedition records to be found by future searchers would be very appropriate. It was a sign that the remaining men now had little hope of escape.

New testimony since Woodman's books by Dorothy Harley Eber indicates that a remanned ship (now identified as *Erebus*) wintered not in Erebus Bay but on the south side of the Royal Geographical Society Islands. The Inuit of Gjoa Haven have identified oil slicks where Franklin survivors cooked seal meat at a campsite on the adjacent Imnguyaaluk Island. Searchers for Captain Crozier's grave and the cement vaults of records might move from Erebus Bay to the south end of Imnguyaalik Island.

17: THE 1850 RETREAT

The most famous piece of Inuit testimony is that first collected by Dr. John Rae in 1854. It described how four years previously, a group of Inuit were hunting seals in the Washington Bay area on the west coast of King William Island, when they encountered a group of European men who were hauling a boat on a sledge with a sail raised. They were accompanied by other men hauling a loaded sledge. This observation was long taken to mean that the meeting was a part of the 1848 retreat. However, Woodman first realised that the encounter probably took place in 1850 and that there was a much longer and more complex history to the lost expedition. Testimony stated that the 1850 retreat was heading for Repulse Bay (Iwillik). Their route would be south following the 1848 retreat as far as Chantrey Inlet – a distance of some 186 miles, and then a straight line march of 267 miles to the east. In contrast, the straight-line distance to Fort Providence on the Great Slave Lake would have been 683 miles. In this reconstruction the 1850 retreat begins at Imnguyaaluk Island, so the encounter at Washington Bay occurred after the men had marched thirty-one miles.

Dr. John Rae's 1854 report

This is the classic encounter first reported by Dr. John Rae. His report will be scrutinised later, when it can be seen to be an interesting composite of many Inuit testimonies. What is remarkable is how much data Dr. Rae was able to gather from the Inuit of the Pelly Bay area on the east side of the Boothian Peninsula, some 150 miles from the line of the Franklin retreat. The Inuit who provided the information to Dr. Rae had not encountered the Franklin Expedition, but heard only of it 'through the grapevine' and were able to trade for useful Franklin relics. In the Rae version, the meeting was believed to have occurred four winters previously (1850) with a party of about forty 'white men' who were hauling a boat on a sledge and camping gear on another sledge. The following year thirty bodies were reported as found on the American continent and a further five on some islands.

McClintock's Report:

> At the time of our interview with the natives of King William Island, Petersen was inclined to think that the retreat of the crews took place in the fall of the year, some of the men in boats, and others walking along the shore.

Tuk-ke-ta and Ow-wer's testimony of the meeting near Washington Bay

The most complete and detailed account of this meeting is presented by David Woodman in his meticulous fifteen-year research work 'Unravelling the Franklin Mystery – Inuit Testimony'. He obtained the fullest account by travelling to the Smithsonian Institution in Washington and re-examining the original notebooks of Charles Francis Hall. His account was found in the Hall Collection, Fieldnotes, Book No.38, dated the eighteenth of May 1869 and was collected from Tuk-ke-ta and Ow-wer. The report is remarkably detailed, including the names and descriptions of the retreating crews, so that Hall believed he had identified the leading officer as Captain Crozier (Aglooka).

Woodman's treatment of this subject is excellent throughout and cannot be bettered. Interestingly, Woodman settles for forty white men at the encounter. In the classic reconstruction of the Victorians, this large party was believed to be the remainder of the large party that retreated south from the ships in 1848. It is also widely believed to be the same party that mainly perished (about thirty bodies) on the American continent at what the Schwatka party would call Starvation Cove. The number of skeletons found did not stand up to Woodman's careful reinvestigation of the Inuit testimony and more recent discoveries of skeletal parts do not support this. Perhaps only six to ten men perished under an upturned boat at Starvation Cove on the Adelaide Peninsula. The following account taken from Woodman with permission, uses the spellings and grammar of Hall.

> Tuk-ke-ta and Ow-wer now tell that they with Too-shoo-art-thar-u and Mong-er, the latter now at Neitchille, were on the west shore of King William Island with their families sealing, & this a long time ago. They were getting ready to move – the time in the morning & the sun high – when Tuk-ke-ta saw something in the distance on the smooth ice that looked white & thought it was a bear. The company had got all ready to start travelling on the land. Soon as Tuk-ke-ta saw this something white, he told his companions of it, when all waited, hoping it was a bear. As they watched, the white object grew larger, for it was coming down towards them. They saw the white thing moving along in the direction of the coast, turning in

a kind of circling way just as the little bay turned. At length they began to see many black objects moving along with what they had first espied as white in the distance. The object that they 1st had seen as white proved to be a sail raised on the boat & as this got nearer saw this sail shake in the wind. On seeing what they did, the object grew plainer and they thought of white men and began to be afraid.

As the company of men (strangers) & what they were drawing got quite near, 2 men came on ahead of all & were walking on the ice & getting near where the Innuits were standing looking out, which was on the land, the 2 men (Koblunas) came walking up to where they were. Too-shoo-art-thar-u and Ow-wer started to meet them, walking there on the ice. When they came to the crack in the ice, they stopped for the two white men to come up. Then the 2 white men came close to Ow-wer and Too-shoo-art-thar-u. One had a gun which he carried in his arms. The crack in the ice separated the meeting natives. The man that carried the gun stopped behind – a little back, while the other man came as close up to Ow-wer & Too-shoo-art-thar-u as the crack in the ice would allow him. The man that came up to the crack had nothing in his hands or on his shoulder. As he stopped, he cried out 'Chi-mo'. The first man that came up then spoke to the man a little behind, when he laid the gun down and came up at once alongside the 1st man.

The 1st man then showed that he had an oo-loo when he stooped down beside the ice crack which divided the white men from the Innuits & began cutting the ice with a peculiar kind of circling motion with the oo-loo (Western mincing-knife or Innuit woman's knife). This peculiar motion now showed by Ow-wer with his oo-loo on the snow floor of the igloo. At the same time, or rather right after this man had made these 'chippings' or 'scratchings' (as you call it) on the ice, he put his hand up to his mouth and lowered it all the way down his neck and breast, as if to say he wanted to get something to eat. Then the two white men moved along the one side, till they found a place where they could pass over to the 2 Innuits – Ow-er and Too-shoo-art-thar-u. On the 2 Kabloonas (white men) getting to them, the 1st man, who was Aglooka, spoke to them, saying, 'Man-nik-too-me' at the same time stroking 1st one and then the other down the breast, and also shook hands with each, repeating 'Man-nik-too-me' several times. The other man with Aglooka did all the same in stroking the breast, shaking hands & speaking 'Man-nik-too-me.'

'After this salutation Aglooka tried to speak with them, but of all he then said, they could only make out one word I-wil-ik. Here some 15- 20 minutes have been spent in Ow-wer's describing in pantomimic way just how Aglooka appeared and repeating his words.

Aglooka pointed with his hand to the southward & at the same time repeating the word I-wil-ik. The Innuits could not understand whether he wanted them to show him the way there or that he was going there. He then made a motion to the northward & spoke the word 'oo-me-en', making them understand there were 2 ships in that direction; which had, as they supposed been crushed by the ice. As Aglooka pointed to the N., drawing his hand & arm from that direction he slowly moved his body in a falling direction and all at once dropped his head sideways into his hand, at the same time making a kind of combination of whirring, buzzing and wind blowing noise. This the pantomimic representation of ships being crushed by the ice. While Aglooka was talking and making motions, the other men Innuits came to where they were.

After this first interview the two men went ashore with the Innuits. While Aglooka was trying to talk with the Innuits (Ow-wer and Too-shoo-art-thar-u), the party with the boat and one other sledge passed by going a little lower down to a point or cape of the little bay where they then were. On getting ashore Aglooka wanted everything – every pack opened & opened them himself, the dogs saddle bag packs, the women's packs and the men's packs, for everything was ready for making a journey across the land. Aglooka wanted meat & for this he wanted every pack opened. The Innuits were all willing he should do as he did.

After each man Innuit had given him some seal meat, it was all put on a (one) dog's back & then by the request of Aglooka all 4 Innuit men with the dog laden with meat went down with Aglooka and the man with him to where the men and the boat were, the men erecting a tent. As they approached the tent, one man came out to meet them. Aglooka spoke to the men when he and the Innuits were near the tent. The men alongside the tent and the men alongside of the boat stood in line holding their arms and open hands above their heads, showing that they had nothing (that is no weapons) about them.

Then Aglooka spoke to one of his men, a short man with a narrow face, prominent nose. Then this man tried to talk with the Innuits. (Jo & Hannah who are my interpreters are almost certain this man was Alexander MacDonald, Assistant Surgeon of *Terror* who had visited the Arctic before). The man who came out to meet Aglooka & Innuits was a tall man and did not laugh or smile. 'Looked kind 'o ugly' as Jo expressed himself. The Innuits Ow-wer and Tuk-ke-ta think he looked so because he was afraid.

The small man that Aglooka told to speak with the Innuits could talk so that they could understand him better than they could Aglooka.

He told the names of Aglooka & the man that was with him on 1st meeting the Innuits, also asked the Innuits their names. Told these the name of one white man was Too-loo-a & another Ill-kern (perhaps Royal Marine Private William Pilkington of *Erebus*). The short man had whiskers and a moustache.

The Innuits took down their tents early the next morning & as they proceeded on their journey passed by Aglooka's tent. Aglooka was standing on the outside of his tent when the Innuits passed it. Aglooka tried to make them stop – put his hand to his mouth and spoke he word 'Netchuk' or 'Nest-chuk' (seal). But the Innuit were in a hurry – did not know the men were starving…

After leaving Aglooka and party never saw anything more of them till some were found starved to death… Too-shoo-art-thar-u never saw Aglooka after the time Ow-wer and Tuk-ke-ta saw him. Aglooka to their knowledge never gave Too-shoo-art-thar-u any papers or package.

The testimony recorded by Hall contains descriptions of some of the surviving expedition men:

Aglooka (Crozier) about my (Hall's) height, hair nearly like mine (auburn) but a little darker than mine & did not stand erect but with head and shoulders dropping forward a little (Something like Captain Christopher Chapel, as Ou-e-la and Jack say) – no gray hair, a scar mark across the small or indent (?) of the nose.

Too-loo-a stood erect, strait up, so strait that a little bent back – that is breasted out, having slight curve inward from hands to shoulders. His hair a little grey. Aglooka's body never found among the dead. Therefore Innuits have always supposed that he got home to his country. Too-loo-a's body found on the isle Kee-u-na & was one of the 5 found there. His skull was seen there of late years with grey hair & with whiskers adhering to the skull.

Hall and his party thought that one of the men who spoke some Inuktitut might be *Terror*'s Assistant Surgeon Alexander Macdonald. The possibility of another being Marine private William Pilkington has been mentioned. Evidence will be presented later that this 'Aglooka' might have been *Terror*'s Marine Sergeant Solomon Tozer. The older Too-lo-a might have been *Terror*'s Ice Master Thomas Blanky (*Erebus* Ice Master James Reid has been provisionally identified as the large body in the stern of the boat found by the McClintock expedition in Erebus Bay after the 1848 retreat).

Other lesser versions of the encounter were collected by Hall and show how much variation in detail exists as the tale was obviously widely passed around by the Inuit. The interest here is in the number of white men met during the encounter. This is because the Inuit estimates of higher numbers are unreliable and reported as 'many'. The other versions in the compilation by Professor Nourse give far less detail, each with different numbers of men in the sighting. Two of these are given below. In addition, Dorothy Harley Eber has collected several versions from the Inuit of Gjoa Haven between 1994 and 2008. However, these reports have been so embellished over time that they are not considered here.

Hall's report of May 8th 1869 of the Washington Bay meeting

The first time Ag-loo-ka came he did not come inside; next morning he entered one of the tents of the four families who were there encamped by the west shore of King William's Land, a little way above Cape Herschel (as pointed out on the chart). His telescope was hung about his neck. Ag-loo-ka and his men had come along, the men dragging a large sledge laden with a boat and a smaller sledge with camp material and provision. Close by the Inuit they erected a tent; some of the men slept in the boat, which was left on the sea ice, all the snow being off the land. On Ag-loo-ka's first meeting with the Inuit he had a gun in his hand. On seeing him lay it down, the Inuit laid down their spears. Then Crozier walked up and said, 'Tij-mo?' 'Man-ik-too-mee?' at the same time brushing his hand down their breasts and shaking hands, Kob-lu-na-way. The time was late in spring – July, Joe and Hannah said it must have been, for the sea-ice was nearly ready to break up; the sun was in sight all the time; the ducks, now-yers (gulls), &c., all in abundance in the pools and lakes. Tee-kee-ta saw Aglooka kill two geese, and his men were busy shooting. Ag-loo-ka tried very hard to talk to the Inuit, but did not say much to them. He had a little book as he sat in Ow-er's tent and wrote notes. The full meaning of what he said about the ice destroying the ship and his men dying was afterward understood. He ate a piece of seal raw, about as big as the fore and next finger to the first joint. He wore no sword. He then said he was going to Iwillik (Repulse Bay), making motions with his hands in that direction. One of his men was very fat, the others all poor; one man with one of his upper teeth gone, and one with marks on the saddle of his nose, and one man squinting or cross-eyed. The Inuit left them although supposing that they were abandoning starved men.

Hall reproved these men sharply for leaving Crozier. Does it not, however, seem probable that those few natives feared that Crozier's large party would starve them out? Hall had difficulty estimating the number of men sighted dragging a sledge on the south side of Washington Bay by the Inuit. As he explains:

> I now got Ow-wer & Tuk-ke-ta to try to tell me how many men were in Aglooka's party when they met it. They say they cannot tell, they were so many. One man a very short man. One man very fat all over. One man with a single upper front tooth gone. One man with very sore bleeding gums – lower gums. One man cross eyed. Ow-wer and Tuk-ke-ta on my getting 4 men to hold up their hands, showing 40 fingers and thumbs, say that they would think perhaps 5 more – that is 4 fingers and a thumb more would represent about the numbers of souls in Aglooka's party.

Further information was gathered by Hall on the eighth of May 1869 from an unspecified source:

> Crozier had a little book as he sat in Ow-wer's tent, and wrote notes. He said, while in the tent, 'Ag-loo-ka wonger', patting his own breast, outside, he said he was going to I-wil-lik (Repulse Bay), making motions with his hand in that direction. No dog with Aglooka's company, now-yers (gulls), geese and ducks hanging to the boat. One man very fat, the others all poor. One man with Crozier in Ow-wer's tent said, Tier-kin wonger. One man with one of his upper teeth gone, and one with marks on the indent or saddle of his nose. Trouble thought to be among the men; but not so. They were putting up the tent and stopped, staring at the Innuits. When Crozier spoke to them, they at once resumed their work. The Innuits left Crozier and men encamped there, and moved inland, suspicious that they abandoned starving men. Crozier described to them the ice destroying his vessel, his men dying, the full meaning comprehended afterwards by the Innuits. An awning over the boat, roof-like. No sword worn by Crozier. In a little bay were Crozier's party when the Innuits first saw them. One man cross eyed or squinted. Same boat found on mainland, (or rather isle, as the tides high on the west side of inlet of Point Richardson).

Crozier, while in Ow-wer's tent, ate a piece of seal, raw, about as big as fore and next fingers to first joint.

Ahlangyah's 1879 testimony of the meeting near Washington Bay

Schwatka in 1879, thirty-one years after the ships were abandoned, heard evidence of another version of the Washington Bay meeting:

> Ahlangyah pointed out the eastern coast of Washington Bay as the spot where she, in company with her husband, and two other men with their wives, had seen ten white men dragging a sledge with a boat on it many years ago. There was another Inuit with them who did not go near the white men.
>
> The sledge was on the ice, and a wide crack separated them from the white men at the interview. The women went on shore, and the men awaited the white people at the crack on the ice. Five of the white men put up a tent on the shore, and five remained with boat on the ice. The Inuit put up a tent not far from the white men, and they stayed together here five days. During this time the Inuit killed a number of seals on the ice and gave them to the white men. They gave her husband a chopping knife. He was the one who had the most intercourse with the white crew. The knife is now lost, or broken and worn out. She has not seen it for a long time.
>
> Some of the white men were very thin, and their mouths were dry and hard and black. They had no fur clothing on. When asked if she remembered by what names the white men were called, she said one of them was called 'Agloocar', and another 'Toolooah'. The latter seemed to be the chief, and it was he who gave the chopping-knife to her husband... another one was called 'Doktook' (Doctor). 'Toolooah' was a little older than the others, and had a large black beard, mixed with gray. He was bigger than any of the others – 'a big broad man'. 'Agloocar' was smaller, and had a brown beard about four or five inches below his chin (motioning with her hand). 'Doc-took' was a short man with a big stomach and red beard, about the same length as 'Agloocar's'. All three wore spectacles, not snow goggles, but, as the interpreters said, all the same seko (ice).
>
> At the end of five days they all started for Adelaide Peninsula, fearing that the ice, which was very rotten, might not let them across. They started at night, because then, the sun being low, the ice would be a little frozen. The white men followed, dragging their heavy sledge and boat, and could not cross the rotten ice as fast as the Inuit, who halted and waited for them at Gladman's Point. The Inuit could not cross to the mainland, the ice was too rotten, and they remained in King William's Land all summer. They never saw the white men again, though they waited at Gladman's Point fishing in

the neighbouring lakes, going back and forth between the shore and lakes nearly all summer, and then went to the eastern shore near Matty Island.

There is some confirmation that the Aglooka at the famous Washington Bay meeting was not Captain Crozier. This is because he was unable to communicate with the Inuit and got another man to take over the conversation. Captain Crozier with his previous experience in the Arctic had learned some of the Inuit language (Inuktitut).

An officer's report of the retreat

Perhaps the most interesting version of these tales is that told by the leader of three or four survivors who arrived on the Boothian Peninsula. The Inuit knew this man as Aglooka and Hall believed he was Captain Crozier. What is of particular interest is the number of men stated to be in the party that set out from Terror Bay. The number was given as seventeen:

> The native stated that when he was a young man in his father's hut three men came over the land towards Repulse Bay and that one of them was a great captain. The other two lived some little time in his father's hut, and he showed Captain Adams the spot on the chart where they were buried. The Esquimaux, continued his narrative, said that seventeen persons started from two vessels which had been lost far to the westward but only three had been able to survive the journey to his father's hut.

The conclusion drawn here is that after two years in the ice near Imnguyaaluk Island and the death of Captain Crozier, a party of either ten, seventeen or forty-five men set out hauling one boat and a sledge with camping equipment. The party was mainly made up of men of *Terror* and they were heading for Repulse Bay. The party was probably led by Ice Master Thomas Blanky and Marine Sergeant Solomon Tozer. In the party were probably Assistant Surgeon Alexander Macdonald and from *Erebus* marine William Pilkington. A boat with the precious box of records was found the following year by the Inuit at Starvation Cove on the mainland near the entrance to the estuary of Back's Great Fish River with fewer than ten bodies of men who perished under the boat. The Inuit believed this was the boat seen the year before at Washington Bay.

Another interesting conclusion is possible from the detailed account given by Woodman of the classic meeting near Washington Bay. The retreating crews spoke almost no Inuit language and communication was mainly by pantomime. This is surprising as it is known from the Fitzjames Journal that when the ships were at the Whale Fish Islands of Greenland, Assistant Surgeon Goodsir of *Erebus*, had started to compile a dictionary of Inuit words. Clearly this operation had ceased and the vocabulary was obviously not available to the retreating crews. This would suggest that Goodsir was probably amongst the nine officers who died before the retreat began, although a facial reconstruction on a skull found at Tulloch Point has been tentatively identified as that of Goodsir. Similarly, Captain Crozier, who spoke Inuktitut, was also much missed for his communication skills.

Remains at the southern entrance to Washington Bay

Learmouth records that a skull and some bones were found on the southern entrance to Washington Bay, just to the north of Cape Herschel in late June 1942. The remains were taken to Gjoa Haven (Map II).

Scattered remains on the south-western part of King William Island

The 1850 retreat appears to have continued south-east along the coast of King William Island, probably until they reached the narrowest point in Simpson Strait. This is the crossing place known a Maleruakik. It is a vital place to the Inuit who waited here each year to ambush the caribou as they arrive and leave King William Island. Here, the retreat split into two parts. One group led by the older officer described as Too-loo-a led the men south along the coast of King William Island. Men died all along the route and a scatter of thirteen graves has been found along the line of retreat on the south western and southern shores of King William Island. This party carried the inflatable Halkett boat.

Opposite the Todd Islets the party divided again and six men went out to the islands. Too-loo-a's body with four others was found as a group on a Todd Islet where they died together. Another man died nearby on another islet. The remnants of the King William Island party, being four men led by Aglooka and carrying the Halkett boat, continued east. They arrived near Boothia later that summer where they met and were befriended by Inuit.

The other group with the wooden boat, crossed Simpson Strait onto the eastern Adelaide Peninsula and continued south. The division probably occurred because they were starving and the hunting was poor. The men were thin, ill and visibly hungry when they met the Inuit in Washington Bay. Splitting up the men increased their chances of improved hunting by increasing the search area, as well as chance encounters with the Inuit. There were several routes that could be followed to Repulse Bay. Ironically the testimony of Aglooka and the three men who arrived in the west near Boothia, reported a fight with Indians possibly in Chantrey Inlet.

The group with the boat and the precious box of records, crossed over Simpson's Strait onto the Adelaide Peninsula (a part of the American continent) presumably at the narrowest point (Maleruakik) and proceeded towards Chantrey Inlet. The retreating group left seven bodies (wearing shoes with brass screws in the soles) on the coast at Thunder Cove. The boat did not reached Chantrey Inlet and was left with six men beneath it at a low muddy inlet later called Starvation Cove by the Schwatka party. A small party moved on on foot. One body was found on the surface a few miles away. A cod fishing line with a striped cotton lure as found at Point Ogle by the Anderson search expedition.

A skeleton found in 1973 between Gladman Point and Tulloch Point

In summer 1973, a military group from the First Battalion, the Royal Canadian Regiment, using assault boats, searched some of the coast of King William Island for Franklin relics. While searching between Gladman and Tulloch Points, Corporal David Williams saw two human leg bones beside a large rock. An almost complete skeleton was recovered along with several shirt and jacket buttons. The latter were identified as of European manufacture in the mid-nineteenth century. The skeleton and artifacts are now in the Museum of Man in Ottawa. The scattered bodies show that the retreat was losing men as it proceeded. This was probably due to starvation as well as illness.

Remains at Tulloch Point

Hall in 1869 visited the area and found a skeleton after digging in snow. Hall had a cairn six feet tall built to contain the skeleton. He did not give good location details but his cairn was found on Tulloch Point by Gibson in 1931 and the disturbed bones reburied.

The Schwatka expedition in 1879 found an opened isolated grave at Tulloch Point. Gilder observed that it:

> Had been made of small stones, although larger stones were lying there, indicating the physical weakness of the retreating men.

In June and July 1931, Chief Trader Paddy Gibson, manager of the Hudson's Bay Company outpost at Gjoa Haven made a search of the south coast of King William Island looking for remains of the Franklin expedition. At Tulloch Point he found the remains of a disturbed cairn and the skeletal remains of a member of the Franklin retreat that had been interred by C.F. Hall in 1866. Gibson repaired the cairn and reinterred its scattered contents. Learmouth (1948) reports that two skulls were found on the beach just west of Tulloch Point and these were forwarded to the R.C.M.P. at Cambridge Bay, where they were buried near the grave of Patsy Klengenberg.

Remains found near the 'Peffer River' including a modern forensic investigation

Inuit led Hall in 1869, to what Hall thought was the left bank of the Peffer River within sight of a Todd Islet. Woodman has disputed the location and believes that Hall could not have reached the Peffer River as the river is further away, so the location is uncertain. There they opened a shallow grave on the Franklin line of retreat. This location is eighty miles from Imnguyaaluk Island. Only the skeleton and some rotted cloth remained. Hall collected these and took them to one of his sponsors in New York, who passed them to Admiral Inglefield of the Royal Navy who took them to England. There, famous biologist Thomas Henry Huxley wrote a report on them and submitted it to the Admiralty. Because of a gold tooth filling and the remains of a silk undervest, the remains were identified as those of an officer. The Admiralty declared them to be the remains of the late Lieutenant Henry Le Vesconte of *Erebus*, without stating how this conclusion was drawn. The remains were buried beneath the Franklin memorial at the Royal Naval College in Greenwich in 1873.

In 2009, renovations to the monument provided an opportunity to look at the skeleton with modern forensic methods and check the identification made 140 years previously. The near-complete skeleton surprisingly revealed no evidence of scurvy, or tuberculosis. Isotopic enamel of the teeth indicated a youth spent, not in Devon where Le Vesconte was raised, but in the north of Britain, suggesting the remains are not those of Le Vesconte.

A facial reconstruction (independent of existing daguerreotypes) proved on completion to be a remarkable likeness to the daguerreotype of Assistant Surgeon and Naturalist Harry Goodsir of *Erebus* (including a deep groove under the lip). Goodsir had been raised in Scotland. But other crew members had also been raised in Scotland, so the evidence is regarded as probable but not certain. The remains had been found buried on King William Island with care and wrapped in a blanket, indicating that the 1850 retreat was still in good order at this point which is at a straight line distance of ninety two miles from Imnguyaaluk Island.

The site was visited by the Schwatka expedition in 1879, and they found a cairn built by Hall with an inscription written by him and the date May the twelfth 1869.

The Inuit had reported to Gibson that there remained a second skeleton at this site. Parts of this were found by Gibson on the shore but most had been washed away.

Remains between the 'Peffer River' and Todd Islets

Hall was unable to get a sun sighting and missidentified the Peffer River so that his locations are unreliable and have been reinvestigated by Woodman. Along a fifteen-mile stretch of coastline Hall interred the remains of three other members of the Franklin expedition. When revisited by William Gibson in the summer of 1931 no traces were found.

Remains found on the east side of the mouth of the 'Peffer River'

Hall wrote:

> The graves of the two men (white) that are buried on the point of King William's Land on the east side of the mouth of the Peffer River were found by Nee-wik-tee-too, a Neitchille Innuit now dead. His widow, the old lady with shaking head at twenty-eighth encampment, whom I saw when there. The bodies buried by placing stones around and over them; the remains facing upward, and the hands had been folded in a very precise manner across the breasts of both; clothes all on; flesh all on the bones. On the back of each a suspended knife found. The bodies perfect when found; but the Innuits having left the remains unburied, after unearthing them, the foxes have eaten meat and sinews all off the bones. A tenting place of the whites close by where these two men were buried. Many needles and one nail found by Innuits at this tenting place.

In 1904 two members of Amundsen's *Gjoa* North-West Passage expedition found two skeletons of Europeans on the ground surface at Hall Point. These were reburied and a small cairn erected. These may have been the remains of the two bodies described above.

Remains on the shore of King William Island north of the Todd Islets

Hall wrote on May 11 1869:

> The grave and remains were in the same perfect methodical state when found as those at the two at the mouth of the Peffer River. This grave on

King William's Land about due north of Kee-u-na (Todd Islets). The body dug up and left by the Innuits. This white man was very large and tall, and by the state of gums and teeth was terribly sick (bad state). As In-nook-poo-zhee-jook testified.

Remains on the Todd Islets

There are five Todd islets, three are very small and two are larger with an area of about a half square mile. Five bodies of the Franklin expedition were found lying together on the top of one of the islets.

Poo-yet-ta's testimony – five bodies, one with an unopened tin of meat, on a Todd islet

Hall gathered testimony on May 11 1869, while camped on the Todd Islets (source unspecified):

> Poo-yet-ta was the Innuit who first found these remains of the five whites. The remains, some not buried, but some found lying down on the high parts of the island, all close together, and each fully dressed, flesh all on the bones, and unmutilated by animals. Next to Too-loo-a's body, was one preserved meat can. This can found by Poo-yet-ta beside the body of Too-loo-a unopened. It was opened by the Innuits and found to contain meat and much tood-noo with it. No bad smell to it. The contents eaten by the Innuits. The meat and fat very sweet and good. A jack knife found in the pocket of one of the five men.

E-vee-shuk's testimony – another description of the five bodies on a Todd islet

Hall gathered further testimony from Tuk-pee-too's wife E-vee-shuk on May 14 1869, while camped in the same place:

> I now, with Jack's assistance as interpreter, ask her two questions: Did you see anything of the men who died on this island? Answer. She has seen five skulls of the white men who died a long time ago here. Did you see Too-loo-ark? Answer. Saw the bodies of four white men in one place on the island, and of Too-loo-ark a little way from the four. When she first saw them flesh and clothing all on the men; the bodies entire; and after making tupiks near, the dogs devoured much of the flesh of the kob lu-nas. It was some time after this that she saw the five skulls she first spoke of as having seen. She saw these bodies entire one winter after Poo-yet-ta found them,

and the clothes these men had on were black, - their kum-mins (boots) those men had on were of the same kind of leather as the belt I have given to In-nook-poo-zhe-jook, tanned leather from the United States. Were these men buried? Answer. No, they were lying as they had died, on the top of the ground. Where are the skeletons now? Answer. On this island, some in one place and some in another, but all are under the snow, having tried to find them since we arrived here, but the snow covers them so deep cannot find even one bone. When snow is gone all the bones can be seen.

Hall was told of five bodies found there by the Inuit, one of which he located and interred. William Gibson, in 1931, searched the Todd Islets. On one of the larger islets near the coast he located two skulls on the highest part and on digging around found the remains of these and other bodies. On the other larger islet about two miles offshore Gibson found a single skeleton with the remains of clothing. He was a very young man with the teeth of both jaws remarkably perfect. Nearby some bones of a second skeleton were found. All skeletal remains were buried by Gibson.

The bones at Booth Point – a macabre tale

Hall, on May 13 1869 visited the narrow spit of Booth Point because the Inuit reported skeletal remains of one of the Franklin expedition there. He was shown the place but everything was hidden under a snow cover.

However, Beattie revisited Booth Point in 1981 and found the remains reported to Hall, undisturbed and on the surface. A single tent ring had a scatter of human bones near the entrance and around it. When subjected to modern forensic research, the bones revealed a macabre story. Thirty-one bone fragments were collected from an area measuring thirty by forty-five feet, centred on a single tent ring of stones. Also found with the bones were a shell button and a clay pipe stem. The bones were those of a Caucasian male aged between twenty and twenty-five years old. Pitting and scaling on the outside of the bones indicated that the young man had suffered from scurvy. The skull fragments lying around the entrance to the stone circle, showed that they had been forcibly broken and the face and both jaws and teeth were missing. The other bones were from arms and legs only. One femur bone showed three knife cuts. Beattie conclude that this was not the site where a young man had died, but rather was the site of a cannibal meal. The skull, arms and legs were the most portable body parts and had been used as a portable food source, while travelling along the south coast of King William Island.

The conclusion is that a small party of starving survivors carrying body parts for food was moving east (away from the estuary of Back's Great Fish River) across the south side of King William Island. This may have been the small party led by Marine Sergeant Solomon Tozer that carried a Halkett inflatable boat. The remains suggest that in the 1850 retreat cannibalism was used by some of the able bodied to continue the retreat when hunting failed. Inuit testimony of the meeting with four men near Boothia confirms that three of the men had been eating human flesh but their leader, who was in very poor shape, had refused to do this. In contrast, the cannibalism at the three 1848 'death camps' occurred where immobile men were left to await rescue by their colleagues who had returned to *Erebus*.

Remains on the eastern Adelaide Peninsula (American mainland) and in Chantrey Inlet (Estuary of Back's Great Fish River)

After the 1850 split up, the group with the wooden boat and the precious box of records, crossed over Simpson's Strait onto the Adelaide Peninsula (a part of the American continent) presumably at the narrowest point and proceeded towards Chantrey Inlet. The narrowest point is known to the Inuit as Maleruakik and is a key place for their survival, as they wait there each year for the caribou to arrive and depart King William Island. The retreat left seven bodies (wearing shoes with brass screws in the soles) on the coast at Thunder Cove. The retreat continued but did not reach Chantrey Inlet. The boat with six men beneath it was abandoned at a low muddy inlet later called Starvation Cove by the Schwatka party. A few stragglers moved on on foot. One body was found on the surface a few miles away.

Nenijook's testimony – seven skeletons on the eastern shore of the Adelaide Peninsula

Learmouth reported that Nenijook, Eyarituk's mother, then about seventy years old, had found when she was a small child, the skeletons of seven men partly clothed in blue serge and partly buried in sand and seaweed on a small island on the east coast of the Adelaide Peninsula. Their hard boots had nails in the soles for gripping on ice while sledge hauling. A search of the area by Learmouth failed to locate any remains. However, Learmouth discovered the remains of three men at Tikeraniyou, together with a George IV half crown and a large ivory sailor's button. The location was a point of land shaped like a crooked finger, where the land bends round to the south west between twelve and fifteen miles west of Starvation Cove. The remains were taken to Gjoa Haven and buried under the beacon there along with other Franklin Expedition bones.

The boat party at Starvation Cove

Dr. John Rae in 1854 brought back the first Franklin relics and a summary of Inuit testimony he made after interviewing Inuit at Repulse Bay for two months. In his report he describes that the bodies of some thirty persons were discovered on the continent. Some of the bodies were under a boat that had been turned over to form a shelter. The remains were first found by an Inut named Poo-yet-ta. The boat was in complete order with many men inside with their hands sawed off at the wrists lying under a tent or awning as if asleep under some blankets. No sledge was found with the boat.

Tooktocheer and her son Ogzeuckjeuwock's testimony – description of things seen at Starvation Cove

The Schwatka expedition next interviewed seventy-year-old Tooktocheer, the widow of Poo-yet-ta and her son Ogzeuckjeuwock:

> She said she had never see any of Franklin's men alive, but saw six skeletons on the main-land and an adjacent island – four on the main-land and two on the island. This she pointed out on the southern coast near ninety-five degrees west latitude. There were no graves at either place. Her husband was with her at the time, and seven other Inuits. This was when she was at the boat place west of Richardson Point. In fact, she seemed to have the two places somewhat mixed up in her mind, and Ogzeuckjeuwock took up the thread of the narrative here. In answer to a question which we asked his mother, he said he saw books at the boat place in a tin case, about two feet long and a foot square, which was fastened, and they broke it open. The case was full. Written and printed books were shown to him, and he said they were like the printed ones. Among the books he found what was probably the needle of a compass or other magnetic instrument, because he said when it touched any iron it stuck fast. The boat was right side up, and the tin case in the boat. Outside the boat he saw a number of skulls. He forgot how many, but said there were more than four. He also saw bones from legs and arms that appeared to have been sawed off. Inside the boat was a box filled with bones; the box was about the same size as the one with the books in it.

[This description seems to be of the boat found in Erebus Bay by

In-nook-poo-zhee-jook in 1861, not the overturned boat at Starvation Cove, suggesting the testimony is a mixture of several]

> He said the appearance of the bodies led the Inuits to the opinion that the white men had been eating each other. What little flesh was still on the bones was very fresh; one body had all the flesh on. The hair was light; it looked like a long body. He saw a number of wire snow goggles, and alongside the body with flesh on it was a pair of gold spectacles. (He picked out the kind of metal from several that were shown him.). He saw more than one or two pairs of such spectacles, but forgot how many. When asked how long the bodies appeared to have been dead when he saw them, he said they had probably died during the winter previous to the summer he saw them. In the boat he saw canvas and four sticks (a tent or sail), saw a number of watches, open faced; a few were gold, but most were silver. They are all lost now. They were given to the children to play with, and have been broken up and lost. One body – the one with flesh on – had a gold chain fastened to gold ear-rings, and a gold hunting-case watch with engine turned engraving attached to the chain, and hanging down about the waist. He said when he pulled the chain it pulled the head up by the ears. This body also had a gold ring on the ring finger of the right hand. It was taken off, and has since been lost by the children in the same way that the other things were lost. His reason for thinking that they had been eating each other was because the bones were cut with a knife or saw. They found one big saw and one small one in the boat; also a large red tin case of smoking tobacco and some pipes. There was no cairn there. The bones are now covered up with sand and sea weed, as they were lying just at the high-water mark. Some of the books were taken home for the children to play with, and finally torn and lost, and others lay around among the rocks until carried away by the wind and lost or buried beneath the sand.

Mangaq's son Iggiararsuk's testimony – remains at Starvation Cove

In 1926 Knud Rasmussen met an Inut called Iggiararsuk whose father Mangaq reported finding a boat with six dead men. He told Rasmussen of four places where skeletal remains of the Franklin expedition could be seen. Rasmussen located the remains of two members of the Franklin expedition identified by remnants of their uniforms. He erected a cairn over the remains. The caption of a photograph of this cairn identifies it as being at Starvation Cove.

Some of the Schwatka party, on their return march, stopped at Starvation Cove and found a skull, a small pewter medal commemorating the launch of Brunel's Great Britain in 1843, and some pieces of blanket. They also learned of a skeleton of a single man found 'five miles inland from Starvation Cove.' The remnants of associated clothing indicated that the individual was not an officer, but a seaman.

Further testimony collected by Hall on May 11 1869 (Hall spelling and grammar)

> The boat on the west side of the inlet - that is, west side of Point Richardson – was found same season of same year as remains at Kee-u-na (Todd Islets). A keg of powder found at the boat, and much of contents emptied on the ground; a gun or two found there. The nature and use of these things not known to Innuits till they saw Dr. Rae in 1854 at Pelly Bay. Poo-yet-ta had seen guns of Aglooka when at Neitchille, but did not know the nature of the black sand stuff (powder}. An igloo was blown to atoms by a little son of Poo-yet-ta and another lad, who were afterwards playing with the powder canister having some of the black stuff in it. They dropped some fire into the canister through the vent or opening, their faces were awfully burned and blackened with the explosion; no one was killed, but the igloo completely demolished.

Enigmatic remains at Montreal Island in the estuary of Back's Great Fish River

At the time of Dr. John Rae's report, Britain was at war (Crimean War – October 1853 to February 1856), and there were no resources to equip another big expedition. So the Hudson's Bay Company was requested to confirm that the Franklin retreat had reached Back's Great Fish River. Dr. Rae declined to lead this party and Mr. James Anderson, a chief factor of the company, took charge. Lady Franklin objected, as she did not believe the party would reach King William Island, and that time would be lost. Regretfully Anderson took no translator. The first Franklin relics were seen on July the thirtieth 1855 at the rapids below Lake Franklin. Anderson wrote in his report:

> On the 30th, at the rapids below Lake Franklin, three Esquimaux lodges were seen on the opposite shore, and shortly after an elderly man crossed to us. After the portage was made we crossed over, and immediately perceived various articles belonging to a boat, such as tent poles and kyak paddles made out of ash oars, pieces of mahogany, elm, oak, and pine; also copper and sheet iron boilers, tin soup tureens, pieces of instruments, a letter nip

dated 1843, a broken hand saw, chisels &c. One man was left at the lodges; but the women, who were very intelligent, made us understand, by words and signs, that these articles came from a boat, and that the white men belonging to it had died of starvation.

The search party finally reached Montreal Island and Anderson wrote:

> There on a high ridge of rocks at the S.E. point of the island, a number of Esquimaux caches were found, and, besides seal oil, various articles were found belonging to a boat or ship, such as chain hooks, chisels, blacksmith's shovel and cold chisel, tin oval boiler, a bar of unwrought iron about three feet long, one and a half inch broad, and a quarter of an inch thick; small pieces of rope, bunting, and a number of sticks strung together, on one of which was cut 'Mr. Stanley' [surgeon of *Erebus* – the sticks were snowshoes]. A little lower down was a large quantity of chips, shavings, and ends of planks of pine, elm, ash, oak, and mahogany, evidently sawn by unskilful hands; every chip was turned over, and on one of them was found the word '*Terror*' carved. It was evident that this was the spot where the boat was cut up by the Esquimaux; but not even a scrap of paper could be discovered, and though rewards were offered, and the most minute search made over the whole island, not a vestige of the remains of our unfortunate countrymen could be discovered.

The search party then continued to Point Ogle, where a search revealed only a short length of cod line and a strip of cotton. From there Anderson sent four men by Halkett boat to search Maconochie Island. Thirty-five years later it was learned that one of these men (Paul Papanakies) had sighted two masts in the distance. He did not report it however, because he was afraid Anderson would insist on visiting the place in the fragile canoes and slowing their return trip. On August 8, (with the canoes in a battered condition) they began retracing their way back, the trip having achieved its objective of showing that the river reported by Dr. Rae was Back's Great Fish River.

The complete absence of any bones or human remains strongly suggests that the reported Franklin relics were most likely obtained by the Inuit from the boat at what Schwatka would name as Starvation Cove. There, a Franklin boat party had mistaken a long blind inlet for Chantrey Inlet – the estuary of Back's Great Fish River. However, the cod line and cotton strip and the isolated skeleton, suggest that some of the survivors of Starvation Cove walked east to the estuary of the Great Fish River and went fishing using cod line with cotton strips for lures.

Sherard Osborn has speculated that the evidence of carpenter's tools, including a broken saw and planks suggests that the boat party waited on

Montreal Island for the ice to melt and open the river. During this time they broke up their boat and with some of the planks carried, built a canoe. How far a small party ascended Back's Great Fish River is unknown, but if they carried Sir George Back's chart and followed his track, their route would not always be that followed by the Anderson search party that deviated considerably. However, this is not a very likely possibility because the boats had already been lightened and converted for use with paddles in order to ascend a river before the retreat began.

Roderic Owen – a descendant of Sir John Franklin – wrote that the Montreal Herald followed by the Times and Examiner newspapers reported that one of the Inuit women communicated by signs to the Anderson party that one of the lost crew died on Montreal Island. He was large and strong and sat on the beach with head resting on his hands and died. The other men died on the coast [Starvation Cove?] having wandered the beach until they lay down and died of starvation and exhaustion.

This report is believed to be fabricated by the press to make more out of the Anderson trip. It does not ring true and the information conflicts with the Inuit testimony of Starvation Cove, where the dead men were well wrapped up and lying under an overturned boat. They had evidently been given the best care possible when they became too ill and weak to continue and the boat and precious box of records had to be abandoned. Later examinations of Montreal Island by McClintock and the Schwatka party also failed to find human remains there.

In May 1859, McClintock made a detour to Montreal Island which he searched along with adjacent islands. His sledge party found only a single Inuit marker and alongside it a cache of a piece of preserved meat tin, two pieces of iron hoop, some scraps of copper and an iron hook-bolt.

Hall wrote a letter dated June 20 1869, to his patron Henry Grinnel from Repulse Bay:

> This day I returned from a sledge journey of 90 days to and from King William Land... The result of my sledge journey... may be summed up thus: none of Sir John Franklin's companions ever reached or died on Montreal Island.

What happened in Chantrey Inlet?

The main event in Chantrey Inlet area was the arrival of a boat (possibly drawn on a sledge) that did not quite reach the Inlet. Around six immobile sick men were abandoned with the boat, much equipment and the precious box of records, at what is now known as Starvation Cove. This is likely to be the same boat earlier encountered by the Inuit near Washington Bay. The survivors obviously too few and weak to haul the boat any further, set off on foot with one seaman dropping by the way some five miles further on. Significantly, he was not buried. The party probably reached the shores of Chantrey Inlet because a cod fishing line was found there in an Inuit cache. Perhaps the small party turned eastwards towards Repulse Bay. Evidently, the struggle was dire and a hand-carried pouch of the records was left in a distinctive shaped cairn.

However, there are echoes suggesting other events occurred in the estuary. There is a distinct possibility that a second boat also arrived, although what year is unknown. Her two masts may have been those seen but not reported by Paul Papanakies of the Anderson Expedition. Dorothy Harley Eber reports that a boat mast was found by Mark Tootiak on an islet near Montreal Island. There are at least two possibilities for a second boat, both from the 1848 retreat. The fourth boat of the 1848 retreat remains unaccounted for. The wood chippings at Douglas Bay may have been the remains of a sledge rather than a boat. The wood chippings on Montreal Island may also be the remains of the sledge that carried the boat to Starvation Cove in 1850.

There is also a hint that a small group of Franklin men may have met hostility in Chantrey Inlet. Sir George Back descended Back's Great Fish River and explored Chantrey Inlet in 1834. On his return trip, unknown to him, some of his men killed three Inuit and may have wounded others near the waterfalls where the Great Fish River entered Chantrey Inlet. Hostility might have existed towards any more western men arriving there. Woodman found in Hall's notebooks some testimony describing fighting between some of Franklin's men and 'Indians'. One was an 'Aglooka' who was reputedly wounded in the forehead by a lance, but killed his attacker. Hall concluded that the fight may have taken place near the entrance to Back's Great Fish River.

A death march

The 1850 retreat was very different to that of 1848. It was now two years since the stores for the expedition had been largely exhausted and the men had eked a living by fishing, hunting birds and caribou in summer and seals in winter. There were probably no food reserves and the men were weak after two years on a starvation diet. Whereas the 1848 retreat was well organised, carried rations for forty days and was disciplined by officers. There was no trail of graves (only three in Erebus Bay and Grover Bay to the north). The men were kept alive and the sick cared for and carried along on the sledges. This continued until the sick reached such proportions that they could no longer be carried and the retreat halted in two parts – Erebus Bay and Terror Bay. It seems possible that it was the two *Erebus* boats that were halted in Erebus Bay, probably by Captain Fitzjames. The two *Terror* boats were likely in the lead driven by the sterner discipline of Captain Crozier. The latter achieved the goal of reaching the summer hunting grounds of south King William Island. Unforunately, their arrival was too early for most of the migrating wildlife with only birds arriving.

Cannibalism occurred at each of the three 'death camps.' This was after the immobile sick had been left with carers and the hunting failed. The men would have known that a half of the retreat had returned to *Erebus* in the hope that she might be released later that summer. So the incentive was to hold on. The descriptions by the Inuit of two of the 'death camps' suggest that when found there as only one complete body of the last cannibal in each and they were festooned with the valuables of the group.

The 1850 retreat in contrast was a very desperate last attempt to escape – a forlorn hope. They took only one wooden boat (and the inflatable Halkett boat) and one sledge anticipating many deaths on the way. Captain Crozier had died and along with his body many paper records were buried indicating that after five years, hope of escape was almost gone. The retreat was likely led by and dominated by *Terror* men and only a very small core of *Erebus* men remained aboard her with their Captain. They did place in the boat a metal box of records measuring two by one foot. Their health was poor because of an inadequate diet based on hunting for two years since their original stores were exhausted. They had learned from the 1848 retreat that April was too early to start, so the encounter in Washington Bay took place in June shortly before the sea ice broke up and a time when the hunting should have been good.

When the men set out for Repulse Bay in a weakened state they knew they had to march or die. But they were going home. This they did and it proved a death march with frequent stops for burials, like the one at Tulloch Point where graves were no longer dug but the body laid on the ground and covered with only small stones. The illness and weakness persisted during the retreat as the Inuit reported to McClintock that:

> they fell down and died as they walked along

The burials indicate that discipline was maintained. They tried splitting up to increase their chances of hunting and bartering with the Inuit. But this failed and the deaths continued (at least thirteen).

Opposite the Todd Islets a crisis occurred when the leader realised that they could go no further. It was likely the lack of food. He and four friends went out to a Todd Islet and sat together on the top of an islet and died together with their unopened tin of pemmican and looking across at the American continent. Probably a straggler had the same idea and went out to another islet.

The remnant led probably by marine sergeant Solomon Tozer (with a Halkett boat and his sword on a sledge) continued. But the party had decided that in order to continue they would eat the dead (as they told their rescuer later). This is a different justification to the cannibalism of the 1948 retreat. Something similar happened to the bodies at Starvation Cove where only the hands were removed so that a last few might continue. Only Sergeant Tozer abstained from the decision to eat the dead as his rescuer could see that when they met. At Booth point a cannibal meal was eaten (the remains found and studied by Owen Beattie). They had almost reached Boothia when they met and were rescued by Too-shoo-ar-thar-i-u. One of the party died soon after not of starvation but of a sickness.

18: THE BLACK MEN

Amongst the testimonies that can be attributed to the stay of the ship at Imnguyaaluk Island are two that describe a ship with one officer and a small crew. One of these testimonies describes the crew in some detail as 'black men'. There is only one place in the sequence of events that can account for such an occurrence. This is *Erebus* at Imnguyaaluk Island after the death of Captain Crozier and after the 1850 retreat, when most of the remaining men had left the ship. What was left aboard of the two crews was the one officer – probably Captain Fitzjames - and about a dozen crewmen who were loyal to him and may have sailed with him on previous trips.

Both pieces of Inuit testimony, result from the work of David Woodman, who went to the Smithsonian Institution in Washington to examine the original Hall notebooks. There he found testimony omitted from the 1879 summary of Nourse, probably because it could not then be understood. Both testimonies are reproduced here with the permission of David Woodman. They were recorded by Hall in a journal dated 'Dec. 6 1864 – May 12 1865' book 6.

Ook-bar-loo's testimony – the Captain's miserable meal, 1849 or 1850

This testimony was given by Ook-bar-loo when talking of an Inut who visited a ship in the ice near a large island. In addition, to visits by her relatives, she reported that the ship was visited by one man travelling alone who became a guest of the great captain (Woodman with Hall's spelling and grammar):

> There was one Neitch-il-le Innuit that visited the ship alone, she (O) did not recollect his name. He went with dogs & sledge on the ice to the ship. The kob-lu-na Esh-e-mut-ta (the white chief or Captain) of ship was very kind to him (the Inut) & gave him many things. The Captain took him down into the Cabin & gave him something to eat & drink & then he went home. Some time after, when the sun was high, that is it was well into spring or summer, the same Inut visited the ship again & the Captain took him down into the Cabin & gave him see-qa-la (Bread-Crackers) to eat & he (the Captain) gave him a long big piece of something that was white – a

good deal of ook-sook (blubber) to it with a little thin bit of meat with bone in it. And this Inut thought something bad about this and did not wish to take it. He thought perhaps it was a piece of the side of an Ek-er-lin (Indian) or perhaps of a Kob-lu-na! He never saw anything like it. He knew it was not of a Ni-noo (Polar Bear) though it looked something like – in fact he never saw anything like it, & could not help thinking it must be a piece of the side of a Indian or Kob-lu-na; it would bend so: it was so white: - it had such thick ook-sook; & had so little meat & bone on it.

As pointed out by Woodman, the Captain offered the Inut some of his own food, almost certainly salt pork. But it was a poor piece of salt pork, lacking meat, and the Inut was unfamiliar with pig meat. The Inut probably did not understand that the food situation aboard the ship was disasterously short and what was left of the salt pork was of very poor quality. The Inut feared the strange meat that he had not seen before was human meat.

Ook-bar-loo's additional testimony – the ship with one officer and a crew of 'black men,' 1849 or 1850

The stories of the unnamed Inut's visits to the ship continue and it is the next story that is of critical importance to understanding the events aboard the reoccupied *Erebus* (Woodman with Hall's spelling and grammar):

Bye & Bye the Innuit went again to the ship with his dogs and sledge. He went on deck, & a great many men - black men – came up right out of the hatch-way & the first thing he (the Innuit) knew he could not get away. These men who were then all around him, had black faces, black hands, black clothes on – were black all over! They had little black noses… & this Innuit was very much alarmed because he could not get away from these black men but especially was he frightened when they made three great noises (three rounds of cheers as Too-koo-li-too thinks these great noises were). When three great noises were made the Esh-e-mut-ta (Captain) came up out of the Cabin & put a stop to it, when all the black men went down the same way they had come up. This Innuit believed these men belonged down among the coals & that they lived there.

Then the Captain took this Innuit down with him into his Cabin & made him many presents, for he [the Innuit] had been frightened so. Before the Captain took him down into his Cabin he told this Innuit to take a look over to the land, the Captain pointing out to him the exact spot where there was a big Tupik (tent). The Captain asked him if he saw the tent, & the Innuit told him he did. Then the Captain told him that black men, such as he had just seen, lived there, & that neither he (this Innuit) nor any of his people must ever go there. After the Innuit had received the presents that the Captain made him, he left the ship & went home; & he would never go to the ship again because of the frightful looking black men that lived there down in the Coal hole.

This testimony is here regarded as the most crucial piece of Inuit testimony in this reconstruction of the lost expedition. The geographical information – being able to see the hospital tent at Terror Bay, indicates that the ship was situated in the Alexandra Channel between Cape Crozier and the Royal Geographical Society Islands. The location has been described in other Inuit testimony above. It also confirms the position of the reoccupied *Erebus* at Imnguyaaluk Island. Coincidentally, the position is also close to where the wreck of *Terror* was found just outside Terror Bay in 2016.

It indicates that *Erebus* had been reoccupied in Spring 1848 and after she had been released in summer 1848 or 1849 was worked some eighty-five miles south along the shore of King William Island, around Cape Crozier (the westernmost point of King William Island) to within sight of the hospital tent in Terror Bay. Other Inuit testimony places the ship on the south side of Imnguyaaluk Island about twenty miles from the hospital tent at Terror Bay (this is about the range of sight from the deck of a ship in clear air). Presumably she was brought there in an attempt to rescue the sick and immobile men left in Erebus and Terror Bays. However, the presence of only one officer and a small number of crew suggests that the Inut's visits to the ship occurred after the death of Captain Crozier and after the 1850 retreat.

The officer is likely to be Captain Fitzjames. What is remarkable is the Captain warning the Inut to keep away from the hospital tent where other 'black men' lived. This could mean that the black men meeting occurred in late 1848 and that one or two men who had turned to cannibalism might still be alive and in such desperate shape that they might regard a visiting Inut as a meal. Alternatively, it could be warning to keep away from the horrors of the hospital tent in Terror Bay in late 1850. Whichever case, it seems that on arrival at Imnguyaaluk Island the two captains had learned of the deaths and cannibalism of the men left in the three camps and had turned the ship away from Terror Bay to anchor in the lee of Imnguyaaluk Island, out of the ice stream that moved south through Alexandra Channel. Sadly it also means that although *Erebus* had come to the rescue, the summer hunting had been so poor, that most of the men left behind had either died or drifted away south in small parties. The few surviving cannibals might have managed to extend their lives ashore from their April departure from the ships, until late August or September. With his own crew on a starvation diet including seal meat, the captain – then Crozier – could not permit a few, now mentally disturbed cannibals, on board.

The likely scenario is that the meeting with the black men took place in 1850 after the death of Captain Crozier and after the 1850 retreat. The deplorable state of the crew being filthy with blackened faces and blackened clothing indicates that the hot water heating and drinking system was no longer fully operating in the ship. The ships had been provisioned only for three years. For the fourth and fifth years of the expedition, the hot water system in the ship would have been out of use most of the time. Only ninety tons of coal were supplied to each ship and very little would have been left after three years. Possibly the remaining coal had been transferred to *Erebus* to assist her in her breakout attempt to reach Bering Strait. Perhaps only wood was available for melting ice for drinking water and cooking in the long dark winter aboard ship.

Thin hungry men with blackened faces and blackened oil soaked clothing can be understood by reading and looking at the Elephant Island photographs of Shackleton's 1914-16 Trans-Antarctic Expedition (Shackleton, 1919, 1982, 1999; Lansing, 1959). Blubber soot and oil were a problem experienced by Sir Ernest Shackleton and his men on the 1914 to 1917 Trans-Antarctic expedition, after their ship *Endurance* was crushed by ice and sank in the Weddell Sea. The men took to the ice and lived on it for five months before reaching Elephant Island.

For this time and the next three months spent of the island, the men, who had no change of clothing, lived off supplies from the ship and seals and penguins that they hunted. Their heat source was blubber. They cooked their food off blubber stoves of their own design. In the two overturned boats in which they lived on Elephant Island, illumination was provided by an improvised blubber oil lamp - a tin can with blubber oil inside and a strip of bandage for a wick. Burning blubber and blubber oil produced blubber soot and oil that clung to everything – clothing and skin. A few men washed it off with handfuls of snow but many preferred to keep it as a possible protection against frost bite. Again without surplus hot water, shaving ceased and most men grew beards.

Shackleton cited a crewman's diary from Elephant Island as saying this:

We are as regardless of our grime and dirt as is the Esquimaux. We have been unable to wash since we left the ship, nearly ten months ago. For one thing we have no soap or towels, and, again, had we possessed these articles, our supply of fuel would only permit us to melt enough ice for drinking purposes. Had one washed, half a dozen others would have to go without a drink all day. One cannot suck ice to relieve the thirst, as at these low temperatures it cracks the lips and blisters the tongue. Still, we are all very cheerful.

Shackleton writes about another party stranded at Hut Point in McMurdo Sound:

> At the Hut he and his companions lived an uneventful life under primitive conditions. Mackintosh records that the members of the party were contented enough, but, owing largely to the soot and grease from the blubber-stove, unspeakably dirty.

The Inut visitor to the ship of 'black men' was evidently terrified by their strange wild appearance and thin hungry forms, black oil-soaked clothing, black faces and hands. Their beards would have enlarged their faces so that their noses looked small. As the Inuit do not grow beards perhaps this change in the crew's appearances was most frightening of all.

Aboard *Erebus*, the Captain in the great cabin had illumination in daylight hours through the cabin windows. So the visiting Inut would not have noticed anything amiss. In contrast, the crew living below decks had no illumination, and their appearance suggested they were using blubber oil lamps, implying that the ship's supply of tallow, candles and lamp oil was exhausted after more than three years. The state of the crew suggests they were spending much of the time hunting for food, being seals from a camp on nearby Imnguyaaluk Island. *Erebus* at this time was barely a naval ship. The Captain alone was maintaining his appearance and the discipline of the ship, but the crew were living as survivors in a long trapped ship that had become a prison.

The crew were evidently delighted with the Inut's visit and raised three cheers, hoping for setting up a trade for food. However, their terrible appearance frightened the Inut. When the Captain saw this he immediately ordered the crew below decks and took the Inut to his cabin and gave him many gifts.

Like Shackleton was to show, survival in extreme conditions depended on the Captain maintained a firm discipline aboard ship, as evidenced by the abrupt disappearance of the crew below decks at the Captains order.

Rear Admiral Wright reports that in summer 1848, there was a tremendous and abnormal breakup and drift of ice in Barrow Strait, far greater than usual. Sir James Clark Ross arriving in summer 1848, was unable to proceed because of the great amount of ice that had moved into and blocked Barrow Strait. This great ice jam broke suddenly on the first of September 1849 and carried Sir James Clark Ross and his ships over 100 miles with the ice out into Baffin Bay, when he abandoned his Franklin search expedition trip and returned to London. So unlike the previous two summers, the big break up of summer 1848 presented the two captains on the reoccupied *Erebus* with the opportunity to escape the ice stream on the coast of north-west King William Land and work the ship south to Imnguyaaluk Island.

At Imnguyaaluk Island, survival conditions aboard *Erebus* must have been deplorable. Only the iron will and courage first of Captain Crozier and later by Captain Fitzjames enforcing naval discipline kept the ship together. When visited by the Inut, the men were facing long months in the ice in the hope of rescue. Their gaunt pinched faces described by the Inuit seen on the 1850 retreat, told of insufficient food. The rum ration was probably long gone. Dr. Cyriax reported that the ships were stored with sufficient rum for full crews for two years and five months. The ships were first abandoned in 1848 after two years and nine months in the Arctic. But almost twenty percent of the men had died by that time. So the rum supply would have lasted a little longer and probably ran out at about the time the ships were abandoned in 1848.

There may well have been a final issue of grog on departure day 1848. This is mentioned in the Peglar papers. It would have marked their bold act of departing the hell ship, but in reality proved to be a case of stepping out the frying pan into the fire. Last toasts might have been raised to their speedy success. Crozier's basic retreat plan was similar to that executed by John Ross, when he abandoned his ship *Victory* in May 1832. It was to get the men to a supply of fresh food and then by using the boats which had been lightened and converted for river use with paddles, to travel to outposts of civilisation.

The filthy state of the crews' clothing suggests that most of the ships surplus clothing was still where it was found by the McClintock expedition in 1849, in a heap four feet high at Crozier's Landing. The heap had probably been inside a store tent that had largely blown away in the intervening years. Here is a hint that there was insufficient time to resupply H.M.S. *Erebus* in summer 1848. She must have been released soon after the men returned. In their haste to get back to the men left in Erebus and Terror Bays, there just was not enough time to get the clothing back on board.

19: THE UTJULIK SHIP

In 1859 McClintock was told by the Inuit of a wreck that was ashore and had been heavily salvaged by them for many years at Utjulik. She had been visited only the previous year by an old lady and a boy who reported that there was not much of her left. The wreck was finally located in 2014 by a consortium led by Parks Canada and identified as *Erebus* (Map II).

After the 1850 retreat from the reoccupied *Erebus* trapped in the ice near Imnguyaaluk Island, the next event was the release of the ship and her hoisting sails and perhaps using her engine. The testimony of Aglooka given to his host, who found the four survivors near Boothia, was that the 1850 retreat party contained seventeen men. Alternatively, Dr. Rae reported forty men. Hall questioned the Inuit closely and concluded that here were forty-five men. Around thirty-seven bodies from the 1850 retreat can be accounted for.

So when *Erebus* left Imnguyaaluk Island the crew would have been very small, perhaps only around thirteen men. She was worked south towards the mapped summer open-water channel along the margin of the North American continent. The testimony of Frank Analok collected by Dorothy Harley Erber describes the Imnguyaaluk ship leaving:

> It has been said that once summer came the ship - with sails, like flags - that wintered left for where we do not know, but perhaps for wherever they had come from, and it is believed all the men left with the ship. Whether they made it I do not know.

Translator Petersen's report on a ship on fire

There is a possibility that *Erebus* might have been seen by the Inuit on her journey south. McClintock in 1859, after crossing from Matty Island, found an Inuit village on the north-east coast of King William Island where he heard of the two ships and purchased many Franklin relics. They all came from the Utjulik wreck.

> They told us it was five days' journey to the wreck – one day up the inlet still in sight and four days overland...they added that but little now remained accessible of the wreck, their countrymen having carried almost everything

away. In answer to an enquiry, they said she was without masts; the question gave rise to some laughter amongst them, and they spoke to each other about fire, from which Peterson thought they had burnt the masts through close to the deck in order to get them down.

Alternatively, the reference to smoke and masts might also have been a description of smoke issuing from the funnel of the steam engine. Similar misinterpretations were made in England, when the smoke was seen from the first steam engines in ships also rigged for sailing.

McClintock's report of two ships

After much anxious enquiry we learned that two ships had been seen by the natives of King William's Island; one of them was seen to sink in deep water, and nothing was obtained from her, a circumstance at which they expressed much regret; but the other was forced on shore by the ice, where they supposed she remains, but is much broken. From this ship they have obtained most of their wood, &c.; Oot-loo-lik is the name of the place where she grounded.

In-nook-poo-zhe-jook's testimony of how the ship was found by the Inuit

Hall wrote:

The ship had four boats hanging at the sides and another was above the quarter deck. The ice about the ship one winter's make; all a smooth floe. A plank was found extending from the ship's side down to the ice.

Gathering into an igloo my interpreters Joe and Jack with In-nook-poo-zhee-jook, and putting before the last named native McClintock's chart, he readily pointed out the place where the Franklin ship sank. It was very near O'Reilly Island. A little eastward of the north end of said island, between it and Wilmot and Compton Bay. A native of the island first saw the ship when sealing, it was far off to seaward, beset in the ice. He concluded to make his way to it, though at first he felt afraid, got aboard, but saw no one, although from every appearance somebody had been living there. At last he ventured to steal a knife, and made off as fast as he could to his home, but in showing the Innuits what he had stolen the men of the place all started off to the ship. The party on getting aboard tried to find out if anyone was there, and not seeing or hearing any one, began ransacking the ship. To get into the igloo (cabin), they knocked a hole through because it was locked. They found there a dead man, whose body was very large and heavy, his teeth very long. It took five men to lift this giant kob-lu-na. He was left where they found him. One place in the ship, where a great many things were found, was very dark, they had to find things there by feeling around. Guns were there and a great many good buckets and boxes. On my asking if they saw anything to eat on board, the reply was there was meat and tood-noo in cans, the meat fat and like pemmican. The sails, rigging and boats – everything about the ship – was in complete order.

From time to time the Neitchilles went to get out of her whatever they could, they made their plunder into piles on board, intending to sledge it to their igloos some time after, but on going again they found her sunk, except the top of the masts. They said they had made a hole in her bottom by getting out one of her timbers or planks. The ship was afterwards much broken up by the ice, and then masts, timbers, boxes, casks, &c, drifted on the shore. A little while after this fresh tracks were seen of four men and a dog on the land where the ship was. In-nook-poo-zhee-jook, who had seen Ross and his party on the *Victory* and Rae in 1854, knew these tracks to be kob-lu-nas, the foot marks were long, narrow in the middle, and the prints like as if of boots found in the two boats found on King William's Land. One man, from his running steps, was a very great runner – very long steps. The natives tracked the men a long distance, and found where they had killed and eaten a young deer.

Another native at this interview told nearly the same story of the ship and of the man found on board, adding that he was found dead on the floor, his clothes all on, that the ship was covered all over with sails or tent stuff. The cabin was down below and not on deck.

The timing of the discovery of the ship by the Inuit was May to June 1. She had evidently arrived in the open water of the previous summer. People had wintered aboard her and she was encased in canvas for winter quarters (1850-1852). Four men and a dog had recently departed leaving a plank alongside to get on and off the ship, and there were sweepings from the deck on the ice alongside. These men were probably at a summer hunting camp not too far away. The story of the making a hole in the bottom and the ship sinking with masts standing above water is not at all compatible with what McClintock learned in 1859 from the Inuit of north-eastern King William Island of the wreck lacking masts. The testimony is mixed with the story of the end of *Terror*.

The footprints of four men and a dog were seen on a nearby small island. The Inuit followed the footprints and found the remains of a shot deer (prints and kill made after the winter snow of 1850-51). The implication is that a very small party led by 'The Hunter', now able to live by hunting had wintered (1850 to 1851) on *Erebus* before finally abandoning her in spring 1851 or later.

McClintock's report that *Erebus* wreck was heavily salvaged by Inuit

they added that but little now remained accessible of the wreck, their countrymen having carried almost everything away... There had been many books, they said, but all have long ago been destroyed by the weather; the ship was forced on shore in the fall of the year by the ice. She had not been visited during this past winter, and an old woman and a boy were shown to us who were the last to visit the wreck; they said they had been at it during the preceding winter (i.e. 1857-58).

This vital record suggests that if after *Erebus* was abandoned for the second and last time, in spring 1851 or 1852, near O'Reilly Island, then she was forced ashore in a summer melt, and remained accessible from the land for possibly seven years, during which time she was heavily salvaged by the Inuit. The sonar images of the wreck of *Erebus* show that her stern has much deck and hull missing and Sir John Franklin's great cabin is open to the sea. Her bowsprit and masts are also missing. This damage fits with Inuit description of salvaging the ship, possibly with the masts burned through. Access into the ship was from the stern through Sir John's great cabin. The ships library was stored in the great cabin and no doubt furnished many books for Inuit play things. Years later (after 1858) the wreck encased in a raft of ice must have broken free of the shore to sink nearby in shallow water with much of the stern missing.

Ek-kee-pee-re-a's testimony – *Erebus* had five boats when found by the Inuit

Hall wrote:

Ek-kee-pee-re-a had lived at Ook-joo-lik (O'Reilly Island), and had heard the natives there tell about the ship that came to their country. The ship had four boats hanging at the sides and another was above the quarter deck. The ice about the ship one winter's make, all a smooth floe. A plank was found extended from the ship's side down to the ice.

Seeuteetuar's wife Koo-nik's testimony – Inuit enter the abandoned *Erebus*

Woodman wrote:

She says that Nuk-kee-che-uk & other Ook-joo-lik Innuits were out sealing when they saw a large ship – all very much afraid but Nuk-kee-che-uk who went to the vessel while the others went to their Ig-loo. Nuk-kee-che-uk looked all around and saw nobody & finally Lik-lee-poo-nik-kee-look-oo-loo (stole a very little or few things) & then made for the Ig-loos. Then all the Inuit went to the ship & stole a good deal – broke into a place that was fastened up & there found a very large white man who was dead, very tall man. There was flesh about this dead man, that is, his remains quite perfect – it took 5 men to lift him. The place smelt very bad. His clothes all on. Found dead on floor – not in a sleeping place or berth… The vessel covered over with see-loon, that is housed in with sails or that material, not boards, but as Jack (Hall's guide Nu-ker-zhoo) says like Capt. Potter's vessel when at Ships Harbour Isles in winter quarters.

The Ig-loos or cabins down below as *Ansel Gibbs* not on deck like *Black Eagle*.

Puhtoorak's testimony – items removed from *Erebus*

Gilder wrote:

> When his people saw the ship so long without any one around, they used to go on board and steal pieces of wood and iron. They did not know how to get inside by the doors, and cut a hole in the side of the ship, on a level with the ice, so that when the ice broke up during the following summer the ship filled and sunk. No tracks were seen in the salt water ice or on the ship, which was also covered in snow, but they saw scrapings and sweepings alongside, which seemed to have been brushed off by people who had been living on board. They found plenty of knives, forks, spoons, pans, cups, and plates on board, and afterward found a few such things on shore after the vessel had gone down. They also saw books on board, and left them there. They only took knives, forks, spoons and pans; other things they had no use for.

McClintock, in 1859 met these people and purchased a lot of silver plate as well as utensils from them. Some of the silver cutlery had crews initials scratched onto them. If the officers silver ware was distributed to the crew in the hope of saving it for the 1848 retreat, then this cutlery would have been brought back to *Erebus* when she was reoccupied. It then remained aboard her until it was removed from the Utjulik ship by the Inuit many years later. The initials scratched on the silver therefore identify two *Terror* men who returned to reoccupy *Erebus* after the 1848 retreat:

Relics obtained from the Esquimaux near Cape Norton, upon the East Coast of King William's Island, in May 1859:- Two tablespoons; upon one is scratched 'W.W.,' on the other 'W.G.'

W.W. was William Wentzall, Able Seaman, H.M.S. *Terror*. W.G. was either William Goddard, Captain of the Hold, H.M.S. *Terror*, or Subordinate Officers Steward William Gibson, H.M.S. *Terror*. The initials confirm that the 1848 retreat set out hoping to reach civilisation and carrying the officers silver. They also show that *Terror* men returned to H.M.S. *Erebus* and not to H.M.S *Terror* so that after 1848 only H.M.S. *Erebus* was occupied and worked as far as Utjulik on the Adelaide Peninsula.

20: LAST ACTIVITIES ABOARD *EREBUS*

It is not known if *Erebus* arrived at what proved to be her final destination, off O'Reilly Island, (where she became the Utjulik ship of Inuit testimony) in summer 1850 or 1851. When she was found by the Inuit abandoned in one year old ice, her decks were covered in by canvas for a winter stay. So presumably some of the crew wintered aboard her, possibly from 1850-51. There is evidence of crew activities on islets around O'Reilly Island. There is also evidence of activities aboard ship after she arrived, but for only a very small number of men – only four hunters and a dog. It is possible to reconstruct some of the final activities of the last of the crew aboard *Erebus*.

Honours for the last officer

The body of a large man with long teeth, found by the Inuit locked into the great cabin of *Erebus* (see Koo-nik's testimony above), is likely to be that of the last officer who brought the remanned *Erebus* south to Utjulik. He had held discipline in very poor conditions to get the ship into the open summer waters along the northern coast of the American continent. He succeeded in this and bought some of his crew another two years of life and hope, after the 1848 retreat turned into a disaster, with about a half of the crews left in what became the three death camps at Erebus and Terror Bays. The death of their leader and last senior officer would have been catastrophic for the few remaining crew. He had held them together and driven them to work the ship south as well as organising hunting trips to supply much needed fresh food. He was also their last navigator and senior officer understanding the handling of sails and courses.

He probably died before *Erebus* came to her final anchorage. But he had succeeded in bringing *Erebus* through the part of the North-West Passage choked by the Beaufort ice stream. His crew accorded him the honor of presenting him with the ship as a fitting tomb and monument as a measure of his great drive, courage and near success.

So it is suggested here that the body was probably that of Captain Fitzjames and the cabin was the great cabin (originally occupied by Captain Sir John Franklin) of *Erebus*. The great cabin is identified as being the only officers' cabin big enough to hold the body of a large man and five Inuit (who lifted the body). Without their leader's drive and skills, there was no other officer to command the ship and in particular navigate her. This was probably why *Erebus* was abandoned the second time.

There is a curious find that may be related to this act of the crew. When Captain Ingelfield and later when Beattie and Geiger exhumed the Franklin graves on Beechey Island, they found buried on top of the coffins copper plates bearing the details of the dead prepared by their fellow crewmen. In summer 1879 the Schwartka expedition recovered a relic from the west coast of the Adelaide Peninsula near where the Utjulik ship sank. It was a piece of black-painted pine board, possibly part of the head of a bunk or the top of a box or locker. It was covered in a heavy black oil cloth in which were set brass-headed tacks forming letters read as 'I F' by Schwatka or 'LF' by Gilder and Klutschak. It was not the custom in the Royal Navy to personalise the head boards of bunks. Woodman came up with a very interesting possible solution. The letters might be 'I.P', and when complete might have read as 'R.I.P'. It might have been placed with the body of the large officer left in the great cabin of *Erebus*.

Erebus was found in fresh ice and probably arrived in summer 1850 or 1851. She was probably winter occupied with summer camps on a nearby island. Inuit testimony tells of her final occupants being four men and a dog. In this reconstruction these were the best hunters with a dog to assist them. These four were likely to be away in summer, hunting with a camp on a nearby islet. They may have wintered aboard *Erebus* for one or two winters, finally abandoning her in 1851 or 1852.

In this reconstruction they left the body of their Captain Fitzjames in the great cabin, possibly with the head board marked 'R.I.P.'. As they could no longer work the ship, and possibly because of Inuit looting while they were away hunting, they eventually left for Repulse Bay/Iwillik and then turned north along the Melville Peninsula where their distinctive track with their dog was seen by the Inuit. When they abandoned *Erebus*, they left the ship neat, tidy and locked up.

Did a boat or sledge party leave *Erebus* to head west?

Erebus most likely arrived near O'Reilly Island in the autumn of 1850, perhaps 1851 with a small crew of only around thirteen men. The men on board no doubt knew of Fitzjames' plan to get the ship to Petro Paulowski [Petropavlovsk] across the Bering Strait, where his mail awaited him and that a fast trip had been arranged for him to cross Russia by land. Was it possible that a boat crew set out in the fall to the west trying to move along the coastline of the American continent. What is known from the Inuit testimony is that only four men and a dog remained aboard by the following spring (1851 or 1852). There is some weak evidence that a boat crew left the ship.

Erebus was likely crewed by only around thirteen men on her arrival at Utjulik – enough to build a three tent campsite on Ook-soo-see-too islet near O'Reilly Island. The following year there were only four men and a dog left aboard. The difference suggests that there were still sufficient men to man a boat or sledge breakout along the summer water channel along the northern margin of the American continent. The presence of a substantial campsite, suggests the boat attempt did not take place and the men concentrated on summer hunting and then wintered aboard *Erebus*. The next opportunity to leave would be the following spring by sledge.

Bering Strait is around 1,700 miles from O'Reilly Island and was obviously beyond the capability of the tiny crew without a senior officer. A more realistic objective would be the Mackenzie River. The Hunter and his small party of four men did not participate and probably decided to remain where they were, because they had learned how to live like the Inuit and were in good health. Testimony (described later) indicates that 'The Hunter' and his three companions and their hunting dog were the last survivors on board *Erebus*. The hunting party would have been engaged in summer hunting of caribou before the sea lanes froze over again.

In 1850 the ship *Investigator* under the command of Commander Robert McClure had shaken off his commanding officer, Captain Richard Collinson, on board *Enterprise*, and was engaged in a solo search officially for the lost Franklin expedition. McClure was very ambitious and was set on finding the North-West Passage and being the first through it. This he did and was knighted but he lost his ship *Investigator*. She was located in 2010 by divers of Parks Canada.

When sailing east along the northern shoreline of the American Continent, a party from *Investigator* went ashore on August 24 1850 to the Inuit settlement of Tooktoyaktuk to the east of the Mackenzie River. The curiosity of the shore party was aroused by a grave with a curious wooden monument. Translator Miertsching asked about it and was told of strangers who arrived without a boat and had built a house out of driftwood on a nearby cape and lived by hunting. However after the birds, seal and reindeer left the area they had all disappeared except for one man who died. The Inuit had found the body of the last survivor and buried it beneath the wooden marker.

Miertsching could not find the date of the burial. Before the conversation could end Captain McClure thought their ship was aground and rushed everyone back to the ship. Next day, the Captain, Miertsching and Dr. Armstrong landed on what they thought was the cape indicated by the villagers some ten miles away and searched it. They found the ruins of two Eskimo winter-houses built of driftwood and other Inuit debris. The complete absence of any western relics suggested that the party that had been there was not from the Franklin expedition. However the search was not persued elsewhere on that coast and so the outcome was not conclusive.

In August 1850 when *Investigator* was offshore of Tooktoyaktuk, the fate of the Franklin expedition was unknown, especially that the crews had retreated south from the ships in 1848 and again in 1850. On both occasions the crews had set out to the south, man hauling boats on sledges. Had these facts been known at the time of *Investigator*'s visit, a more thorough questioning of the villagers and search of the coastline might have been undertaken. If the stranger who died came from a sledge party from the reoccupied *Erebus*, then he would have died at the latest in Autumn 1849 after leaving the ship either as part of the 1848 retreat or another party in Summer 1849, perhaps before she reached Utjulik.

In 1859, at a meeting of the Royal Geographical Society, Captain F.L. McClintock presented his findings on his successful search for the lost Franklin Expedition. It was a particularly interesting meeting chaired by Vice President Sir Roderick Murchison with Captain McClintock and three other leaders of his expedition in the *Fox*, Commander Hobson, Dr. Walker and Captain Allen Young. Also present were many leaders and participants of other Franklin Relief Expeditions: Sir Edward Belcher; Captain R. Collinson; Captain Sherard Osborn, Mr. Parker Snow; Mr. Kennedy; Dr. R. King.

In the discussion afterwards Mr Kennedy reported:

> He had heard a rumour in the Red River colony that some time ago Europeans had been seen in the direction of the Mackenzie River. He imagined these were some of the 105, and that there was a likelihood that some of them were yet alive.

Also in 1850 an interpreter who had been with John Ross reported that white men had traded arms for food but had died and were buried near the Mackenzie River.

There were other rumours of white men in the vicinity of the Mackenzie River. Dr. John Richardson reported meeting over 200 esquimaux in kayaks plus another thirty women and children in three umiaks. The location was at the mouth of the Mackenzie River on the third of August 1848. An Inuit told him that white men were living nearby on Richard's Island and offered to take him to meet them. He reported they had been living there the previous winter. Richardson had been on the island the day before and believed the Inut was lying and trying to lure him there to rob him. The story is repeated by Dr. John Rae:

> When Sir John Richardson descended the Mackenzie River in 1848, a great number of Esquimaux came off in their canoes; they told us that on an island to which they pointed, a number of white people had been living for some time; that they had been living there all winter, and that we ought to land there to see them. Their story was altogether so incredible, that we could not have a moments doubt or difficulty in tracing its object. They wished to get us on shore in order to have a better opportunity to pillage our boats as they did those of Sir John Franklin; for it must be remembered that the Esquimaux at the Mackenzie and to the westward are different from any of those to the eastward. The former, notwithstanding the frequent efforts of the Hudson's Bay Company to effect a peace, are at constant war with the Louchoux Indians, and consequently with the 'white men', as they think the latter by supplying guns and ammunition to the Louchoux, are their allies.

The story requires the 'white men' to have arrived in the autumn of 1847. This is unlikely to be a party from the Franklin ships as they were not abandoned until April 1848.

The last act of defiance

There is a traditional last act of defiance by a crew abandoning ship. This is to nail the colours to the mast. This happened when Sir John Ross abandoned his ship *Victory* in 1832. It was repeated by Captain Henry Kellett, when he abandoned *Resolute* in 1852.

Sir John Ross and his nephew Sir James Clark Ross were trapped together for four winters in Prince Regent Inlet (1829 to 1833). Their paddle ship *Victory* was abandoned in 1832. On the twenty-ninth of May 1832 the colours were hoisted and nailed to the mast and parting glasses were drunk to the ship.

In 1852 five ships of the Royal Navy were sent in search of the lost Franklin expedition under the command of Sir Edward Belcher. Two years later four of the ships were trapped in the ice and Belcher ordered them to be abandoned and the expedition return home in the last freely moving ship. He was court marshalled for the loss of the four ships. This decision did not sit well with Captain Kellett who wanted to sit out the winter aboard his ship *Resolute* as he felt the ship would be freed in the summer thaw. However he had to follow orders. Before abandoning his ship Captain Kellett had her put in good order, with the decks swept, the cabins locked and all flags were flying. He inspected the ship including the lower deck and holds. After drinking a glass of wine to the old *Resolute* and her crew, the decks were cleared, the main hatchway secured and she was abandoned. However sixteen months later in September 1855, *Resolute* was found 1000 miles to the east by an American whaling ship after she had drifted free. She was sailed to New London, Connecticut and purchased by the U.S, government and refitted. She was then sailed back to Portsmouth and presented as a gift to Queen Victoria and the British government.

So both *Erebus* and *Terror* were probably abandoned with their flags flying. Certainly *Erebus* was honoured by a last act of defiance by her crew and left clean, her decks swept, cabins and hatchways secured and with their officer's body secure in the great cabin. The latest news of *Terror* (March 2017) is that her hatches are closed and the crew's personal possessions were removed.

Remarkably in 1851, Dr. Rae of the Hudson's Bay Company reached a point only sixty miles west of where *Erebus* and *Terror* had been first abandoned, only three years before. He planned to cross to King William Island, but the heavy ice and strong winds prevented him, so he retreated along his route. He met Inuit but they had no Franklin relics nor knowledge of the ships. However on the south coast he found wreckage. One was the base of a flagpole five feet nine inches long, which had white rope attached to it by two copper nails. The pole was marked with the broad arrow of the British Navy and the rope had a red thread in it. Both these features were typical of government property of the British Navy. The location at lat. 68 deg 52 min N., 103 deg 20 min W., is only eighty miles west of where *Terror* is believed to have sunk after 1850 near Terror Bay. *Erebus* was at Utjulik. The flagpole was almost certainly from one of the two ships and suggests that the colours had been nailed to the mast.

Erebus was lost to western people until the summer of 2014.

The Hunter and his three companions

The fireplace trail indicates that some of the crew of the reoccupied *Erebus* became successful seal hunters during the winters of 1848-50 when *Erebus* was frozen in off Imnguyaaluk Island. This would have required some friendly cooperation with the Inuit who could have taught them how to use a dog to smell out seal breathing holes. It seems likely from Inuit testimony that the dog used by the hunting party was not an Inuit dog, but possibly Neptune, the Newfoundland brought out from England on the ships. This cooperation may have begun in summer 1848 with a joint summer hunt with the Inuit for caribou.

Inuit testimony suggests that 'The Hunter' and three companions were the last men to leave *Erebus*. These four were likely to have been the most skilled of the hunters and had fully regained their health and physical activity from their new lifestyle. It is likely they were led by one man who was the chief hunter. There is some Inuit testimony collected recently by Dorothy Harley Eber that may describe an encounter with this small group. It is enigmatic for it describes a small group of fit and healthy men encountered by Inuit near the Etuk Islands near the Adelaide Peninsula. It contrasts greatly with the descriptions of weak and emaciated men of the boat party encountered in Washington Bay.

Nicholas Qayutinaq's testimony via Mark Tootiak – a description of 'The Hunter' and his companions

Eber wrote:

> This group of Inuit was at a sealing camp in the month when the young seals are already born, hunting around the Etuk Islands off the Adelaide Peninsula, when they saw something black, a small group of people. Before they arrived, there was a shaman with the Inuit who said, 'They are different people, they might be different people.' The Inuit found out they were friendly and someone put up a small igloo for them. They gave them what they could, a little of what they could, because they didn't have much. One of the men was a big man and very friendly. He was hairy, they touched his skin and he had hair on his chest, a big man and friendly. After a few days they treated him specially – they gave him a woman. The Inuit were getting along well with the strangers and they might have stayed longer but they left – they themselves were so poor they could not take any of the strangers with them.

There is more testimony describing this small group of hunters (described later) who are known from their footprints in the snow on Ook-soo-see-too island, they were accompanied by a dog. The trail was followed by the Inuit to a place where the hunters had killed a young deer and eaten it. The presence of a dog with the last survivors is a particularly interesting. *Erebus* carried a dog (also a cat and a monkey) when she sailed from England. It is possible that the dog with the last survivors was Neptune. Neptune might be expected to have died aboard ship, when being used to test the quality of the canned food. A dog might not be expected to have survived the starvation of the crew during the retreat. A dog is essential to the Inuit way of seal hunting to sniff out the breathing holes of the seals that are often hidden beneath a snow cover. Inuit dogs are also trained to carry backpacks and to haul sledges. The presence of the dog indicates that the winter seal hunting parties from *Erebus* had encountered Inuit also seal hunting.

Erebus was found in fresh ice and probably arrived in summer 1850 or 1851. She was probably winter occupied with summer camps on a nearby island. Inuit testimony tells of her final occupants being four men and a dog. In this reconstruction these were the best hunters with a dog to assist them. These four were likely to be away in summer, hunting with a camp on a nearby islet. They may have wintered aboard *Erebus* for one or two winters, finally abandoning her in 1851 or 1852.

In this reconstruction the crew left the body of their Captain Fitzjames in the great cabin, possibly with the head board marked 'R.I.P.', as a token of their respect for the man who had taken them back from a death march in 1848 and fought the ship south through the ice leads each summer to give them life and hope of escape for another two or three years. As they could no longer work the ship, and possibly because of Inuit looting while they were away hunting, they eventually left for Repulse Bay/Iwillik and then turned north along the Melville Peninsula where their distinctive track with their dog was seen by the Inuit, as was the dog. When they abandoned *Erebus*, they left the ship neat and tidy and locked up.

The unusual position of the *Erebus* wreck

Details of the exact location of the *Erebus* wreck have not been released, in order to protect the wreck, her last position is approximately known from Inuit testimony. She was first seen abandoned in young ice about three miles north of O'Reilly Island. She drifted or was ice rafted south and beached herself on a small island near O'Reilly Island where she remained for a number of years. Possibly her bow end was submerged and the Inuit extensively salvaged her stern end. Eventually she floated free in an ice raft before sinking in shallow water with her decks only ten feet below the water surface.

Her position near O'Reilly Island requires some explanation. If under the command of Captain Fitzjames, he would have attempted to work her along the northern margin of the American continent, westwards to Bering Strait (his mail awaited him in Petro Paulowski [Petropavlovsk] in Kamchatka). However, the wreck position is too far to the east, if this was the objective. She is close in to the west side of the Adelaide Peninsula in a bay. A course for Bering Strait should never have brought her into this bay. From Cape Crozier the route should have been southwest along the Victoria Strait and then turn west into Dease Strait between Victoria Island and the mainland of the American continent. It is possible, but unlikely, that the only leads in the ice took her to her final position.

There is another possibility. Her position today suggests she turned south east and got as close as possible to the estuary of Back's Great Fish River. There is a hint here that there might have been a change of plan. If the single officer died on route to her final resting place, then the remaining crew would not have the navigational skills to get the ship the 1,700 miles west, along the north coast of the American continent to Bering Strait. Perhaps the remaining crew led by 'The Hunter' decided to put the ship as close as possible to the good hunting grounds of the Adelaide Peninsula and Back's Great Fish River. There she could act as a base for the last few survivors, who now lived largely by the Inuit hunting lifestyle.

Two campsites and a skull on Ook-soo-see-too Islet.

A scatter of Franklin relics exists on the islets near O'Reilly Island and on O'Reilly Island itself and on the west coast of the Adelaide Peninsula. These are mainly objects transported by the Inuit from the time they salvaged *Erebus* (the Utjulik ship), but some are clearly from Franklin survivors, including a substantial campsite.

David Woodman has given brief accounts of the search expeditions for the Utjuklik ship and of islands in the O'Reilly Island area on Russell Potter's website (www.ric.edu/faculty/rpotter/woodman). A small islet identified as Ook-soo-see-too has produced interesting results. A spike with a broad arrow was found there in 1965. A copper belaying pin and barrel staves were found in 1967. A skull was found there in 1997, that proved to be of a young Caucasian male. The 2002 Irish-Canadian Franklin Search Expedition identified a campsite with three large rectangular tent sites that were of non-Inuit origin. The islet was identified as Ook-soo-see-too being the place where Inuit had found the footprints of the last survivors of *Erebus* and reported them to Hall. In 2002 a tent site and an optical prism were found there. Eight kilometres to the east on the western shore of the Adelaide Peninsula, a wooden mast was found but might have come from *Erebus* or a 1926 wrecked barge

The presence of a campsite, or two camp sites, one with three large tent bases is particularly interesting as it suggests that after *Erebus* arrived at her final destination, there were enough crew surviving to build a substantial summer camp. This might have been in summer 1850 or 1851. The fact that there are two campsites at a time when few men were left, raises the possibility that they were both summer hunting camps of the last survivors for two consecutive years. One might have been for autumn 1850 and the other might have been as late as summer 1851 or 1852. Interestingly there are no reports of the ground being saturated in blubber oil from blubber cooking fires. The lack of oil saturated ground would suggest that the two campsites were summer hunting and convalescent camps.

Ook-soo-see-too islet seems to be the place where the last act of the Franklin Expedition was played out. The last place where the crew camped together. After this the majority of the men vanish, and there is only the small group of four hunters and a dog, that soon diminishes to three hunters.

The probable last activities aboard *Erebus*

The Inuit testimonies give glimpses of a story of great hardship, endurance, fortitude and courage. A small crew probably led by Captain James Fitzjames had remained with their ship - *Erebus* - for five long years. They had survived the loss to the expedition of *Terror*, the catastrophic 1848 retreat, the deaths of Sir John Franklin and Captain Crozier and resisted later escape attempts. The ship had been provisioned for only three years. They had eked out a very poor existence particularly for the last two years, rather like Shackleton's men on Elephant Island by hunting. The crew were thin, hungry, bearded and filthy with blubber soot and oil and their health was poor. Some are remembered by the Inuit – 'Meetik' (the duck) and 'Qoitoyok' (the pisser – possibly a warrant officer who would wet his bed at night), and of course the great Esh-e-muta – the Captain in the Great Cabin.

The few left after the 1850 retreat got their ship through the North-West Passage into the summer water channel along the northern shore of the American continent – a distance of about sixty miles. They did this probably in 1850 – the first ship ever to do so. What elation there must have been on board. But then disaster struck once more when their captain – the only man with the navigation skills – died. The few crew were too weak and lacking navigation skills to fight the ship the 1,700 miles along the summer water channel to Bering Strait which had been the dream of their Captain. So the last crew probably turned the ship away from Bering Strait and sailed her to the good hunting grounds of the Adelaide Peninsula and anchored her there in Wilmot and Compton Bay near O'Reilly Island where her wreck was found in 2014.

Conclusions

Erebus was found in fresh ice and probably arrived in summer 1850 or 1851. She was probably winter occupied with summer camps on a nearby island. Inuit testimony tells of her final occupants being four men and a dog. In this reconstruction these were the best hunters with a dog to assist them. These four were likely to be away in summer, hunting with a camp on a nearby islet. They may have wintered aboard *Erebus* for one or two winters, finally abandoning her in 1851 or 1852.

In this reconstruction the crew left the body of their Captain Fitzjames in the great cabin, possibly with the head board marked 'R.I.P.', as a token of their respect for the man who had taken them back from a death march in 1848 and fought the ship south through the ice leads each summer to give them hope of escape for another two years. As they could no longer work the ship, and possibly because of Inuit looting while they were away hunting, they eventually left for Repulse Bay/Iwillik and then turned north along the Melville Peninsula where their distinctive track with their dog was seen by the Inuit, as was the dog. When they abandoned *Erebus*, they left the ship neat and tidy and locked up.

21: THE ARRIVAL OF A DESERTED SHIP WITH BODIES ABOARD, SOUTH OF CAPE CROZIER

Inuit find a deserted ship with many bodies aboard in Victoria Strait

There are several testimonies of the Inuit finding a solitary deserted ship in the ice with many bodies aboard and these are given below. In this reconstruction, at the time of the 1848 retreat, the damaged *Terror* was lying on her beam ends not far from *Erebus* in the Victoria Strait. Over winter 1847-1848 *Terror* had been used as a mausoleum ship. The 1848 Report stated that at the time of the retreat, the total number of deaths was nine officers and fifteen men. Three men died on Beechey Island and Sir John Franklin died on June 11 1847; so that another eight officers and twelve men died between June 1847, and the time the retreat began in April 1848. Many of these twenty bodies were likely placed, in the depths of winter, aboard the abandoned, overturned *Terror*, so she became a mausoleum ship. The *Chieftain* Report indicates that *Erebus* and *Terror* were both in the ice, with *Terror* still on her beam ends, in Spring 1849.

Two brothers' testimony of finding a deserted ship with many bodies aboard

Rasmussen collected the following testimony:

> Two brothers were out hunting seal to the northwest of Qequertaq (King William's Land). It was in the spring, at the time when the snow melts about the breathing holes of the seal. They caught sight of something, far out on the ice; a great black mass of something, that could not be any animal they knew. They studied it and made out at last that it was a great ship. Running home at once, they told their fellows, and on the following day all went out to see it. They saw no men about, it was deserted; and they therefore decided to take from it all they could find for themselves. But none of them had ever before met with white men, and they had no knowledge as to the use of all the things they found.

One man, seeing a boat that hung out over the side of the ship, cried: 'Here is a fine big trough that will do for meat! I will have this!' And he cut the ropes that held it up, and the boat crashed down endways on to the ice and was smashed.

They found guns, also, on the ship, and not knowing what was the right use of these things, they broke away the barrels and used the metal for harpoon heads. So ignorant were they indeed, in the matter of guns and belonging to guns, that on finding some percussion caps, such as were used in those days, they took them for tiny thimbles, and really believed that there were dwarfs among the white folk, little people who could use percussion caps for thimbles.

At first they were afraid to go down into the lower part of the ship, but after a while they grew bolder, and ventured also into the houses underneath. Here they found many dead men, lying in the sleeping places there, all dead. And at last they went down also in a great dark space in the middle of the ship. It was quite dark down there and they could not see. But they soon found tools and set to work and cut a window in the side. But here those foolish ones, knowing nothing of the white men's things, cut a hole in the side of the ship below the water-line, so that the water came pouring in, and the ship sank. It sank to the bottom with all the costly things; nearly all that they had found was lost again at once.

In another version Rasmussen added that the ship was out in the ice between King William Island and Victoria Land and that the Inuit could see that the many dead men had died of a sickness.

Amundsen's report – a deserted ship off Cape Crozier with tinned meat that poisoned some Inuit

Testimony for the presence of a ship off Cape Crozier, the westernmost point of King William Island and directly opposite the Royal Geographical Society Islands was collected by Amundsen in 1905.

The ship was deserted when found and Inuit entered her. They found and ate some tinned meat and became ill and several died:

> One of the ships had driven down towards Ogluli and was found by the Eskimo one winter's day when they were seal fishing on the south coast of Cape Crozier, the most westerly point of King William Land. They had then removed all the iron and wood work they could remove, and when spring came and the ice broke up the ship sank. At this time the Eskimo had eaten something from some tins which were like ours, and it made

them very ill: indeed some had actually died. They knew nothing of the other vessel.

Implications of the deserted and isolated mausoleum-ship south of Cape Crozier

The testimonies describe only a single ship with many bodies inside. *Erebus* and *Terror* were both beset some seventeen miles off the west coast of King William Island, and drifted slowly south down Victoria Strait. In this reconstruction *Terror* was pushed over by the ice onto her beam ends in the summer of 1847. During winter 1847-1848 she was used as a mausoleum ship for those who died during the winter, aboard the crowded *Erebus*, before the 1848 retreat. The description of the central hold and a normal waterline suggest the ship on arrival in the ice south of Cape Crozier was once again upright. This suggests that in an earlier summer thaw, the ship was released by the ice and became upright again.

The *Chieftain* report suggests that the two ships were seen with one still on her beam ends in spring 1849. *Erebus* was reoccupied in summer 1848, after the retreat failed. In order to arrive at one ship with bodies, the implication is that in the summer breakup of 1848, the remanned *Erebus* was released and worked some way to the south to become first the Imnguyaaluk ship, and then two years later when she was worked further south, the Utjulik ship. The arrival of a deserted ship with many bodies aboard (*Terror*) in the ice south of Cape Crozier would have to have been after the reoccupied *Erebus* at Imnguyaaluk Island had been freed from the ice and worked ninety sixty miles south to Utjulik, probably after 1850 or 1851.

Whether the Inuit cut a hole through the side of the ship, might be revealed shortly as Parks Canada divers examine the *Terror* wreck found intact in 2016. It would have been no simple matter to cut through the side of such a ship. *Erebus* and *Terror* had been specially strengthened to withstand ice pressure. Cookman describes the ships as former bomb vessels with ribs and beams of English oak one and a half feet square. The ships sides were of three inches of English oak to which two layers of African oak were added, each one and a half inches thick and arranged diagonally against each other. To this was added two layers of Canadian elm, each two inches thick. The five layers of timber made the ships sides ten inches thick. An easier method of making a hole would have been to work through a damaged part of the hull.

A remarkable sea saga

In the days of the sailing ships the roles played by the wind and the sea led to many mysterious and strange events for these ships and their crews. Mysteries such as the Marie Celeste occurred. The 1000 mile voyage of the unmanned *Resolute*, abandoned in the Arctic by the Belcher search expedition has already been described. It is only today following the publication of the critical testimony of the ship at Imnguyaaluk Island by Dorothy Harley Eber in 2008 and the discovery of the wreck of *Terror* off Terror Bay that another remarkable sea saga is revealed.

This is the voyage of *Terror*, abandoned in 1848 lying on her port side with a crew of dead officers and men lying in her bunks. Sometime after *Erebus* left for the south, *Terror* was freed from the ice and came upright again. Then with no one at the helm she drifted in the ice along the coast of King William Island, for ninety-sixty miles to the entrance of Alexandra Strait. Then she turned south for twenty miles and then turned again in an arc to be carried north-east almost inside Terror Bay. She had sailed herself 103 miles passing through Alexandra Strait (around Cape Crozier) and finally due to vagaries of the wind had almost entered Terror Bay (Map II).

She was mainly following the route of *Erebus*. But the fickle winds turned her almost into Terror Bay, where she was found by the Inuit who holed her and she sank with her mast tops above water. Even more remarkable is that about a century and a half later (around 2007) an Inuit from Gjoa Haven – Sammy Kogvit - was out hunting and saw one of her masts standing though the ice and had himself photographed on it. Unfortunately he lost his camera and this almost unbelievable photograph. But he led a search vessel there seven years later and *Terror* was found.

In this reconstruction Terror Bay was the place where the 1848 retreat stopped. About fifteen men were left immobile and weak in a tent awaiting the return of *Erebus*. The latter did arrive but too late for the men had died. But Captain Crozier turned *Erebus* away from Terror Bay and the horrors of the cannibalised remains of the men there. He anchored *Erebus* on the south side of Imnguyaaluk Island in the lee of the island protected from the ice stream.

Erebus remained trapped there for another two years, but with friendly relations with the Inuit in their hunting grounds. So only today has the remarkable voyage of a ship crewed only by dead men sailed herself south for 103 miles and almost into a bay where many of her crew had died awaited rescue in vain. It is another remarkable tale of the sea and the men who sailed the wind ships. These men believed their ships had personalities and referred to them as 'she' and would not have been surprised at this event.

22: 1851 TO 1854 - THE LAST SURVIVORS

The subject of the possible last survivors of the Franklin expedition is very much the work of David Woodman in his 1995 book on the Lost Franklin Expedition 'Strangers among us'. In it he examines in great detail, testimony collected by Hall that is often omitted from the 1879 Nourse compilation of Hall's work. There are two major topics. First is the arrival of four survivors in the Boothia region to the east of King William Land. These men were cared for by an Inut through the winter. Next year they hunt with the Inuit and then head south for Fort Churchill, but never arrive.

The second are Inuit testimonies of strangers on the Melville Peninsula. The latter is a particularly exhaustive study as the area was mapped by Dr. John Rae and his party and visited by the second Parry expedition of 1821 to 1823 (including a youthful midshipman Crozier). Woodman has convincingly unravelled the various testimonies and in both cases is left with a residue of testimony that can only be attributed to Franklin survivors. However these men also failed to reach their objective that was probably Repulse Bay. The reader is referred to Woodman's excellent books for the full reasoning. Here, only a selection of testimonies is given to outline the struggles of the last survivors. In addition, weak reports of a third possible group in the Mackenzie River area have already been considered.

Hall, in September 1864 at the start of his second expedition, was put ashore in the wrong place some forty miles short of his destination of the Wager River on route to Repulse Bay. The party travelled by small boat northwards and stopped when they met a party of Inuit led by Ouela. Hall asked about white men being lost long ago, and was astonished to get new information immediately.

Ouela's testimony – four men did not die
Hall wrote:
> ... they at once told me that there were two ships lost near Neitchille many years ago, and that a great many kabloonas (white men) died – some starved and some were frozen to death – but that there were four that did not die. How astounded I was as Too-koo-li-too (the best interpreter

of Inuit language into our vernacular that ever accompanied an Arctic expedition) told me this! Little did I expect to find so soon natives that seemed to know a volume of interesting and important facts bearing on the Franklin Expedition.

Later, when in winter quarters, Hall wrote a full account of his findings to his friend Captain Chapel of the whaling ship Monticello. This letter is included here in full. In it he follows his interpretation that anyone named 'Aglooka' by the Inuit was Captain Crozier – a view no longer held today. Owen who is a descendant of Franklin wrote of this letter that Hall was either exceptionally gullible or really on to something. He also wrote that the kobloonas were at liberty to believe what they chose of any of this nonesense.

Letter from C.F. Hall dated 10th December 1864

WINTER QUARTERS, IN IGLOO,
NOO-WOOK, WEST END OF ROWE'S WELCOME
Lat. 64 deg. 46 min. N., Long. 87 deg. 20 min. W., Friday, December 10, 1864.

DEAR FRIEND CHAPEL: In this letter I have some deeply interesting intelligence to communicate to you. Since falling in with the natives I have not been idle. Nothing in Parry's narrative of second voyage for the discovery of the North-West Passage relating to the Eskimos of Winter Island and Igloolik but these natives are perfectly posted up in. Indeed, I find through my superior interpreter, Too-koo-li-too, that many deeply interesting incidents occurred at both named places that never found their place in Parry's or Lyon's works. But the great work already done by me is the gaining little by little from these natives, through Too-loo-li-too and Ebierbing, news relating to Sir John Franklin's Expedition. This, you know was the great object of my mission to the north. I cannot stop to tell you now all I have gained from this people – no not one hundredth part. (The natives are now loading sledge; it is 7 o'clock 30 minutes a.m.)
I will give you very briefly what the people of England and America will be most interested to learn. When I come down I shall bring my dispatches and journals up to the time of writing you, and these will be committed to your care for transmitting to the States. The most important matter that I have acquired related to the fact that there may yet be three survivors of Sir John Franklin's Expedition, and one of these Crozier, the one who succeeded Sir John Franklin on his death. The details are deeply interesting,

but this must suffice until I come down: Crozier and three men with him were found by a cousin of Ouela (Albert), Skoo-ski-ark-nook (John), and Ar-too-a (Frank), while moving on the ice from one igloo to another; this cousin having with him his family and engaged in sealing. This occurred near Neitchille (Boothia Felix Peninsula). Crozier was nothing but 'skin and bones', was nearly starved to death, while the three men with him were fat. The cousin soon learned that the three fat men had been living on human flesh, on the flesh of their companions who all deserted the two ships that were fast in mountains of ice; while Crozier was the only man that would not eat human flesh, and for this reason he was almost dead from starvation. This cousin, who has two names (but I cannot stop to get them now) took Crozier and the three men at once in charge. He soon caught a seal and gave Crozier quickly a little – a very little piece, which was raw – only one mouthful the first day. The cousin did not give the three fat men anything, for they could well get along, till Crozier's life was safe. The next day the cousin gave Crozier a little larger piece of same seal. By the judicious care of this cousin for Crozier, his life was saved. Indeed, Crozier's own judgement stuck to him in this terrible situation, for he agreed with the cousin that one little bit was all he should have the first day. When the cousin first saw Crozier's face, it looked so bad – his eyes all sunk in, the face so skeleton like and haggard, that he did not dare look upon Crozier's face for several days after; it made him feel so bad! This noble man, whom the whole civilized world will ever remember for humanity, took care of Crozier and his three men, save one who died, through the whole winter. One man, however, died a short time after the cousin found them, not because he starved, but because he was sick. In the spring, Crozier and the remaining two men accompanied this cousin on the Boothia Felix Peninsula to Neitchille, where there were many Inuit. Crozier and each of his men had many guns and plenty of ammunition, and many pretty things. They killed a great many ducks, nowyers (gulls), &c with their guns. Here they lived with the Inuit at Neitchille, and Crozier became fat and of good health. Crozier told this cousin that he was once at Iwillik (Repulse Bay), at Winter Island and Igloolik, many years before and at the last two named places he saw many Inuit, and got acquainted with them. This cousin had heard of Parry, Lyon and Crozier, from his Innuit friends at Repulse Bay, some years previous, and therefore when Crozier gave him his name he recollected it. The cousin saw Crozier one year before he found him and the three men, where the two ships were in the ice. It was there that he found out that Crozier had been to Igloolik.

Crozier and the two men lived with the Neitchille Inuit for some time. The Inuit liked him (C.) very much, and treated him always very kindly. At length, Crozier with his two men and one Inut, who took along a ki-ak (an Indian rubber boat, as Eberbing thinks it was, for all along the ribs there was something that could be filled with air), left Neitchille to try to go to the kobluna's country, taking a south course.

When Ouela (Albert) and his brothers in 1851, saw their cousin that had been so good to Crozier and his men, at Oekky Bay that is not far from Neitchelle, the cousins had not heard whether Crozier and the two men and Neitchille Innuit had ever come back or not. The Inuit never think they are dead – do not believe they are. Crozier offered to give his gun to the cousin for saving his life, but he would not accept it, for he was afraid it would kill him, it made such a great noise and killed everything with nothing. Then Crozier gave him a long, curious knife (sword, as Ebierbing and Too-koo-li-too say it was), and many pretty things beside (the dogs are all in harness, and sledges loaded, and Inuit waiting for my letters. I promise to be ready in 30 minutes.) Crozier told the cousin of a fight with a band of Indians – not Inuit, but Indians. This must have occurred near the entrance of Great Fish or Back's River. More of this when I see you.

God bless you. C.F. Hall

Later Hall became sceptical of this report. It is however correct when it states that Parry, Lyon, Crozier (and James Clark Ross) had participated together in an earlier Arctic Expedition at Repulse Bay (Parry's second expedition of 1821 to 1823).

The sentence:

> The cousin saw Crozier one year before he found him and the three men, where the two ships were in the ice. It was there that he found out Crozier had been to Igloolik

is particularly interesting. It suggests Inuit contact with the two ships in the ice in 1849-1850 at Imnguyaaluk Island after the 1848 retreat. Such contact including joint hunting trips was not unusual at that time.

Ook-bar-loo's testimony about the arrival of Aglooka and companions in the east

Hall wrote:

> Mother Ook-bar-loo continued – One man would not eat the flesh of his frozen and starved companions, and therefore when her nephew,

Too-shoo-ar-thar-i-u, found Aglooka (Crozier) and three other Koblunas with him, Aglooka, who was the one that would not eat human flesh, was very thin and almost starved. One of the three men with Aglooka died, for he was very sick. He did not die from hunger, but because he was very sick.

Ouela and his brothers' testimony about the arrival of Aglooka and companions in the east

Hall wrote:

> This evening I have had another talk with Ou-e-la, Shoo-she-ark-nuk and Ar-too-a about some of the men of Franklin's Expedition. The man who caught seals for Ag-loo-ka (Crozier) and some of his men – the three with him – is their cousin. His name is Too-shoo-ar-thar-i-u. When he first found Crozier and the three men with them, Crozier's face looked bad – his eyes all sunk in – looked so bad that their cousin could not bear to look at his face. Their cousin gave Crozier a bit of raw seal meat as quick as he could when he first saw him. Did not give any to the other three, for they were fat and had been eating the flesh of their companions. It was near Neitch-il-le that this occurred on the ice. This cousin is now living at Neitch-il-le. When Too-shoo-ar-thar-i-u first saw Crozier and the men with him, he was moving, having a loaded sledge drawn by dogs; he was going from place to place, making Igloos on the ice – sealing – he had with him his wife, whose name is E-laing-nur and children. Crozier and his men had guns and plenty of power, shot and ball. The cousin took Crozier and his men along with him, and fed them and took good care of them all winter. Beside a high cliff Inuit saw something like Now-yers (gulls) fall down to the ground, dead, and would not touch them, for Crozier had done something to them – they (the Inuit) knew not what. In the summer Crozier and his men killed with their guns a great many birds, ducks, geese and rein-deer. Crozier killed many – very many of the latter. The Inuit saw him do it.

Aglooka gives his sword to his rescuer Too-shoo-ar-thar-i-u

Hall in his letter to Captain Chapel (above) states that 'Aglooka', before he departed for the south, gave his sword to Too-shoo-ar-that-i-u. This was a fitting gift to the man who had saved their lives and fed them through the winter (his first offer of a gun was declined as the Inut had no knowledge of them). A sword was presented to Hudson's Bay Chief Factor Roderick

MacFarlane from an old Inut man who said it had been given to him in 1857 by a 'great officer'.

The sword is kept in the Manitoba Museum in Manitoba. The sword is shown in a photograph in Potter's recent book with a detailed description. Potter drew a surprising conclusion. The basket work on the sword's hilt identifies it as a British infantry sword and not a naval sword. For the Franklin Expedition such a sword could be carried only by the Royal Marines. However there were no Royal Marine officers on the expedition. Aboard *Erebus* were Sergeant Daniel Bryant, Corporal Alexander Paterson and five privates (one of whom William Braine had died and was buried on Beechey Island). Aboard *Terror* were Sergeant Solomon Tozer, Corporal William Hedges and four privates.

The four survivors including the officer Aglooka were a remnant of the party encountered by the Inuit near Washington Bay. Inuit descriptions suggest they were led by a young officer and an older man with grey hair and a beard. The latter is suggested here to have been *Terror*'s Ice Master Thomas Blanky who died with four companions on a Todd Islet. Facial reconstruction work has suggested that Ice Master James Reid of *Erebus* died at one of the boat places in Erebus Bay in 1848. He was found in the stern of a pinnace from *Erebus* with a loaded shotgun on either side of him. He had probably volunteered to remain behind to look after the immobile *Erebus* sick left with their halted boat.

There is a distinct possibility, if the sword is that presented to Too-shooar-that-i-u, that the 'great officer' who led his colleagues almost as far as the Boothian Peninsula on route to Repulse Bay, was Royal Marine Sergeant Solomon Tozer of *Terror*. So it seems possible that after Captain Crozier died, many of the survivors aboard *Erebus*, perhaps mainly *Terror* men, made a last effort to escape to Repulse Bay in 1850, led by Ice Master Thomas Blanky and Marine Sergeant Solomon Tozer.

According to Lloyd-Jones, Sergeant Solomon Tozer was from Somerset, born in Axbridge near Cheddar in around 1815, although his exact age is uncertain as in 1833 his age was eighteen years and two months, but in the 1853 list of officers and crew, his age in 1845 is given as thirty-four years. Lloyd-Jones accepts his age as thirty years in 1845. He was promoted to sergeant in the 48th Company on October 26 1844.

The area of the Franklin retreat was occupied by two tribes of Inuit and their distribution is shown on the maps of Schwatka. To the west and north-west of Chesterfield Strait lay the hunting grounds of the fierce Kin-na-pa-too Inuit and to the north-east of Chesterfield strait were those of the friendly Iwillik Inuit. Dorothy Harley Eber records that:

McClintock met terror-stricken Inuit who 'would give him no information', and 'Colonel Gilder(of the Schwatka expedition) believed that certain Eskimos would gladly have killed him and other members of his party in order to obtain their equipment.

The Schwatka expedition discovered that the friendly Utjulingmiut of the Adelaide Peninsula area in the time of Franklin, had been driven out by the more hostile Netsilingmiut.

Hall receives a warning

In April 1866, Hall met a group of Inuit led by Kok-lee-arng-nun and receive news that caused him to turn back from King William Island and return to Repulse Bay. He planned to make another attempt the following year bringing some western whaling men with him.

> But other news received from these strangers was anything but gratifying. It effectively barred further progress to King William's Land for the year 1866. The first words to Nu-ker-zhoo, Mammark and Ar-mou told of the loss of their friends and relatives some years before by starvation, murder and cannibalism. This was followed by such accounts of the dangers awaiting them if they went to Pelly Bay and Oot-goo-lik, as to throw a damper on the whole party except Hall himself. The old chief said that a very old and infirm man on removing to Oot-goo-lik had been immediately murdered with his whole family; that very recently there had been fights between the Neit-tee-lik Inuit for a woman, and one of them had been killed to get his wife; that some of the Pelly Bay natives who were without wives and who being aided by the friends in their attempts to steal wives from their husbands, would certainly carry off Mam-mark, and that he himself was leaving his own country for Repulse Bay through fear especially of the See-nee-mee-utes............Three men of Kok-lee-arng-nun's party, one by one confirmed all that their chief had said of the bad state of affairs among the natives northward and westward, and added that since a recent fight about a deposit, in which the See-nee-mee-utes had lost two men by the Neit-tee-liks, they were burning to wreak vengeance on somebody.

Too-shoo-ar-thar-i-u's testimony - Aglooka and two men set off to the south

Hall wrote:

A Neitchille Inut went with Crozier and his remaining two men when they started to go to their country. They had a kiak with which to cross rivers and lakes. They went down toward Ook-koo-seek-ka-lik (the estuary of Back's Great Fish River). Their cousin liked Crozier very much. Crozier wanted to give their cousin his gun, but he would not accept it, for he was afraid of it, he did not know anything about how to use it. Crozier gave him his long knife (sword, as Too-koo-li-too and Ebierbing interpret it) and nearly everything he had. He (C,) had many pretty things. Crozier told Too-shoo-ar-thar-i-u all about what had happened, but he could not understand all. The cousin is now alive, and knows all what he saw and what Crozier told him.

The story now is, that Crozier with his two men and a Neitch-il-le Inuit started from Neitch-il-le – started in the summer or fall – for the Kob-lunas' country, travelling to the southward on the land. They had a small boat that had places on the sides that would hold wind (air) (Ebierbing said to me). From their (our informer's) description, the boat must have been an India rubber one, or something like it, with hollow places in the sides for wind (air) to hold it up when in the water. (By this it would seem that Franklin must have had in his vessels a boat or boats called Halkett's air-boats, or its equivalent. But I do not recollect of ever reading or hearing about this particular; however, I believe that he (Franklin) must have had something of this kind aboard his ship). There were sticks or holes for this boat, to keep it open (spread) when needed.

This small boat was wrapped or rolled up in a bundle or pack, and carried on the shoulder of one of his men. The sides of this boat, something like Inuit 'drugs' that could be filled with air.

Kok-lee-arng-nun's testimony - Aglooka and one man continue to the south

When Hall reached Pelly Bay in April 1866, he met Inuit with much information about the Franklin expedition. One reported:

> Ag-loo-ka and one other white man – the latter called Nar-tar, a pee-ee-tu (steward) started and went toward Oot-koo-ish-ee-lee (Great Fish or Back's River), saying they were going there on their way home. That was the last they saw of them, but heard of them some time after from a Kin-na-pa-too, who said he and his people heard shots or reports of guns of strangers somewhere near Chesterfield Inlet. On getting the Innuits to try to pronounce the word 'doctor,' they invariably said 'nar-tar.' This made Hall think that

the white man with Ag-loo-ka was someone called 'doctor' – perhaps Surgeon Macdonald, of Franklin's ship *Erebus*.

Too-koo-li-too's testimony - Aglooka and one man arrived amongst the hostile Kin-na-pa-toos

Woodman explains that the Kin-na-pa-too were the Qairnirmiut Inuit who lived near Baker Lake and hunted the Chesterfield Inlet area. This report of Hall was published by Nourse:

> The astounding news that Ag-loo-ka (Crozier) arrived with one man, amongst the Kin-na-pa-toos, his powder and shot nearly all gone! I must give the particulars of the above startling news, as given me a few moments ago. At the time I got the above information there were, as usual through the day and evening, several Innuits in our igloo. The An-nat-koo's (Ar-too-a's) wife, and the wife of --------, and the old man, See-gar, were all seated on the dias or bed platform, while Too-loo-li-too was at her place by her fire lamp, engaged telling these visitors about Ag-loo-ka (Crozier). Too-koo-li-too had just made the sympathetic remark – 'What a pity it is that Ag-loo-ka and the two men who started together from Neitchille for the purpose of getting to the kob-lu-nas country had never arrived', Old See-gar listened, as did the other Inuit present, to all that Too-koo-li-too said, and when she made the last remark, See-gar sprang from his seat, quick as a flash, and looking staringly at Too-koo-li-too, exclaimed with great force and surprise, 'What! Ag-loo-ka not got back! Why,' continued See-gar, 'the Kin-na-pa-toos (Inuit who belong to Chesterfield Inlet) told me several years ago that Ag-loo-ka and one man with him arrived among their (the Kin-na-pa-toos) people, and that they (Ag-loo-ka and his men) had gone to where the Kob-lu-nas live further down the Big Bay' (to Churchill or York Factory, as Too-koo-li-too thinks See-gar tried to explain it). I was greatly interested as well as surprised, in what See-gar said, as now recorded. I at once had Too-koo-li-too ask old See-gar several questions, which he answered by communicating the following:
> Ag-loo-ka, of whom he (See-gar) had heard Too-shoo-ar-thar-i-u tell all about at the same time that Ou-e-la and his brother saw him, arrived among the Kin-na-pa-toos, having one man with him, and his powder and shot were nearly all gone. The Kin-na-pa-toos told him (See-gar) about this before, See-pee-lar (Captain E. A. Chapel) and his brother came the first time into this bay (which was in 1860). The kin-na-pa-too Innuits said that Ag-loo-ka and his man had gone on and had arrived at the nearest place where Kob-la-nas live, which must mean Fort Churchill.

Too-shoo-ar-thar-i-u told him (See-gar) (this was in the winter of 1853-4 at Pelly Bay) that Ag-loo-ka would probably get home to where the Kab-lu-nas live, unless somebody killed him, for he (Ag-loo-ka) knew all about how to hunt and kill took-too [rein deer] and nearly everything else that the Inuit could kill; knew how to keep himself warm, how to live just as the Inuit do; as he (E.) had lived and hunted with him (Too-shoo-ar-thar-i-n) and with many others of the Neitchille Innuits. Ag-loo-ka knew all about everything that the Inuit knew. The Kin-na-pa-too Innuits told him (See-gar) about Ag-loo-ka and his men; did not see them; but said that they had their information from others of their people who did.

The death of Aglooka

Hall could not understand how Aglooka, knowing everything about Arctic survival and taught by the Inuit, could have failed to reach Fort Churchill. He suspected that the men had been murdered by the Kin-na-pa-toos whom the other Inuit regarded as a treacherous people.

Woodman discovered in Hall's unpublished notebooks, information from a Captain Fisher of the whaler *Ansel Gibbs*, collected shortly before Hall left the Arctic. Captain Fisher obtained his information from the Kin-na-pa-toos – the Inuit who live along the Chesterfield Inlet - during a visit to the whaling ships in winter quarters at Marble Island, in winter 1868-1869. The testimony was that a white man had arrived amongst the Kin-no-pa-toos many years before. He was finally murdered or rather starved to death which was the same thing. Another white man was with him but died before reaching the Kin-na-pa-toos. Captain Fisher believed the man murdered was Captain Crozier but gave no reason.

Strangers on the Melville Peninsula

Woodman has examined many of Hall's Inuit testimonies of strange white men on the Melville Peninsula, usually carrying guns slung over their shoulders. In addition, there are testimonies describing campfires with red painted tins, strange cairns and even human excrement that was quite different to that of the Inuit. There were tracks of distinctive white man footprints, with gunshots being heard in the same areas. Some tracks were accompanied by those of a dog, including one sighting of a non-Inuit type dog pursuing two deer.

It took Woodman a lot of careful work to separate the testimonies of Parry, Lyon and Crozier from their 1821 to 1823 expedition from the two mapping trips of Dr. John Rae. The latter thought some of the testimonies described his two expeditions of 1846-47 and 1854. The Inuit had thought these men to be Et-ker-lin or Indians before they learned about the Franklin Expedition. The Inuit were very aware of the visit of Parry and the two visits of Dr. John Rae and dated the strangers' activities relative to these visits. There was also the possibility of unrecorded visits by whalers who kept their explorations secret.

However, there was testimony from places where the western explorers had not been. Woodman's careful analysis concluded that there were possible Franklin survivor sightings that were restricted to two periods. The first set are timed between the two visits of Dr. John Rae and were shortly before or two years before his second visit, being 1852. Other testimonies seem to centre on 1855 to 56. Attempts by Hall to date the testimonies by counting the years backwards yielded dates of 1855 to1864.

'The Hunter', companions and dog arrive on the Melville Peninsula

After the 1848 retreat, the priority on board the reoccupied *Erebus* would be hunting to increase the food supply that had almost run out after three years in the Arctic. The fireplace trail indicates that some of the crew of the reoccupied ship became successful seal hunters during the winter of 1848-9 and 1849-50. There is also the testimony of the successful joint summer hunt with the Inuit for caribou. During this time of friendly cooperation with the Inuit a group of hunters emerged. There is testimony to suggest that the last few men aboard *Erebus* (when she had reached the Adelaide Peninsula) were four hunters and a dog that must have been used as a hunting dog to smell out the fur seal air holes that are often covered with drifting snow. This cooperation may have begun in late summer 1848 with a joint summer hunt with the Inuit for caribou.

Inuit testimony suggests that 'The Hunter' with three companions were the last men to leave *Erebus*. They were known from Inuit testimony of their footprints and those of their dog on Ook-soo-see-too Island. Nourse wrote:

> fresh tracks were seen of four men and a dog on the land where the ship was... the foot marks were long, narrow in the middle, and the prints like as if of boots found in the two boats found on King William's Land. One man from his running steps, was a very great runner – very long steps...

These four were likely to have been the most skilled of the hunters and had fully regained their health and physical activity from their new lifestyle. It is likely they were led by one man who was the chief hunter. Inuit testimony collected by Dorothy Harley Eber has already been given describing an encounter with this small group. It is enigmatic for it describes a small group of fit and healthy men encountered by Inuit near the Etuk Islands near the Adelaide Peninsula.

The likely fate of The Hunter, his party and their dog

So if the *Erebus* Hunter, with companions and a dog reached Repulse Bay (Iwillik), then there were two possible routes to places where white men might be met. From Repulse Bay it is 250 miles north to the settlement on Igloolik Island. Inuit there visited Ponds Bay and Admiralty Inlet to hunt whales or meet with whaling ships as described by the second Parry expedition of 1821 to 1823. Alternatively, it is 600 miles south to the Hudson's Bay Company post at Fort Churchill.

Woodman describes three testimonies of the men and their dog that indicate three different positions on the Melville Peninsula. It seems the party travelled 360 miles east from *Erebus* on the west side of the Adelaide Peninsula, then across the southern ends of Pelly and Committee Bays to Repulse Bay. This route was used by Hall in 1869 when he made a return trip to King William Island. Woodman reports that Hall considered it an excellent escape route for the Franklin survivors because in the three months of his trip, his party killed seventy-nine musk oxen, eighteen caribou and two seals. Next, they chose the shorter route north to Igloolik island. This involved a tortuous coastal route up the east coast of the 233 mile long Melville Peninsula. They reached Kee-wee-gee island on the east coast off the Amitoke Peninsula. They are next reported at the west end of Fury and Hekla Strait. They may have been lost at this stage, as Igloolik Island lies at the east end of Hekla and Fury Strait. The testimonies also indicate that during this journey their numbers decreased, so that only two men and the dog arrived at Fury and Hekla Strait. The story fades there, and no more is known of this group.

Other strangers on the Melville Peninsula

In a second book, Woodman has presents an exhaustive study of Inuit encounters with strangers and the remains of their campfires etc. and concludes that some of the testimony relates to the Parry's second expedition of 1821 to 1823, others to the two visits of Dr. John Rae in 1846 to 1847 and 1854. There is a residue of testimony possibly describing strangers in 1855 to 1856. If these men were Franklin survivors, then they too would have followed the route east to Repulse Bay/Iwillik on the Melville Peninsula, but moved up the west coast of the peninsula and possibly lived in the area for some years. However, nothing is conclusive and so these surprisingly late testimonies are not repeated here.

23: SOME EVENTS AT HOME

From the time of the last sighting of the expedition on July 26 1845 there was no news until August 1850. The mightiest of searches was conducted by the Admiralty, by private expeditions, friends of Sir John Franklin, private American expeditions and the Hudson's Bay Company. But all were to no avail for no ships or men were found. In 1850, the search ships found the 1845 - 46 winter quarters of the Franklin expedition on Beechey Island off the south-west corner of Devon Island at the junctions of Lancaster Sound and Wellington Channel. Regrettably, no record was found telling where the expedition had been nor which way it was heading.

On March 31 1854, nine years after the expedition sailed, the Admiralty removed the names of the officers and men of the Franklin expedition from their books and declared the men dead. The Crimean war had broken out in October 1853 and continued until February 1856, and in this time the Admiralty had no more men and ships to spare on the searches. In October 1854, the first real news of the fate of the expedition was brought home by Dr. John Rae, more than nine years after they had sailed. He had found the missing piece of the puzzle. The expedition had retreated south towards the estuary of Back's Great Fish River. The expedition had gone to the one place that most experts agreed it would not go.

Because of the war effort, the Admiralty requested the Hudson's Bay Company to send men down the Great Fish River to confirm Dr. Rae's report. This was carried out in summer 1855 by Chief Factor Anderson and a small party in two frail bark canoes. They were able to collect more Franklin expedition relics and confirm Dr. Rae's information, but little more. It fell to Lady Jane Franklin to raise funds for a private expedition to try to recover the lost records and log books. She purchased the yacht *Fox* and accepted the voluntary offer to command her by then-Captain F. Leopold McClintock. The expedition in 1859 became the first by western men to visit the line of the Franklin retreat and brought home numerous relics and a brief written record that remains the only written information from the lost expedition up until the present day.

Letter from Lady Jane Franklin to Zachery Taylor, President of the United States of America, requesting assistance for the search for the lost Franklin Expedition

The very capable Lady Jane Franklin was an eloquent letter writer. It was her skill in this direction, when she assisted her husband as Governor of Van Diemen's Land with his official government dispatches, that incurred the wrath of Colonial Secretary John Montagu. The long drawn out dispute led eventually to Sir John being recalled. After the Franklin Expedition sailed, Lady Jane became a very prominent activist calling for searches for the lost expedition. Her courage and determination to discover the fate of her husband and the lost expedition and her failure to give up hope, led to her becoming one of the best know Victorian ladies. She wrote many letters, not only to the British Prime Minister and the Admiralty, but to President Zachary Taylor of the United States of America, the Czar of Russia and numerous people in various countries, requesting searches of the northern shores of their continents. The following letter to the President of the United States is a good example of her eloquence.

The Lady of Sir John Franklin to the President of the United States of America.

Spring Gardens, London.

December 11th 1849.

Sir,

I had the honor of addressing you, in the month of April last, on behalf of my husband. Sir John Franklin, his officers and crews, who were sent by Her Majesty's Government, in the spring of 1845, on a maritime expedition for the discovery on the North-West Passage, and who have never since been heard of.

Their mysterious fate has excited, I believe, the deepest interest throughout the civilised world, but nowhere more so, not even in England itself, than in the United States of America. It was under the deep conviction of this fact, and with the humble hope that an urgent appeal to those generous sentiments would never be made altogether in vain, that I ventured to lay before you the necessities of that critical period, and to ask you to take up the cause of humanity which I pleaded, and generously make it your own. How nobly you, sir, and the America people, responded to that appeal, how kindly and courteously that response was conveyed to me, is known wherever our common language is spoken or understood; and though difficulties, which were mainly owing to the advanced state of the season, presented themselves after your official announcement had been made known to our government and prevented the immediate execution of your intentions, yet the generous pledge you had given was not altogether withdrawn, and hope still remained for me that, should the necessity for renewed measures continue to exist, I might look again across the waters for the needed succour.

A period has now, alas! arrived, when our dearest hopes as to the safe return of the discovery ships this autumn are finally crushed by the unexpected, though forced, return of Sir James Ross, without any tidings of them, and also by the close of the Arctic season. And not only have no tidings been brought of their safety or of their fate, but even the very traces of their course have yet to be discovered; for such was the occurrence of unfortunate and unusual circumstances attending the efforts of the brave and able officer alluded to, that he was not able to reach those points where indications of the course of the discovery ships would most probably be found. And thus, at the close of a second season since the departure of the recent expedition of search we remain in nearly the same state of ignorance respecting the missing Expedition as at the moment of its starting from our shores. And in the meantime, our brave countrymen, whether clinging still to their ships or dispersed in various directions, have entered upon a fifth winter in those dark and dreary solitudes, with exhausted means of sustenance, while yet their expected succour comes not!

It is the time, then, of their greatest peril, in the day of their extremist need, that I venture, encouraged by your former kindness, to look to you again for some active efforts which may come in aid of those of my own country, and add to the means of search. Her Majesty's ministers have already resolved on sending an expedition to Bering's Strait, and doubtless have other necessary measures in contemplation, supported as they are, in every means that can be devised for this humane purpose, by the sympathies of the nation and by the generous solicitude which our Queen is known to feel in the fate of her brave people imperilled in their country's service. But whatever be the measures contemplated by the Admiralty, they cannot be such as will leave no room or necessity for more, since it is only by the multiplication of means, and those vigorous and instant ones, that we can hope, at this last stage, and in this last hour, perhaps, of the lost navigators' existence, to snatch them from a dreary grave. And surely, til the shores and seas of those frozen regions have been swept in all directions, or until some memorial be found to attest their fate, neither England, who sent them out, nor even

America, on whose shores they have been launched in a cause which has interested the world for centuries, will deem the question at rest.

May it please God to move the hearts and wills of a great and kindred people, and of their chosen Chief Magistrate, that they may join heart and hand in the generous enterprise! The respect and admiration of the world, which watches with growing interest every movement of your great republic, will follow the chivalric and humane endeavour, and the blessing of them who were ready to perish shall come upon you!

I have the honor to be, sir, with great respect,

Your grateful and obedient servant,

JANE FRANKLIN

To His Excellency the President of the United States.

The many searches for the lost Franklin Expedition

An immense effort was made in the search for the lost expedition and it continues today. A vast library records this effort. Ross in 2002 identified for the period 1847 to 1859, twenty search expeditions, eleven supply expeditions, one relief expedition and four bipurpose expeditions that contributed in some way, being a total of thirty-six expeditions. In addition, three aborted search expeditions failed to reach the Arctic. Beattie and Geiger listed twenty-five major search expeditions between 1846 and 1880. Potter, in his recent book, omits the unsuccessful early searches and begins a list with Dr. John Rae's 1854 discovery, so that his list is for expeditions that reached the search area of the line of retreat of the Franklin Expedition. Between 1854 and 2015, Potter lists sixty-five search expeditions. A modern era of search expeditions aimed at finding the lost ships, followed the publication of David Woodman's 1991 book 'Unravelling the Franklin mystery.' These were superseded by consortiums led by Parks Canada in 2008. Apart from 2009, these became an annual event and led to the discovery of *Erebus* in 2014 and *Terror* in 2016. Much information of these later searches is available on internet websites such as Russell Potter's 'Visions of the North' at www.visionsnorth.blogspot.com and William Battersby's www.thefranklinsite.com

Private expeditions organised and often funded by Lady Jane Franklin

Hindsight is a wonderful thing and today looking back on what was an enormous effort to find the lost Franklin Expedition, it is possible to see who amongst the many involved had the right ideas. The Admiralty, Sir John Franklin's friends (especially Sir John Ross) and American sponsored searches, all sought the advice of experts on where the expedition might have gone. The failure to find a message at the 1845-46 winter quarters on Beechey Island (discovered in 1850) resulted in much effort being wasted on the Wellington Channel and north-west. The Admiralty made use of their Arctic 'champions' known as the 'The Arctic Council' comprising Sir George Back, Sir William Edward Parry, Captain Edward Joseph Bird, Sir James Clark Ross, John Barrow, Lt.-Col. Edmund Sabine, Captain William Alexander Baillie Hamilton, Sir John Richardson, Sir Francis Beaufort and Captain Frederick William Beechey. A magnificent oil painting of these heroes and experts of the Arctic known as 'The Arctic Council planning a search for Sir John Franklin' (measuring 46.5 by 72.13 inches) by Stephen Pearce was presented to the National Portrait Gallery (portrait 1208) by Sir John Barrow and can be seen today at Graves and Company in Pall Mall. The result of the considerable effort of the searches yielded only the 1845-46 winter quarters.

However, there were two people who guessed correctly where the Franklin expedition might be. These were Lady Jane Franklin and Dr. Richard King. The latter had accompanied Sir George Back on his descent of Back's Great Fish River in 1833 to 1835. The expedition descended the river and the length of its estuary - Chantrey Inlet - (including mapping and naming Montreal Island) where they saw in the distance what would later be known as King William Island.

Let us consider first the efforts of Dr. Richard King, because those of Lady Jane lasted longer and included six privately funded expeditions. Dr. Richard King was a difficult person being conceited and overconfident in his abilities and highly critical of others. He managed to antagonise most people with whom he dealt. Nevertheless, he was a very gifted and perceptive man who worked hard on the Back expedition and won the affection and respect of the men under his command. After the expedition down the Great Fish River, he wrote his own book about the expedition and alienated himself by criticising the leadership of Sir George Back and the management of the Hudson's Bay Company. Dr. King believed strongly that the best way to explore for the North-West Passage was by small overland expeditions as used by Sir George Back, and Dr. Rae. He saw Back's Great Fish River as a gateway to Arctic exploration by land. He thought the use of large naval ships far too risky because of the danger of besetment in ice.

As early as 1846 Dr. King wrote a series of letters to the Colonial Office suggesting that the Franklin Expedition must be icebound near Melville

Island. He offered to lead a party in canoes down Back's Great Fish River to locate them and bring information on the locations of food depots put out for them. The suggestion died when Sir John Ross observed that after descending 600 miles down the river with such limited means, King would probably be in need of assistance himself, rather than being able to offer it. Also the Admiralty saw no need to worry about the Franklin Expedition after an absence of only twenty-four months, as the expedition had been supplied for three years. The possibility of getting some sort of relief expedition to the mouth and estuary of Back's Great Fish River in 1847 was therefore lost.

The Admiralty did however listen to other advice and set about organising a relief expedition to be led by Sir James Clark Ross with two ships *Enterprise* and *Investigator* to search from the east (1848-49). Also for Sir John Richardson and Dr. John Rae to lead an overland expedition to the Coppermine – Mackenzie River area (1847- 49). Lady Jane Franklin offered to join the latter expedition, but was rejected by Sir John Richardson. Neither expedition had any success in locating the missing Franklin Expedition.

In 1848, Dr. King again offered to lead an expedition down Back's Great Fish River, but the Arctic experts all thought that Franklin would be further west. This time Sir George Back stated that Sir John Franklin after his catastrophic 1821 experience in the barren lands, would never again attempt them on the continental shore east of the Mackenzie River.

Lady Jane Franklin spent a large part of her fortune in fitting out and sending six expeditions in search of the lost expedition. Before he sailed, Sir John had shown his wife and several other people, a partially completed map of the Arctic (as it was at the time, but now the Canadian Arctic). He pointed to Simpson Strait (the north end), along with the south part of Victoria Strait that was to be mapped by the Franklin Expedition. These water channels separated King William Land from Victoria Island and the Adelaide Peninsula of the American continent. This was a gap of only 100 miles between the southern mapping of Simpson and Dease in 1839 and the northern mapping of James Clark Ross in 1830. Sir John had said that if he could only get to Simpson Strait, his troubles would be over because of the summer open water channel along the northern margin of the American continent. Simpson Strait linked with Chantrey Inlet – the estuary of Back's Great Fish River.

Lady Jane knew that Franklin's goal was the Simpson's Strait area. To get there and follow his instructions, she thought he could have turned south or south-west from Barrow Strait. Also if his ships were trapped in the ice, he could make for the estuary of Back's Great Fish River, where in summer, herds of caribou and musk oxen had been reported along with abundant fish. However, the Admiralty ignored her suggestions and followed the advice of Parry and James Clark Ross, who thought the ships might be trapped in the ice stream further west, and likely make for the Mackenzie or Coppermine Rivers.

The Admiralty was sufficiently concerned by March 1849 to offer a reward of £20,000 to any ship assisting the lost expedition. Lady Jane decided that to get the Simpson Strait – Estuary of the Great Fish River area searched she would have to mount her own expedition. Her first attempt failed in May 1849, when the Admiralty refused to sell her two dockyard lighters that she wanted to fit out at her expense for a search expedition.

Later that year in Londonderry, Ireland, a four-year-old girl called Weasey Coppin died of gastric fever, but her presence remained with her brothers and sisters who received prophecies from her. One of these appeared in writing stating '*Erebus* and *Terror*. Sir John Franklin, Lancaster Sound, Prince Regent Inlet, Point Victory, Victoria Channel.' This was remarkable for it was later found that the ships were trapped in Victoria Channel or Strait, seventeen miles off Victory Point. The prophecy was communicated to Lady Jane who saw it as confirmation of her belief of where the ships were. However at that time the sea route from Prince Regent Inlet to Victoria Strait had not yet been discovered.

The narrow twenty-mile long channel was later found by one of Lady Jane's search expeditions, and named Bellot Strait. No one has seriously considered that the Franklin Expedition could have used this route as it differed greatly from the Admiralty orders, that were to first pass Cape Walker at the north end of Somerset Island, before turning south-west. However, at the time the Franklin expedition sailed, some thought that Boothia and North Somerset were a large island and that the western sea could be accessed from the south end of Prince Regent Inlet. Later mapping by Dr. John Rae in 1847 proved that this was not the case. Today it is generally considered that the lost expedition did follow orders and discovered and sailed south down Peel Sound.

1850 proved to be the peak year for search expeditions with a total of thirteen ships in the Arctic seeking the lost expedition. That year Lady Jane had sent her first private expedition with William Penny, to search for the missing ships, or their crews who might have abandoned them and be heading for Back's Great Fish River. But Penny explored Wellington Channel. The Franklin Expedition ships were first abandoned in April 1848 but were reoccupied and a second retreat took place in 1850 leaving only

Erebus with a small crew. But by 1851 only a few survivors lived, some with the Inuit near Boothia and others aboard *Erebus* at Utjulik.

Lady Jane bought a ninety ton pilot boat and renamed it *Prince Albert*. With the help of friends she supervised the fitting out. She appointed volunteer Captain Charles C. Forsyth in command with an odd assortment of crew. *Prince Albert* sailed on June 5 1850. It was planned that the *Prince Albert* was to sail down Prince Regent Inlet, then send a party across North Somerset and then head south to the area reached by James Clark Ross. This late instruction was based on the information obtained from the Coppin family. If followed, it would have led to the discovery of the lost expedition. Unfortunately, Forsythe returned the *Prince Albert* after an absence of only four months, without following his instructions. He had entered Prince Regent Inlet but retreated to North Devon and Beechey Island, where the other search ships were gathering at Franklin's first winter quarters. The early return of *Prince Albert* was a great disappointment to Lady Jane.

In November 1851, The *Prince Albert* sailed again. Lady Jane had replaced Forsyth with William Kennedy, a former Hudson's Bay Company fur trader, who was half Orkney man and half Cree who had sailed to England to volunteer. Second in command was Joseph Rene Bellot, a volunteer and decorated junior officer in the French Navy. Before sailing Lady Jane had sent Kennedy to meet the Coppin family. The *Prince Albert* travelled down Prince Regent Inlet to Fury Beach then on south and discovered Bellot Strait. They sledged along the sixteen miles of its length to find themselves at the junction of Franklin Strait and Peel Sound.

Kennedy thought he could see land to the north across what is Peel Sound. Believing that Franklin could not have come this way, he abandoned his orders to proceed south and the party crossed Peel Sound to Prince of Wales Land. They crossed the latter looking for a southbound channel. They reached Ommanney Bay on the west side and then returned east to Browne Bay and then north to Cape Walker, returning to the ship after crossing the northern end of Peel Sound. Later in 1852 when the ice broke up they proceeded to Beechey Island and met the *North Star*, a depot ship of the Sir Edward Belcher's search expedition, and then they returned home.

Lady Jane purchased the steam yacht *Isabel*, that sailed in summer 1852 under the command of Commander Edward A. Inglefield on the condition the ship be used for the search for Sir John Franklin in Smith and Jones sounds and the west coast of Baffin bay. No signs of the lost expedition were found but a volume resulted.

In 1853, *Isabel* sailed again, but this time under the command of William Kennedy and for the New Siberian Islands via the Pacific route. Much of the cost of his expedition came from the colonists of Van Diemen's Land who had raised and gifted £1,700 for the search for Sir John Franklin. The expedition failed when most of the crew mutinied in Valparaiso, claiming the ship was too small for the mission. Kennedy remained two years on the coast of South America, but was unable to find a replacement crew to go to the Arctic and so brought the ship home.

On October 22 1854, the Admiralty received a letter from Dr. John Rae written in Repulse Bay informing them of his findings about the loss of the Franklin expedition. Dr. John Rae had mapped the west shore of the Isthmus of Boothia between the mapped area of Simpson and Dease at the mouth of the Castor and Pollux River to Bellot Strait. Dr. Rae had discovered that King William's Land was an island separated from Boothia by a North-West Passage later used by Amundsen in *Gjoa*. He also learned about the fate of the Franklin Expedition and bought relics from the Inuit.

Lady Jane finally accepted the fact of the death of her husband and the loss of the entire expedition. She experienced a profound sadness and a great relief that nine years of false hopes and pain were ended. Britain at the time was engaged in the Crimean War and had no resources to spend on the lost expedition. Now that the location of the disaster was known, it fell to Lady Jane to organise another expedition with the hope of bringing back any survivors and the lost log books and records of the expedition. She provided funds and obtained public subscriptions and donations. The brothers and sisters of John and Thomas Hartnell, who had sailed aboard *Erebus*, contributed £5.

Lady Jane purchased the *Fox*, a 177-ton yacht, and had her fitted out for Arctic work. The Admiralty provided all the equipment necessary including Arctic clothing, guns, ammunition and three tons of pemmican. The Board of Trade provided the meteorological and nautical instruments. The Captain was Royal Navy volunteer Francis Leopold McClintock and second in command was Lieutenant William Robert Hobson. *Fox* sailed in June 1857, but failed to cross Baffin Bay due to heavy ice. *Fox* was trapped in the pack ice for the winter and drifted with it. After 250 days in the ice-pack of Baffin's Bay and Davis' Strait and drifting 1,194 geographic miles backward, *Fox* was released in April 1858. McClintock was not a man to turn back and *Fox* proceeded. She entered Lancaster Sound and proceed to Peel Strait, but found it blocked by ice. *Fox* then went back to Prince Regents Inlet and wintered at Port Kennedy at the eastern entrance to Bellot Strait.

In April 1859 McClintock and Hobson each led a sledge party from the ship to King William Island. The two parties independently found the track of the Franklin retreat with relics, graves, skeletons, campsites and a boat on a sledge. The brief 1847 and 1848 records were also found, so that the fate of Sir John Franklin and the expedition was finally learned. As McClintock wrote:

> So sad a tale was never told in fewer words.

They completed their round sledge journeys of over 800 miles, with Hobson carried back on the sledge with severe scurvy. McClintock became famous for his dogged achievement. He was knighted on his return and went on to become Rear Admiral Sir Leopold McClintock. His book however demonstrates his tact and diplomacy for the word 'cannibalism' never appears. He was a very different man to the tactless Dr. Richard King.

News at last – Dr. Rae's 1854 report and the reaction of Victorian Society

After completing his explorations in 1851 of Wollaston and Victoria Lands (and proving that Victoria Island existed as one mass), Dr. Rae put forward a plan to the Hudson's Bay Company to complete the mapping of the American continent by mapping the unknown coastlines of the Boothia region. His objective was purely scientific and it was thought there was no possibility of finding Franklin relics in the area. By early 1854 he had crossed the Simpson Peninsula and arrived at Pelly Bay to the east of the Boothia Peninsula. There he met an Inut – In-nook-poo-zhe-jook – who was wearing the gold cap band of a lost Franklin officer and who told him that he had heard of a party of white men who had died some four years earlier, beyond the mouth of a great river, many days journey to the west.

Dr. Rae purchased the officers gilt cap band. He offered rewards for more information and artifacts and continued with his planned survey. In-nook-poo-zhe-jook was to become a famous source of information on the lost Franklin expedition, not only for the information he supplied Dr. Rae, but because twenty-five years later, he met the American searcher Charles Francis Hall, who took copious notes of his testimony. Dr. Rae was criticised for not going immediately to the site of the lost expedition, and it would be another five years before McClintock reached the area. If Dr. Rae had proceeded there directly, he might have recovered some of the records of the lost expedition.

Dr. Rae's survey demonstrated that King William Land was not a part of the Boothian Peninsula, but an island. He returned to Pelly Bay and spent two months there collecting much information and relics of the lost expedition. Although he had no knowledge of the £10,000 reward for information of the lost expedition, he decided to return to London as soon as possible to stop the expensive and wasted search expeditions of much of the Arctic. From Repulse Bay he wrote a letter on July 29 1854 to the Admiralty in London.

On Sunday October 22 1854 Dr. John Rae returned to England. The Admiralty released his unedited report to the Times newspaper. The report states:

> Sir, - I have the honor to mention, for the information of my Lords Commissioners of the Admiralty, that during my journey over the ice and snow this spring, with a view to completing the survey of the west shore of Boothia, I met with Esquimaux in Pelly Bay, from one of whom I learned that a party of 'white men', (Kablounans) had perished from want of food some distance to the westward, and not far beyond a large river, containing many falls and rapids. Subsequently, further particulars were received, and a number of articles purchased, which places the fate of a portion, if not of all of the then survivors of Sir John Franklin's long-lost party, beyond a doubt – a fate as terrible as the imagination can conceive.

The substance of the information obtained at various times and from various sources, was as follows:

> In the spring, four winters past (spring 1850), a party of 'white men' amounting to about forty, were seen travelling southward over the ice dragging a boat with them, by some Esquimaux, who were killing seals near the north shore of King William's Land, which is a large island. None of the party could speak the Esquimaux language intelligibly, but by signs the party were made to understand that their ship, or ships, had been crushed by ice, and that they were now going to where they expected to find deer to shoot. From the appearance of the men, all of whom, except one officer, looked thin, they were then supposed to be getting short of provisions, and purchased a small seal from the natives. At a later date the same season, but previous to the breaking up of the ice, the bodies of some thirty persons were discovered on the Continent, and five on an island near it, about a long day's journey to the N.W. of a large stream, which can be no other than Back's Great Fish River (named by the Esquimaux Doot-ko-hi-calik), as its description, and that of the low shore in the neighbourhood of Point Ogle and Montreal island agree exactly with that of Sir George Back. Some of the bodies had been buried (probably those of the first victims of the famine), some were in a tent or tents, others under the boat, which had been turned over to form a shelter, and several lay scattered about in different directions. Of those found on the island, one was supposed to

have been an officer, as he had a telescope strapped over his shoulders, and his double-barrelled gun lay underneath him.

From the mutilated state of many of the corpses and the contents of the kettles, it is evident that our wretched countrymen had been driven to the last resort – cannibalism – as a means of prolonging existence.

There appeared to have been an abundant stock of ammunition, as the powder was emptied in a heap on the ground by the natives out of kegs or cases containing it; a quantity of ball and shot was found below the high water mark, having probably been left on the ice close to the beach. There must have been a number of watches, compasses, telescopes, guns (several double barrelled), etc., all which appear to have been broken up, as I saw pieces of the different articles with the Esquimaux, together with some silver spoons and forks. I purchased as many as I could get. A list of the most important of these I enclose, with a rough sketch of the crests and initials of the forks and spoons. The articles themselves shall be handed over to the Secretary of the Hudson's Bay Company on my arrival in London. None of the Esquimaux with whom I conversed had seen the 'whites', nor had they ever been to the place where the bodies were found, but had their information from those who had been there, and who had seen the party when travelling.

I offer no apologies for taking the liberty of addressing you, but as I do so from belief that their lordships would be desirous of being put in possession at as early a date as possible, of any tidings, however meagre and unexpectedly obtained, regarding this painfully interesting subject.

I may add, that by means of our guns and nets, we obtained an ample supply of provisions last autumn, and my small party passed the winter in snow houses in comparative comfort, the skins of the deer shot affording abundant warm clothing and bedding. My spring journey was a failure, in consequence of accumulation of obstacles, several of which, my former experience in Arctic travelling had not taught me to expect. – I have, &c.

John Rae, M.D.,

Commanding Hudson's Bay Arctic Expedition.

Dr. Rae added a little more in his journal and listed his purchases of Franklin relics:

From what I could learn, there is no reason to suspect that any violence had been offered to the sufferers by the natives.

List of articles purchased from the Esquimaux, said to have been obtained at the place where the bodies of the persons reported to have died of famine were found, viz.: - 1 silver table fork – crest, an animal's head, with wings extended above; 3 silver forks – crest, a bird with wings extended above; 1 silver table spoon – crest, with the initials 'F.R.M.C.' (Captain Crozier, *Terror*); 1 silver table spoon and 1 fork – crest, bird with laurel branch in mouth, motto, 'Spero meliora;' 1 silver table spoon, 1 tea spoon, and 1 desert fork – crest, a fish's head looking upwards, with laurel branches on each side; 1 silver table fork – initials, 'A.M'D'. (Alexander M'Donald, assistant surgeon, *Terror*); 1 silver table fork – initials, 'G.A.M.' (Gillies A. Macbean, second master, *Terror*); 1 silver fork – initials, 'J.T.'; 1 silver dessert spoon – initials, 'J.S.P.' (John S. Peddie, surgeon, *Erebus*); 1 round silver plate, engraved, 'Sir John Franklin, K.C.B.;' a star or order, with motto, 'Nec aspera terrent, G.R. III., MDCCCXV.'

Also a number of other articles with no marks by which they could be recognised. But which will be handed over with those above-named to the Secretary of the Hudson's Bay Company.'

John Rae. MD

Repulse Bay, July 1854

Charles Dickens' tirade against Dr. Rae's report of cannibalism and the Inuit

Charles Dickens, at the urging of Lady Jane, wrote a surprising tirade published in his popular magazine Household Words, under the title of 'The Lost Arctic Voyagers'. The article was in two parts and totalled eleven and a half pages of double column print. Its purpose was to discredit Dr Rae's report especially the part about cannibalism. The tirade also accused the Inuit of murdering Franklin's men so there was no cannibalism. It is quite remarkable to see how Victorian England's greatest writer used his considerable literary skills for such a dishonorable action, rather than use his reasoning powers to get to the truth. It demonstrates the great power of Victorian Society. Dr John Rae replied in the same journal in two lengthy parts, totalling six pages of double column. But he never recovered from the damage inflicted by Dickens' tirade and was not knighted for his great services to Arctic exploration and mapping. Today Household Words is online and can easily be perused.

Dickens wrote:

Dr. Rae may be considered to have established, by the mute but solemn testimony of the relics he has brought home, that SIR JOHN FRANKLIN and his party are no more. But, there is one passage in his melancholy report, some examination into the probabilities and improbabilities of which, we hope will tend to the consolation of those who take the nearest and dearest interest in the fate of that unfortunate expedition, by leading to the conclusion that there is no reason whatever to believe, that any of the members prolonged their existence by the dreadful expedient of eating the bodies of their dead companions. Quite apart from the very loose and unreliable nature of the Esquimaux representations (on which it would be necessary to receive with great caution, even the commonest and most natural occurrences), we believe we shall show, that close analogy and the mass of experience are decidedly against the reception of any such statement, and that it is in the highest degree improbable that such men as the officers and crews of the two lost ships would, or could, in any extremity of hunger, alleviate the pains of starvation by this terrible means.

Before proceding to the discussion, we will premise that we find no fault with Dr. Rae, and that we thoroughly aquit him of any trace of blame. He has himself openly explained, that his duty demanded that he should make a faithful report, to the Hudson's Bay Company or the Admiralty, of every circumstance stated to him; that he did so, as he was bound to do, without any reservation; and that his report was made public by the Admiralty: not by him. It is quite clear that if it were an ill-considered proceeding to disseminate this painful idea on the worst of evidence, Dr. Rae is not responsible for it. It is not material to the question that Dr. Rae believes in the alleged cannibalism; he does so merely "on the substance of information obtained at various times and various sources," which is before us all. At the same time we will most readily concede that he has all the rights to defend his opinion which his high reputation as a skilful and intrepid traveller of great experience in the Arctic Regions combined with his manly, conscientious, and modest personal character – can possibly invest him with. Of the propriety of his immediate return to England with the intelligence he had got together, we are fully convinced. As a man of sense and humanity, he perceived that the first and greatest account to which it could be turned, was, the prevention of the useless hazard of valuable lives; and no one could better know in how much hazard all lives are placed that follow Franklin's track, than he who has made eight visits to the Arctic shores. With these remarks we can release Dr. Rae from this inquiring, proud of him as an Englishman, and happy in his safe return home to well-earned rest.

The following is the passage in the report to which we invite attention: "Some of the bodies had been buried (probably those of the first victims of the famine); some were in a tent or tents; others under the boat, which had been turned over to form a shelter; and several lay scattered about in different directions. Of those found on the island, one was supposed to have been an officer, as he had a telescope, strapped over his shoulders, and his double-barelled gun lay underneath him. From the mutilated state of many of the corpses and the contents of the kettles, it is evident that our wretched countrymen had been driven to the last resource – cannibalism – as a means of prolonging their existence. None of the Esquimaux with whom I conversed had seen the 'whites', nor had they ever been to the place where the bodies were found, but had their information from those who had been there, and who had seen the party when travelling."

We have stated our belief that the extreme improbability of this inference as to the last resource, can be rested, first on close analogy, and secondly, on broad general grounds, quite apart from the improbabilities and incoherencies of the Esquimaux evidence; which is itself given, at the very best, at second-hand. More than this, we presume it to have been given at second-hand through an interpreter; and he was, in all probability, imperfectly aquainted with the langusage he translated to the white man. We believe that few (if any) Esquimaux tribes speak one common dialect; and Franklin's own experience of his interpreters in his former voyages was, that they and the Esquimaux they encountered understood each other "tolerably" – an expression which he uses frequently in his book, with the evident intention of showing that their communication was not altogether satisfactory. But even making the very large admission that Dr. Rae's interpreter perfectly understood what he was told, there yet remains the question whether he could render it into language of corresponding weight and value. We recommend any reader who does not perceive the difficulty of doing so and the skill required, even when a copious and elegant European language is in question, to turn to the accounts of the trial of Queen Caroline, and to observe the constant discussions that arose – sometimes, very important – in reference to the worth in English, of words used by the Italian witnesses. There still remains another consideration, and a grave one, which is, that ninety-nine interpreters out of a hundred, whether savage, half-savage, or wholly civilised, interpreting to a person of superior station and attainments, will be under a strong temptation to exaggerate. This temptation will always be strongest, precisely where the person interpreted to is seen to be the most excited and impressed by what he hears; for, in proportion as he is moved, the interpreter's importance is increased. We have ourself had an opportunity of enquiring whether any part of this aweful information, the unsatisfactory result of "various times and various sources", was conveyed by gestures. It was so, and the gesture described to us was often repeated – that of the informant setting his mouth to his own arm – would quite as well describe a man having opened one of his veins, and drunk of the stream that flowed from it. If it be inferred that the officer who lay upon his double-barrelled gun, defended his life to the last against ravenous seamen, under the boat or elsewhere, and that he died in so doing, how came his body to be found? That was not eaten, nor even mutilated, according to the description. Neither were the bodies, buried in the frozen earth, disturbed; and it is not likely that if any bodies were resorted to as food, those the most removed from recent life and companionship would have been the first? Was there any fuel in that desolate place for cooking "the contents of the kettles"? If none, would the little flame of the spirit lamp the travellers may have had with them, have sufficed for such a purpose? If not, would the kettles have been defiled for that purpose at all? "Some of the corpses," Dr. Rae adds, in the letter to the Times, "had been sadly mutilated, and had been stripped by those who had the misery to survive them, and who were found wrapped in two or three suits of clothes." Had there been no bears thereabout, to mutilate those bodies; no wolves, no foxes? Most probably the scurvy, known to be the dreadfullest scourge of Europeans in these latitudes, broke out among the party. Virulent as it would inevitably be under such circumstances, it would of itself cause dreadful disfigurement - woeful mutilation - but, more than that, it would not only annihilate the desire to eat (especially to eat flesh, of any kind), but would annihilate the power. Lastly, no man can, with any show of reason undertake to affirm that this sad remnant of Franklin's gallant band were not set upon and slain by the Esquimaux themselves. It is impossibole to form an estimate of the character of any race of savages, from their deferential behaviour to the white man while he is strong. The mistake has been made again and again; and the moment the white man has appeared in the new aspect of being weaker than the savage, the savage has changed and sprung upon him. There are pious persons who, in their practice, with a strange inconsistency, claim for every child born to civilisation all innate depravity, and for every savage born to the woods and wilds all innate virtue. We believe every savage to be in his heart covetous, treacherous, and cruel; and we have yet to learn what knowledge the white man – lost, houseless, shipless, apparently forgotten by his race, plainly famine-stricken, weak, frozen, helpless, and dying – has of the gentleness of Esquimaux nature.

Dickens continues by arguing that a man like Franklin would infuse the expedition with his character, discipline, patience and fortitude to set against 'the wild tales of a herd of savages'. Franklin, along with Richardson and Back, in his 1818-22 Arctic expedition, had already experienced starvation and had eaten boots and old leather, but they did not eat their dead companions. He noted that on one of Sir John Franklin's earlier arctic Expeditions that one man – an Iroquois hunter - was believed to have killed and eaten men. He was executed by Sir John Richardson.

Dickens goes on to consider instances of where English men had survived ordeals with little food and water, without resorting to cannibalism. His first example was the feat of Captain Bligh who imposed a stern discipline on the men cast adrift with him after the mutiny of the Bounty and brought them to safety. Second, he considered the survival of eleven men in a pinnace, survivors of the Centaur man-of-war for fifteen days with little food and water. Third, he considered the case of the Pandora that sank leaving 110 men in boats. Fourth was the Juno. The fifth case was the Peggy, a ship on the high seas that ran out of food. Cannibalism occurred, and Dickens attributed this to the fact that the starving crew drank heavily of the cargo of wine and brandy and were at all times intoxicated. The sixth case was the Thomas, where cannibalism occurred and Dickens attributed this to the crew being of 'inferior class'. Next two more cases of cannibalism were considered – the Nautilus, a sloop of war, and the raft of the Medusa. The latter had 150 persons on board, but after thirteen days only fifteen survived. Dickens concluded that the 'scourged and branded sweepings of the galleys of France, in their debased condition' could not be compared with 'the flower of the trained adventurous spirit of the English Navy, raised by Parry, Franklin, Richardson and Back.'

Dickens then considers seven cases: the Jacques; an Elizabethan wreck; the Wager; an East Indiaman bound for Jiddah; the Philip Aubin; the Tyrel; and a party of seven missionaries left on the coast of Patagonia. In all cases the majority died of starvation, but there was no cannibalism. These examples were considered as strong support for the Dickens view. He next considered four other cases: the New Horn; six deserters from the English artillery on St. Helena; the Nottingham galley; and the St. Lawrence. In all cases cannibalism occurred or was planned. He concluded that the influence of great privation upon the lower and least disciplined class of character seem to induce hallucinations and delusional behaviour, absent from men such as Bruce and Mungo Park and particularly by Franklin as demonstrated by his writing of his early disastrous Arctic expedition.

The measured response of Dr. John Rae to Mr. Charles Dickens

Observing, in the numbers of this journal dated the second and ninth of this month, a very ably-written article on the lost Arctic voyagers, in which an attempt was made to prove that Sir John Franklin's ill-fated party did not die of starvation, but were murdered by the Esquimaux; and consequently that they were not driven to the last dread alternative as a means of protracting life, permit me to make a few remarks in support of my information on this painful subject – information received by me with the utmost caution, and not one material point of which was published to the world without my having some good reason to support it.

First, as regards my interpreter. To compare either Augustus or Ouligback (who accompanied Sir John Franklin and Sir John Richardson in their overland journeys) with William Ougligback, my interpreter, would be very unfair to the latter. Neither of the first two could make themselves understood in the English Language and did not very perfectly comprehend the dialect of the natives of the coast westward of the Coppermine River. William Ougligback speaks English fluently, and perhaps more correctly than one half of the lower classes of England or Scotland.

As I could not, from my ignorance of the Esquimaux tongue, test William Ouligback's qualifications, I resorted to the only means of doing so I possessed. There is an old servant of the company at Churchill, an honest and trustworthy, who has acquired a very fair knowledge of both the Esquimaux character and the Esquimaux language. This man informed me that young Ouligback could be perfectly relied on; that he would tell the Esquimaux exactly what was said, and give the Esquimaux reply with equal correctness, that when he had any personal object to gain, he would not scruple to tell a falsehood to attain it, but in such a case the untruth was easily discovered by a little cross-questioning. This description I found perfectly true.

Again: the natives of Repulse Bay speak precisely the same language as those of Churchill, where young Ouligback was brought up.

The objection offered that my information was received second-hand, I consider much in favour of its correctness. Had it been obtained from the natives who had seen the dead bodies of our countrymen, I should have doubted all they told me, however plausible their tale might have appeared; because had they, as they usually do, deposited any property under stones in the neighbourhood, they would have had a very excellent cause for attempting to mislead me.

That ninety-nine out of a hundred interpreters are under a strong temptation to exaggerate, may be true. If so, my interpreter is an exception, as he did not like to talk more than he could possibly help. No doubt had I offered him a premium for using his tongue freely he might have done so; but not even the shadow of a hope of a reward was held out.

It is said that part of the information regarding cannibalism was conveyed to me by gestures. This is another palpable mistake, which is likely to mislead. I stated in one of my letters to the Times that the natives had preceded me to Repulse Bay; and, by signs, had made my men left in charge of the property there (none of whom spoke a word of Esquimaux) comprehend what I had already learnt through the interpreter.

I do not infer that the officer who lay upon his double-baralleled gun defended his life to the last against ravenous seamen; but that he was a brave, cool man, in full possession of his mental facilties to the last; that he lay down in this position as a precaution, and, alas! Was never able to rise again; and he was among the last, if not the very last, of the survivors. The question is asked, was there any fuel in that desolate place for cooking the contents of the kettles? I have already mentioned in a letter to the Times how fuel might have been obtained. I shall repeat my opinion with additions: - When the Esquimaux were talking with me on the subject of the discovery of the men, boats, tents, &c., several of them remarked that it was curious no sledges were found at the place. I replied that the boat was likely fitted with sledge runners that screwed on to it. The natives answered that sledges were noticed with the party of whites when alive, and their tracks on the ice and snow were seen near the place where the bodies were found. My answer then was, that they must have burnt them for fuel; and I have no doubt that the kegs or cases containing the ball and shot must have shared the same fate.

Had there been no bears thereabouts to mutilate the bodies – no wolves, no foxes? Is asked; but it is a well-known fact that, from instinct, neither bears, wolves, nor foxes, nor that more ravenous of all, the glutton or wolverine, unless on the verge of starvation, will touch a dead human body; and the carnivorous quadrupeds near the Arctic sea are seldom driven to that extremity.

Quoting again from the article on the lost Arctic voyagers. "Lastly, no man can with any show of reason undertake to affirm that the sad remnant of Franklin's gallant band were not set upon and slain by the Esquimaux themselves?"

This is a question which like many others is much more easily asked than answered; yet I will give my reasons for not thinking, even for a moment, that some thirty or forty of the bravest class of one of the bravest nations in the world, even when reduced to the most wretched condition, and having firearms and ammunition in their hands, could be overcome by a party of savages equal in number to themselves. I say equal in number, because the Esquimaux to the eastward of the Coppermine, seldom, if ever, collect together in greater force than thirty men, owing to the difficulty of obtaining the means of subsistence. When Sir John Ross wintered three years in Prince Regent's Inlet, the very tribe of Esquimaux who saw Sir John Franklin's party were constantly or almost constantly in the neighbourhood. In the several springs he passed there, parties of his men were travelling in various directions; yet no violence was offered to them, although there was an immense advantage to be gained by the savages in obtaining possession of the vessels and their contents.

In eighteen hundred and forty-six-seven I and a party of twelve persons wintered at Repulse Bay. In the spring my men were divided and scattered in all directions; yet no violence was offered, although we were surrounded by native families, amongst whom there were at least thirty men. By murdering us they would have put themselves in possession of boats and a quantity of cutlery of great value to them. In the same spring, when perfectly alone and unarmed, except with a common clasp knife, which could have been of no use, I met on the ice four Esquimaux armed with spear and bow and arrow. I went up to them, made them shake hands; and, after exchanging a few words and signs, left them. In this case no violence was used; although I had a box of astronomical instruments on my back, which might have excited their cupidity. Last spring, I, with seven men, was in almost constant communication with a party four times our number. The savages made no attempt to harm us. Yet wood, saws, daggers and knives were extremely scarce with them, and by getting possession of our boat, its masts and oars, and the remainder of our property, they would have been independent for years.

What appears to me the most conclusive reason for believing the Esquimaux report, is this: the natives of Repulse Bay, although they visit and communicate for mutuaol advantage with those further west, both dislike and fear their neighbours, and not without cause; as they have behaved treacherously to them on one or two occasions. So far do they carry this dislike, that they endeavoured, by every means in their power, to stimulate me to shoot several visitors to Repulse Bay, from Pelly Bay, and from Sir John Ross's wintering station in Prince Reget's Inlet.

Now, is it likely that, had they possessed such a powerful argument to excite – as they expected to do – my anger and revenge as the murder of my countrymen, would they not have made use of it by acquainting me with the whole circumstances, if they had any such to report?

Again, what possible motive could the Esquimaux have for inventing such an awful tale as that which appeared in my report to the secretary of the Admiralty. Alas! These poor people know too well what starvation is, in its utmost extremes, to be mistaken on such a point. Although these uneducated savages – who seem to be looked upon by those who know them not, as little better than brutes – resort to the "last resource" only when driven to it by the most dire necessity. They will starve for days before they will even sacrifice their dogs to satisfy the cravings of their appetites.

Dr. Rae continued by stating that Inuit he had known had died of starvation. Some had killed themselves as they were unable to watch the children starving. Only a few resorted to cannibalism. Rather than telling lies, the Inuit geographic information had always proved correct by later mapping. Dr. Rae cited other examples of information, he had received from the Inuit, that later proved to be correct.

Inuit falsehoods were unlike those of western people. They were silly and ridiculous and easily discovered (what today might be called 'transparent liars'). He then gave two examples, one concerning Sir John Richardson and the other, Captain McClure.

Dr. Rae considers the Esquimaux character to be superior to all the tribes of red-men in America. They have dutiful sons and daughters, kind brothers and sisters and affectionate parents, who will be looked after in old age by the childen. At the Hudson's Bay Company establishments they are highly regarded. Moravian missionaries on the Labrador coast employ the Esquimaux constantly, as they find them honest and trustworthy.

About the shipwreck cases raised, where cannibalism was not resorted to in times of extreme want, none of the cases represent the probable position of Sir John Franklin's party. In the shipwreck cases there was starvation and lack of water. The latter would have been readily available to Franklin's men. The much cited former disasterous journey of Franklin is not a parallel case, as pieces of old leather, tripe de roche and infusions of tea were available. The moral character and admirable discipline of the Franklin crews has been emphasised. However, their conduct at the very last British port they entered would not encourage 'the high eulogium passed upon them in Household Words'. Nor can one say how in extreme cases of privation, the men would respond. Dr. Rae regrets the recent disagreements between Arctic officers. A ship soon to return will have two or three courts martial. Seamen, once they have lost their ship and set foot ashore, generally, consider themselves free of the strict discipline enforced aboard ship.

Dr. Rae finished with:

> That my opinions remain exactly the same as they were when my report to the Admiralty was written, may be inferred from all I have now stated. That twenty or twenty-five Esquimaux could for two months together, continue to repeat the same story without variation in any material point, and adhere firmly to it, in spite of all sorts of cross-questioning, is to me the clearest proof that the information they gave me was founded on fact. That the 'white men' were not murdered by the natives, that they died of starvation, is, to my mind, equally beyond a doubt.

Letter from Dr. Rae to Captain McClintock

The views of Dr. John Rae are surprisingly modern and different compared with the Victorian outlook. He wrote to Captain McClintock who included his undated letter in the introduction of his book:

> As my name is mentioned in connection with the subject of cannibalism. I must state that when I came home in 1854 I felt bound to report in as condensed a form as possible all the information given us by the Esquimaux, including the most painful part. I would have felt it my duty to do this even had my dearest friends been amongst the lost ones, for had I withheld any part of the sad story, it would have come to light through my men, and I should have been accused, with some show of justice, of garbling my report. I consider it no reproach when suffering the agony to which extreme hunger subjects some men, for them to do what the Esquimaux tell us was done. Men so placed are no more responsible for their actions than a madman who commits a great crime. Thank God, when starving for days, and compelled to eat bits of skin, the bones of ptarmigan up to the beak and down to the toe-nails, I felt no painful craving; but I have seen men who suffered so much that I believe they would have eaten any kind of food, however repulsive.

It is particularly interesting that McClintock never mentioned cannibalism. He rose rapidly to become Admiral Sir Leopold McClintock - another Arctic hero of the Victorians. In contrast, honest Dr. John Rae bore the stigma of intense Victorian criticism and was never recognised in his lifetime for his remarkable achievements in Arctic mapping. Indeed unlike the huge Franklin retreat party of 105 men, who failed to gather enough food, his small parties (like that of Lieutenant Schwatka later on) were able to travel rapidly and live successfully off the land by hunting.

McClintock's description of the one boat he found in Erebus Bay with two skeletons, is somewhat ambiguous about the disturbance of bones by 'wild animals.' Both skulls were also missing but surprisingly were found with the same bones by the Schwatka expedition and buried. The bones were recently exhumed and subjected to modern forensic investigation including modern facial reconstructions. One wonders what McClintock might have written had he found the second boat or the two campsites on the islets of Erebus Bay, or the hospital tent at Terror Bay. These sites were hidden beneath snow at the time of his visit, but all showed abundant evidence of cannibalism, as described by the Inuit and confirmed by modern forensic studies.

Captain McClintock's comments on Charles Francis Hall's investigations

In 1881, McClintock wrote a supplementary chapter that was added to the fifth edition of his book. It is called 'Hall's Relief Expedition'. In it he summarised his views of Hall's records of Inuit testimony which included detailed descriptions of the remains of cannibalism:

> Hall acquired a vast deal of information respecting Esquimaux modes of life, and he wrote down with greatest care all the information he could gather from them of Franklin's people. But his simple and enthusiastic mind received as truths many absurd fables, and thus he fell into many errors, and lost a whole year by his unnecessary exploration of Hecla and Fury Strait.

This was probably written in support of Lady Jane Franklin as another case against cannibalism.

Sir John Franklin promoted and the crews of *Erebus* and *Terror* officially pronounced dead on 1st March 1854

On October 26 1852, Sir John Franklin was promoted to rear Admiral of the Blue. It was only in 1859, when the McClintock expedition recovered the brief 1848 and 1849 records, that it was finally known for certain that this was a posthumous promotion, as Franklin had died on June 11 1847.

On January 12 1854, Sir James Graham wrote to Lady Jane that the names of the expedition members of *Erebus* and *Terror* would be removed from the Admiralty books on March 31 1854 (nine years after the expedition provisioned for three years had sailed). It would mean that the men were officially dead and their families would receive back pay owed to that date. Lady Jane was considerably upset. When the Admiralty notice was gazetted on the thirty-first, she changed her clothing from the black of mourning to bright colours – green and pink. In contrast, her step daughter's family changed to the black of mourning. Lady Jane refused to accept a widow's pension. She argued that it would be acting a falsehood and a gross hypocrisy to put on mourning, when she had not yet given up hope. Further she could not do it on the day and month that suited the Admiralty's financial convenience. Lady Jane wrote a strong letter of protest to the Admiralty about abandoning the men who had served their country, and urged that their country ascertain their fate.

The Admiralty decision caused considerable problems for Lady Jane in the matter of Sir John Franklin's will. Franklin's first wife's daughter Eleanor Isabella (Franklin's only child) had married family friend the Reverend John Phillip Gell in 1849. They had seven children. Sir John had obtained considerable property from his first marriage. Before Sir John sailed he had given Lady Jane power of attorney to use the income from the estate as she wished. On Sir John's death the property and income would go to the Gells.

Eleanor supported by her husband, felt that Lady Jane was squandering her inheritance with her searches for the lost expedition. The Gells managed to stop Drummond's Bank from honouring Lady Franklin's cheques. They argued that Sir John Franklin was dead and therefore his first wife's property, from which Lady Franklin was still drawing the income, was theirs. They also claimed that landed property in Van Dieman's Land and Australia passed to them on his death. The latter was a very weak claim as the will had been made ten years before the property was bought and because the property had been bought by a gift to Lady Franklin from her father. At the time, the law was such that everything a wife possessed was legally her husbands. The matter was resolved by an out of court settlement of £12,000 to the Gells. Eleanor Gell died in 1860 at the age of thirty-six of scarlet fever. She contracted it while nursing one of her children.

The Admiralty decision also caused problems for the family of Lieutenant James Walter Fairholme of *Erebus*. His uncle Adam Fairholme of Greenknowe, Berwickshire died on May 23 1853. He had conveyed his estate, valued at £37,500 to trustees and willed it to be passed to Lieutenant Fairholme as first beneficiary, but if not then to his brother George Fairholme as second beneficiary. Scottish Law did not recognise the Admiralty decision, so the legal question was raised as to whether Lieutenant Fairholme had survived his uncle, in which case he would have inherited the estate. If not then his brother George would inherit the estate.

There followed a court case in which many eminent Arctic experts testified. It was concluded that even if Fairholme had survived until 1850 and was one of the party met by Inuit in Washington Bay, it was extremely lightly that he had not survived until 1853. The court ruled that he had probably predeceased his uncle. However, as Dr. John Rae had testified under cross examination that there was some possibility that a few might have survived, the court awarded the estate to Lieutenant Fairholme's brother George. However they did require him to pay a bond as an insurance to protect the Fairholme trustees should Lieutenant Fairholme reappear one day.

Preface to McClintock's book by Sir Roderick Murchison

In the preface to the 1908 edition of McClintock's 'The Voyage of the '*Fox*' in Arctic Seas,' Sir Roderick I. Murchison, President of the Royal Geographical Society wrote:

> To the honour of the British nation, and also, let it be said, to that of the United States of America, many have been the efforts made to discover the route followed by our missing explorers. The highly deserving men who have so zealously searched the arctic seas and lands in this cause must now rejoice that, after all their anxious toils, the merit of rescuing from the frozen North the record of the last days of Franklin has fallen to the share of his noble-minded widow.
>
> Lady Franklin has indeed, well shown what a devoted and true-hearted Englishwoman can accomplish. The moment that relics of the expedition commanded by her husband were brought home [in 1854] by Rae, and that she heard of the account given to him by the Esquimaux of a large party of Englishmen having been seen struggling with difficulties on the ice near the mouth of the Back or Great Fish River, she resolved to expend all her available means (already much exhausted in four other independent expeditions) in an exploration of the limited area to which the search must thenceforward be necessarily restricted.

Letter from The Admiralty to Captain McClintock

For Captain Leopold McClintock who had volunteered to go without pay, there was much praise and a letter from the Admiralty.

To Captain L. McClintock, R.N.

Admiralty, London,

24th Oct. 1859.

SIR,

I am commanded by my Lords commissioners of the Admiralty to acquaint you that, in consideration of the important services performed by you in bringing home the only authentic intelligence of the death of the late Sir John Franklin, and of the fate of the crews of the '*Erebus*' and '*Terror*', Her Majesty has been pleased, by her order in Council of 22nd instant, to sanction the time during which you were absent on these discoveries in the Artic Regions, viz., from the 30th June, 1857, to the 21st September 1859, to reckon as time served by a captain in command of one of Her Majesty's ships, and my Lords have given the necessary directions accordingly.

I am, Sir,

Your very humble servant,

W.G. ROMAINE,

Secretary to the Admiralty

24: SOME NARROW MISSES IN LOCATING THE LOST EXPEDITION

There were some narrow misses in locating the lost expedition before Dr. Rae returned with the first information in 1854. They are listed below chronologically.

Dr. Richard King's offers of 1845 and 1847

Dr. King was an argumentative surgeon/naturalist who accompanied Lieutenant (later Admiral, Sir) George Back down the Great Fish River to Chantrey Inlet where they saw King William Land in 1834. He wrote his own account of the expedition in which he criticised his commander. King saw the Great Fish River as a gateway to exploring the Arctic regions. When the 1845 expedition was proposed, Dr. King wrote to Lord Stanley, the Secretary of State for War and the Colonies (the same man who fired Sir John Franklin as Lieutenant Governor of Tasmania) proposing that the sea expedition be supported by a land expedition, that he would lead down Back's Great Fish River. His offer was declined but he repeated the offer in 1847 to lead an expedition down the river in 1848 with information of relief supply depots at Hudson's Bay posts and others deposited from ships in Barrow Strait. Some extracts follow from his lengthy letter to Lord Stanley, Secretary for State for War and the Colonies, dated 10th June 1847:

> Page 12: My Lord, One hundred and thirty-eight men are at this moment in imminent danger of perishing from famine. Sir John Franklin's expedition to the North Pole in 1845, as far as we know, has never been heard of from the moment it sailed...

> P.13: It is greatly to be regretted that Lord Stanley did not entertain the plan which I proposed for acting by land in concert with Sir John Franklin's expedition by sea.

> P.25: Information of such provision having been made should be conveyed, in the course of the summer of 1848, by a small party provided with Indian guides – in case it should be desirable to convey the lost party to the Hudson's Bay depots on the Mackenzie or the Great Slave Lake, instead

of to the southern boundary of Barrow Strait in search of the provision vessels. Such a party, my Lord I will undertake to lead...

Dr. King believed that the Franklin expedition was trapped somewhere in the ice between Somerset and Banks Islands and could escape to either the north into Barrow Strait or to the south to one of the Hudson's Bay outposts along one of the rivers on the north American continent. Had he descended Back's Great Fish River in the summer of 1848 by boat, he would have been too late to meet the 1848 retreat that took place before the thaw. But he could have sailed north along Chantrey Inlet and along the western coastline of King William Island, where he might have encountered the reoccupied *Erebus* with about a half of the expedition members still alive. The distance along Chantrey Inlet to the position where the ships were abandoned was 350 miles. The information of new food depots would have been invaluable to the lost expedition who had reoccupied *Erebus*. Unfortunately, Lord Stanley did not approve any of Dr. King's offers.

Lady Franklin's repeated efforts

As we've seen (above), Lady Jane privately organised six expeditions to search the Victoria and Simpson Straits area. In 1849 she was unable to purchase the ships she wanted, but later succeeded and sent out a search ship in each year from 1850 to1853. But none of the ships reached the area she had correctly specified. A few men and a dog led by 'The hunter', were probably still living aboard *Erebus* at Utjulik perhaps as late as 1852. She finally succeeded with the *Fox* expediton.

The *Chieftain* Report of 1849
This is the work of David Woodman.

As already described, in summer 1849 Captain Ker of the whaling ship *Chieftain* at Ponds Bay was handed a drawing by a visiting Inuit. Regrettably there was no interpreter present, but the whalers thought he was explaining that four ships were in Prince Regent Inlet and that those in the west had been in the ice for four years (one lying on her side) and those in the east for one year. They thought the Inut had been aboard all four ships during the previous spring and that they were safe. The whalers recognised that the western ships were probably *Erebus* and *Terror* and the eastern ships *Enterprise* and *Investigator* - a search expedition under Sir James Clark Ross that wintered 1848 – 1849 at Port Leopold.

Woodman points out that the lines in the centre of the map are most likely the Boothian Peninsula and this reinterpretation provides an accurate and dated report of where the four ships were in spring 1849. Unfortunately, when James Clark Ross returned home he reported meeting no Inuit and the report was disregarded. Following Woodman's reinterpretation, the map is a key part of the present reconstruction and probably shows the ships in spring 1849. This is after the 1848 retreat.

A strange grave marker found by *Investigator* in 1850

In 1850, *Investigator* under the command of Commander Robert McClure, sailed east along the northern shoreline of the American Continent. A party from *Investigator* went ashore on August 24 1850 to the Inuit settlement of Tooktoyaktuk to the east of the Mackenzie River. Their visit was brief but they saw a curious wooden monument. Translator Miertsching learned of strangers who had arrived without a boat and lived by hunting. After the birds, seal and reindeer left the area they had all disappeared except for one man who died. The Inuit had found the body and buried it beneath the wooden marker.

At the time it was not known aboard *Investigator* that the Franklin expedition had retreated south from their ships and only a brief followup was made. If the stranger who died had been from a sledge party from *Erebus*, then they would have left the area at the latest in Autumn 1849 after leaving the ship during the 1848 retreat or in Spring 1849.

Dr. Rae finds relics on the east shore of Victoria Island in 1851

In 1851, Dr. Rae of the Hudson's Bay Company was instructed to search the shores of Wollaston - Victoria Island for traces of the Franklin Expedition. After strenuous exploration he reached Cambridge Bay (on the south east corner of Victoria Island) in the summer by boat and entered Victoria Strait. He reached a point only sixty miles west of where *Erebus* and *Terror* had been abandoned, only three years before. He planned to cross to King William Island, but the heavy ice and strong winds prevented him, so he retreated along his route. He met Inuit but they had no Franklin relics nor knowledge of the ships.

However, on the south coast he found two pieces of wreckage. One was the base of a flagpole five feet nine inches long, which had white rope attached to it by two copper nails. The pole was marked with the broad arrow of the British Navy and the rope had a red thread in it. Both these features were typical of government property of the British Navy. A half mile further along he found a three foot eight inch long piece of oak, partly squared that he identified as a ship's stanchion. Dr. Rae was uncertain of the origin of the relics as other ships had been lost in the Arctic and with difficulty in stormy weather he returned. However, their location at lat. 68 deg 52 min N., 103 deg 20 min W., is only eighty miles west of where *Terror* is believed to have sunk after 1850 near Terror Bay.

McClintock learned in 1859 that *Erebus* had been ashore at Utjulik in 1858. The flagpole was almost certainly from one of the two ships and suggest that the colours had been nailed to the mast.

Captain Penny recovers charred elm wood on Cornwallis Island in 1851

Captain William Penny with the *Lady Franklin* and Captain Alexander Stewart with the *Sophia* wintered 1850 – 1851 at Assistance Bay on Cornwallis Island. In June and July 1851 Captain Penny explored by boat the east coast of Cornwallis Island. Captain Penny found a block of elm wood charred at one end on Cornwallis Island. Sir John Richardson examined it in England and concluded that it was English elm and that it had no connection with the lost expedition. However, Captain Penny firmly believed that it indicated the passage of Franklin's ships in the neighbourhood of Baillie Hamilton Island where it was found and that the Franklin expedition had ascended the Wellington Channel. Unfortunately, the evidence was inconclusive and no location was found where the Franklin ships might have stopped and scientific specimens had been collected. Penny was proved correct only when the McClintock expedition found the 1847 record in 1859.

Enterprise reports a ship in the ice and finds part of a magnetic observatory in 1853

In 1852/3 Captain (later Admiral Sir) Richard Collinson on board *Enterprise* wintered in Cambridge Bay on the SE corner of Victoria Land only 100 miles west of King William Island. This was the same stretch of coast visited by Dr. Rae in 1851. Captain Collinson planned two sledge trips on either side of Victoria Strait, but cancelled the one for the east side (King William Island, where the much sought after remains of the Franklin Expedition lay) when he saw the rugged ice packed into Victoria Strait – the same ice that trapped *Erebus* and *Terror*.

During frequent encounters with the Inuit (during which the ship had no interpreter), one of the officers - Mr Arbuthnot - obtained a report of a ship in the ice. Unfortunately, Captain Collinson rejected it as probably a repetition of a question. Rear - Admiral Noel Wright was most scathing about this:

> But this interesting item of news was ignored by Captain Collinson; an act of stupidity he afterwards attempted to justify by saying that the Eskimo had drawn a chart which afterwards turned out to be incorrect, and so caused doubt to be thrown on his whole story.

In the spring of 1853 a further clue was obtained when a fragment of a hatchway or door frame with brass and copper fittings from a Royal Navy ship was found washed ashore. Captain Collinson though it was part of a magnetic observatory.

Collinson describes it as:

> It is composed to two pieces of fir nailed together, the largest piece being fifty-one inches long by three and three quarters in its broadest part and three quarters of an inch thick. The back has been painted lead colour and then black; and 13 inches from one end is the copper hasp for securing the latch of a door, fastened by three screws, and with the Queen's mark (broad arrow) on it; the edge next to the hasp has been painted, while the irregularity of other side shows it has been split from a broader piece. On the inside, three inches from the end, is a batten, twenty-four inches long, two and a half wide, three quarters thick, chamfered at both ends, secured to the larger piece by copper nails, but with the marks of one or two iron ones; the batten is painted white as is part of the lower side of the larger piece, which has originally had a coat of light green.

The ship is likely to have been *Terror* (as *Erebus* had moved south to Utjulik and was ashore there in 1858) and the debris likely to be a part of one of the magnetic observatory huts.

25: THE PRESENT LEVEL OF KNOWLEDGE ABOUT THE FATE OF THE LOST FRANKLIN EXPEDITION

There has been a vast outpouring of writing about the lost Franklin expedition, but most of it is fragmentary and deals only with small aspects of the whole. Reconstructions of the expedition's history are remarkably few. The Victorians followed the simple version first put forward by Rear Admiral Leopold McClintock, who being a friend and supporter of Lady Jane Franklin omitted the word 'cannibalism' from his most excellent book. It was really the work of David Woodman that revived modern interest in the lost expedition by making a study of the original notebooks of Charles Francis Hall in which he found more information than in the 1879 summary by Professor Nourse.

Unlike the Victorians, who had rejected Inuit testimony because of the issue of cannibalism, Woodman sifted the testimonies carefully to eliminate other expedition stories. He made the first modern reconstruction of the history of the lost expedition. He granting them another two years, by realising that the Washington Bay meeting was in 1850 as stated by Inuit testimony, rather than the retreat of 1848 as recorded in the 1848 Record. In his second volume Woodman, extended the history of the expedition by another few years by sifting and sorting out testimonies of the last few survivors.

Woodman's work was followed by a serious but fictional attempt by Canadian author John Wilson. The present volume is the latest up to date version utilising much new evidence that has emerged over the past quarter century. This includes new Franklin testimony collected by Dorothy Harley Eber from the residents of Gjoa Haven. It also includes modern forensic studies including of the site in Erebus Bay discovered by Barry Ranford. Finally, there has been the discovery of the wrecks of both *Erebus* and *Terror* by a consortium led by Parks Canada, so that general descriptions and videofilms of the ships are available before any excavation work. Hopefully the wrecks will yield preserved written records or buried records may yet be found frozen in the permafrost.

What the Victorians understood had happened to the Franklin expedition

The families of the lost expedition had to be content with the rather meagre information brought back by Dr. John Rae in 1854, together with the brief record and observations of Captain McClintock's 1859 *Fox* expedition. Sadly, Dr. Rae's 1854 report of cannibalism was immediately released by The Admiralty to the press. 129 men were missing and Dr. Rae's report accounted for only forty men hauling sledges and a boat in Washington Bay, thirty bodies (presumably the same men) on the mainland and five bodies on the Todd Islets - perhaps only forty to forty-five men. The Inuit testimony collected by Charles Francis Hall added a few more bodies and confirmed the reports of cannibalism.

The Victorian or classic interpretation of what happened after the 105 men abandoned ships on April 22 1848 follows. In that month, the men assembled into their teams each hauling a boat on a sledge, others with sledges of camping equipment. McClintock concluded that the sledges were overloaded, so that on arriving at Crozier's Landing much was discarded, including a great mound of clothing and equipment. At Erebus and Terror Bays, the retreat paused and hospital tents were set up for the sick and exhausted. A portion of the retreat continued and met with Inuit near Washington Bay. As they progressed men died and were buried in shallow graves. On the southern coast of King William Island they divided, some continuing as far as Booth Point. Others with a boat crossed over to the Adelaide Peninsula on the mainland, where about thirty men died at Starvation Cove. In several places the immobile sick resorted to cannibalism to prolong life. The deaths occurred in 1848.

The reconstruction of David Woodman

Captain, writer, harbour master and Franklin searcher David Woodman has published two excellent Franklin books, worked with the original Hall notebooks, and led searches for the wreck of the Utjulik ship. She was eventually found in the search area in 2014 by a Parks Canada led consortium. Contrary to expectations she proved to be *Erebus*. His books include the only modern reconstruction of the expedition's history to date.

The Woodman interpretation hinges on two key pieces of information. First is the testimony collected by Dr. John Rae in 1854 that reported the classic meeting of the Inuit with a Franklin party, man hauling a boat on a sledge near Washington Bay, as occurring only four years previously. This places the classic meeting in 1850, some two years after the 1848 record reporting the retreat occurring in April 1848. Woodman believes that when the crews discovered that they could cover no more than three miles a day (so that the 1200 miles retreat to the nearest Hudson's Bay Company post was impossible), almost all of the crew returned to the two ships within a month. As proof that the crew returned to the ships, Woodman cites the dubious identification of Lieutenant Irving's grave at Crozier's Landing. The 1848 record mentions that Lieutenant Irving was sent to recover the 1847 record from a location some miles to the north. Woodman has restated his case in a letter included in Russell Potters Blog of the sixth of January 2010.

A second crucial conclusion by Woodman is that there was no contact between the Franklin expedition and the Inuit until after the 1848 retreat began. This is because the Inuit did not know of the valuable materials left by the retreat north of Erebus Bay, until informed by the McClintock sledge party in 1859. This in turn dictates that Sir John Franklin's burial could not have been observed by the Inuit. The Inuit witnessed a military burial that was therefore after the 1848 retreat and was not that of Sir John Franklin.

Woodman thought that the two remanned ships had drifted south in the ice until they reached Erebus Bay. There boat parties went ashore and established what would become the three death camps. They met with the Inuit and jointly successfully hunted caribou. Also a senior officer died and was buried with full military honours that was witnessed by the Inuit. He was buried in a fissure in the ground sealed with cement. Nearby many paper records were buried in cemented vaults. The senior officer whose burial was observed by the Inuit was suggested by Woodman to be Captain Crozier.

Inuit observed one of the ships crushed by ice that sank quickly, so that many supplies and some men were lost. Some of the crew moved ashore at Erebus and Terror Bays. In 1850 a group set off to the east, probably heading for Inuit settlements at Igloolik or the shipping lanes in Barrow Strait. For the remaining men, discipline broke down, some remained in the camps and others returned to the ship. The men ashore died there after practicing cannibalism. Most deaths took place in 1850.

Finally, the ice broke up and released the intact *Erebus* with its small crew that reached Utjulik, where she was anchored near a small island in Wilmot and Crampton Bay in Queen Maud Gulf. The few remaining crew wintered aboard her and then left for an overland trip in the following spring. Inuit testimony puts the last survivors on the Melville Peninsula possibly as late as 1852 or even 1856.

The present reconstruction

Potter has published maps of the two death camps in Erebus Bay and they can be seen to be very insubstantial – each merely a tent site with a boat nearby. The 1997 forensic publication of Keenleyside and others gives further detail on the two abandoned boat sites at Erebus Bay. The three 'death camps' are here not regarded as permanent camps from 1850 that were repeatedly visited. Each is a time capsule of the 1848 retreat with only relics belonging to that retreat. They are regarded as formed in 1848 and mark the furthest points of the 1848 retreat, where up to fifty percent of the men became too ill to either continue or to return to the ships.

The camps show where about a half of the men were left in sick tents with carers, one of whom was probably *Erebus* Ice Master James Reid, as suggested by a 2016 facial reconstruction. Most men left in the camps died in 1848 soon after the forty days rations finished as the paucity of animal bones suggests that the hunting failed. This was probably because of their early arrival before the main summer migration of wildlife occurred. Only about a half of the men returned to reman *Erebus*. It was in these camps that a few men prolonged their existence by cannibalism hoping for a return of their comrades with the ship. The *Chieftain* report suggests *Terror* was still on her beam ends in spring 1849.

Vital new testimonies were recently collected by Dorothy Harley Eber that identify the remanned *Erebus* as spending much time not in Erebus Bay, but at the south end of Imnguyaaluk island (the smaller of the two Royal Geographical Society Islands). This ship is believed to have spent about two years in the area, before escaping south to become the 'Utjulik ship'. Captain Crozier kept the crew of the reoccupied *Erebus* away from the death camp nearby at Terror Bay by forming a camp on Imnguyaaluk Island. The site was identified by present day Gjoa Haven Inuit by the presence of oil soaked ground from blubber fires.

There was much interaction with the Inuit and their testimonies describe some of the crew. This interaction taught some of the crew how to live Inuit style by hunting. Dorothy Eber's new information on the fireplace trail explains how the crew of the reoccupied *Erebus* fed themselves in part by winter hunting the bearded seal and cooking over blubber fires. There is also testimony of joint summer hunting of caribou with the Inuit. This enabled the remaining crew to survive for some years after the expedition's three year food supply ran out.

It was during this stay at Imnguyaaluk Island that Captain Crozier died and was buried along with records in cement vaults near the camp on the south part of the island, where the raised beach ridges run east-west. The burial of the records indicates that the men had little hope of escaping after five years in the Arctic. The 1850 retreat is believed to have occurred shortly after the burial of Captain Crozier and was dominated and led by *Terror* men. This would have left a very small crew aboard *Erebus*.

The testimony of the 'black men' recovered by Woodman from the original papers of Hall, has been reinterpreted by comparison with the men of Sir Earnest Shackleton's 1914-17 Trans Antarctic expedition who were stranded on Elephant Island, living under two overturned boats and hunting birds and seals and gathering shellfish and seaweed. They cooked on improvised blubber stoves and used blubber oil in improvised lamps. The resulting oil and blubber soot covered them, so they became 'black men'. They were thin from the poor diet and had to grow beards as there was insufficient fuel to melt ice for water to wash. This is regarded as a good description of the last crew aboard *Erebus* with a single officer in summer 1850, after the 1850 retreat.

Miraculously, the ship was released in the summer thaw and the tiny crew worked her south to the summer open-water channel along the northern coast of the American continent. She had become the first ship to sail through the North-West Passage. Sadly the last officer, believed to be Captain Fitzjames, died and was honoured by the crew who laid his body in the great cabin of the ship he had fought for so hard. The small weakened crew had neither the strength nor the navigational skills to sail *Erebus* the 1,700 miles to the Bering Strait, so they turned her west and took her into Wilmot and Compton Bay on the coast of the Adelaide Peninsula - a good hunting ground.

A boatload of men may have attempted to escape west along the open water channel. Four men, the hunters, and the ships dog Neptune remained aboard the ship and wintered there before setting out for the Melville Peninsula. Dorothy Harley Eber has also provided Inuit testimony of the final group of survivors from *Erebus*, who were led by a strong healthy man who is 'The Hunter' in this reconstruction.

Erebus was located in 1851/52 by the Inuit, when she was in perfect shape with her doors locked. Inuit salvaged her for at least seven years. During that time she drifted ashore on an islet and probably partly sank so that only the stern remained accessible. After 1858 she was ice rafted offshore and sank in only thirty feet of water, to be found in 2014 by a Parks Canada led major search consortium. The condition of the wreck, is poor with bowsprit, masts and much of the stern missing. This might be the result of the salvage work of the Inuit (more than ice), as wood and iron were highly prized for tools and hunting equipment.

After the reoccupied *Erebus* had finally escaped from Imnguyaaluk Island and sailed south to Utjulik, a deserted ship with many bodies aboard was ice rafted south of Cape Crozier and drifted almost into Terror Bay. She is identified as *Terror* – a mausoleum ship since winter 1847-48. There she was found by Inuit who cut a hole through her side so she sank leaving the tops of her masts standing out of the water. It was Inut Sammy Kogvat from Gjoa Haven who around 2007 saw one of her masts still standing through the ice that led to her discovery.

Testimony by Kok-lee-arng-nun describing a ship being overwhelmed by ice and sinking, taking some crew with her was accepted by Woodman but is rejected here.

THE END

APPENDIX 1: CREW LISTS

These are the 129 men who went into the ice. When the expedition departed there were 134 men but 5 were repatriated from Stromness and Disko Island.

H.M.S. *EREBUS*

OFFICERS
Captain and Expedition Leader	Sir John Franklin
Commander	James Fitzjames
Lieutenants	Graham Gore,
	Henry Thomas Dundas Le Vesconte,
	James Walter Fairholme
Mates	Robert Orme Sargent,
	Charles Frederick Des Voeux,
	Edward Couch
Second Master	Henry Collins
Surgeon	Stephen Samuel Stanley
Assistant Surgeon	Harry D.S. Goodsir
Paymaster and Purser	Charles Hamilton Osmer
Ice-Master	James Reid

WARRANT OFFICERS
Boatswain	Thomas Terry
Carpenter	John Weekes
Engineer	John Gregory

PETTY OFFICERS
Boatswain's Mate	Samuel Brown
Carpenter's Mate	Thomas Watson
Captain of the Forecastle	Philip Reddington
Quartermasters	Daniel Arthur,
	William Bell,
	John Downing
Sailmaker	John Murray
Caulker	James W. Brown

Blacksmith	William Smith
Leading Stoker	James Hart
Cook	Richard Wall
Captain's Coxswain	James Rigden
Captain of the Maintop	John Sullivan
Captain of the Foretop	Robert Sinclair
Captain of the Hold	Joseph Andrews
Caulker's Mate	Francis Dunn
Captain's Steward	Edmund Hoar
Gun-room Steward	Richard Aylmore
Paymaster and Purser's Clerk	William Fowler
Subordinate Officer's Steward	John Bridgens
Stokers	John Cowie, Thomas Plater

ABLE SEAMEN

Charles Best	Thomas McConvey
William Closson	John Morfin
Charles Coombs	William Orren
Robert Ferrier	Francis Pocock
Josephus Geater	Abraham Seeley
John Hartnell	John Stickland
Thomas Hartnell	Thomas Tadman
Robert Johns	George Thompson
Henry Lloyd	George Williams
William Mark	Thomas Work

ROYAL MARINES

Sergeant	David Bryant
Corporal	Alexander Paterson
Privates	William Braine, Joseph Healey, Robert Hopcraft, William Pilkington, William Reed

BOYS

George Chambers,	David Young

H.M.S. *TERROR*

OFFICERS
Captain .... Francis Rawdon Moira Crozier
Lieutenants .... Edward Little,
George Henry Hodgson,
John Irving
Mates .... Frederick John Hornby,
Robert Thomas
Second Master .... Gillies Alexander MacBean
Surgeon .... John Smart Peddie
Assistant Surgeon .... Alexander Macdonald
Clerk in Charge .... Edwin James Howard Helpman
Ice-Master .... Thomas Blanky

WARRANT OFFICERS
Boatswain .... John Lane
Carpenter .... Thomas Honey
Engineer .... James Thompson

PETTY OFFICERS
Boatswain's Mate .... Thomas Johnson
Carpenter's Mate .... Alexander Wilson
Captain of the Forecastle .... Reuben Male
Quartermasters .... David Macdonald,
John Kenley,
William Rhodes,
Caulker .... Thomas Darlington
Blacksmith .... Samuel Honey
Leading Stoker .... John Torrington
Cook .... John Diggle
Captain's Coxswain .... John Wilson
Captain of the Foretop .... Harry Peglar
Captain of the Hold .... William Goddard
Caulker's Mate .... Cornelius Hickey
Captain's Steward .... Thomas Jopson
Gun-room Steward .... Thomas Armitage
Subordinate Officers' Stewards ...... William Gibson,
Edward Genge
Stokers .... Luke Smith,

William Johnson

ABLE SEAMEN

John Bailey	David Leys
John Bates	Magnus Manson
Alexander Berry	Henry Sait
George J. Cann	William Shanks
Samuel Crispe	David Sims
John Handford	William Sinclair
William Jerry	William Strong
Charles Johnson	James Walker
George Kinnaird	William Wentzall
Edwin Lawrence	

ROYAL MARINES

Sergeant .... Solomon Tozer
Corporal .... William Hedges
Privates .... James Daly,
                                                          John Hammond,
                                                          William Heather,
                                                          Henry Wilkes

BOYS

Thomas Evans,   Robert Golding

Note: Name spellings follow Cyriax (1939).

APPENDIX 2:
SOME NUMERICAL ESTIMATES.

Date	Situation	Number of men aboard ships
12th July 1845	Departure from Greenland	129
-- July 1846	Departure from Beechey Island	126
11th June 1847	Death of Sir John Franklin	125
24th May 1848	Ships abandoned - retreat (9 officers and 15 men dead)	105
August 1848	Erebus Bay NgLj-1	(6 to 14 dead)
August 1848	Erebus Bay NgLj-2	(minimum of 11 dead)
August 1848	Erebus Bay NgLj-3	(3 dead)
August 1848	Terror Bay	(Perhaps 15 dead, including 3 graves)
August 1848	Douglas Bay	(7 dead)
August 1848	Retreat	dead total around 47
July 1848	Return to *Erebus*	around 58
July/Aug 1848	*Erebus* released and sails to Imnguyaaluk Island	
July 1849	Departure of boat to north	51
1850?	Captain Crozier dies	50
May 1850	1850 retreat	(between 17 and 45 men depart)
August 1850	Todd Islets	(6 men dead)
August 1850	Scattered graves KWI	(around 13 dead)
August 1850	Thunder Cove	(7 dead)
August 1850	Starvation Cove	(7 dead)
August 1850	Boothia	(4 men arrive)
August 1851	Retreat; dead around 37	13
July 1850/51	*Erebus* released and sails to Utjulik	13

July 1850/51	Last officer dies, placed in Great Cabin	12
July 1850/51	Boat departure to west with 8 men	4
May 1852	Four hunters and dog depart Eebus	0

APPENDIX 3: SOME SUGGESTIONS FOR FUTURE DIRECTIONS OF SEARCH FOR THE LOST FRANKLIN RECORDS AND HISTORY

At Crozier's Landing, a magnetometer search for the buried scientific reports and specimens might reveal excavated sites. The latter will include bottled preserved animals and plants, geological specimens (indestructible) especially fossils from the limestones of the area including Beechey and King William Islands, maps and short reports of discoveries. Possibly also officer's diaries. These would likely have been buried in wooden boxes clenched by nails or screws, possibly bound by metal strips and maybe with a lock. They should have been wrapped inside oiled canvas covers. It is the metal content that could be detected. They presumably were buried in the 10 foot raised beach where the stores were stacked well above the tidal waters.

A similar search might be carried out on south Imnguyaaluk island behind the campsite there.

A search of *Erebus* and *Terror* looking for the geological samples which are indestructible, possibly also glass bottles of preserved animals. If they are absent from the ships, then this would suggest that the collections were buried ashore.

At the south end of Imnguyaaluk Island (the smaller of the two Royal Geographical Society Islands), an archaeological team could investigate the campsite identified by an area where the ground is saturated in seal oil from cooking seal meat over seal blubber fires.

A search around the campsite (above) for the cemented grave of Captain Crozier in a ground fissure. Also for the cement vaults nearby in which paper records were deposited.

A check on the stumps of the masts and bowsprit of HMS *Erebus* to see if they were burned through by the Inuit to get the wood or whether they were broken off by winter ice.

A careful search of the bunks of HMS *Terror* to look for burial clothing and cloth strips that bound dead men lodged there

Appendix 3: Some Suggestions For Future Directions of Search

A search in the hold of HMS *Terror* to see if there is a window cut through the ships side by the Inuit that led to her sinking.

Is there evidence inside *Terror* of heavy objects being displaced to the port side, if she was thrown onto her beam ends.

A search again for the site of Sir John Franklin's grave - probably the stone lined cyst found by Supunger and his uncle who removed the covering slabs of stone allowing mud and water to enter the cyst.

A low level air photograph survey of Crozier's Landing and the campsite at Imnguyaaluk Island. In the wilderness the natural stone surface has a regular pattern. Every animal track, campsite, fire site, or other surface disturbance is recorded by movement of the stones from their natural pattern. Land utilisation maps can be prepared of these critical areas showing artificial disturbances.

APPENDIX 4: TWO REJECTED TESTIMONIES

Almost all available Inuit testimony believed to be related to the Franklin expedition has been included in this volume. However there are two testimonies of uncertain provenance that are included below. The first of these collected by Hall in 1866 was accepted by David Woodman in his book 'Unravelling the Franklin Mystery- Inuit testimony'. Both are rejected here.

Inuit testimonies have already adequately explained the fates of both H.M.S. *Erebus* and H.M.S. *Terror* at the locations where the ships were found in 2014 and 2016. The testimonies are in general in good agreement with the state of the wrecks. *Erebus* after many years of being ashore and being plundered for wood and metal, was found in poor condition with much of the stern and great cabin missing. The masts and bowsprit are also missing, either burned off by the Inuit or broken off by ice rafting. The destruction of the stern including the great cabin of Sir John Franklin is consistent with the wreck lying stern to the shore with the forepart submerged and better preserved. In this manner the years of Inuit salvage work were confined largely to the stern of the ship.

Terror in contrast, was found to be in very good shape with her masts and bowsprit standing, hatches battened down, and her crews possessions removed. She had not been extensively salvaged. Her appearance is more consistent with minor pillaging only and it is possible that a hole (cut by the Inuit) might be found in her hull near the waterline.

Kok-lee-arng-nun's further testimony – a ship crushed and sunk by the ice that took some of the crew down with her. (Nourse 1879, p.255):

> Kok-lee-arng-nun, their head man, showed two spoons which had been given him by Ag-loo-ka (Crozier), one of them having the initials F.R.M.C. (Francis R. M. Crozier) stamped upon it. His wife Koo-narng, had a silver watch-case. This opened up the way for immediate enquires. Through Too-koo-li-too who as usual soon proved a good interpreter, it was learned that these Inuit had been at one time on board of the ships of Too-loo-ark, (the great Esh-e-mut-ta, Sir John Franklin), and had their tupiks (tents)

on the ice alongside of him during the spring and summer. They spoke of one ship not far from Ook-kee-bee-jee-Iua (Pelly Bay), and two to the westward of Net-tee-lik, near Ook-goo-lik.

The old man and his wife agreed in saying that the ship on board of which they had often seen Too-loo-ark was overwhelmed with heavy ice in the spring of the year. While the ice was slowly crushing it, the men all worked for their lives in getting out provisions, but before they could save much, the ice turned the vessel down on its side, crushing the masts and breaking a hole in her bottom and so overwhelming her that she sank at once, and had never been seen again. Several men at work on her could not get out in time, and were carried down with her and drowned. 'On this account Ag-loo-ka's company had died of starvation, for they had not time to get the provisions out of her.' Ag-loo-ka and one other white man – the latter called 'nar-tar', a pee-ee-tu (steward) – started and went toward Oot-koo-ish-ee-lee (Great Fish or Back's River) saying they were going there on their way home. That was the last they saw of them, but heard of them some time after from a Kin-na-pa-too, who said he and his people heard shots or reports of guns of strangers somewhere near Chesterfield Inlet.

The above testimony is here rejected as the description of the two wrecks found in 2014 and 2016 does not suggest a dramatic sinking with men still on board. Also there is a problem with the timing of Kok-lee-arng-nun testimony. As described in an earlier chapter Kok-lee-arng-nun's age suggests that the encounters he described probably occurred around 1822 to 1831. This was well before the time of the Franklin expedition and corresponds to the *Victory* expedition of Sir John Ross (1828 to 1833).

Kok-lee-arng-nun's statement that it was Too-loo-ark's ship that was overwhelmed by ice and was seen to sink by the Inuit has long led Franklin researchers to believe that it was *Erebus* that was crushed and sank, so that the Utjulik ship was probably *Terror*. However the recent discovery of both wrecks shows this to be incorrect.

The testimony of Adam Beck

In 1850 an Inut called Adam Beck provided a similar dramatic testimony to Sir John Ross during the latter's search for the lost expedition (Woodman, 1991, p. 57). His testimony was that two ships had been lost and the crews came ashore. The ships were not whalers, as the officers wore epaulettes. Some of the crew were drowned and the survivors lived for some time in huts or tents. They had guns but no balls and were in a weak exhausted condition. They were all killed by the natives with darts and arrows.

Beck was regarded as a liar by some British naval officers, but a later interview by Charles Frances Hall led Hall to conclude that Beck was reporting only what he had heard. Woodman (1991) has made a lengthy study of Beck's testimony with inconclusive results.

The dramatic testimony of Kok-lee-arng-nun together with the somewhat similar version by Beck were probably in circulation with the Inuit; but may not refer to the lost Franklin expedition, and are here dismissed. This results in some significant differences in the present reconstruction of the history of the lost expedition from that of Woodman (1991). It must be remembered that the old and blind Kok-lee-arng-nun also provided the graphic testimony describing what might have been a meeting with Sir John Franklin. This latter interpretation was rejected by Woodman (1991), who concluded that there was no meeting between the lost expedition and the Inuit until after the 1848 retreat.

ACKNOWLEDGEMENTS

This work was made possible by the internet where many obscure and out of print books are available. Amazon.com also provided an excellent rapid book service. Blogspots by Russell Potter, William Battersby and Peter Carney were helpful. Professor Nourse's compilation of Charles Francis Hall's note books provided a start. The many publications by Richard Cyriax clarify many points. The outstanding work of David Woodman, especially additional information that he obtained from the unpublished notebooks of C.F. Hall, was essential, although his interpretations were not always followed. Similarly Dorothy Harley Eber's new Franklin testimonies provided much new critical information. The staff at the National Maritime Museum at Greenwich kindly answered several questions. The author thanks Dr Russell Potter and David Woodman, for permission to cite from their work. He also thanks his wife, Dr. Anne Roobol for help in obtaining some books and scientific papers. My gratitude to Nic Nicholas for her careful and excellent work on the index. My thanks to my editor and publisher James Essinger for his enthusiastic support and also to Charlotte Mouncey for typesetting the manuscript and the cover design.

NOTES ON SOURCES

Flyleaf: Lieutenant Hobson's 1859 description of King William Island, Stenton, 2014, p. 518.

CHAPTER 1.
Fox Expedition: McClintock, 1860, McClintock 1908.
Parry's first voyage: Parry, 1821.
John Ross's escape: Ross, 1835.
Twenty-five expeditions: Beattie and Geiger, 1987, Appendix 2.
The Austen Relief Expedition: Simmonds, 1852, p. 246; Savours, 1999, p. 194.
Dr. Rae's letter to the Admiralty: Rae, 1880.
C.F. Hall's five year search: Nourse, 1879.
Lte. Schwatka's search: Gilder, 1881.
Major Burwash: Burwash, 1931.
Paul Fenimore Cooper: Cooper, 1961.
Roald Amundsen: Amundsen, 1908, Amundsen and Hansen, 1908.
David Woodman: Woodman, 1991; Woodman 1995.
Dorothy Harley Eber: Eber, 2008.

CHAPTER 2.
Roderic Owen 'nonesense': Owen, 1978, p. 411-412.
Halls books: Hall, 1862; Nourse, 1879.
Arsenic poisoning: Loomis, 2010.
Hudson and son: Eber, 2008, p.137.
Hall's notebooks published by Nourse: Nourse, 1879.
Gilder, 1881, p. 90.
Woodman, 1991; Woodman 1995.
Anne Keenleyside: Keenleyside and others, 1997.

CHAPTER 3.
Paul Fenimore Cooper, 1961.
Dried fish: Klutschak, 1987, p. 109.
Cycles of birthing: Nourse, 1879, p. 239.

McClure, 1860.
Utjulik area: Eber, 2008, p. 93.
John Ross, Victory 1829: Ross, 1835.
Back 1834: Back, 1836.
Simpson, 1843.
Ross on ice stream: Ross, 1835, p. 291.
Amundsen *Gjoa*: Amundsen 1908, Amundsen and Hansen, 1908.
McClure North-West Passage: McClure, 1865.
Austen Relief Expedition: Simonds, 1852, p. 246; Savours, 1999, p. 195.
Captain Ommanney: Savours, 1999, p. 193, p. 198.
Sherard Osborne on ice stream: Osborne, 1865.

CHAPTER 4
Baffin's voyage: Savours, 1999.
Ross's Croker Mountains: Ross, 1819.
Parry's first voyage: Parry, 1821.
Parry's second voyage: Parry, 1824.
Parry's third voyage: Parry, 1826.
Franklin's first Arctic mapping expedition: Franklin, 1823.
Franklin's second Arctic mapping expedition: Franklin, 1828.
John Knight expedition: Simmonds, 1852, p. 213; Geiger and Beattie, 1993.
John Ross, Victory: Ross, 1835.
Tennent Island: Ross, 1835, p. 410.
Victory Point: Ross, 1835, p. 418; Cyriax, 1952.
Cape Herschel: Simpson, 1843.

CHAPTER 5.
James Clark Ross, Antarctica: Ross 1969, Palin, 2018.
Sir John Franklin: Wilson, 2001.
Franklin First Arctic mapping expedition: Franklin, 1823.
Franklin's second Arctic mapping expedition: Franklin, 1828.
Clash with Montagu: McGoogan, 2006, p. 254.
Franklin's Justification: Franklin, 1845.
Captain Crozier: Smith, 2014.
Crozier's letters to Ross: Fluhmann, 1976, p. 77.
Commander Fitzjames: Battersby, 2010.
Lte. Graham Gore: Cyriax, 1997, p.208; Battersby, 2010, p. 159.
Dr Harry Goodsir: Cyriax, 1997, p.210; Battersby, 2010, p. 159.

Thomas Blanky: Cyriax, 1997, p. 214; Battersby, 2010, p. 160.
James Reid: Cyriax, 1997, p. 212; Battersby, 2010, p. 160.
The Halkett boat: Battersby, 2010, p. 273.

CHAPTER 6.
Fitzjames journal: Fitzjames, 1852; Mangles, 1852.

CHAPTER 7.
Letter from Sir John Franklin: Simmonds, 1852, p.162.
Letter to William Coningham: Mangles, 1852, p. 85.
Letter from Thomas Blanky: Blenky (different spelling) 1852; Mangles, 1852, p. 85.
Letter from Captain Crozier: Fluhmann, 1976, p. 90 – 93.
Fitzjames mail to Petropavlovsk, Coningham letter: Mangles, 1852, p. 85.
Fitzjames plans overland return home: Battersby, 2010, p. 168.

CHAPTER 8.
Lte. Griffiths comments: Battersby, 2010, p. 178.
Captain Martin's report: Penny, 1852; Fluhmann, 1976, p. 93.
Fitzjames last journal entry: Fitzjames, 1852; Mangles, 1852.
Prince of Wales sighting: Fluhmann, 1876, p. 93.
Captain Ommanney Cape Riley: Savours, 1999, p.193, p.198.
Captain Penny Beechey Island: Savours, 1999, p.198.

CHAPTER 9.
The 1847 and 1848 records: McClintock, 1860; 1908.
Lte. Hobson's account: Stenton, 2014.
Peglar papers: McClintock, 1860; 1908, Cyriax and Jones, 1954.
The Franklin graves on Beechey Island: Beattie and Geiger, 1987.
Franklin's Beechey Island camp: Simmonds, 1852, p. 293; Cyriax, 1939, p. 105-108; Woodman, 1991, p. 70.
Cape Riley: Simmonds, 1852, p. 277.

CHAPTER 10.
Alternative route: Hickey and others, 1993.
Erebus draught: Fitzjames, 1852, p. 200; Mangles, 1852.
Terror draught: Crozier's letter to James Clark Ross: Fluhmann, 1976, p. 90 – 93.

Ross's Croker Mountains: Ross, 1819.
Rae's 1854 mapping: McGoogan, 2001, p. 181.
Amundsen's *Gjoa* passage: Amundsen, 1908; Amundsen and Hansen 1908; Woodman, 1991, p. 76.
Ross, Victory Point: Ross, 1835, p. 418; Cyriax, 1952.
Back beaches *Terror*: Savours, 1999, p. 144-146.
Ross, magnetic pole, 1830: Ross, 1835.
Pelly Bay men see ship: Nourse, 1879, p. 259-260.
Ship aground: Burwash, 1930, p. 60.
A sunken 'ship': Burwash, 1931, p. 72; Woodman, 1991, p. 77-80.
Enukshakak and Nowya's testimony: Burwash, 1931, p. 72; Woodman, 1991, p. 77.
Tommy Anguttitauruq's testimony: Eber, 2008, p. 99.

CHAPTER 11.

McClintock's Camp Felix: McClintock, 1875, p. 300.
Schwatka's Camp Felix: Gilder, 1881, p. 133.
Minuteness of search: Gilder, 1881, p. 136.
Inspector Larsen's visit: Cyriax, 1939, p. 214.
Photo of Larsen's bone collection: Potter, 2016, p. 150.
Kok-lee-arn-nun's testimony: Nourse, 1879, p. 255.
Happy voyage out, Fitzjames journal: Fitzjames, 1852; Mangles, 1852; Battersby, 2010.
Potter mixed testimony: Potter, 2016, p. 109.
McClintock's report of wreck ashore: McClintock, 1908, p. 194.
Hobson's lack of vegetation: Stenton, 2014, p. 512.
Hobson's barren north: Stenton, 2014, p. 519.
Old man's testimony: Klutschak, 1987, p. 72.
Kok-lee-arng-nun's testimony: Nourse, 1879, p. 258.
McClintock ink study: McClintock, 1860; 1908.
Cyiax, mistake: Cyriax, 1979.
Ross's saga: Ross, 1835.
Point Culgruff: Ross, 1835, p. 419.
Cape Herschel: McClintock, 1908, p. 212.
Sketch of Simpson's cairn: McClintock, 1908, facing p. 202.
Sir John's monuments: Woodward, 1951, p. 349, p. 362 and p. 364: Rawnsley, 1923, p. 192.
Plans for preservation of *Erebus* and *Terror*: Kirwan, 1959, p. 165.
Gore's mistake: McClintock, 1860; 1908.

McClintock, Victory Point: McClintock, 1908, p. 59-61.
Cyriax, Victory Point: Cyriax, 1952.
Sir John's adventures, Fitzjames journal: Fitzjames, 1852; Mangles 1852; Battersby, 2010.
Crozier burial: Woodman, 1991.
Beechey Island graves: Beattie and Geiger, 1987.
Supunger and uncle: Potter, 2016, p. 161-164.
Tom Gross: Potter, 2016, p. 218.
Lte. Irving's grave: Gilder, 1881, p. 124.
Klutschack's description: Klutschak, 1987, p. 83.
Okamawole's testimony: Gilder, 1881, p.110.
Grave, Franklin Point: Klutschak, 1987, p. 81; Gilder, 1881, p. 285.
Grave, Point Le Vesconte: Gilder, 1881, p. 289.
Grave, Point Le Vesconte: Klutschak, 1987, p. 286.
Grave, Tulloch Point: Gilder, 1881, p. 286.
Photo of grave at Crozier's Landing: Potter, 2016, p. 176.

CHAPTER 12.
Endurance trapped: Shackleton, 1919; 1999, Lancing, 1959.
Stephen Goldner: Cookman, 2000.
Under-cooking: Cookman, 2000.
Tinned meat poisons Inuit: Eber, 2008.
Drift measuring pillar: Gilder, 1881, p. 134.
Too-koo-li-too's testimony: Nourse, 1879, p. 569.
Chieftain Report: Woodman, 1991, p. 211.
Admiralty orders Article 21: www.arcticwebsite.com/Franklinorders.com
Crozier's Landing by McClintock: McClintock 1860, p. 259.
Crozier's Landing by Burwash: Burwash, 1831, p. 504; Cyriax, 1952, p. 504.
Map of Crozier's Landing: Burwash, 1931, p. 96.
Crozier's Landing by Larsen: Cyriax 1952, p. 505; Cyriax, 1969, p. 24.
Shackleton's Endurance: Shackleton, 1919; 1999, Lansing, 1959.
Peglar Papers: Cyriax and Jones, 1954; Battersby, 2010, p.187.
Shackleton's Endurance: Shackleton, 1919; 1999; Lansing, 1959.
Polar Bear, Beechey Island: Battersby, 2010, p. 188.
Items with owner's names: McClintock, 1908, p. 231; Gilder, 1881, p. 126.
Food and fuel: Cyriax, 1945, p. 153; p. 179; Cyriax, 1962, p. 36.
Boots: McClintock, 1875, p. 252; Cookman, 2000, p. 159.
Pinnace by McClintock: McClintock, 1908, p. 248.

Sledge by McClintock: McClintock, 1908, p. 250.
Peglar Papers: Cyriax and Jones, 1954; Battersby, 2010.
Camping equipment Washington Bay: Woodman, 1991, p. 127.
24 paddles: Wright, 1949, p.93.

CHAPTER 13.
Lead poisoning: Beattie, 1985; Beattie and Geiger, 1987.
400 bone fragments: Keenleyside and others, 1997.
Lead source: Beattie and others, 1990.
Lead in tins: Battersby, 2008.
Lead match with solder: Beattie and others, 1990.
Alternative source: Battersby, 2008.
Lead study: Millar and others, 2015.
Tommy Anguttitauruq's testimony: Eber, 2008, p. 75.
One ounce daily: Cyriax, 1939, p. 139.
Scurvy reappraisal: Mays and others, 2011.
Tinned meat poisons Inuit: Amundsen, 1908,
Beechey Island exhumation: Beattie and Geiger, 1987.
Ikinnelikpatolok's testimony: Gilder, 1881, p. 78.
Ice Blink: Cookman, 2000.
Peglar papers: Cyriax and Jones, 1954; Potter, 2016, p. 42.
McClure, trapped: McClure, 1856.
Tuberculosis: Beattie and Geiger, 1987.
Dental problems: Keenleyside and others, 1997.
McClintock's report: McClintock, 1863, p. 249.
Richard King's book: King, 1836.
Arctic sledging: Cyriax, 1963.
Parry's second Arctic expedition: Parry, 1824.
Ross's Victory expedition: Ross, 1835.
McClintock's sledge journey: McClintock, 1859b, p. 6.
Forty days rations: McClintock, 1875, p. 313.
Proposed sale of stores from Fury Beach: Fluhmann, 1976.
McClure's book: McClure, 1856, p. 131.
Back's book: Back, 1836.
King's book: King, 1836.
Dease and Simpson report: Simpson, 1843.
Richardson's suggestion: Richardson, 1861, p. 169.
Cyriax, food stores: Cyriax, 1939, p. 153.
Hall testimony: Woodman, 1991, p. 124; Hall Collection, Book A, p. 47.

CHAPTER 14.
Hobson's report: Stenton, 2014, p. 518.
In-nook-poo-zhe-jook's finds: Nourse, 1879, p. 405.
Beattie finds: Beattie, 1983.
Potter's map and photo: Potter, 2016, Figure 23, p. 158-159.
Forensic study: Keenleyside and others, 1997.
Site NgLj-3: Stenton, 2015.
McClintock's boat place: McClintock, 1859; Gilder, 1899, p. 155.
Schwatka's bone find: Gilder, 1881, p. 156-157.
Cranial reconstruction: Stenton and others, 2016.
The pinnace in Erebus Bay: McClintock, 1908, p. 221-226.
James Reid: Stenton and others, 2015.
In-nook-poo-zhe-jook's testimony: Nourse, 1879, p. 405; p. 419.
Schwatka's report: Gilder, 1881, p. 155.
Site NgLj-2: Keenleyside and others, 1997.
Ranford's find: Ranford: 1994.
Beattie's find: Beattie and Geiger, 1987.
Site NgLj-2: Keenleyside and others, 1997.
McClintock's statement: McClintock, 1908, p. 182.
Fairholme rescued: Battersby, 2010.
In-nook-poo-zhe-jook's testimony: Hall, 4th May 1869, in Nourse, 1879, p. 405.
In-nook-poo-zhe-jook's additional testimony: Hall, 2nd July 1869 in Nourse, 1979, p. 420.
In-nook-poo-zhe-jook's mother in law's testimony: Hall, 2nd July 1869 in Nourse 1879, p. 420.
Ahlangyah's testimony: Gilder, 1881, p. 92.
Ranford's find: Keenleyside and others, 1997.
Camp site by Potter: Potter, 2016, figure 23, p. 158-159.

CHAPTER 15.
Cyriax, stores: Cyriax, 1939.
Vegetation change: Klutschak, 1987, p. 100.
Douglas Bay: Gibson, 1932.
Sea poem: Cyriax, 1954.
Iggiararsuk's testimony: Rasmussen, 1926, p. 138; Cooper, 1961, p. 245.
Tommy Anguttitauruq's testimony: Eber, 2008, p. 76.
Douglas Bay: Gibson, 1932.
Boat description: Rasmussen, 1927, p. 240.

Rae's problem with Lady Jane: McGoogan, 2001.
Hall's five year stay: Nourse 1879.
Pot boiling: May and Beattie, 2016, p. 778-786.

CHAPTER 16.
Chieftain Report: Woodman, 1991, p. 211.
Fireplace trail: Eber, 2008, p. 87.
Admiral Wright: Wright, 1969, p. 37.
Campsite Imnguyaaluk Island: Eber, 2008.
Deserted ship with bodies aboard: Rasmussen, 1925, p. 138.
Patsy Topilikton's testimony: Eber, 2008, p. 86.
Description of crew: Eber, 2008, p. 86.
Frank Analok's testimony: Eber, 2008, p.85.
Summer hunt: Nourse, 1879, p. 256; Woodman, 1991, p. 227.
Tommy Anguttitauruq's testimony: Eber, 2008, p. 90.
Michael Angottittauruq's (different spelling) testimony: Eber, 2008, p. 87.
Mate Graham Gore, hunting: Back, 1838.
Kok-lee-arng-nun's testimony: Nourse, 1879, p. 256.
Burwash photo: Potter, 2016, p. 142-143.
Burwash, Jamme report: Burwash, 1931, p. 112.
Jamme Report, Victory Point: Burwash, 1931, p. 90.
Map of graves: Burwash, 1931, p. 114; Woodman, 1991, Figure 3.
Cooper, Victory Point: Cooper 1961.
Search for Crozier's grave and buried records: Potter, 2016, p. 219.

CHAPTER 17.
1850 retreat in 1850: Woodman, 1991.
Dr. Rae's report: Rae, 1880.
McClintock's report: McClintock, 1859, p. 248.
Tu-ki-ta and Ower's testimony: Woodman, 1991, p. 124.
Hall's report: Nourse, 1879, p. 406.
Hall's numbers estimate: Nourse, 1879, p. 403; Woodman, 1991, p. 140.
Hall's further information: Nourse, 1879, p. 606.
Ahlangyah's testimony: Gilder, 1881, p. 90-91.
An officer's report: Woodman, 1995, p. 308.
Fewer than ten bodies: Woodman, 1991, p. 308.
Crozier absent: Woodman, 1991, p. 124.
Fitzjames journal: Fitzjames, 1852; Mangles, 1852.
Skull and bones find: Learmouth, 1948.

Too-loo-a: Woodman, 1991, p. 127.
1973 skeleton: Walsh, 1974.
Hall in 1869: Nourse, 1879, p. 286.
Remains at Tulloch Point: Gilder, 1881, p. 286.
Gibson, Tulloch Point: Gibson, 1932.
Near 'Peffer River,' Hall collects skeleton: Woodman, 1991, p. 160.
2009 forensic investigation: Mays and others, 2011.
'Peffer River' to Todd Islets: Hall in Nourse, 1881, p. 401-402.
Remains east of 'Peffer River': Hall in Nourse, 1879, p. 606.
Poo-yet-a's testimony: Nourse, 1879, p. 606.
E-vee-shuk's testimony: Nourse, 1879, p. 608.
Bones at Booth Point: Beattie and Geiger, 1987.
Nenijook's testimony: Learmouth, 1848; Woodman, 1991, p. 149.
Starvation Cove, Rae's report: McClure, 1854.
Tooktocheer and Ogzeuckjeuwock's testimony: Gilder, 1881, p. 106-108.
Iggiararsuk's testimony: Rasmussen, 1926, p. 138.
Single skeleton: Gilder, 1881, p. 210.
Hall 11th May 1869: Nourse, 1879, p. 607.
First Franklin relics: McClure, 1856, p. 219.
Montreal Island: McClure, 1856, p. 319.
Paul Papanakies: Woodman, 1991, p. 279.
Sherard Osborn: McClure, 1856, p. 327,
Roderic Owen: Owen, 1978.
Hall letter: Nourse, 1879, p. 415.
Hostility in Chantrey Inlet: King, 1836, p. 68-69; Woodman, 1991, p. 66 and p. 310.

CHAPTER 18.
Two testimonies: Woodman, 1991, p. 204 – 205, from Hall journal dated December 6 1864 – May12 1865, book 6.
Ook-bar-loo's testimony, the miserable meal: Woodman, 1991, p. 204-205.
Ook-bar-loo's testimony, the 'black men': Woodman, 1991, p. 205.
Blubber soot: Shackleton, 1919; 1999; Lansing, 1959.
Elephant Island diary: Shackleton, 1999, p. 161.
Hut point diary: Shackleton, 1999, p. 173.
Rear Admiral Wright: Wright, 1949, p. 37.
Cyriax stores: Cyriax, 1947.

CHAPTER 19.
Frank Analok's testimony: Eber, 2008, p. 86.
Peterson's report: McClintock, 1908, p. 201.
McClintock's report of two ships: McClintock, 1908, p. 194.
In-nook-poo-zhe-jook's testimony: Nourse, 1879, p. 404.
Footprints: Nourse, 1879, p. 404.
McClintock, heavily salvaged: McClintock, 1908, p. 201.
Ek-kee-pee-re-a's testimony: Nourse, 1879, p. 404.
Koo-nik's testimony: Woodman, 1995, p. 250.
Puhtoorak's testimony: Gilder, 1881, p. 79.
Initials on silver: McClintock, 1908, p. 287.
Koo-nik's testimony: Woodman, 1995, p. 250.
Captain Inglefield: Savours, 1999, p. 199.
Beattie and Geiger: Beattie and Geiger, 1987.
Relic: Gilder, 1881, p. 104.
Woodman, R.I.P.: Woodman, 1991, p. 254.

CHAPTER 20.
Ook-soo-see-too islet: www.ric.edu/faculty/rpotter/woodman
McClure abandons *Investigator*: McClure, 1856.
Tooktoyakbuk visit: Miertsching, 1967, p. 53; Neatby, 1970, p.172.
Royal Geographical Society meeting: McClintock, 1859.
Mr. Kennedy's report: McClintock 1859, p. 12.
Dr. Rae's report: Rae, 1854, p. 457.
Captain Kellett abandons Resolute: Savours, 1999, p. 264-265.
Sir John Ross abandons Victory: Ross, 1835.
Admiral Belcher abandons four ships: Savours, 1999, p. 266-267.
Dr Rae finds flagpole: Rae, 1851.
Nicholas Qayutinaq's testimony: Eber, 2008, p. 80.
Ook-soo-see-too islet: www.ric.edu/faculty/rpotter/woodman
R.I.P.: Woodman, 1991, p. 254-255.

CHAPTER 21.
Two brother's testimony: Rasmussen, 1931, p. 130; Klutschak, 1968, p. 209.
Many dead men: Rasmussen, 1925, p. 138.
Amundsen's report: Amundsen and Hansen, 1980, v. 2, p. 61.

CHAPTER 22.
Ouela's testimony: Nourse, 1879, p. 64.
Letter from Hall: Nourse, 1879, p. 107-109.
Owen, Hall gullible: Owen, 1978, p. 411.
Ook-bar-loo's testimony: Nourse, 1879, p. 591.
Ouela and his brother's testimony: Nourse, 1879, p. 591.
Aglooka gives sword: Woodman, 1991, p. 132; Potter, 2016, p. 182.
Tozer from Somerset: Lloyd-Jones, 2004.
Terror-stricken Inuit: Eber, 2008, p. 82.
Netsilingmiut: Rasmussen, 1926, p. 135.
Hall warning: Nourse, 1879, p. 258.
Too-shoo-ar-thar-i-u's testimony: Nourse, 1879, p. 591.
Kok-lee-arng-nun's testimony: Nourse, 1879, p. 257.
Too-koo-li-to's testimony: Nourse, 1879, p. 593.
Kin-na-pa-too: Woodman, 1995, p. 113.
Death of Aglooka: Woodman, 1995, p. 128.
Strangers in 1852 and 1854 to 1864: Woodman, 1995.
Footprints: Nourse, 1879, p. 404.
Other strangers, 1855 to 1856: Woodman, 1995.

CHAPTER 23.
Anderson's river trip: Anderson, 1969.
Letter from Lady Jane: Rawnsley, 1923, p. 197.
The many searches: Ross, 2002.
Potter's sixty-five expeditions: Potter, 2016, Appendix, p. 221-232.
King's book: King, 1836.
Sir James Clark Ross: Ross, 1835.
Richardson and Rae's expedition: Richardson, 1854.
Simpson Strait: Simpson, 1843.
Weasey Coppin: Woodward, 1951, p. 267.
Beechey Island: Snow, 1851.
Kennedy, Peel Sound: Kennedy, 1853.
Inglefield search: Inglefield, 1853.
McClintock's comment: McClintock, 1908, p. 219.
Dr. Rae's report to Admiralty: McClure, 1854.
Dr. Rae's additional information: McClure, 1854, p. v.
Charles Dickens' tirade: Dickens, 1854, no. 245, p. 361-365 and no. 246, p. 385-391.
Dr. Rae's reply: Rae, 1854, no. 248, p. 433-437 and no. 249, p. 457-459.

Letter from Dr. Rae to Captain McClintock: McClintock, 1908, Introduction.
Captain McClintock's comments on Hall's investigations: McClintock, 1908, supplementary chapter, p. 49.
Sir James Graham: Woodward, 1951, p. 285.
Gell dispute: Woodward, 1951, p. 276, p. 282 and p. 285.
Sir Roderick Murchison: McClintock, 1908, Preface.
Admiralty letter: McClintock, 1908, Preface.

CHAPTER 24.
Dr. Richard King: King, 1855.
Chieftain report: Woodman, 1991, p. 211.
Tooktoyaktuk: Miertsching. 1967; Neatby, 1970, p. 172.
Dr. Rae, Victoria Land: Rae, 1851.
Captain Penny, Cornwallis Island: Sutherland, 1852, v. 2, p. 246.
Mr. Arbuthnot's report of a ship: Collinson, 1889, p. 331.
Captain Collinson: Collinson, 1889, p. 278.
Rear-Admiral Noel Wright: Wright, 1949, p. 25.

CHAPTER 25.
Woodman: Woodman, 1991.
Wilson, 2000.
Woodman: Woodman, 1995.
Potter's map: Potter, 2016, p. 158-159.
James Reid, possible facial reconstruction: Stenton and others, 2016.

REFERENCES

Amundsen, R., 1908, The North West Passage. VI: Being the record of a passage of the ship *Gjoa*, 1903-1907. E.P. Dutton & Co., New York, vol. 1, 335 p. Reprinted 2014, Cambridge University Press.

Amundsen, R. and Hansen, G., 1908, The North West Passage – Being a record of a voyage of exploration of the ship *Gjoa* 1903-1907: vol. 2. Archibald Constable and Co. Ltd., London, Reprinted 2014, Cambridge University Press.

Anderson, J., 1969, The Hudson Bay Expedition in search of Sir John Franklin. Introduction by S. Mickle: Reprinted from Canadian Women's Historical Society (Transaction 20). Toronto: Canadiana House 1969.

Anderson, J., 1940 and 1941, Chief Factor James Anderson's Back River Journal of 1855: Canadian Field Naturalist 54 (May-Dec. 1940): 63-7, 84-9,107-9, 125-6, 134-6, and 55 (Jan-March 1941): 9-11, 21-26, 38-44.

Back, G., 1836, Narrative of the Arctic Land Expedition to the Mouth of the Great Fish River: John Murray, London. Reprinted 1970, Hurtig, Edmonton.

Back, G., 1838, Narrative of an expedition in H.M.S. '*Terror*': John Murray, London.

Ball, B., 1881, Lieut. John Irving, RN of H.M.S. *Terror*: David Douglas, Edinburgh.

Banfield, F.H., 1960, The oldest Canned Food in the World?: The New Scientist, May 1960, p.1138-1140.

Barrow, J., 1818, A chronological history of voyages into the Arctic regions; Reprinted 2011, Cambridge University Press.

Barrow, J., 1846, Voyages of discovery and research in the Arctic regions, for the years 1818 to the present time: John Murray, London. Reprinted 2011, Cambridge University Press.

Battersby, William, 2008, Identification of the Probable Source of the Lead Poisoning Observed in Members of the Franklin expedition: Journal of the Hakluyt Society, September 2008, p.1-10.

Battersby, William, 2010, James Fitzjames: the mystery Man of the Franklin Expedition: The history press Co., and Dundum Press, Canada, 224 p.

Beattie, O., 1983, A Report on Newly Discovered Human Skeletal Remains from the Last Sir John Franklin Expedition: Muskox, vol. 33, p. 68-77.

References

Beattie, O.,1985, Elevated Bone Lead Levels in a Franklin Expedition Crewman: In: Sutherland, P.D., Ed., The Franklin era in Canadian History, 1845-59; National Museum of Man, Ottawa, p.141-148.

Beattie O., and Geiger, J., 1987, Frozen in time: Unlocking the Secrets of the Franklin Expedition: Western Producer Prairie Books, Saskatoon, Saskatchewan.

Beattie O., Kowal, W., and Baadsgard, H., 1990, Did solder kill Franklin's Men?: Natures, vol. 343 (January 1990), p. 319-320.

Beattie, O., and Savelle, J.M., 1983, Discovery of Human remains from Sir John Franklin's Last Expedition: Historical Archeology vol. 17, p. 10-105.

Bell, B., 1881, Lieut.John Irving, R.N. of H.M.S. *Terror* in Sir John Franklins Last expedition to Arctic regions - A Memorial Sketch with Letters: David Douglas, Edinburgh.

Blenky, E.,1852, Mrs. Blenky's letter to the 'Morning Herald.' In; Mangles, J. (Ed,), 1852, Papers and Despatches relating to the Arctic Searching expeditions of 1850-51-52. Francis and John Rivington, London, p. 85-86.

Brandt, A., 2011, The man who ate his boots – the tragic history of the search for the Northwest Passage: Jonathan Cape, London, 441p.

Burwash, L.T., 1930, The Franklin Search: Canadian Geographical Journal, 1 (November 1930), p. 507-603.

Burwash, L.T., 1931, Canada's Western Arctic: Report on Investigations in 1925-26, 1928-29 and 1930. Ottawa, F.A. Acland, King's Printer.

Collinson, R., 1889, Journal of H.M.S. *Enterprise* on the expedition in search of Sir John Franklin's ships in Behring Strait, 1850-55: Sampson Low, Marston, Searle and Rivington, London. Reprinted 1976, AMS Press, New York.

Cookman, Scott, 2000, Ice Blink – The tragic fate of Sir John Franklin's lost Polar expedition: John Wiley and Sons, New York, 244p.

Cooper, P.F., 1961, Island of the lost: G. P. Putnum's, New York, 256 p.

Cooper, P.F. 1955a, A trip to King William Island in 1954: Arctic Circular 8, No. 1, p. 8-11.

Cooper, P.F., 1955b, A second trip to King William Island: Arctic Circular 8. No. 4, p. 78-79.

Cyriax, R.J., 1939, Sir John Franklin's Last Arctic Expedition: Methuen and Company, London. Reprinted 1977, The Arctic Press, Plaistow and Sutton Coldfield, 222p.

Cyriax, R.J., 1944, Captain Hall and the So-Called Survivors of the Franklin Expedition: Polar Record, 4, p. 170-185.

Cyriax, R.J., 1945, Centenary of the sailing of Sir John Franklin with the *Erebus* and *Terror*: Geographical Journal, London, vol. 106, p. 169-180.

Cyriax, R.J., 1947, A Historic Medicine Chest: Canadian Medical Association Journal, 57, p. 295-300.

Cyriax, R.J., 1951, Recently Discovered Traces of Sir John Franklin's Expedition: Geographical Journal, 117 (June 1951), p. 211-214.

Cyriax, R.J., 1952, The Position of Victory Point: Polar Record, 6, p. 496-507.

Cyriax, R.J., 1965, Two notebooks of C. F. Hall: Geographical Journal, 131, p. 90-92.

Cyriax, R.J., 1969, The Unsolved Problem of the Franklin Expedition Records Supposedly Buried on King William Island: Mariner's Mirror, 55, p. 23-32.

Cyriax, R. J., and A. G. E. Jones, 1954, The Papers in the possession of Harry Peglar, Captain of the Foretop, HMS *Terror* 1845: Mariner's Mirror, 40, p. 186-195.

Day, A.E., 1986, Search for the Northwest Passage: An Annotated Biography. Garland. New York.

Dease, P.W. and Simpson, T., 1841, Narrative of the Progress of Arctic Discoveries on the Northern Shore of America, in the summer of 1839: Royal Geographical Society Journal, v. 10, p.268-274.

Dickens, C., 1854, The Lost Arctic Voyagers. Household Words: Part 1, v. X, no. 245, 2nd December 1854, p.361-365; Part 2, v. X, No. 246, 9th December 1854, p. 385-391.

Eber, D.H., 2008, Encounters on the passage: Inuit meet the explorers: University of Toronto Press, 168 p.

Fitzjames, J., 1852, Journal of James Fitzjames aboard *Erebus*, 1845: Nautical Magazine and Chronicle, 21, p.158-165, p. 195-201. Also: Mangles, J. (Ed.), 1852, Papers and Despatches relating to the Arctic searching expeditions of 1850-51-52. 2nd Edition, Francis and John Rivington, London, p.76-88.

Fluhmann, M., 1976, Second in command: NWT Dept. of Information, 162p.

Franklin, J., 1823, Narrative of a journey to the shores of the Polar Sea in the Years 1818-20-21-22: John Murray, London. Reprinted 1969 Hurtig, Edmonton. Reprinted 2012, Cambridge University Press.

Franklin, J., and Richardson, J., 1828, Narrative of a second expedition to the shores of the Polar Sea, in 1825-27: John Murray, London. Reprinted 1971, Hurtig, Edmonton. Reprinted 2012, Cambridge University Press.

Franklin, Sir J., 1845 and 1967. Narrative of some passages in the history of Van Diemen's Land during the last three years of Sir John Franklin's administration of its government: Platypus Publications, Hobart, Tasmania.

Geiger, J. and Beattie, O., 1993, Dead silence: Bloomsbury Publishing Ltd., London, 219 p.

Gibson, William, 1932, Some further traces of the Franklin Retreat: Geographical Journal, v. LXXIX, No. 5, May issue, p. 402-208.

Gibson, William, 1937, Sir John Fanklin's Last voyage: The Beaver, p. 44-75.

Gilder, William H., 1881, Schwatka's Search: Sledging in the Arctic in Quest of Franklin Records: Charles Scribner's Sons, New York, 316 p.

Gilder, William H., 1899, The Search for Franklin, A Narrative of the American Expedition under Lieutenant Schwatka: Nelson and Sons, Reprinted 2014, Cambridge University Press.

Gould, R.T., 1927, Admiralty Chart 5101, Chart showing the vicinity of King William Island, with the various positions in which relics of the Arctic Expedition under Sir John Franklin have been found: Compiled by Lieut. Commdr. R.T. Gould.

Hall, Charles Francis, 1862, Life with the Esquimaux: A Narrative of Arctic Experience in Search of Sir John Franklin's Expedition: Sampson, Low, Sons and Marston, London. Reprinted 1970, Hurtig, Edmonton.

Harris, J., 1982, Without trace – The last Voyages of eight ships: Book Club associates, London, 244p.

Hickey, C.G., Savelle, J.M. and Hobson, G.B., 1993, The Route of Sir John Franklin's Third Arctic Expedition: An Evaluation and Test of an Alternative Hypothesis: Arctic, Vol. 46, No. 1 (March 1993), p. 78-81.

Inglefield, E.A., 1853, A summer search for Sir John Franklin: Thomas Harrison, London.

Kane, E.K., 1856, Arctic Explorations - The second Grinnell Expedition in search of Sir John Franklin 1853, '54, '55: Childs and Peterson, Philadelphia, 467 p.

Kennedy, W., 1853, A short narrative of the second voyage of the *Prince Albert* in search of Sir John Franklin: W.H. Dalton, London. Reprinted 2010, Cambridge University Press.

King, R., 1836, Narrative of a Journey to the Shores of the Arctic Sea under the Command of Captain Back, RN: Richard Bentley, London.

King, R., 2014, The Franklin Expedition from First to Last: Reprinted Fogotten Books, 2012, 224 p.

Knowles Bolton, Sarah, 1893, Famous voyagers and explorers: Thomas Y. Crowell & Co., New York.

Keenleyside, A., Bertulli, M., and Fricke, H.C., 1997, The final days of the Franklin expedition: new skeletal evidence: Arctic. vol. 50, no.1, (March 1997), p.36-46.

Kerr, R., 1954, Rae's Franklin Relics: Beaver, March 1954, p. 25-27.

Klutschak, H., 1987, Overland to Starvation Cove: with the Inuit in search of Franklin. Translated and edited by William Barr. University of Toronto Press, Toronto 261 p.

Lansing, A., 1959, *Endurance*: Reprinted 2014 by Basic Books, New York, 357 p.

Larsen, H., 1954, Northwest Passage: The Voyage of the *St. Roch*. Vancouver: Queen's Printer.

Learmouth, L.A., 1948, Notes on Franklin relics: Arctic, p. 122-123.

Lloyd-Jones, R., 2004, The Royal Marines on Franklin's last expedition: Polar Record, v. 40, p. 319-320.

Lloyd-Jones, R., 2005, The men who sailed with Franklin: Polar Record, v. 41, p. 311-318.

Mangles, J., 1852, Papers and Despatches relating to the Arctic Search expeditions of 1850-51-52: Francis and John Rivington, London.

Mays, S., Ogden, A., Montgomery, J., Vincent S., Battersby, W., and Taylor, G.M., 2011, New light on the personal identification of a skeleton of a member of Sir John Franklin's last expedition to the Arctic, 1845: Journal of Archaeological Science, v. 38, issue 7, p. 1571-1582.

Mays, S., Maat, G.J.R. and de Boer, H.H., 2015, Scurvy as a factor in the loss of the 1845 Franklin expedition to the Arctic: a reconsideration: International Journal of Osteoarchaeology, vol.25, issue 3, p. 334-344.

Mays, S., and Beattie, O., 2016, Evidence for End-Stage Cannibalism on Sir John Franklin's Last Expedition to the Arctic, 1845: International Journal of Osteoarchaeology, vol.26, issue 5, p. 778-786.

McGoogan, K., 2001, Fatal Passage: Harper Collins Publishers, Canada; Bantam Edition, 2002, 328p.

McGoogan, K., 2005, Lady Jane's revenge: Harper Collins, Toronto, 468 p.

McKenzie, W. G., 1969, A Further Clue to the Franklin Mystery: Beaver, 299 (Spring 1969), p. 28-32.

McClintock, F.L., 1859, The Voyage of the *Fox* in the Arctic Seas - A Narrative of the Discovery of the fate of Sir John Franklin and his companions: John Murray, Albemarle Street, London. Reprinted 2005, Elibron Classics Series, Adamant Media Corporation, 403 p. Reprinted 2012, Cambridge University Press.

McClintock, F. L., 1859, Discoveries by the late Expedition in Search of Sir John Franklin and his Party: Royal Geographical Society Proceedings, v. 4, 2-13.

McClintock, F. L., 1860, The voyage of the *Fox* in the Arctic Seas: A Narrative of the Discovery of the Fate of Sir John Franklin and his Companions: Porter and Coates, Philadelphia. Reprinted 1972 by Hurtig Publishers, Edmonton.

McClintock, F. L., 1861, Narrative of the Expedition in Search of Sir John Franklin and his Party: Royal Geographical Society Journal , v. 31, p. 1-13.

McClintock. F.L., 1875, Voyage of the *Fox* in the Arctic Seas in search of Franklin and his companions: John Murray, Albemarle Street, London, 336p.

McClintock, F.L., 1908, The voyage of the *Fox* in Arctic seas in search of Franklin and his companions: John Murray, Albemarle Street, London, 303p.

McClure, R., 1854, Melancholy fate of Sir John Franklin and his party as disclosed in Dr. Rae's report together with dispatches and letters of Captain McClure and other officers employed in the Arctic Expeditions: John Betts, Strand, London.

McClure, R., 1856, The discovery of the North-West Passage by H.M.S. *Investigator*, Capt. McClure, 1850, 1851, 1852, 1853, 1854: Edited by Commander Sherard Osborn, Longman, Brown, Green and Longman, London. Reprinted 1969, Hurtig. Reprinted 2013, Cambridge University Press.

Miertsching, J., 1967, Frozen Ships -The Arctic diary of Johann Miertsching, 1850-1854: Translated from the German and published with an introduction and note by L.H. Neatby. Macmillan, Toronto, 254 p.

Millar, K., Bowman, A.W., and Battersby, W., 2015, A re-analysis of the supposed role of lead poisoning in Sir John Franklin's last expedition: Polar Record, v. 51, issue 03, p. 224-238.

Neatby, L.H., 1958, In Quest of the North West Passage: Constable and Company, London, 194 p.

Neatby, Leslie H., 1970, The Search for Franklin: Arthur Barker Ltd., London, 281 p.

Nourse, J.E., Ed., 1879, Narrative of the Second Arctic Expedition Commanded by Charles Francis Hall: Washington, Government Printing Office, 778p. Reprinted by Nabu Public Domain Reprints. Lightning Source UK Ltd., Milton Keynes, UK.

Osborn, S., 1860, The career, last voyage and fate, of Captain Sir John Franklin: Bradbury and Evans, London.

Osborn, S., 1865, Stray leaves from an Arctic Journal: Longman, Brown, Green, and Longmans, London.

Owen, R., 1978, The Fate of Franklin: The Hutchinson Publishing Group, London.

Palin, M., 2018, *Erebus* – The story of a ship; Hutchinson, London, 334 p.

Parry, W.E., 1821, Journal of a voyage for the discovery of a North-West Passage in 1819-20 in HMS *Hecla* and *Griper*: John Murray, London. Reprinted 1968, Greenwood Press, New York.

Parry, W.E., 1824, Journal of a second voyage for the discovery of a Northwest Passage performed in the years 1821-22-23 in HMS *Fury* and *Hecla*. John Murray, London. Reprinted 1969, Greenwood Press, New York.

Parry, W.E., 1828, Journal of the 1st, 2nd and 3rd voyages for the discovery of a Northwest Passage from Atlantic to Pacific in 1819-20-21-22-23-24-25 under orders of Captain W.E. Parry. John Murray, London.

Penny, W. 1852, Captain Penny to the Editor of the 'Times'. In: Mangles, J. (Ed.), 1852, Papers and Despatches related to the Arctic Searching Expeditions of 1850-51-52: 2nd Edition, Francis and John Rivington, London, p. 90-91.

Rae, J., 1850, Narrative of an Expedition to the Shores of the Arctic Sea in 1846 and 1847: John Murray, London. Reprinted 1970, Canadiana House, Toronto.

Rae, J., 1851, Letter to Hudson's Bay Company dated 25th Sept. 1851. Published April 5th 1852.

Rae, J., 1854, The Lost Arctic Voyagers: Household Words: Part 1, v. X, no. 248, 23rd December 1854, p. 433-437; Part 2, v. X, No. 249, 30th December, 1854, p. 457-459.

Rae, J., 1880, Letter of Dr. John Rae to the British Admiralty: American Geographical Society of New York, Journal 1880, 12, p. 284-288.

Rasmussen, K. J., 1926, The Fifth Thule Expedition: Geographical Journal, v. 26, p.133-128.

Rasmussen, K.J, 1931, The Netsilik Eskimos: Social Life and Spiritual Culture, Report of the 5th Thule Expedition; Glydensdalke Boghandel, Nordisk Forlag, Copenhagen, Reprinted 1976 AMS Press, New York.

Rawnsley, W.F. 1923, The life, diaries and correspondence of Lady Jane Franklin 1792 – 1875: Erskine, MacDonald, Ltd., London: Reprinted 2014, Cambridge University Press, 242 p.

Richardson, Sir, J., 1854, Arctic searching expedition, New York.

Richardson, Sir J., 1861, The Polar Regions: Adams and Charles Black, Edinburgh.

Ross, James Clark, 1969, Voyage of Discovery and Research in the Southern and Antarctic Seas. 1847. Reprinted 1969, David and Charles Reprints, London. Reprinted 2011, Cambridge University Press, 334p

Ross, Sir John, 1819, A voyage of discovery made for the purpose of exploring Baffin Bay, London: Longman, Hurst, Rees, Arme and Brown.

Ross, Sir John, 1835, Narrative of a second voyage in search of a North-West Passage: and a residence in the Arctic regions during the years 1829, 1830, 1831, 1832 1833, including the report of Commander, now Captain, James Clark Ross, R.N., F.R.S., F.L.S, &c. and the discovery of the Northern Magnetic Pole: 2 volumes, Webster, Regent Street, London. Reprinted 2012, Cambridge University Press.

Ross, J, Rear-Admiral, 1855, A Narrative of the circumstance and causes which led to the failure of the searching expeditions sent by government and others for the rescue of Sir John Franklin: Reprinted 2012, Cambridge University Press.

Ross, W.G., 2002, The type and number of expeditions in the Franklin Search 1847 – 1859. Arctic, v. 55, no. 1, p. 57-69.

Schwatka, F., 1882, The search for Franklin; a narrative of the American expedition under Lieutenant Frederick Schwatka, 1878-1880, London.

Shackleton, E. H. Sir, 1919, South; the story of Shackleton's 1914-1917 expedition. Century Publishing, London.

Shackleton, E.H., Sir, 1999, South. The story of Shackleton's last expedition 1914-1917. Edited by Peter King. Pimlico Edition, 1999, 207 p.

Simmonds, P.L., 1852, Sir John Franklin and the Arctic regions, Republished 2005, Nonsuch Publishing, Gloucestershire, UK, 313 p., Reprinted 2012, Cambridge University Press.

Simpson, T., 1843, Narrative of discoveries on the north coast of North America during the years 1836-1839: Richard Bentley, London.

Smith, M., 2006, Captain Francis Crozier - Last man standing? The Collins Press, Cork, 242 p.

Snow, W.P., 1851, The voyage of the *Prince Albert* in search of Sir John Franklin: Longman, Brown, Green, and Longmans, London. Reprinted 2010, Cambridge University Press.

Stackpole, E. (Ed.), 1977, The Long Arctic Search: the Narrative of Lieutenant Frederick Schwatka, USA. 1878-1880, seeking the records of the lost Franklin expedition: Pequod Press, Connecticut.

Stenton, D.R., 2014, A most inhospitable coast: The report of Lieutenant William Hobson's 1859 search for the Franklin expedition on King William Island. Arctic, v. 67, No. 4, p. 511-522.

Stenton, D.R., Keenleyside, A., and Park, R.W., 2015, 'The Boat Place' Burial: New Skeletal Evidence from the 1845 Franklin Expedition: Arctic, 68, no.1, p. 32-44.

Stenton, D.R., Keenleyside, A., Trepkov, D.P., and Park, R.W., 2016, Faces from the Franklin expedition? Craniofacial reconstructions of two members of the 1845 Northwest Passage Expedition: Polar Record, v. 52, No. 1, p 76-81.

Walsh, R.T.,1974, Quest in the North: Sentinel , v. 10, no. 5, p. 23-24.

Wilson, J., 2000, North with Franklin: Fitzhenry & Whiteside, USA and Ontario, 305 p.

Wilson, J., 2001, John Franklin, Traveller of Undiscovered Seas: XYZ Publishing , Montreal, Canada, 175 p.

Woodman, D. C.,1991, Unravelling the Franklin Mystery – Inuit Testimony: McGill-Queens University Press, Montreal & Kingston, London, Buffalo, 390 p.

Woodman, D. C., 1995, Strangers among us: McGill-Queen's University Press, Montreal & Kingston, London, Buffalo, 166 p.

Woodward, Frances J., 1951, Portrait of Jane – A Life of Lady Franklin: Hodder and Stoughton, London, 371p.

Wordie, J. M., 1945, The Northwest Passage since the last Franklin Expedition: Geographical Journal, London, vol.106, p. 180-197.

Wright, Noel, 1959, Quest for Franklin: Heinemann, London, 124 p.

MAPS

MAP I

Part of the Canadian Arctic showing areas unknown in 1845, the ice river extending from the Beaufort Sea to King William Island and the route of the 1845 expedition.

MAP II

The King William Island - Adelaide Peninsula area showing locations of remains of the Franklin retreats.

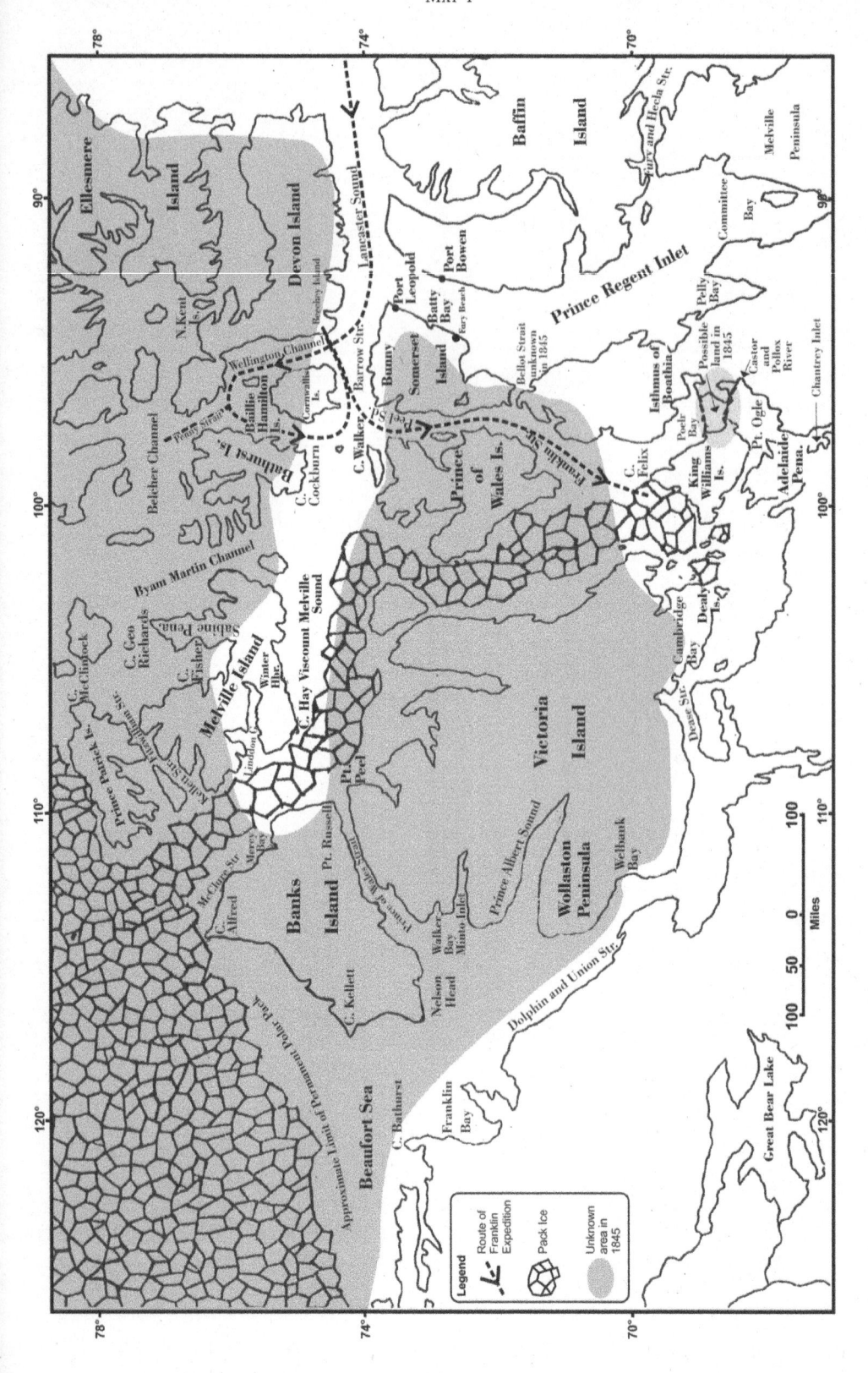

Map I

MAP II

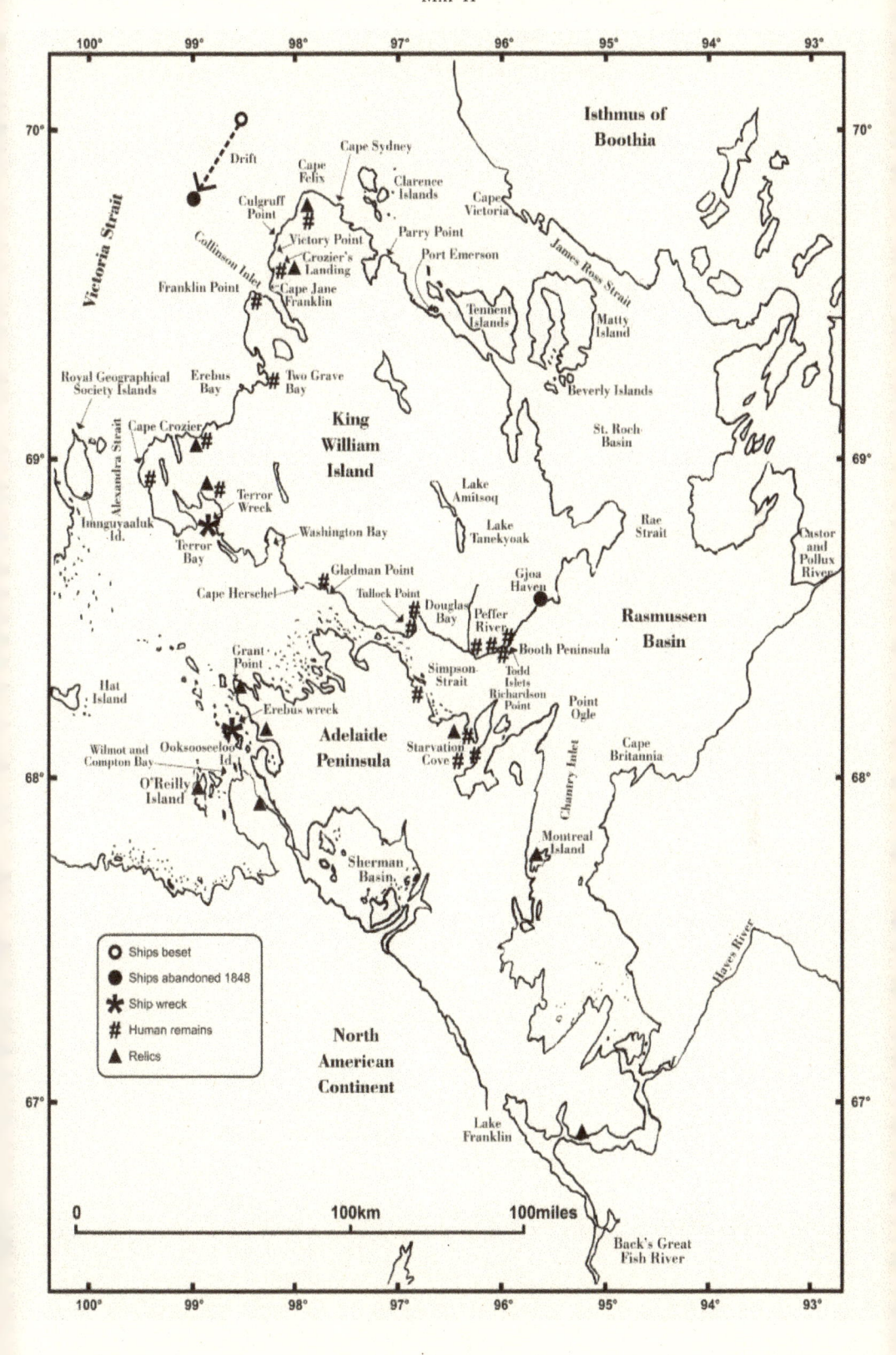

INDEX

Sir John Franklin is referred to as JF throughout.

A
Abernathy, Thomas 115, 116, 171
Adelaide Peninsula 112, 214, 229–30, 235–6, 264
Admiralty, The
　Article 21: 64, 89, 110, 119, 141–2, 146
　lack of emergency plans 150
　and Lady Franklin 291
　letter to McClintock 309–10
　and North-West Passage 46–7
　overconfidence of 81–2
　search ships sent 83, 90, 293–4
　and *Victory* 51
Advance, U.S.S. 91
Aglooka *see* Crozier, Capt Francis R.M.
Ahlangyah (Inut) 193–4, 227–8
Albany (ship) 47
Alexandra Channel 246
Amundsen, Roald
　Gjoa expedition 44, 96–7, 100, 101
　and Inuit testimony 32, 137
　report on Inuit discovery 164–5
　and Royal Geographical Society Islands 211
　on tinned meat eaten by Inuit 268–9
Analok, Frank 211–12, 250
Anderson, James 238–9, 240, 285
Angottitauruq, Michael (Inut) 214–15

Anguttitauruq, Tommy (Inut) 101, 162, 203–5, 213–14
animals aboard ship 66, 74, 212, 262–3
Ansel Gibbs (whaling ship) 281
Arbuthnot, G. 314–15
'*Arctic Council planning a search for Sir John Franklin*' (Pearce) 289
Arctic Council, The 289
Arctic Research Foundation 35
Armitage, Thomas 85, 156
Armstrong, Dr. Alexander 259
Assistance Bay 314
Assistance, H.M.S. 90, 91
Austin, Capt Horatio 29, 90
Austin Relief Expedition 45, 83
autopsies 18, 162, 165, 167
Aveomavik Island 214–15
Aylmore, Richard 61

B
Back, Capt (Sir) George
　author 169–70, 175
　and Chantrey Inlet 241
　mapping 28, 240, 289
　search expedition 43
　Terror expedition 97
Back's Bay *see* Collinson Inlet
Back's Great Fish River 43, 87, 160, 172, 175–6, 289–91
Baffin Bay 50, 51, 83, 249, 293
Baillie Hamilton Island 314
Ball, Nick 186–7
Balsillie, Jim 35
Banks Island 44
Banks, Sir Joseph 65
Barretto Junior, H.M.S. 67, 75, 81, 153

Barrow, Sir John 27–8, 53, 61, 96, 174, 289
Barrow Strait 53, 92–3
Bathurst Island 90
Battersby, William 60, 61, 148, 161–2, 190, 288
Bayne, Capt Peter 137, 217, 218
Beagle, H.M.S. 54, 65
Beattie, Dr. Owen
　Booth Point 234
　Crozier's Landing 144
　Erebus Bay finds 179, 187, 198
　exhumations 91, 123, 165
　forensic investigation 47, 161
Beaufort ice stream 42, 43, 94, 97, 103, 160
Beck, Adam (Inut) 331–2
Beechey Island 83, 84–93
Belcher, Sir Edward 260–1
Belcher Relief Expedition 45
Bellerophon, H.M.S. 55
Bellot, Joseph Rene 292
Bellot Strait 48, 49, 291
Bering Strait 90, 113, 176, 258
'black men' 244–9, 320
Blanky, Thomas
　cautiousness of 113, 119
　ice experience 63, 82, 102
　and Inuits 224, 277
　leadership 228
　letter to wife 78
　previous expeditions 65, 115, 169, 175
Blenky, Esther (wife of Thomas Blanky) 78
Blenky Island 101
blubber, use of
　'Fireplace Trail' 214–15
　for fires 23, 42, 202, 247
　use aboard ship 211–12
Boat Island 70
boat teams 158, 158–9
boats, and sledges
　carried by ships 153–4

Index

Douglas Bay 205–6
  head west 257–60
  sent north for help 213–14
  'sledge boats' 170–1, 197
  bomb vessels 95
bones/bone fragments, forensic examinations of
  cut marks on 188, 207, 234
  DNA matching 180
  by Keenleyside 179
  modern 33
  teeth/jawbone 167, 188
  See also lead poisoning; scurvy
Booth, Felix 48
Booth Point 234–5, 243
Boothia Felix 48, 272, 274
boots 25, 155–6, 198, 230, 234, 235
botulism poisoning 136, 152, 166, 174
Braine, William 88, 123, 130
brass cylinders, progress messages and 83, 85–6, 89, 114–15, 116, 118
British Trans-Antarctic Expedition 134–5, 147, 149
Buchan, Capt David 55
burials
  along death march 242–3
  Beechey Island 123
  Cambridge Bay 231
  found 179
  King William Island 168
  officers and 32, 122, 217–18, 231
Burwash, Maj Laughlin Taylor 31, 99–100, 122, 137, 143, 216–18

C

Cambridge Bay 231, 313, 315
Camp Terror 148–9
camping equipment 156–7
campsites
  Beechey Island 91, 92
  Camp Terror 148–9
  Crozier's Landing 142, 144, 147, 151
  hunting-observatory 105–6, 107–8
  Imnguyaaluk Island 211
  Jamme map 218–19
  Ook-soo-see-too Islet 264–5
Canadian Government 14, 27, 33
cannibalism
  1848 retreat 196, 243
  and 'black men' 246–7
  cut marks on bones 188, 207, 234
  in death camps 242
  Dickens on 297–301
  Franklin and 206–7
  Inuits and 162
  outcry over 13–14, 29–30
  preferred to seal 205
  response from Dr. Rae 302–6
Cape Bowden 92
Cape Crozier 114, 190, 209, 210, 246, 268–9
Cape Farewell 72
Cape Felix 41, 42, 49, 95, 105–8
Cape Herschel 43, 49, 53, 113, 114, 116
Cape Jane Franklin 116, 122, 143
Cape Riley 83, 91, 92
Cape Victoria 99
Cape Walker 90, 94
Carney, Peter (blogger) 95, 96, 162
cases, stacked wooden 99–101
Castor and Pollux River 96
Cator, Lt J. Bertie 90
Chantrey Inlet 43, 159, 169, 176, 230, 239–41
Chapel, Capt Christopher 224, 273
charts 98–9, 157
Chieftain (whaling ship) 140–1, 146, 269, 312–13
cholera, suggestion of 168
Clarence Islands 97, 99
clothing
  found 182
  future searches 328
  Inuit 156
  officer 231
  snow goggles 157
  surplus 249
  unsuitable 154–5
coastline, mapping 28
Coleman, Pat 217
Coleville Bay 98
Collins, Henry 70
Collinson, Capt (*later* Adm) 70, 90, 258, 314–15
Collinson Inlet 116, 122, 214
Colville Bay 112
compass, use of 138, 205–6
Coningham, Elizabeth 68
Coningham, William 77
Cook, Capt James 65
Cookman, Scott, *Ice Blink* 135–6, 152, 153, 158, 174, 269
Cooper, Paul Fenimore 32, 40, 219
Coppermine River 55, 176
Coppin, Weasy 291, 292
Cornwallis Island 87, 90, 314
Couch, Edward 61, 73
Cracroft, Sophia 58, 59, 64, 65
Creswell's Tower 92
Crimean War 30, 285
Croker Mountains 46, 96
Crozier, Capt Francis R.M.
  and 1850 retreat 228
  'abandon ship' 148, 150
  'Aglooka' meaning 110
  background 57–8, 57–9
  burial of 123, 158, 218
  cautiousness of 82, 104, 113
  character 57, 173–4, 200
  death and burial 215–16, 281
  description of 109, 224
  discipline aboard ship 66–7
  final letter to J. Ross 78–80

359

and Fitzjames 69–70, 199–200
and 'Fox' (dipping-needle) 59, 69, 70, 76
gives sword to Inuit 275, 276–7
and Gore 117, 119–22
Hall on 273–5
and ice streams 97, 102
interaction with other officers 62–5, 67
and Inuit language 228
and Inuit 108–9, 222–4, 273–7, 279–81
and J. Ross 174
letter to J. Ross 58–9, 64, 66–7, 104
possessions 297, 330
previous expeditions 54, 103
reasoning behind early retreat 174–7
on retreat 188–91
and sledging 172
takes command of expedition 87, 88–9, 109–10, 135, 197
and terrestrial magnetism 59
at Washington Bay 225–6
Crozier Strait 90
Crozier's Landing
to Chantrey Inlet 176
cylinders found 85
depot camp 117, 151
descriptions of 142–8
future searches 328–9
graves at 123, 130, 131–2
interpretation of 147–8
position of 121
Cyriax, Dr. Richard
1847/48 records 86, 115
'Croziers Encampment' 147
food supply study 92, 151–2, 176, 199–200
and Larsen 107, 144
on sledging 170
Victory Point 120, 121–2

D

Darwin, Charles 65

De Haven, Edwin J. 91
Dease, Peter Warren 27, 175
death camps 192–6, 201, 209, 242, 246, 319
death march 190, 191, 200, 241–3
deaths, expedition
high rate of 20, 137, 152, 167–8, 174, 268
numbers of 88, 135, 160, 220
officially pronounced 307–9
Starvation Cove 240
defeat, captains face 199–208
dental problems 167, 188
Des Voeux, Charles
1847 record 86, 88, 137
Cape Felix 107
and Fitzjames 61, 73
and sledge exploration 113
Devon Island 83
diaries, future search for 328
Dickens, Charles 30, 207, 297–301
dipping-needle ('Fox') 58, 59, 69, 70, 76
disaster planning 82–3
discipline 63
Discovery (ship) 47
Disko Island, Greenland 61, 66, 82
dogs 118, 212, 215
See also 'Neptune' (dog)
Douglas Bay 158, 197, 202, 205–6, 241

E

E-vee-shuk (Inut) 233–4
Eber, Dorothy Harley,
Encounters on the passage ...
on Amundsen 137
on boat mast 241
book 14
definition of 'Utjulik' 42
'Fireplace Trail' 214–15

Inuit testimony 32, 36–8, 210, 211, 250, 319 *See also* individual testimonies
Egerton, Lord Francis 119
Ek-kee-pee-re-a (Inut) 253
Elephant Island 135, 149, 247–8
emergency plans, lack of 150
Emerson Harbour 97, 103
Endurance H.M.S. 134–5, 147, 149
Enogeiaqtuq Island 214
Enterprise, H.M.S 81, 90, 140, 141, 258, 314–15
Enukshakak (Inut) 99–101
equipment
camping 156–7
latest 27
scientific 76
survival 157
Erebus Bay 84, 158, 167, 173, 179–87, 206–8
Erebus, H.M.S
abandoned 87–8, 149–50
accommodating both crews 146, 151
atmosphere aboard 75–7
Barrow's proposals 53–4
boats from 153–4, 242, 253
coal supply 247
crew members 70–3, 277
discipline aboard 63, 248, 249, 256
discovered 33–5, 42, 109
drifting 145–6
'on fire' 250–1
future searches 328
health problems 160
heavily laden 95, 98
illness aboard 135, 162–4
Jacko (ship's monkey) 66, 73
last activities 256–66
last sightings of 81–3
latest equipment 27
leaves *Terror* 270
library 168–9, 175, 182
moved south 109
nailing colours to mast 260–1, 313–14

officers aboard 81
pinnace (boat) 154
previous expeditions 54, 58
ran aground 111
remanning 201, 209–10, 212, 269
rope store 145
rum supplies 249
scientific collections from 36
sonar images 253
steam engine 95, 152, 162
still intact 191
trapped 102–4, 138–42, 141, 142
visited by Inuit 215
wreck 14, 263–4, 320
See also 'Utjulik ship'
Etuk Islands 262
Euphrates, River 60
exhumations 31, 37, 91, 123, 161, 165
expeditions
  future 328–9
  private 30, 214, 285, 288–94
  search 288, 291–4, 311–15
exploration
  budget 35
  program 160

F

facial reconstructions 179, 184, 229, 231
Fairholme family 308–9
Fairholme, Lt James Walter
  and Fitzjames 61, 70
  letter from 75
  magnetic work 107
  possible leader 190
  and *Terror* 66
  will 308–9
Felix Harbour 48
Felix (schooner) 91
finger posts 91
'Fireplace Trail' 214–15, 261–2, 282
fires, blubber 42
firewood 153
Fisher, Capt 281

Fitzjames, Cdr James
  'All well' 85, 87, 104, 114, 219
  background 59–62, 60–1
  and 'black men' 246
  character 28, 59–60
  on colleagues 68–74, 244
  and Crozier 191, 199–200
  discipline aboard ship 66–7
  final letter from 75, 77
  glory hunter 61–2
  honours and awards 60
  on icebergs 72, 77
  identification of 190
  interaction with other officers 62–5, 67, 198
  journal 54
  magnetic work 107
  and mail 257
  messages written 86, 89, 121
  overconfidence of 82
  polar novice 55
  previous expeditions 60–1
  'remains' 256–7
  second in command of expedition 88–9
  and sledging 172
  taking risks 103
  written records 85, 228–9
Flinders, Capt Matthew 55
floes, ice 36, 97, 146, 147
fog 91, 206
food poisoning 136, 137, 152, 160
food supplies
  abandoned 82, 167
  abandoned ships 150, 183
  amount carried 151–2, 174
  Blenky Island 133
  Cyriax study of 151–2, 176, 199–200
  discovered 100, 101
  fresh 165, 172, 175–6, 203–5, 241
  men refusing seal 203–5
  pemmican 23, 97, 100, 152
  rationing 166–7, 178, 203
  rum supplies 249

tinned 101, 135–6, 137, 164, 166, 233
tins of meat 92
footwear 25, 155–6, 198, 230, 234, 235
forensic examinations, of bones/bone fragments
  cut marks on bones 188, 207, 234
  DNA matching 180
  by Keenleyside 179
  modern 33
  teeth/jawbone 167, 188
  See also lead poisoning; scurvy
forensic investigations, full 47
Forsyth, Cdr Charles 91, 292
Fort Providence 176
'forty days' calculation' 168–73, 174, 175, 191
'Fox' (dipping-needle) 58, 59, 69, 70, 76
Fox (ship) 84, 180, 259, 285, 293
Frankin Point 124
Franklin, Lady Jane (née Griffin) (JF's widow)
  and the Admiralty 291, 307–8
  and Hall 38
  letter to President Taylor 286–8
  marriage 56, 57
  Memorial Expedition 214
  Murchison on 309
  near misses locating expedition 312
  and niece 59
  objects to Anderson expedition 238
  outcry over cannibalism 29–30, 206–7
  prophecy from dead girl 291
  raising funds 285, 288–94
  sends search ship 90–1
  sponsors expeditions 13, 30, 290–3
  and stepdaughter 308
Franklin, Sir John

background 27, 55, 56
burial 217
cabin of 253
character 122
death 30, 87, 88, 118–19, 122–3
Fitzjames on 68–9
future search for grave 329
Governor of Van Diemen's Land 56–7, 67, 69
and Greece 56
honours and awards 29, 56, 307
interaction with other officers 62–5
Inuit description of 108–9, 216
last official letter from 75–7
letter to Lady Jane 65, 75
'the man who ate his boots' 45, 55
marriages 56
overconfidence of 81
possessions 297
previous expedition leader 28, 47
previous expeditions 55–7
Simpson Strait 290
taking risks 103, 104
and Van Diemen's Land 56
will 308
Franklin memorial, Greenwich 231
Franklin Point 122, 128
Franklin Strait 94, 95, 157
Franklin Trail project 32
Frobisher, Martin 37
fuel 152–3
Fury Beach 46, 48, 50, 52, 171, 175
Fury (ship) 46–7, 48, 58, 64, 104

G
gales 172, 178
Gambier, Sir James 60–1
Gambier, Robert 60–1
Gannet, H.M.S. 85

Geiger, John 47, 144, 161, 165, 198
Gell, Eleanor Isabella (née Franklin) (JF's daughter) 308
Gell, Rev John Phillip 308
Gibson, William 'Paddy' 205–6, 230–1, 232, 234, 255
Gilder, William Henry
 Cape Felix camp 106, 137–8
 Crozier's Landing 143
 on graves 126, 128–9, 230
 and Inuit 38, 127–8, 254, 278
 O'Reilly Island 165–6
Gjoa Haven 42, 99
Gjoa (ship) 44, 96–7, 98, 100, 101, 102
Gladman's Point 227
Goddard, William 255
Goldner, Stephen 135–6, 161–2, 166
Goodsir, Dr. Harry D. S.
 Crozier on 79
 on *Erebus* 65
 Fitzjames on 71–2
 Inuit dictionary 229
 letter from 75
 'remains of' 231
 scientific collections 157
Gore, Lt (*later* Cdr)
Graham
 background 65
 Cape Felix 107
 cylinders deposited 86, 88
 death 137, 188–9
 Fitzjames on 70
 and Franklin 66
 'The Hunter' 215, 258, 261–3, 282–3
 'mistake' 118–22
 personal effects 185, 196
 'remains found' 132, 179–80
 sledge exploration 113–17
 and Victory Point 117
Gore Point 85, 116
Graham Gore Peninsula 200

Graham, Sir James 307
graves
 Beechey Island 29, 33, 86, 88, 91
 Cape Felix 137
 Crozier's Landing 123, 130, 131–2
 digging 47
 elaborate 124–5
 Erebus 31
 estimated location of Franklin's 129–30
 Franklin Point 128
 Gilder on 126, 128–9, 130
 headboards on 83, 91, 123
 on King William Island 107
 King William Island 229
 location of Franklin's 122–3
 marker 313
 medals found at 126, 127
 officers' 123–4, 126–7, 131
 Peffer River 232
 Point Le Vesconte 128–9
 significance of different types of 130–2
 Tooktoyaktuk (Inuit settlement) 258
 Tulloch Point 230–1
Great Slave Lake 43, 176
Greenhithe, Kent 66
Greenland 48
Griffin, Jane (JF's 2nd wife) *see* Franklin, Lady Jane (JF's widow)
Griffin, Lt S.O. 91
Griffiths, Lt Edward 67, 69, 76, 81
Grinnel, Henry 91, 240
Griper (ship) 46
Gross, Tom 125

H
Halkett, Peter 66, 229
Hall, Charles Francis
 and Crozier 177, 226
 on escape route for Franklin 283

hires hunters 217
inscriptions by 232
Inuit testimony 30–2, 36–8, 43, 207, 230–4 *See also* individual testimonies
and Inuit 98–9, 112–13
letter to Chapel 273–5
letter to Grinnel 240
notebooks 38, 124–5, 221–4, 244, 281
and Peffer River 231–2
poisoned 37
receives warning 278
report of Washington Bay meeting 225–6
search expedition 13
Hall Point 232
Harper, Stephen 33, 34
Hartnell family 293
Hartnell, John 88, 123, 130, 165
health problems 160–77
Hearne, Samuel 47
Heather, William 151
Hecla (ship) 47, 58, 64
Hedges, William 151
Helpman, Edwin 61
Hickey, C.G. 94
Hobson, Lt William R.
  on bad weather 5
  finds boat 180, 182
  finds camp 105–6
  Fox expedition 27, 293
  on Inuit 111
  on May weather 178
  sledge exploration 13, 84–5
Hodges, William 142
Hodgson, Lt George 61, 69
Hooker, Joseph 65, 79
Hornby, Fredrick John 151
hospital tents 192–4, 206–8, 217, 246
Household Words (Victorian magazine) 297
Hudson, Henry 37–8
Hudson, John 37–8
Hudson's Bay Company 47, 87, 91, 230, 238, 285
Hudson's Bay Fort Resolution 43

'The Hunter' 215, 253, 258, 261–3, 282–3
hunting
  Inuit 215
  with Inuit 212–13, 217, 218, 262, 274–5
  lifestyle 264
  success 201, 241, 282–3
  time spent 248
Hut Point, McMurdo Sound 248
Huxley, Thomas Henry 231

I

ice streams
  Beaufort 42, 43–5, 94–6, 103, 160
  caught in 67, 102–4, 248–9
  King William Island 82, 87
icebergs 72, 77
Iggiararsuk (Inut) 202, 237
Ikinnelikpatolok (Inut) 165–6
immobile sick 190–1, 198, 206–8, 242
Imnguyaaluk Island
  Erebus anchored off 36, 139, 218, 219
  future searches 328
  Inuit testimony 210–12, 244, 246
  living conditions 249
In-nook-poo-zhe-jook (Inut) 38, 179–80, 185–6, 192, 194, 251–2
Indians, fight with 241, 275
Inglefield, Capt (*later* Adm) E.A. 165, 231, 257, 292
Intrepid, H.M.S. 90
Inuit
  and 'black men' 244–9
  and boat sightings 158
  booties 155
  clothing 156
  and communication 75
  and Crozier 189
  description of JF 108–9
  drawing of ships 140–1, 141

eating tinned meat 268–9
fights with Franklin's men 241
finding a box full of papers 158
food offered to 245
Gjoa Haven 210–11
helping *Albany* sailors 47
hunting 41, 212–3
killed by Back's men 241
lifestyle 40–5
and methods 28, 49
oral tradition 40
on Poet's Bay 97
Rae on 302–6
rejected testimonies of 330–2
reliability of testimony 37–9
relics purchased from 84, 98
settlements 277–8
and shipwrecks 99
testimony of 14, 29, 31–3, 84, 164, 210–13
trading with 47, 50
Investigator, H.M.S.
  abandoned 167
  discovered 35–6
  search expedition 44–5, 90, 140–1, 258–9, 313
Irish-Canadian Franklin Search Expedition 264–5
Irving Bay 121, 122
Irving, Lt John
  death 137
  finds 1847 record 87, 88, 120
  'grave' 125, 126, 131, 156
  honours and awards 127, 131
  'identified' 31, 121
  remains of 121
Isabel (ship) 292, H
Isthmus of Boothia 28, 44, 48, 95, 96, 141

J

James Ross Strait 44, 95, 96, 97–8
Jamme Report 217–18
Jenny Lind Island 42, 213

363

Jepson, Thomas 61
Jones Sound 90
Jopson, Thomas 80, 156

K
Kamchatka 24, 61, 63
Kane, Dr. Elisha Kent 91
Keenleyside, Anne 161, 167, 187–8, 201, 319
Kellett, Capt Henry 260–1
Kennedy, William 292
Ker, Capt 312
Kin-na-pa-toos (Qairnirmiut Inuit) 280–1
King, Dr. Richard 169, 175, 176, 289–90, 311–12
King William Island
  and Hall 37
  'island' 28
  north and south 198
  north-west 111, 218–19, 267–8
  passing 35, 169
  Ross discovers 49
  route to 94–5
  searches 31–3
  seasons and ice stream of 40–5
  study of 114
  in summer 200
  three-man sledge party and Inuits 202–3
Kirkerktak see King William Island
Klengenberg, Patsy 231
Klutschak, Heinrich 41, 112, 126–9
Knight, James 47
Kogvit, Sammy 35, 270
Kok-lee-arng-nun (Inut) 98, 108–10, 112–13, 216, 278–80, 330–1
Koo-nik (Inut) 253–4
Krusenstern (ship) 48, 110

L
Lady Franklin, H.M.S. 90, 314
Lancaster Sound 46, 51, 53, 90, 96
land depot 151

Larsen, Insp Henry Asbjorn 31–2, 107, 122, 143–4
Le Vesconte, Lt Henry Thomas Dundas
  and Fitzjames 61, 70
  and Franklin 75
  magnetic work 107
  on Reid 65
  'remains of' 31, 231
  on *Terror* 66
lead poisoning 33, 91, 144, 161–3, 187, 188
leadership 53–67
Learmouth, L.A. 42, 229, 231, 235
Leopold Island 140
letters, final (sent by expedition members) 75–80
line of retreat
  found by expeditions 30
  Hall and 31
  relics found 84
  tinned food 137
  undisturbed 111
  Woodman and 32
Little, Lt Edward 69
Lloyd-Jones, Ralph 277
log books 157
looting 213–14, 239, 251–2, 253, 268, 330
'The Lost Arctic Voyagers' (Dickens) 297–301

M
MacBean, Gilles Alexander 297
McClintock Channel 94
McClintock, Capt (*later* Adm Sir) Leopold
  books 207, 309
  comments on Hall's records 307
  on Crozier's Landing 142–3
  description of Erebus Bay boat 154, 180–4, 187, 197
  finds boat 31
  on food remains 164
  Fox expedition 13, 27, 84–5, 285, 293–4
  hears about wrecks 42

hunting-observatory camp report 105–6
and Inuit 250, 278
letter from Dr. Rae 306–7
and looting by Inuit 253
Montreal Island detour 240
presents findings to RGS 259
on record errors 87, 89, 114
relics purchased from Inuit 254
report 221, 251
skeletons found at Erebus Bay 179
sledge exploration 92, 98, 111, 116–17
sledging technique 171–2
Voyage of the Fox 14
McClure, Capt Robert 44–5, 90, 167, 258–9, 313
MacDonald, Alexander 92, 223, 224, 228, 280, 297
MacFarlane, Roderick 276–7
Mackenzie River 176, 258, 259–60
McMurdo Sound 248
McNeish, Henry 'Chippy' 149
Maconochie Island 239
magnetic
  North Magnetic Pole 50, 98, 102, 133, 217
  observations 71, 92, 148, 315
  poles 206
  South Magnetic Pole 54
Maleruakik (crossing place) 229, 230, 235
mapping
  Canadian Arctic 46, 57
  land utilisation 329
  North-West Passage 105–21, 113, 114
  progress of 96
  of unknown lands 157
Marble Island 47
Mark, William 142
Martin Bergmann (research vessel) 35

INDEX

Martin, Capt Robert 81
Mary (yacht) 91
mast, nailing colours to the 260–1, 313–14
Matty Island 44, 95, 98, 99, 115, 133–4
mausoleum ship, *Terror* as 146, 167–8
Mays, Simon 163
medals, found at graveside 126, 127
Melville Island 29
Melville Peninsula 263, 272, 281–3
Mercy Bay, Banks Island 35
messages, progress 83, 85–6, 89, 114–15, 116, 118
Michell, Jeremy 153
Miertsching, Johann 258–9, 313
Millar, Keith 162
Montagu, John 56
Montreal Island 159, 169, 238–40, 240
Murchison, Sir Roderick 309
Musk Ox Lake 169
mutinies 293

N

National Maritime Museum, Greenwich (NMM) 85, 86, 157, 186–7
naval dockyards 145
Neitchille *see* Boothia Felix
Nelson, Horatio 27, 55
Nenijook (Inut) 235–6
'Neptune' (dog) 66, 212, 262, 263, 281, 282–3
Netchelu Tribe (Inuits) 99
Netsilingmiut Inuit 111, 112–13, 278
Newfoundland Banks 36
newspaper reports 29, 240, 295–6
North Devon Island 91
North Magnetic Pole 50, 98, 102, 133, 217
North Star (ship) 292
North-West Passage
  dream of a 46–52
  and Larsen 143
  mapping 49, 86, 105–21
  routes 96
Nourse, Prof J.E. 31, 32, 38, 124, 185
Nowya (Inut) 99–101

O

Ocean Camp 149
Ockarnawole (Inut) 127–8
officers, senior
  deaths 88
  details of 53–67
  divided command 89, 103, 199, 200
  honours for the last 256
  interactions between 62–5, 201
  'with long teeth' 35, 189–90, 256–7
Ogle Point 214
Ogzeuckjeuwock (Inut) 236–7
Ommanney, Capt Erasmus 29, 45, 83, 85, 90, 91
Ook-bar-loo (Inut) 139, 192–3, 244–6, 275
Ook-soo-see-too Islet 262, 264–5, 282
O'Reilly Island 34, 164, 165
Osborn, Capt Sherard 45, 90, 175, 239–40
Osmer, Charles Hamilton 72–3, 75, 151
Ouela (Inut) 272–3, 276
Ougligback, William 302
Ow-wer (Inut) 221–6
Owen, Roderic 37, 64, 240

P

Papanakies, Paul 239, 241
papers, burial of 122–3
Parks Canada, Canadian Government 33, 34, 35, 269, 288
Parry, (Sir) William Edward
  expeditions 58, 64, 90, 96, 101, 275
  and Fitzjames 62
  on Franklin 55
  ice streams 44
  and Inuits 282
  naval expeditions 29, 46
  sledging pioneer 170–1
Pearce, Stephen, '*Arctic Council planning a search for Sir John Franklin*' 289
Peddie, John S. 297
Peel Sound 45, 93, 94, 157, 214, 292
Peffer River 148, 231–2
Peglar, Harry 85, 148, 156
'Peglar Papers'
  departure day 249
  found 155
  information from 85, 166
  poem from 201–2
  'Terror Camp' 108, 146, 148
Pelly Bay 98, 108, 113, 202, 279
pemmican 23, 97, 100, 152
Penny, Capt William 83, 90, 291, 314
Petersen, Johan 221, 250–1
Petro Paulowski [Petropavlovsk] 28, 61
photography 126, 179, 196, 217, 329
Pilkington, William 224, 228
pillar, drift measuring 137–8
pinnace (boat) 170
Pioneer, H.M.S. 90
Poet's Bay (Poctes) 82, 96–8, 101–4, 115, 152
Point Culgruff 115–16
Point Le Vesconte 124, 128–9
Point Ogle 230, 239
Point Richardson 236, 238
polar explorers 28
Poo-yet-ta (Inut) 233
Porden, Eleanor (JF's 1st wife) 56
Port Emerson 49, 95
Potter, Russell (blogger)
  book 288
  Crozier's sword 277
  expedition lists 288
  findings 123–6

365

and Inuit 110, 112
and Larsen's report 107
maps and photos 179, 196, 217, 318–19
Prince Albert, H.M.S. 91, 292
Prince of Wales, H.M.S 81, 83
Prince of Wales Island 45, 95, 214, 292
Prince Regent Inlet 46, 95, 140
Puhtoorak (Inut) 254

Q
Qairnirmiut Inuit 280–1
Qayutinaq, Nicholas (Inut) 262
Queen Maud Gulf 34, 112

R
Rae, Dr. John
  charts 98–9
  honours and awards 30, 207
  and Inuit methods 28
  and Inuits 29, 38, 194, 236
  letter to Admiralty 293
  letter to McClintock 306–7
  mapping 96, 282, 293
  Pelly Bay 238
  and relics 13, 296–7, 313–14
  reports 29, 206–7, 220, 295–6
  response to Dickens 302–6
  on Richardson 260
  search expedition 91, 261
Ranford, Barry 179
Rasmussen, Knud 32, 167–8, 202, 206, 237, 267–8
rationing 166–7, 178, 203, 212
reconstructions, facial 179, 184, 229, 231
records, written 84–90
  1847 record 86–7, 89–90, 113, 115, 116, 137

1848 record 87–9, 101, 103–4, 114–17, 120, 173
reefs 49, 55, 96, 99, 100, 101–2
Reid, James
  Fitzjames on 70, 72
  and Gore's personal effects 185, 196
  ice experience 65, 97, 102, 103
  identification of 184–5
  lost way 67, 82
  'remains found' 179
relics found
  on abandoned boat 183
  Adelaide Peninsula 235
  black pine board 257
  by Burwash 217
  Cape Felix 105–6
  Cape Riley 91
  charred elm wood 314
  Crozier's Landing 142–3, 217
  Erebus Bay 187–8
  Erebus, H.M.S 185
  by *Fox* expedition 30
  by Hall 31
  from land depot 151
  on line of retreat 84
  Ook-soo-see-too Islet 264–5
  'Peglar Papers' 85
  Starvation Cove 237
  Terror Bay 194
  Victoria Island 313–14
  Willow Pattern crockery 107
relief expeditions 176, 259, 260–1
remains, human
  Adelaide Peninsula 165, 215, 235–6
  along retreat 30–1
  Beechey Island 130, 167
  Booth Point 234–5
  and boots 155
  Camp Terror 148
  Cape Felix 137, 143
  Chantrey Inlet 235–6
  death camps 196
  Douglas Bay 202, 205–6

Erebus Bay 178–80, 181–2, 186, 187–8, 201, 307
Hall Point 232
King William Island 229–30, 232–3
lead in bone fragments 33, 91, 144, 161–3
missed 184
Montreal Island 238–40
officer 35, 85, 189–90, 256–7
Peffer River 231–2
and 'Peglar Papers' 156
Starvation Cove 228, 236–8
Terror Bay 192–4
Todd Islets 164, 233–4
Tulloch Point 229, 230–1
Washington Bay 229
See also graves
Repulse Bay 113, 210, 225, 240, 283, 304
rescue expeditions 29
Resolute, H.M.S. 45, 90, 260–1, 270
retreats 178–98, 220–43, 250
rewards offered 29, 53, 291
Richard's Island 260
Richardson, Sir George 30
Richardson, Sir John 34, 92, 175, 259–60, 301, 314
Riedel, Doreen Larsen 107
Romaine, W.G. 309–10
rope 144–7, 145, 151
Ross, Cdr James Clark
  and Blanky 119
  and Crozier 63
  description of 110
  expeditions 43
  final letter from Crozier 78–80
  honours and awards 96
  and ice 248–9
  and ice streams 97
  and Inuit 140
  letters from Crozier 58–9, 64, 66–7
  and magnetic pole 50
  mapping by 27

previous expeditions 54, 58
sledge exploration 44, 49, 95, 96, 115–18
Victory expedition 42, 48, 115
and Victory Point 89, 113
western sea 171
winter plans 50
Ross, Capt (Sir) John
author 169
description of 110
expeditions 29, 43, 46, 58
precedent set by 48–52
search expeditions 91
search for 169–70
Victory expedition 42, 44, 115, 171, 260
Victory Point pillar 88, 89, 115, 120
Ross, W.G. 288
Royal Canadian Mounted Police (RCMP) 107, 231
Royal Canadian Regiment 230
Royal Geographical Society Islands 36, 158, 209, 210–13
Royal Naval College, Greenwich 231
Royal Navy
exploration program 27, 28, 53
ill-equipped for Arctic 28
Rub Al Khali Desert, Arabia 214

S
St. Roch (RCMP ship) 107, 143
Sargent, Robert Orme 73
Savours, Ann 165
Schimnowski, Adrian 35
Schwatka expedition
find tinned food 164
graves found 126, 128–9, 179, 193–4, 201
ice breakup 135
Inuit testimony 38, 112, 165–6
map from 121
on McClintock boat 186–7
Starvation Cove 237–8
Schwatka, Lt Frederick
Cape Felix search 137
Crozier's Landing 142
expedition 13, 31, 121, 123–4
at graveside 129
and Washington Bay meeting 227–8
scientific collections 36, 157–8
scientific equipment 76
scientists, expeditions and 65
Scott Polar Institute 86
Scott, Robert Falcon 109
scurvy
background to 163–4
major outbreak 50, 51, 152
prevention 27, 175
scarring caused by 187, 234
seasonal changes, island 40–5
Shackleton, Sir Ernest 134–5, 147, 149, 247–8
'shakedown cruise' 66
shelters 50–1
Simpson Strait 41, 43, 229–30
Simpson, Thomas 27, 43, 96, 113, 117, 175
sites
Erebus Bay finds 179
Erebus Bay NgLj-1 180, 184, 187, 194, 196
Erebus Bay NgLj-2 179, 180, 187–8, 194, 196, 198
Erebus Bay NgLj-3 179, 196
skeletons *see* remains, human
sledge explorations
different 95–6, 98, 101
dogs and 118
food supplies 136
Fox expedition 293–4
southern 113–17
tracks from 92
sledges, boats and
carried by ships 153–4
Douglas Bay 205–6
head west 257–60
sent north for help 213–14
'sledge boats' 170–1, 197
snowstorms 91, 154, 172, 178
Somerset House (shelter) 50–1
Sophia, H.M.S. 90, 314
South Baffin Island 37
South Magnetic Pole 54
specimens 71, 92, 157, 328
Spence Bay 98
Stanley, Edward, Lord 56, 311–12
Stanley, Dr. Stephen Samuel 61, 71, 159, 239
Starvation Cove 31, 32, 158, 195, 221, 236–8
Stenton, D.R. 184
Stewart, Capt Alexander 90, 314
Stokes, Capt John Lort 54
Stromness 66
Su-pung-er (Inut) 123, 124–5
surveys
foot 107
geophysical 32
helicopter 94–5
island 34
submarine 33
survival equipment 157
survivors, last 272–84

T
Tasmania *see* Van Diemen's Land (Tasmania)
Taylor, Zachery (US President) 286–8
Tennent Island 49, 95
territorial claims 33
Terror Bay
1848 retreat stopped 270
camp 197
Crozier and Fitzjames meeting 199, 200

hospital tent 192–4, 206–8, 246
hunting on 111
Inuit testimony 35
reaching 173
retreat halts at 190–5
Terror, H.M.S
  abandoned 87–8
  atmosphere aboard 78–80
  Barrow's proposals 53–4
  boats from 153–4
  coal supply 247
  damage to 97, 146
  discipline aboard 63
  discovered 35, 267–70, 315
  drifting 145–6
  future searches 328
  heavily laden 95, 98
  illness aboard 135, 162–4
  last sightings of 81–3
  latest equipment 27
  library 168–9, 175
  nailing colours to mast 261, 313–14
  overturned 141, 142
  possible shipwreck 99
  preparation for abandoning 149–50
  previous expeditions 54, 58, 97
  and reefs 101
  rum supplies 249
  steam engine 95, 152, 162
  thrown on beam ends 140–1, 148, 269
  trapped 102–4, 138–42
  used to store bodies 146, 167–8, 210, 267, 268
  voyage of 270
  wreck 14, 246
Thunder Cove 230, 235
Todd Islets 137, 164, 205, 229, 233–4, 243
Too-koo-li-too (Inuit) 139, 273, 280–1, 330
Too-loo-a (possible JF) 229
Too-shoo-ar-thar-i-u (Inuit) 243, 276–7, 278–9
Tooktocheer (Inut) 236–7

Tooktoyaktuk (Inuit settlement) 258, 259, 313
Tootiak, Mark 241, 262
Topilikton, Patsy 210–11
Torrington, John 88, 123, 130, 161
Tozer, Solomon 224, 228, 235, 243, 277
Trafalgar, Battle of 27, 55
Trent, H.M.S. 55
tuberculosis 167
Tuk-ke-ta (Inut) 221–6
Tulloch Point 123, 124, 129, 130–1, 205

U
United States Naval Observatory 38
United States Navy 91
Utjulik 42, 212–13
'Utjulik ship' 109, 111, 148, 166, 184, 250–5
Utjulingmiut Inuits 112, 278

V
Van Diemen's Land (Tasmania) 56–7, 58, 65, 293
Victoria Island 42, 264, 290, 294, 313–14
Victoria, Queen 61, 261
Victoria Strait 27, 33–4, 70, 267, 313
Victorian Society 28, 33, 46, 297–301, 317
Victory expedition 171
Victory (paddle steamer) 42, 44, 48–52, 110, 169, 175
Victory Point
  Burwash lands at 31
  examining 218–19
  and J. Ross 97
  locating 89, 120
  naming 42, 95
  problem 115–17
  Ross expedition to 49–50
Victory Point pillar 88, 89, 115–16, 120–2
volcanoes 54

W
Waigat Channel 70
Washington Bay 116, 156, 158, 195, 220, 225–8
Weddell Sea 134
Wellington Channel 89–90, 93, 157, 291
Wentzall, William 255
Whale Fish Islands 67, 70, 107, 229
whaling ships
  encounters with 29, 52, 81, 152
  missing 58
  size of 158
  sunken 101
  wreck of 214
Wilkes, Henry 127, 151
Williams, Cpl David 230
Wilson, John 316
Woodman, David
  and 1848 record 101
  and *Chieftain* report 146, 312–13
  and Crozier 216
  and Crozier's Landing 121
  on death camps 195
  disputing Hall 231
  and *Erebus* 218
  interpretation of events 32–3, 36, 317–18
  Inuit testimony 38, 99, 109–11, 221–4, 244, 254, 316
  and Inuit 122–3
  photo of Irving's grave 126
  and Su-pung-er 124, 125
  and *Terror*, thrown on beam ends 140–1
  'Strangers among us' 14, 272, 283
  'Unravelling the Franklin mystery' 14, 186, 288
Woolwich 48, 66
Wright, Rear Adm Noel 35–6, 158, 248, 315

Y
Young, Allen 45